Murder in Our Midst

Murder in Our Midst

Comparing Crime Coverage Ethics in an Age of Globalized News

ROMAYNE SMITH FULLERTON AND
MAGGIE JONES PATTERSON

OXFORD

UNIVERSITY PRESS

OXFORD
UNIVERSITY PRESS

Oxford University Press is a department of the University of Oxford. It furthers
the University's objective of excellence in research, scholarship, and education
by publishing worldwide. Oxford is a registered trade mark of Oxford University
Press in the UK and certain other countries.

Published in the United States of America by Oxford University Press
198 Madison Avenue, New York, NY 10016, United States of America.

Library of Congress Cataloging-in-Publication Data
Names: Fullerton, Romayne Smith, author. | Patterson, Maggie Jones, author.
Title: Murder in Our midst : comparing crime coverage ethics in an age of
globalized news / by Romayne Smith Fullerton, Maggie Jones Patterson.
Description: New York : Oxford University Press, 2021. |
Includes bibliographical references and index.
Identifiers: LCCN 2020022909 (print) | LCCN 2020022910 (ebook) |
ISBN 9780190863531 (hardback) | ISBN 9780190863548 (paperback) |
ISBN 9780190863562 (epub)
Subjects: LCSH: Journalistic ethics—Europe, Western—History—21st century. |
Journalistic ethics—North America—History—21st century. |
Crime and the press—Europe, Western—History—21st century. |
Crime and the press—North America—History—21st century. |
Journalism—Objectivity—Europe, Western—History—21st century. |
Journalism—Objectivity—North America—History—21st century.
Classification: LCC PN4756 .F85 2020 (print) | LCC PN4756 (ebook) | DDC 174/.907—dc23
LC record available at https://lccn.loc.gov/2020022909
LC ebook record available at https://lccn.loc.gov/2020022910

DOI: 10.1093/oso/9780190863531.001.0001

1 3 5 7 9 8 6 4 2

Paperback printed by LSC Communications, United States of America
Hardback printed by Bridgeport National Bindery, Inc., United States of America

For Greg, who always keeps me well-fed and hydrated so I can work,
and for Aidan, whose smarts inspire me every day to learn something new.
—RSF

For Rob Ruck, whose faith in me makes all this possible, and Alex Ruck,
our wonderful son, and Alison Perrotti, his wonderful wife,
who bring joy to life.
—MJP

Contents

Acknowledgments

Many people helped us with this project. To begin, we owe an enormous debt of gratitude to all those who agreed to be interviewed (listed in the Appendix), many of whom also suggested other people to whom we might speak and outlined additional cases and material to consider. In each country, we always found knowledgeable people who were interested in our work. They pointed us toward thought-provoking stories, made introductions to facilitate our interviews, and answered our sometimes basic questions with patience: in the Netherlands, Bart Brouwers and Daphne Koene; in Sweden, Esther Pollack; in Germany, Ivana Ebel, Stephan Russ-Mohl, Izabela Schlindwein, and Katrin Voltmer; in Ireland, Gerry Curran; in England, Jon Brown, Chris Frost, and Mike Jempson; in Portugal, Luis de Sousa; in Spain, Jorge Tuñón Navarro; and in Italy, Fabrizio Tonello. In our home countries of Canada and the United States, we often bent our friends' and colleagues' ears about our work—you know who you are, and we will thank you in person when next we meet. In some of the countries, we needed the help of a translator, or, more accurately, someone we would call a "fixer" in the journalism biz: in Portugal, Miguel Pais; in Spain, Jorge Tuñón Navarro; in Germany, Izabela Schlindwein, Josepha Kirchner, and Anja Neidhardt; in Italy, Fabio Benincasa and Ornella Sinigaglia; in the Netherlands, Elke Bun. To ensure our general accuracy and our understanding of the letter or the spirit of media law, we enlisted the help of knowledgeable people: in Germany, Christine Kensche; in Portugal, Francisco Teixeira da Mota; in Italy, Fabrizio Tonello; in Spain, Carlos Maciá-Barber; in England, Chris Frost; in the Netherlands, Thomas Bruning. All errors or omissions are our own.

No research project can be undertaken without the support of graduate assistants: In Canada, Chris Richardson and Gemma Richardson worked on some of the earliest material; Kate Hoad-Reddick offered insight about literary tropes and organized our vast and growing files; Jenny Poon conducted the initial research about media law in the countries we planned to visit; Percy Sherwood and Aidan Fullerton formatted our work for several conferences; Evin Ellwood helped format the manuscript submission; Zahra Khozema checked the accuracy of early chapters. In the United States, Emalee Sekely,

Megan Amrich, and Jacques Hinkson-Compton worked in various capacities to support research and facilitate the project's completion. We would also like to thank Rob Ruck, who took notes and helped with the interviews in Italy, and Robert Sutton, who read and reread drafts of all the chapters and generously offered his insights about overall coherence, interest, and readability. Bernard Haggerty and Niklas Frykman of the University of Pittsburgh's history department generously shared their knowledge of European culture and attitudes, and Daniel Nagin of Carnegie Mellon University helped us with international comparisons of crime and statistics.

The authors gratefully acknowledge various sources of financial assistance: The Social Science and Humanities Research Council of Canada, Morton Weismann private endowment, the Faculty of Information and Media Studies at the University of Western Ontario, the National Endowment for the Humanities, and Faculty Development funds at Duquesne University.

1

Introduction

Crime stories rivet public attention and create social buzz. As a genre, they continue to enjoy tremendous popularity across time, countries, and increasingly fragmented populations.[1] They also serve as a prism for citizens' anxieties about perceived threats to norms and institutions. As immigration, technological change, and globalization reshape the world, widespread anxiety grips Western Europe and North America and gives rise to populism and political extremism. Because journalism plays a central role in shaping how the public adjusts to moral and material upheaval, this unease raises the stakes for news. Reporters have choices: They can spread panic and discontent or encourage adaptation and reconciliation by the ways they tell these stories. Ethical decisions are inherent in these options about how and how best to tell these tales. At a time when there is more information available than ever, but people are less well-informed and perhaps more tribal, we need a journalism that both opens conversations in local communities and bridges the many differences among nations in a culturally sensitive, thoughtful manner.[2] This challenge may prove particularly difficult, given our contention—one that emerged early in our work—that increasingly globalized media threaten to erase national differences about how crime stories are told and suggest that crime coverage practices are under various pressures to default to the American or British "tell-all" style.

Murder in Our Midst: Comparing Crime Coverage Ethics in an Age of Globalized News employs a comparison of mainstream media crime coverage in ten developed Westernized democracies as a key to consider culturally constructed concepts like privacy, public, public right to know, and justice. Under consideration are Canada, the United States, the United Kingdom, Ireland, Sweden, Germany, the Netherlands, Italy, Portugal, and Spain. How deviance is reported can fan or quell public fears, yet research shows reporters often select frames based on long-standing habits, rather than concern for social consequence. Gaye Tuchman in *Making News* called these often unexamined news practices "rituals" because they are repeated with almost religious dedication.[3]

Murder in Our Midst. Romayne Smith Fullerton and Maggie Jones Patterson, Oxford University Press (2021). © Oxford University Press. DOI: 10.1093/oso/9780190863531.003.0001.

Working from sample news coverage, national and international codes of ethics and style guides, and personal interviews with news professionals and media experts, our work offers fertile material for a provocative international conversation. Together, these primary and secondary sources show that crime news reporting practices differ in both subtle and extreme ways among advanced capitalist democracies that, at first glance, may seem similar; moreover, these stories both reflect and shape each nation's attitudes about these concepts in unique, challenging, and sometimes overlapping ways.

Consider the reporting rituals in these divergent examples:

- The Netherlands, Queensday, 2009: As Karst Tates tried to assassinate Queen Beatrix by smashing a car through police barriers, photojournalists documented the calamity and videographers broadcast it live. Tates killed seven people and injured ten others before crashing into a monument and sustaining a fatal head injury. The story was carried around the world, yet many Dutch media, including the national news service Algemeen Nederland Persbureau (ANP), identified the culprit only as Karst T. They wanted, reporters and editors told us, to protect his family from harmful publicity.[4]
- Bristol, England, Christmas 2011: After 25-year-old Joanna Yeates' body was found near a quarry, police arrested her landlord, Christopher Jefferies. Although he was ultimately cleared of all suspicion, the British tabloids and even reputable papers called him weird-looking, effeminate, blue haired, and perhaps a pedophile. In the lead up to the Leveson Inquiry into the Culture, Practices and Ethics of the British Press, which was prompted by the *News of the World* phone-hacking scandals, Jefferies won significant libel settlements against eight tabloids, and two papers were fined for contempt of court. He told the Inquiry that despite the settlements, he would never fully recover from the effects of media coverage.
- Spain 2015: A 13-year-old Barcelona schoolboy fatally stabbed a teacher and wounded several other teachers and students while wielding a crossbow, knives, and a Molotov cocktail. Respecting both law and custom, Spanish news media protected the boy's identity, referring to him only as "M." However, in 2009 neither teenager Miguel Carcaño of Seville nor his victim, Marta del Castillo, was afforded such deference

when Carcaño confessed to murdering Castillo, his 17-year-old girlfriend. In that instance, Spanish news media milked the social media
site Tuenti to publish intimate photos of Carcaño and Castillo, as well as
private message exchanges among them and their friends. Such inconsistent media behaviors reflect some moral ambivalence on the part of
journalists and editors.

As these brief anecdotes illustrate, distinctive crime coverage practices char-
acterize every country's journalism; such stories served as starting points in
the ten countries we considered, beginning with the Netherlands in 2010
and ending with Germany in 2018. These are not "ordinary" crime stories,
if such can be said to exist; rather, they are tales that everyone is discussing
and dissecting, regardless of whether they regularly consume mainstream
news. Such cases represent what Martin Innes and Nigel Fielding call
"signal crimes."[5] They coined the term "to capture the social semiotic processes by which particular types of criminal and disorderly conduct have
a disproportionate impact upon fear of crime."[6] Innes describes the way
certain crime stories articulate "popular fears about the seeming encroachment of the forces of disorder" and draw upon "inchoate existential anxieties about the state of contemporary society."[7] In this book, we explore how
journalists construct signal crime stories and how those constructions connect to public conversations, politics, and culture, both contemporary and
historic. In almost all instances, these tales became larger than the details
or the specifics because they had both a personal and a communal resonance.[8] Each criminal act is accompanied by "widespread popular concern
that signals that something is wrong with . . . society and its criminal justice process, which requires some form of corrective response."[9] In this
way, crime coverage serves as an ideal exemplar for unlocking the cultural
assumptions behind differing journalistic practices. As Richard V. Ericson
et al. argue in their book, *Representing Order: Crime, Law, and Justice in the
News Media*, "conceptions of deviance and control not only define the central object and character of news stories, but are woven into the methodology of journalists, influencing their choices from assignment through the
selection and use of sources, to the final composition of the story."[10] Thus,
comparison of differing crime coverage practices allows us to glimpse each
country's underlying values and attitudes, and consider whether such reporting rituals aid democracies' many and varying functions.

Goals and Methodology

Murder in Our Midst is the culmination of an eight-year international research project. Our initial goals for the project were two: First, to outline journalistic crime coverage practices and understand their motivations within a selection of liberal market democracies of Western Europe and North America. Second, to use our findings to initiate a conversation among journalism practitioners, academics, and the public about what these differences suggest about current ethical and cultural attitudes toward justice, privacy, and, by extension, the role of journalism in democracies.[11] Daniel Hallin and Paulo Mancini, in *Comparing Media Systems: Three Models of Media and Politics*, write: "Comparative analysis makes it possible to notice things we did not notice and therefore had not conceptualized, and it forces us to clarify the scope and applicability of the concepts we do employ."[12] We concur. Little comparative work has been written about the substantially different ways that advanced capitalist democracies cover criminals and crime in the news media. And journalism practitioners, scholars, and journalism educators rarely, if ever, discuss whether North American and British naming—and blaming—of accused and/or criminals raises ethical concerns. In fact, our research demonstrated most U.S. and Canadian journalists—seasoned and green—as well as their academic colleagues who educate up-and-coming news professionals, are largely unaware of their counterparts' opposing habits across the waters.[13] All the established democracies in our sample share a commitment to a free press, justice, the presumption of innocence, the right to privacy, and the public's right to know; but the weighing and balancing of these values vary widely in ways marked by each country's history, politics, and economic institutions.[14] In part, we hope our work will address these gaps in knowledge so professionals and scholars can consider whether what their crime coverage practices emphasize is consistent with their communal ethical ideals and to consider others' approaches as a way to better inform their own decisions.

While the analysis in this book is, in part, an empirical look at varying journalistic practices, its methodological approach falls firmly within the field of arts and humanities. We offer an ethical evaluation, based on a variety of textual analyses, of whether particular storytelling approaches serve the exercise of democracy. We would also foreground the idea, articulated by Clifford Christians et al., Katrin Voltmer, Stephen J. Ward, and others, that democracies can be broadly defined, and their variants are highly diverse.[15]

And while we build on descriptions of crime coverage practices to offer an exploration of differing democratic values that may be reflected in these journalistic products and approaches, we are not suggesting that one reporting approach is "best" or "most ethical." As we will outline in the book's three parts, in each instance, some values are clearly emphasized and others fade to the background.[16]

This work offers a comparison of crime coverage practices among ten countries: Canada, the United States, the United Kingdom, Ireland, Sweden, the Netherlands, Germany, Italy, Portugal, and Spain.

Our inspiration for this selection of countries came from Daniel Hallin and Paulo Mancini's *Comparing Media Systems: Three Models of Media and Politics*.[17] They group countries in North America and Western Europe into similar geographic models based upon the news media's shared history, economic foundations, and political relationship to government in these regions. In short, they argue, borrowing from Fred Siebert et al.'s *Four Theories of the Press*, that media systems take on the form and color of the political and social systems in which they operate: (1) The North Atlantic Liberal model (Britain, the United States, Canada), characterized by market mechanisms and a press that has been politically independent and privately owned. (2) The North/Central European Corporatist model (the Netherlands, Scandinavia, Germany, Austria, Switzerland, Belgium), where commercial media coexist with news organizations affiliated with churches and political groups. History and culture differ from their neighbors like the United Kingdom, and some journalistic practices are governed by law, but the state has a limited role in media. (3) The Mediterranean or Polarized Pluralist model (Italy, Spain, Portugal, Greece, and France) where media have historically been affiliated and aligned with political parties. In these countries, the state has played a strong role. We chose representative sample countries from each of their models. While Hallin and Mancini's work looks at historic and current social, political, and economic patterns in media, they do not touch upon journalistic practices, policies, or ethics.[18] We borrowed their comparative approach in anticipating that practice follows the historic structures they identified, and, as we will discuss throughout the book, largely it did. In short, we relied on the geopolitical categorization of press systems established in *Comparing Media Systems* and its articulation of the public service ethic as a development of media accountability within the professionalization movement. While Susanne Fengler et al., as well as others, note Hallin and Mancini's theory has some internal inconsistencies, their categorizations gave us a place to start and allowed us the flexibility to draw from some of their generalizations and apply them to the specifics of journalistic ethics practices across the models.[19] To better manage the amount of material we would have to cover, we narrowed our theme to a consideration of crime coverage and began initially with a specific topic for comparison: How do mainstream media routinely handle names and identifying characteristics of those accused of serious crimes? While this often formed a starting point in each of our investigations, our conversations and explorations extended far beyond what such a seemingly simple and straightforward query might suggest.[20]

We chose to look at high-profile crime stories (mostly murder) in particular because we believe they are of broad interest to all publics and because they play a key role in how a nation's values are discussed, reaffirmed, and changed. As American sociologist Jack Katz pointed out, crime stories define the behavioral borders of society by exploring what conduct is deemed unacceptable, as well as indicating how rule breakers are treated.[21] Crime narratives pull audiences into the process of redrawing these socially constructed borders and influence the ways in which those borders shift over time. By doing so, crime journalism both reflects the culture in which it is embedded and plays an important role in constructing it. In "What Makes 'Crime' News?" Katz pinpoints what lies behind the public's never-flagging interest in stories that are, he argues, remarkably similar and largely formulaic: They constitute a society's "daily moral workout."[22] We build on this argument to add that geography once contained this ongoing exercise within the limited reach of news distribution; each country or community could follow its own daily routine. But as we will discuss, the Internet now routinely breaks through geographic and linguistic borders, with varying effects.

Our method was the same in each country under consideration. Because ethical choices can be exercised only within a framework of what is legislatively permitted, we began by identifying each country's legal requirements with respect to media reporting of crime stories and covering court. Next, we consulted ethics codes—national and regional, as well as style guides or manuals offered by journalists' unions, press councils, and/or by media institutions. While codes can be ignored, they point to professional ideals and outline normative practices, as well as offer a reference point for discussions with practitioners, most of whom were crime reporters, media experts, or academics. Additionally, understanding both legal requirements and usual accountability practices enabled us to understand the ethical expectations and the institutional frameworks of the journalistic practices we encountered. We chose not to interview bloggers, freelancers, or those who produce news solely for small niche websites because these practitioners are not bound by ethics codes in the same manner as persons employed by large media institutions.[23] This project focused on institutions, particularly the institution of journalism, which carries history and tradition in its practices, and we believe that the attitudes of institutions are best reflected in the professionals who are employed by them.

With the assistance of news professionals or academics in each country, we chose several high-profile cases that conformed to Innes' definition of "signal crimes," and, using Lexis Nexis, we read a random sample of coverage to familiarize ourselves with the names of crime reporters and the details of the stories they were likely to discuss. In some instances, we identified reporters by their story bylines and contacted them directly. Through reporters or other contacts, we also spoke to editors, who oversaw coverage of the signal crimes that served as our case studies, and ombudspersons or members of press councils who examined reporters' practices on behalf of citizens. To enlarge our sample, we contacted industry experts and academics through appeals to newsrooms, schools of journalism, and professional organizations. Often interview subjects would suggest other people to whom they thought we ought to speak.[24]

Our sampling method allowed us to focus on the specific decisions of a few cases, as well as the broader dimensions that reflected attitudes toward crime, journalism's role, and the media's ability to govern itself. While our sample interviews cover a wide spectrum of age and experience, and gender is nearly equally reflected, we acknowledge we were less successful gaining the participation of tabloid employees.[25] And thus, most of our interview subjects came from mainstream news organizations, including print and broadcast media—both public, like the British Broadcasting Corporation (BBC), the Canadian Broadcasting Corporation (CBC), the Nederlandse Publieke Omroep (NPO), as well as private, for profit corporations like the *Washington Post*, the *New York Times*, *Süddeutsche Zeitung*, *Dagens Nyheter*, and so on.[26]

We traveled to each country to conduct the discussions face-to-face, and rather than using a standardized questionnaire, we chose open and in-depth interviews with reporters and editors whose work we had identified and analyzed. Each interview began with an exploration of how a signal crime was covered. For example, in the Netherlands, we first asked each subject to describe how decisions were made about coverage of the Queensday incident in 2009. Follow-up questions were based on the journalist's answers, and we would request further elaboration, explanations, and examples. Thus, the body of the interview was held within the frame the subject provided. By using this open, exploratory approach to interviewing, we were applying Anselm L. Strauss and Barney Glaser's grounded theory, which allows a thesis to arise from the data, rather than precede it.[27] Under this approach, the interview subjects tell their own stories about their coverage and share with us their own perceptions, reflections, and involvement. This method also adheres to the ideas of Walter Fisher, who articulates, in *Human Communication as Narration: Toward a Philosophy of Reason, Value, and Action*, the need to respect the narrative framing of interview subjects who thus own the stories of why they act as they do.[28] Grant McCracken in *The Long Interview* calls this style of interviewing "one of the most powerful methods" in qualitative research because it allows researchers to "step into the mind of another person, to see and experience the world as they do themselves."[29] Being experts at the interviewing process, journalists quickly pointed out when some particular behavior deviated from their standard practice. They explained why such deviations were warranted. Much press behavior is performed in an almost ritualistic way, but, with some probing, media professionals would explain what values they found reflected in their standard practices and why those values mattered to them and, they believed, to their audiences. These discussions always held clues, if not forthright statements, about how journalists saw their duty to cover crime in their democracies. Afterward, we performed close readings of the narratives we gathered, identifying recurring words and phrases, references to ethics policies or laws, media organizational policies, and unique statements for what they collectively revealed about foundational journalistic values beneath these distinct ethical practices.

Our most important finding emerged early in our data collection, and it will be explored throughout this book: New and increasingly globalized media threaten to erase national distinctions in how crime stories are told. In some instances, a country's practices are being challenged, or even overridden, by technologies and ownership decisions that breach national boundaries and ethics codes, ignore differences in reporting rituals, and lead to a default reporting style that mimics that of Britain and the United States.

One such example of how the Internet and globalization are erasing storytelling distinctions is the coverage of Dominique Strauss-Kahn, a case outlined in some detail in Chapter 7 of this book. In May 2011, the then head of the International Monetary Fund (IMF) was dragged from his hotel room in New York City and paraded in front of news photographers for the "perp walk"—a distinctly American practice where police display an accused person, bound and shackled, on the way to jail. Charged with the sexual assault of a hotel maid, DSK was legally presumed innocent, but nonetheless publicly shamed and embarrassed by the news media. The perp walk offers the American people the opportunity to see its justice system in action, according to its defenders, but these images swiftly circulated across the Atlantic. French television stations ran the footage of DSK, and a swift and furious reaction from French commentators and politicians followed. Former Justice Minister Elisabeth Guigou called the images "brutal, violent and cruel."[30] As justice minister, she had overseen the implementation of a law that forbids photographing criminal suspects in handcuffs because the French believe these visuals can undermine the presumption of innocence. As we will explore in the first part of this book, if DSK's arrest had happened in Paris or Stockholm, it might well have been ignored because the alleged crime was arguably not directly related to his public office. The charges against Strauss-Kahn were ultimately dropped because of inconsistencies in the complainant's story and a lack of physical evidence, but his political career was over and his reputation irretrievable. As other alleged DSK victims came forward and investigations in France continued, the incident gave rise to a cross-Atlantic debate. For the French, the circulation of this story served as a social catalyst, a tale injected into French culture and politics from the outside, but DSK's arrest raised other concerns. As a result, he stepped down as head of the IMF and bowed out of his projected candidacy for president of France. To some, the American tell-all style of crime coverage had raised French awareness that predatory behaviors were not a branch of sensuality but a form of aggression and clearly not a private matter. To others, the incident had cost that nation the leadership of a valued economist and politician. Technology had broken through French boundaries, side-stepped their laws, and disrupted their reporting customs. Such incidents wrest control over journalistic practices and over the local and national conversations about which ethical values should prevail. These breakdowns are likely to be mindless and heedless of cultural difference, driven solely by technology or profit, or both, but not by ethical or cultural values.

Our Findings: Three Media Models of Crime Coverage

We acknowledge that media generally, as well as each organization's crime coverage practices on a case-by-case basis, can differ widely, even within the countries themselves. Public and commercial broadcasters often contrast in goals and styles, as do broadsheets and tabloids, national and regional media. Yet, what emerged from all facets of our research was a fundamental pattern about the values of ritual reporting practices that spanned differences within each country and distinguished one country and one media model from the next. What we ultimately saw were three discernable, although loosely defined, ethical approaches in our sample countries, which cluster in geographic patterns; we outline each in the corresponding three parts of this book:

- *The Protectors of Northern and Central Europe*: The Netherlands, Sweden, and Germany. In these locales, reporters follow practices that seek to preserve the reputations of accused and even convicted criminals, as well as their families, to allow for presumption of innocence before conviction, and then rehabilitation and reintegration into society if a guilty verdict is delivered.
- *The Watchdogs of Canada, the United States, the United Kingdom, and Ireland*, where journalists firmly believe in an ethical obligation to inform the public and keep a watchful eye on police and the criminal justice system. Their stories often outline as many details as legally possible about anyone arrested or convicted under newsworthy circumstances. Harm to defendants' reputations and possible shaming of their families through publicity is seen sometimes as regrettable collateral damage. The push is to publish.
- *The Ambivalents of Southern Europe*: Italy, Spain, and Portugal. Here, police and prosecutors keep arrest and pretrial records under wraps to protect the accused's presumption of innocence. Journalists profess their agreement with these legal protections, yet they routinely skirt them by obtaining information from eyewitnesses or from police and prosecutors, who provide leaks and exclusives, often in exchange for positive publicity or other compromising arrangements.

This book makes several arguments about ethics. First, in each of the three sections, we suggest that a distinct ethical approach is employed when journalists cover crime. We argue that the countries' practices in each grouping are guided by an often-unacknowledged ethic that nonetheless makes some approaches routine in one model and completely alien in another; moreover, as we will explore, each approach suggests underlying cultural attitudes about the value of privacy, presumption of innocence, public right to know, justice, and who "belongs." In the *Protectors* model, we suggest that an ethic of care has traditionally molded their crime coverage practice of routinely not naming or identifying persons accused and, in some instances, convicted of serious crimes. This is a sharp contrast to what we identify as an Enlightenment approach, characterized by the individualist, justice-based values exemplified by the tell-all journalistic crime coverage rituals of the *Watchdog* model. The *Ambivalents*, we argue, are aptly named because their practitioners borrow elements from both ethical frameworks of the other two models but without a real consensus on how either or any ethics might, in fact, best advance the cause of democracy for Portugal, Spain, or Italy. These countries, where the last century's dictatorships are still within the reach of memory, are caught in the crossfire and caught at a crossroads. Their journalists need to consider carefully what their citizens truly value and then which crime coverage practices will best encourage, sustain, and uphold those values. Otherwise, they risk being subsumed by a variety of commercial pressures, as well as an ongoing—and for democracy, an ultimately unsustainable—climate of clientelism.

Second, a more abstract ethical argument informs and underlies the entire book. Our overall findings have led us to the conclusion that journalism ethics must turn its attention to two goals that might seem contradictory: On the one hand, the field must strive to agree upon universal codes of media behavior; on the other, it must simultaneously seek to preserve the right of every country and culture to hold onto its own hierarchy of values, for reasons we will outline. The challenge of meeting both these aspirational aims is what Carol Gilligan and Jane Attanucci refer to as the highest ethical order, one in which decision-makers both adhere to Enlightenment principles of justice and equal treatment, while simultaneously showing care and responsibility for difference and the integrity the other. While each nation in our sample has its own unique legal, economic, and historical relationship with its press, all bear the weight of working out journalism's role in the democratic process where the right of a free press must be balanced by privacy and fair trial rights, as well as by commercial pressures. Stephen J. Ward, in his book *Ethical Journalism in a Populist Age*, makes an argument that assists in advancing our perspective.[31] He suggests that democracies are being undermined largely from within and that the press has played a role in this erosion; democracies usually do not end by a coup d'état or external forces, but rather by slow internal degeneration.[32] Events erode political diplomacy and civility; leaders do not act in democratic ways and people lose their belief in the institution itself. What Ward is proposing is a new way forward for journalism—one that, like our own approach, is based on pairings of terms that, at first glance, appear to be oxymoronic or contradictory.[33] He lays out an ethic for a democratic journalism in a global public sphere, but one that is flexible and practical. "I argue that we should replace the idea of 'journalism of fact' with the idea of an interpretive 'journalism beyond facts,' and we should replace the idea of neutral stenography with the idea of impartially engaged journalism for democracy."[34] The onus for upholding, defending, and even advocating for democracy and its institutions would thus fall on journalists. "I propose that journalists become global patriots for humanity and redefine journalism ethics from this global perspective."[35] We applaud this impulse and its daring. In our book, we will argue that placing the ideals of democracy—differently defined and experienced in each country—at the forefront of considerations about journalistic practices will encourage all practitioners to employ best practices, ones that are not dulled by economic or competitive challenges or driven by self-indulgent desire for career successes.

Ethics texts and codes have consistently defined journalism's mission in terms of public service or public trust; this approach is both well-established and widely acknowledged. As Bill Kovach and Tom Rosenstiel argue in *The Elements of Journalism*, "the primary purpose of journalism is to provide citizens with the information they need to be free and self-governing."[36] Ward points out that these values are aspirational. "The dream is this: The purpose of mass news media is to accurately and objectively inform the public at large so they can be self-governing. The media will help the people form rational decisions and affirm the best policies, in a spirit of compromise and devotion to the common good."[37] The details of enacting this commitment vary with each culture, but a vibrant press plays a central role in the give-and-take dialogue of every democratic society. We see this notion of a conversation as the thread that runs through James Carey's *Communication as Culture*.[38] As G. Stuart Adam writes in his foreword to Carey's fifth edition: "The experience matters—in fact, the events that define experience—occurs when it is reflected upon, symbolized, and expressed. The process has special weight and significance in the democratic world that Carey constructs and cherishes."[39] In *Communication as Culture*, he details what he sees as one of the greatest challenges facing communication studies today: That, largely, North Americans view communication from a transmission perspective, one that emphasizes the here and now, the measurable, and the concrete.[40] And, we would add, the limits that are inherent in such an approach. In contrast, Carey argues many Europeans view communication through a ritual lens. He writes, "If the archetypal case of communication under a transmission view is the extension of messages across geography for the purpose of control, the archetypal case under a ritual view is the sacred ceremony that draws persons together in fellowship and commonality."[41] In terms of an ethical perspective, this latter approach views "the original or highest manifestation of communication is not in the transmission of intelligent information, but in the construction and maintenance of an ordered, meaningful cultural world that can serve as a control and container for human action."[42]

How journalists view the process of communication, its practices, products, motives and goals, implies a set of values that encourages individualism on the one hand, or concern for the group or community on the other. We argue that these two differing attitudes are manifested in our first two media models: The Watchdogs' crime coverage practices are largely illustrative of the former, and the Protectors' approach most closely follows the latter. As we will show, however, the transmission and ritual models are behavioral tendencies, rather than absolutes, as Carey implies. Watchdog reporters show a commitment to reinforcing cultural norms. They see their watchdog function as a public trust, an outgrowth of citizens' mistrust of government and commercial concentrations of power. Keeping the public's business before the public is not merely a job. It is a sacred duty, which they believe is violated—in Canada, for example—when press access to public documents is blocked by court-imposed publication bans. Similarly, Protector journalists acknowledge a commitment to transmitting accurate information. The Ambivalents, too, employ some aspects of each, but they have not yet developed a mature approach to their practice.

Carey, borrowing from Canadian communications scholar Harold Innis, emphasizes the importance of discussion and dialogue in creating and maintaining democratic societies and in developing a sense of community where values can be asserted, disputed, reaffirmed, or rearranged. He wrote that "in the end, journalism simply means carrying on and amplifying the conversation of the people themselves."[43] Journalists are not, and ought not to be, stenographers. They gather the facts: The Who, What, Where, Why, When, and How of an event, but then they fashion those facts into a narrative. The Who becomes character, the What is plot, the Where is the setting, and Why constructs the theme. At the heart of all journalistic enterprise lies the telling of true tales, and this undertaking is an ethical pursuit. As Walter Fisher argues in *Human Communication as Narration*, humans are storytelling animals, and the tales they tell about themselves and each other both reflect and shape the communities in which they live.[44] But when the telling ceases to be their own, as in the case of Strauss-Khan, when others usurp their storytelling power, a community's ability to conduct its public business is in jeopardy; as Gilligan, initially, and then many other feminists asserted, persons being denied their own voice cannot undertake the individual or communal task of becoming moral beings.[45] Such denial or repression of voice is an attack on identity.

Fisher notes, using some ideas first advanced by John Dewey, there is no community if people are not genuinely concerned with and interested in other people and focused on participating in public discussions, conjointly and cooperatively.[46] "Democracy is not an alternative to other patterns of associated life. It is the idea of community itself."[47] The storytelling function, the public aspect of this telling, is central to encouraging people to learn about each other, share meaningful experiences, and work out together how best to live a shared existence. The ethics, in this instance, is inherent in the narrative: "Regardless of form, discursive or non-discursive texts are meant to give order to life by inducing others to dwell in them to establish ways of living in common, in intellectual and spiritual communities in which there is confirmation for the story that constitutes one's life."[48] The implication of this conception of communication is that news serves not only as a way for individuals to define themselves but also as a means for societal definition—for defining themselves as a people. Defining themselves, however, is challenging in an environment where others impose their media ethics about how crime ought to be covered. As a result, foreign attitudes can overshadow indigenous views and news practices. Part of the appeal of Fisher's narrative paradigm is the idea that ordinary people are "experts" about their own affairs and do not need special training to judge a representation's authenticity or its legitimacy because every person is familiar with the nature and inherent value of one's own story. Thus the onus moves onto citizens who, we suggest, are capable of deciding for themselves whether stories are true and cohere with their own experiences and then judging them accordingly.

A Brief Overview of the Book

We have organized *Murder in Our Midst* around our three media models, and at the beginning of each section, we introduce a selection of signal crimes that served as jumping-off points in our interviews or became central in ensuing discussions or both. We thread through all three parts the idea that journalism has a moral obligation to tell stories about its communities in ways that reflect and shape the unique realities and aspirations of those who live there. In Chapter 2, "What the Protectors Protect," we introduce the crime coverage practices of Sweden, the Netherlands, and Germany. Although a suspect's name and other identifying details are part of the public record or supplied to reporters by police, news media in these three countries routinely protect suspects and even convicted criminals from public exposure. In these locales, journalists said they always weigh their obligation to inform the public against (1) protecting the defendants' families—especially if they have children; (2) respecting the right to the presumption of innocence; and (3) avoiding dissemination of information that could damage the defendant's reputation and/or chance for reintegration. Protector countries share a faith that many criminals can be successfully reintegrated into society. Journalists are most likely to protect a private person accused of a crime in the private sector and least likely to protect a public figure or official accused of a public crime. Chapter 3, "Threats to and Benefits of the Protective Policies," suggests journalism practices in Protector countries are deeply rooted in the once largely homogenous cultures from which they developed and remain a part. Globalization, most intensely focused on crime and immigration and the tell-all reporting style popular on the Internet and social media platforms, threatens the embedded sense of who a people are, how they treat one another, and how they ought to address the challenges of difference. In this chapter, we consider how immigrants have been framed as a threat across these nations. We examine the varying responses from news outlets, as well as press councils, about how best to outline, advance, and maintain these public conversations, as well as considering which details ought to be included, and why. To conclude this first section, Chapter 4, "Protectors' Accountability," outlines the makeup of the press councils in Germany, Sweden, and the Netherlands, and their accountability systems. News organizations in Protector countries earn trust, at least in part, by acknowledging that the public has the right to a voice in how news is produced and presented. The nature and effects of story frames are discussed.

The coverage of the years-long trial in Germany of the National Socialist Underground (NSU) members accused of killing immigrants is explored for what it says about immigration and mainstream media's handling of it. We consider how globalization and immigration threaten both the posture of criminal justice systems and the protective press practices that reflect and reinforce those policies. The ethic of care is central to our explorations in this part; Gilligan argues that justice and care are not wholly oppositional, but she also argues they cannot be joined. At its foundation, this feminist approach repositions moral development from concern for agreed-upon ethical standards to the personal in relation to others. This latter attitude is central to the moral philosophy of Emmanuel Levinas, whose ideas about a primary duty to the other animates aspects of the discussion. Borrowing ideas from James Carey about the ways in which types of communication give rise to differing cultural values, we explore the ethical grounds for policy in these countries and consider the comparative work about prisons and attitudes toward crime by Michael Tondry and his colleagues.

Chapter 5 is the first offering in the second model, "The Watchdogs," comprising the United Kingdom, Ireland, Canada, and the United States. Titled, "What the Watchdogs Watch, Why, and Why Watching Matters," this chapter contrasts Watchdog reporters' crime coverage practices with those of the Protector countries; while the latter largely trust their institutions and government officials, Watchdogs do not. Thus, they routinely publish extensive details about an offense, an alleged perpetrator, and victims. We outline how, on the one hand, these details can lead to an exploration of larger social issues, but, on the other hand, they can also lead to sensationalism. Watchdogs want few limits on transparency, but they can lose sight of what people need to know and cater to capitalist ends, rather than sound journalistic ones. Journalists in this model see their primary obligation as informing the people because sunlight is the best disinfectant. Using an historical perspective, we outline how the principles of the Enlightenment, the emphasis on the individual, and an abiding belief in peoples' ability to be rational, underlie this ethical perspective and influence crime coverage choices. The title of Chapter 6, "Risks and Challenges for the Watchdogs: Competition, Demonization, and Productive Examination," suggests the broad outline: Based on sound Enlightenment ideals, Watchdog journalists' push is to publish names of accused persons and details of crimes. And the approach has merit: Citizens are seen as rational and considered capable of deciding for themselves whether and how to act on information. Yet, the biggest threats to the commitment to giving citizens the information they need to be free and self-governing are economic ones. We outline how, in this model, crime coverage decisions can be swayed, consciously or not, by considerations like competition, ownership, shrinking job markets and newsrooms, technology, globalization, and social media. In some instances, accused persons are "monstered" by news coverage for sensationalist ends. Drawing on work by Gilligan, Robert Reiner, and others, we argue that the justice orientation central to Enlightenment beliefs must be complemented by a responsibility orientation where people acknowledge their connections to each other as part of the larger social fabric. The best crime coverage practices are those that keep the public interest, rather than merely what interests the public, at the fore. The concluding piece for the Watchdogs' section is "Accountability: Resistance and Reconciliation." Crime coverage practices vary widely among the models, but these variations are under threat in an increasingly globalized context. To consider what is at stake, this chapter details some of the threats to preserving cultural difference, and then we suggest each Watchdog country consider borrowing aspects of Ireland's approach as one possible way to push back as a profession against government threats of legislation, business incursions, profit motivations, and, most importantly, to counter, in ways unique to each country, inappropriate outside influence on crime coverage. We discuss the professionalism of journalism and accountability measures like news ombudspersons and press councils to better include voices of citizens and shore up flagging credibility. Finally, we assert the importance of maintaining locally determined crime coverage practices because, without a distinct voice, they risk devolving to the "tell-all" American or British style that is synonymous with, and driven by, the Internet, not by best practices.

Chapter 8, "Ambivalent Behavior in Portugal, Spain, and Italy: The Commitment to Maybe" is the first in this third part of the book. In the three countries that make up our Ambivalent model, police may or may not choose to inform crime reporters when a suspect has been arrested. Arrest records do not generally become public until official charges are filed and the prosecutor/judge determines that the suspect will be held for trial.[49] This relatively closed approach protects both the police investigation and the suspect's right to the presumption of innocence, but unofficial actions on the part of both the institutions of justice and the press reflect a lack of clear commitment to those purposes. The seal on records can spring leaks. Police and prosecutors dole out details about the accused and the alleged crime to journalists—but they often favor news outlets whose coverage they like. Reporters, in turn, court police for such favors with the stories they produce. If police are not forthcoming, reporters often seek details from witnesses and hope police will confirm what they find. Chapter 9, "Threats, Harms, and Benefits: At a Crossroads or in a Crossfire?," begins by noting that democratic institutions in Portugal, Spain, and Italy are younger than those in the Protector and Watchdog countries; unsurprisingly, journalism ethics and professionalism are less established than those in the other two models we consider. The Ambivalent journalists' eagerness to tell crime stories even when official information is unavailable indicates a leaning toward Watchdog values: seeing their primary professional duty as informing the public and keeping a wary eye on the criminal justice; however, Ambivalent reporters' faith in protecting accused persons' presumption of innocence by shielding their identities signals a sympathy with Protector countries' codes. Their "ambivalence" may allow journalists to embrace aspects of *both* Watchdog and Protector systems and create something new, but news practices are still deeply rooted in a partisan past. Autonomy is receding further as layoffs and newsroom closings make employment more precarious. In this environment, the Internet is a mixed blessing. It opens up new opportunities for expression, even as it undermines the news media's traditional economic foundation. Chapter 10 tries to answer the question posed in its title, "Is There a Way Forward for Ambivalent Journalists? Yes, No, and Maybe." An emergent journalism may blend the best practices of the Watchdog and Protector models and inspire a more mature journalistic approach. Ethical hierarchies are used to critique current practices and suggest better ways of covering crime. Journalism, hampered by a relatively opaque legal system, is tempted to over-dramatize stories. History and politics help explain a system of clientelism in reporting: a partisan and competitive news media, weak professionalism, and a definition of "public interest" that fails to fully embrace journalism's mission in shaping an informed citizenry. News organizations bear the mark of a press once owned by political parties or interests that weaponized them in ideological battles. This history prevents journalists from readily reaching common professional ground. But we conclude this part on a positive note: Serious reforms that ground journalism in public service are developing. Elements of both a morality of justice and a morality of care are nascent in current practices and reform movements.

In Chapter 11, the "Conclusion," we endeavor to draw together the threads of the entire book. Comparison across national borders lifts the blinders that lead journalists to assume that their particular crime coverage practice is the right—or only—one. Contrasting approaches show differences and similarities and make visible journalism's shared mission: to provide citizens with the information they need for reasoned discussion and self-determination. In order to keep the public trust, the press must weigh the public's need (not want) to know, against the harm publicity can cause. That need is the information that will allow audiences to address what is unraveling the edges of the social fabric. The Internet now carries crime stories across geographic boundaries. Journalists are obliged to deal with diversity inside and outside their own countries. When a community loses control because others usurp its storytelling power, that community's ability to conduct its public business is jeopardized. We assert that conversations about crime coverage decisions across boundaries must be undertaken both within each country and among them in order to best address what threatens the right to self-definition and self-determination.

PART 1

THE PROTECTORS

Sweden, the Netherlands, and Germany

Preface to the Protectors Section

A few of the signal crime stories served as starting points for our explorations and interviews in the Protector countries.

Stockholm, Sweden, September 2003: Anna Lindh, Sweden's foreign minister, was attacked in a Stockholm department store where she was shopping for clothes to wear later that evening in a televised debate about Sweden's adoption of the euro. Lindh was repeatedly stabbed in the chest, arms, and stomach, and she died the next day. Her assassin, Mijailo Mijailovic, who was born in Sweden to Serbian parents, was arrested a few days later, and after a psychiatric evaluation in which he was found to be mentally ill, he was sentenced to life in prison. Many in Sweden were shocked by this violent crime in what had usually been a relatively crime-free country. The circumstances of Lindh's death and lack of security for politicians drew comparisons with the unsolved murder of Prime Minister Olof Palme, killed in 1986.

Apeldoorn, the Netherlands, April 2009: It was Queensday, a national holiday Dutch people set aside to celebrate their queen's birthday. While television cameras rolled and news photographers snapped photographs to document what is usually a happy event, a man drove a small car through two police barriers and into a crowd of spectators who were lining the parade route and hoping to catch a glimpse of the royal family procession in an open-air bus. Using the car as a weapon, the man killed seven people and seriously injured ten more before he ran into a large stone memorial. He died the next day of head injuries sustained in the crash, but not before he confessed to police that he had intended to assassinate Queen Beatrix.

Delmenhorst, Germany, 2005: A nurse, initially named as Niels H. by journalists, was arrested after he was caught injecting a patient with a drug that causes arrhythmia; Niels H. was convicted of attempted murder and sentenced to nearly eight years in prison. Many families became suspicious and pressed for more inquiries. In 2014–2015 during a second trial, Niels H. was found guilty of two murders and two attempted murders, and his sentence became life imprisonment. But during the trial, he also admitted to administering 90 unauthorized injections, from which 30 people had died and 60 needed resuscitation. After more investigations, in May 2019, police concluded this nurse was the most prolific serial killer in Germany, with as many as 300 victims over a 15-year time period. While German journalists usually identify accused persons by first name and last initial only, once the magnitude of his crimes became evident, almost all media organizations named Niels Högel in full.

2

What the Protectors Protect

The countries in the Protector model historically have been tolerant of others' differences, and laws have allowed largely unfettered access to information, both public and personal. Germany, under the leadership of Angela Merkel, welcomed nearly a million migrants and asylum seekers as part of what she called the "*Willkommenskultur*," the culture of welcoming.[1] Sweden's press freedom laws are the oldest in the world. In December 1766, Sweden included freedom of the press into its Constitution. The Swedish Freedom of the Press Act also initiated the principle of public access to information, which made it legal to publish and read public documents.[2] Given this historic and cultural context, it may be surprising to learn that names and identifying features of those accused and, in some cases, convicted of serious crimes in these countries are routinely withheld from the public. What it is that the Protector journalists routinely choose to protect, and why, is outlined in this chapter.

Like many Dutch people, Fleur Halkema was at home watching television as Queen Beatrix and her family glided gently along the streets of Apeldoorn, the Netherlands, in an open-air bus, waving to well-wishers gathered to celebrate her birthday on April 30, 2009. Suddenly, the crowd chatter amplified into shouts and screams. Television cameras swirled, then refocused on a car careening along the parade route and finally crashing into a monument. The cameras panned back to the car's wake where prostrate bodies and mangled bicycles lay across the wide street. The royal family stood, gasping for a few seconds before their bus whisked them away as the national holiday turned tragic.

Halkema, a crime reporter for the Dutch national news service Algemeen Nederland Persbureau (ANP) with headquarters in The Hague, put down the laundry she had been folding and called into work.[3] Police soon released the car driver's name, Karst Tates. He confessed to police that he had intended to assassinate the queen. He had rammed a late model black car through parade barricades and mowed down bystanders, killing seven and injuring ten. Tates himself died the next day of the head injuries sustained when he collided with the obelisk-shaped royal monument, De Naald.

Murder in Our Midst. Romayne Smith Fullerton and Maggie Jones Patterson, Oxford University Press (2021). © Oxford University Press. DOI: 10.1093/oso/9780190863531.003.0002.

The story of this disastrous assassination attempt broke into news cycles around the world; however, ANP, writing for the audience closest to the event, left key details out of its account: Its stories referred to the would-be assassin only as Karst T. and buried other identifying information. Dutch news outlets that subscribe to ANP's newsfeed had the option of opening a separate computer file attached to the story, which contained Tates' full name if they chose to use it or to store the information for the historic record. Media decisions about whether to name this man—who both confessed to police and later died of head injuries sustained in the crash—varied. The normative practice, outlined in the Dutch Press Council Guidelines, suggests that unless the name of a person is vital to a crime story, journalists "must prevent information or images from being published as a result of which suspects and convicted persons can be easily identified and traced by the public at large."[4] While the usual practice of protecting the accused by not publishing the person's full name or giving other identifying details was followed by ANP, other news organizations chose differently.[5] Many media people to whom we spoke saw this incident as an exceptional case, based in part on the public nature of this crime, and they chose to publish his full name; Dutch public television made this choice. Others withheld the name, feeling bound by the ethics practice that generally characterizes their crime coverage.

While most often, the full name and other identifying details are either part of the public record or supplied to reporters by police, news media in the Netherlands, Sweden, and Germany routinely protect suspects, convicted criminals, and their families from public exposure. The most surprising characteristic of this routine practice—at least to North American, Irish, and U.K. ears—is that reporters voluntarily withhold the full or partial names from news reports. Most of these protective policies are choices, not required by legislation. As we will explore in more detail in the next section of the book, reporters we spoke with in the Watchdog countries found this habit astonishing, even unethical by their standards. Yet, in each of our interviews in the three Protector countries, reporters and experts consistently backed their belief in the normative aspects of the practice, even as they noted their ability to make their own decisions, and made clear that a unified approach is not "required." While every interview took on its own character, the subjects spoke with remarkable consistency about their commitment to their protective practice and their purposes.

When they report on newsworthy criminal cases, journalists within the Protector model told us, they always weigh their obligation to inform the public of a person's name against three concerns, each of which carried slightly different weight and emphasis from one country to the next: (1) protection for the defendants' families—especially if they have children; (2) respecting the right of an accused to the presumption of innocence; and (3) avoiding dissemination of information that could damage the defendant's reputation and/or chance for reintegration. These aspirational journalistic commitments run deep, even now as they bump into challenges brought about by globalization and technology; few can imagine reporting any other way. Usually, journalists fully identify suspects only when they believe the public's need to know outweighs privacy considerations. Even using initials is an exception to the norm in Germany, said Hendrik Rasehorn, reporter for the *Braunschweiger Zeitung* in Wolfsburg. Most German reporters refer to "the accused" or "the defendant." Their commitment to these principles holds fast, but disruptive factors in these societies—particularly immigration and the Internet—are sometimes tilting the ethics scale.

Reasons for Protection

Concern for Innocent Family Members

Thomas Bruning was general secretary of the Dutch Journalists Union when we interviewed him in 2010, and he remained in that position, serving as the union's leader and spokesman, when we returned for a follow-up in 2018. He outlined, in our initial meeting, that most discussions about whether to fully identify accused or convicted criminals focus on "the privacy of the family, on the people who have not chosen to be part of the problem." Of course, the local community will always know the suspect's identity, Bruning pointed out, which is why, in part, some of his contemporaries labeled the Dutch ethics policy "hypocritical."[6] But Bruning and many others believe the principle is larger than its contradictions. Reporters in Sweden voiced similar agreement with this ideal.

When the Tates family granted ANP an exclusive interview after their son's funeral, his parents asked for, and were granted, continued anonymity by the news co-operative. "[The family] needed some peace and quiet and didn't want to be haunted by journalists all the time," said Halkema. "Normally when suspects die, we do use their names, but in this case, it was a favor to the parents. . . . It was quite an exception." When told that American reporters routinely report a suspect's full name, address, and perhaps a mugshot, and video or photo of the "perp walk" (the suspect in handcuffs being escorted by police), ANP editor Liesbeth Buitink put her hand across her mouth. "Why would you do that?" she asked, gasping. "What if they had children?"

The fact that numerous private citizens in addition to the Tates family objected when NOS, Dutch public television, put Tates' full name in its news accounts of the attack and the fallout would seem to indicate that a portion of the public in the Netherlands supports the default Dutch practice. Protection of the offender's privacy is the starting point for discussion, but not an absolute principle, NOS editor-in-chief Hans Laroes blogged in defense of his choice to name names in this instance. Some crimes, he explained, shock the public or have a political motive. On such occasions, the perpetrator becomes part of the public debate. "It is, in short, a trade-off, and that can turn out to the detriment of the perpetrator/suspect," Laroes wrote.

Arendo Joustra, editor-in-chief at *Elsevier* weekly magazine and former chair of the Dutch Society of Editors-in-Chief, endorsed Laroes' argument. "My view is that by killing a major politician [in this instance, an attempt to kill the Queen], you intervene in the public debate. Then your name should be published in full. If you kill your wife, that is a private act, but if you kill a public person, then you become public."

Thomas Mattsson, of *Expressen,* one of two national tabloid evening newspapers based in Stockholm, vouched for the system of protection in Sweden, even though his colleagues criticize him for choosing to violate the norm often.[7] "In general, I would say the system works pretty well, and it enables children and wives, more often than husbands, to carry on with their lives without . . . being shamed in the newspaper," he said.

Even after a person has been found guilty in a court of law, and sentenced, "We have to weigh that pain we inflict to the person and their family, against the benefits society can render from naming," said Morgan Olofsson, who spent 20 years as a foreign correspondent and head of *Rapport,* Sweden's largest news magazine, on Sveriges TV. "It is not about how keen people are to know, but how important it is for people to know. . . . It is especially hard if the suspect has school-age children." In each Protector country we surveyed, an active press council, staffed largely by journalists and sometimes lawyers, writes codes of ethics supplying suggested ideals. All the codes in the Protector countries grant wide latitude to individuals and organizations, and journalists to whom we spoke stressed the importance and obligation to weigh the merits of each case individually, balancing a public need to know against concerns about the privacy of those involved. There is no blanket rule. And indeed, in the Netherlands, the paper that enjoys the highest daily circulation is a broadsheet with a right-wing populist bent, called *De Telegraaf*; it chooses to name and identify people in full, following a practice more akin to that of England or the United States than to that of its Dutch peers.[8] While there is evidence that Dutch media professionals value the protection of names and identifying characteristics, a case could be made that citizens are voting with their wallets with little to no regard for the larger cultural issues that are at stake.

Presumption of Innocence

US Chief Justice Earl Warren once expressed the sentiment that the law is a public sanction for certain social and moral values. In all ten countries in our sample, the law holds sacred the belief that criminal suspects are presumed to be innocent until proven guilty; it is a hallmark principle of democracy. Inevitably, news media practices reflect the depth of their own and their country's commitment to that principle. In the Protector countries, journalists shoulder a greater share of the responsibility for preserving that right than do their colleagues in the other two models. Their trust in institutions—government, the justice system, the police—is high. Because laws exert minimal control over the news media and reporters have relatively free access to information about suspects, ethical principles largely govern journalistic decision-making. In Germany, "you always are *not* guilty until you are proven guilty, and that is the heritage of the Third Reich and Hitler's Germany," a time when criminal charges, trials, and accusations against families were corrupted by politics, said Annette Ramelsberger, crime and court reporter for *Süeddeutsche Zeitung* in Munich.

None of the Protector countries in our sample have jury trials, so unlike publication bans enacted to protect this process in some Watchdog countries, consideration of jury selection plays no part in whether to name or publicize.[9] In our interviews, German journalists put protection of the presumption of innocence at the top of their list of reasons for anonymizing suspects. Dutch and Swedish journalists positioned it just behind protection of family members. For most mainstream news media in the Netherlands, Sweden, and Germany, valuing this principle means not just withholding the name of the accused but also editing out identifying and potentially damning facts, such as criminal histories, and obscuring any images of a suspect with pixilation or a black strip across the eyes. Accused persons are not shown in handcuffs or prison garb. In Sweden, the landmark case that many mentioned to us in their interviews was that of the shooting of Swedish Prime Minister Olof Palme in 1986. The crime was an enormous shock to the Swedish public, and interest in the case was high. There was an initial arrest two months after the murder, but the name of the suspect was not made public. He was referred to as "the 33-year-old man." He was released without charge, and a second suspect was charged two years later. This second man was found guilty but later ruled not guilty on appeal. Although most media provided intense coverage of the court case, journalists did not name the second defendant until he was found guilty. The case happened before the Internet era, and most citizens in Sweden knew the accused only as "the 41-year-old man," despite that other countries named him in full. Lennart Weibull and Britt Börjesson surveyed Swedish journalists to gauge whether they supported their country's ethical approach using this case as a base; their finding was that "there was almost full agreement regarding this practice."[10] They wrote, "56% of journalists agreed that when he was sentenced in the first court was the correct time [to name him]; 4% felt it should have been published immediately and 26%, when he was first brought to court; 9% felt the correct time would have been when he was later tried in the court of appeal and 5% felt that his name should never have been made public."[11] It is evident that within the context of Protector countries, there can still be various interpretations of what exactly that protection might entail, and when, how, and under what circumstances such details might be released.

While all members of the European Union agree to abide by privacy laws, for the most part, these statutes do not infringe on freedom of the press, or particularly, on the right to report names and details of those connected with allegations of criminal activity.[12] In Germany, however, press laws are more stringent. As of 2012, the German courts developed a "general right of personality" (*Allgemeines Persönlichkeitsrecht*). This law guarantees the protection of human dignity and the right to freely develop one's personality.[13] In addition, journalists unions and press council codes of ethics prescribe adherence to principles of privacy and protection without stipulating particular practices.

The idea that media coverage ought not to be a form of punishment came up frequently in all Protector countries. "We have this value that the court decides the punishment, and there shouldn't be extra punishment by publication," said Daphne Koene, general secretary of the Netherlands Press Council. Bernadette Kester, assistant professor in the Department of Media and Communication at Erasmus University in Rotterdam, agreed: "We would say it is totally unfair to be condemned by media." Kester, who was educated in the United States, thought the American news media were "totally unfair" in their habit of showing suspects in handcuffs and disclosing their names and addresses. "The media accuse and punish the alleged perpetrator.... That is a contradiction. That is not justice," she said.

Thomas Bruning, in illustrating the degree to which this approach is taken seriously, noted that the Dutch courts, on occasion, have also seen publicity as punishment. For example, he said, businessman Jan-Dirk Paarlberg was so confident he would be vindicated in an investigation of money laundering and tax evasion that he told news organizations to quote him by name and use his photograph. But despite Paarlberg's cool assurance, he was convicted in June 2010. To some reporters' amazement, the judge proclaimed that the negative publicity from media coverage that specifically named him was the equivalent of time served and shaved nearly half a year off his sentence.[14]

Rehabilitation and Resocialization

Protector countries share a faith that many criminals can and should be successfully reintegrated into society; it is both a practical and a moral approach.[15] As a result, consideration for accused persons in these countries stretches from pretrial publicity through conviction and extends to after a sentence is served. For German reporters, "resocialization" is what they cite as their primary concern when explaining their protectionist practices at time of a prisoner's release.[16] The defendant's full name might be used in reporting on a conviction because it is of a timely nature and thus relevant, "but when [the prisoner] is coming to the end of his sentence, and it's time for getting back into society, then we have [legal] restrictions to close his name [to the public] because he has the right to go back to society without being stigmatized," German reporter Annette Ramelsberger explained. The restrictions result from a 1973 Federal Constitutional Court ruling known as "Lebach." Named for the town of Lebach, the case was brought by one of three men convicted after a robbery on an army base in which four sleeping soldiers had been killed. As the man reached the end of his prison sentence, a German public television network prepared a documentary about the notorious crime and was set to broadcast it at the time he was released. The court agreed with the prisoner that his right to personality—that is, in German law, his right to develop as a person, to control public information about himself, and to maintain his honor—outweighed the waning news value of reporting on a past crime.[17] The right to personality in Germany affects crime coverage at all stages of the justice process as journalists, the press council, and the courts weigh it against news value and public interest.[18] The press has a legitimate interest in reporting on a crime when it occurs, the Lebach decision conceded, but afterward, public interest declines. The court issued an injunction blocking broadcast of the documentary, a serious imposition of prior restraint in a country that prides itself on its free press rights.[19] In addition to acknowledging the convicted man's claims, the court also recognized the community's stake in its decision:

> Viewed from the perspective of the community, the principle of the social state requires public care and assistance for those groups in the community who, because of personal weakness or fault, incapacity or social disadvantage, were adversely affected in their social development; prisoners and ex-prisoners also belong to this group. Not least, re-socialization serves the protection of the community itself: it lies in its distinct interest that the offender will not re-offend.[20]

As a result of this and related court pronouncements, German news media generally fall silent as an incarcerated person's release draws close, and most German reporters expressed agreement with the legal practice—as do the Dutch. "When a criminal has done time, he or she has the right to be reintegrated into society" without being crushed under a damaged reputation, Daphne Koene, secretary of the press council, said. Bruning, journalists union head, put it even more succinctly: "In Holland, you have the right to start again." Mats J. Larsson, political reporter and former editor of Sweden's largest morning newspaper, *Dagens Nyheter*, also said that the belief in a second chance governs mainstream journalistic conduct in his country: "If you are a criminal when you are twenty, maybe that will change." In a larger context, Larsson said, the goal of Sweden's extensive social welfare system is to make individuals free, including freeing them from conditions for which they are not at fault. "Maybe they had a bad upbringing . . . and you need to be forgiving," he said.

Morgan Olofsson of Sweden's Sveriges TV, put it differently: "I wouldn't call [our policy] sympathy [for the criminal]—maybe consideration." The policy is not so much a reflection of Sweden's soft attitude toward criminals, said Martin Jönsson of Stockholm's *Svenska Dagbladet.* "It is about the families—they have kids, wives, siblings who will be affected too. . . . Of course, they are much more hurt by the crime itself, but there is seldom a need to give that publicity. In most cases, it is possible to tell the story without the name." Judgment belongs to the courts, said Liesbeth Buitink of ANP, not to the press, or by extension, to the public at large. When you name someone in the news, you "scapegoat" them and give them a different sort of life sentence, she said.

Exceptions

While protection of accused and in some cases convicted persons and their families remains the usual practice for most mainstream news organizations, insight into journalists' thinking can be drawn from how they draw exceptions. Reasons reporters and editors gave for lifting protections varied slightly more from one country to the next than did their reasons for having them in the first place, yet their history and reasoning remain remarkably consistent within this model.

The threat of restrictive privacy legislation perpetually looms over the press in these countries. Swedish press associations negotiated with the Swedish Riksdag (Parliament) in the 1960s about what should be made into law and what left to ethics, according to Lennart Weibull, founder and senior researcher at the SOM (Society, Opinion, Media) Institute and professor in the Department of Journalism, Media, and Communication at Gothenburg University. The result was a compromise in which "you might be able to publish [identifying details] if it were a public person and public event, but not a private person and a private event," Weibull said, as he drew a version of the diagram Figure 2.1 depicts.[21]

1 Private person/Private event	3 Public person/Private event
2 Private person/Public event	4 Public person/Public event

Figure 2.1 This figure represents how Swedish journalists conceptualize the right to privacy and the public's need to know identifying information about alleged criminals. Lennart Weibull explained the sentiment among journalists remains that criminal events in quadrant one, a private person committing a private crime, should not be published. More difficult questions arise in situations that fit into quadrants two and three—private person/public event and public person/private event. These categories are generally where discrepancies and differing crime coverage choices arise.

Reproduced by permission from Lennart Weibull and Britt Börjesson, *Publicistiska seder: Svensk pressetik I teori och praktik 1900–1994* [Publishing traditions: Swedish press ethics in theory and practice 1900–1994]. Stockholm: Tidens förlag, 1995.

Although social and technological forces may now be pushing to weaken this policy, Weibull argued, the sentiment among journalists remains that criminal events in quadrant one, a private person committing a private crime, such as domestic violence, should not be published. On the other hand, those in quadrant four, a public person committing a public crime—a public official engaged in fraud with public monies—should be publicized, and the offender should be fully identified. The same stance is taken in Germany. "We do not protect people who are elected," said Sonja Volkmann-Schluck, public relations officer for the German Press Council. An official's personal life can become public if it affects their role in public office, she said. She offered the explanation of different kinds of illness. "If a mayor is [affected by] dementia, that could affect his job, but if he has cancer, then not." The former would be identified, and the latter would not.

More difficult questions arise in situations that fit into quadrants two and three—private person/public event and public person/private event; these categories are generally where discrepancies and differing crime coverage choices arise. For example, the crime of Karst Tates on Queensday in the Netherlands would fit into private person/public event, and the Dutch news media's decisions about how to handle it were mixed: some named him; some did not. Tates was a private person without public notoriety, but the event, which was televised nationally, could not have been more public. A celebrity or public official caught engaging in domestic violence would fit into quadrant three, public person/private event; we would suggest that the allegations of sexual assault against Dominique Strauss-Kahn, discussed briefly in the Introduction, and considered in more detail in Chapter 7, would fit in this quadrant. Many, but not all news media, in the Protector countries might ignore such a situation. In this regard, the judgments of Protector news media are quite distinct from those in Watchdog countries where the choice falls most often on the side of full disclosure; transparency and full reporting of happenings, especially those concerning prominent people, are valued highly by Watchdog journalists.[22] As we will explore in the Watchdogs chapters, most news professionals in these countries would not consider that public persons are entitled to much privacy.

Any exception to the general principle of protecting a suspect's or defendant's identity "has to have journalistic relevance and that can come at any time in the story, but it has to have public interest and relevance, not just curiosity," said Martin Jönsson, of Stockholm's daily *Svenska Dagbladet*. As an editor, he made such decisions frequently. "I would say that several times a week, editors come to me and ask, 'How do we handle this?'" he said. "We recently had a local elected official who for the second time in a month was found naked and drunk in his office. We had to publish his name.... It would have been stupid not to have done so. We can't say a man who was drunk and naked, a high-ranking government official." Clearly, that would implicate too many people. Jönsson also described the case of a high-ranking police officer suspected of statutory rape and buying the services of prostitutes. The man worked with police ethics. It was impossible to tell this story and protect his identity because he was suspected of using his position to arrange meetings with women, children, and other men, he explained. Not only would the story be incomplete without the officer's name, Jönsson said, but also the public might suspect innocent officers.

Although Weibull's interview, and thus his diagram, focused on Sweden and its practices, Dutch and German journalists described similar criteria in their decision-making. Some stories go beyond the routine crime, "and you want the background—who they are, how they were brought up. You need a name and a picture in the paper," said Thomas Mattsson of Sweden's *Expressen*. He believes the individual's background can open an exploration of larger social issues; a view shared by many Watchdog journalists. A few journalistic colleagues have criticized Mattsson for revealing identities too often, but others see his point. Tim Overdiek of NOS, Netherlands public broadcasting, saw Karst Tates as part of a "broader debate in society: Was this a medical case or political?" Investigations showed Tates was a loner with financial problems, Overdiek said. "So it seemed to be the last attempt of a desperate person to go out with a bang." The impact of Karst Tates' assassination attempt, the fact that he had died, and his indisputable guilt all contributed to the decisions by many Dutch news media to treat his case as an exception to standard protective practice.

Germans emphasized the seriousness of the crime in their decision-making—whether it was "a case for the history books."[23] Generally, their journalistic choice is to use no name, and juveniles are granted special legal protections, which make exceptions all the more surprising.[24] The bloody and public murder of a teenage German girl by an Afghan asylum seeker warranted his identification in many news outlets as Abdul D., despite the fact that he was assumed to be a juvenile. The tabloid *Bild* even showed a large photograph of him without pixilation or a strip over his eyes. "Abdul D.'s age was not a factor" in *Bild*'s decision to run this coverage, according to Ernst Elitz, the newspaper's reader ombudsman. More important was that he was accused of a capital offense, and he was likely to be found guilty, Elitz explained. A juvenile can be identified if the case is considered part of contemporary history. While *Bild*, Germany's most popular daily, and also a tabloid, takes more liberties with identification than most German news outlets, many of our German sources emphasized the serious nature of the crime as a factor when they choose to abandon anonymity.

Germany has also been making an exception in its protective juvenile policies for school shootings, a crime that is relatively rare compared with the United States. Tanjev Schultz, *Süddeutsche Zeitung* reporter and journalism professor at Johannes Gutenberg University Mainz, argued that the practice of naming these young people does real harm by lionizing them and encouraging imitators. Melanie Verhovnik, a research associate in the School of Journalism Catholic University Eichstätt-Ingolstadt, studied the coverage of school shootings for her doctoral dissertation. She underscored what Schultz said, adding that evidence shows that students who commit school violence hope to be remembered.[25] These students research shooters' methods, including the way these youths have manipulated the media coverage. They imagine themselves, Verhovnik said, "in a row of perpetrators . . . in a kind of 'hall of fame'" for school shooters. She herself briefly accessed a site on the "dark web" devoted to school shootings under an alias to try to better understand its functioning and gain some sense of the participants, until she was blocked. There, she saw apparent wannabees hoping to top previous "performances" and garner admiration, especially of the like-minded others on this site. Media coverage, which now travels around the globe, fans this fervor, she said, when it puts perpetrators' names in the headlines and draws attention to how their shocking actions put them "in the history books." American journalism names alleged perpetrators, reports these shockingly frequent occurrences in great detail, and sometimes broadcasts the events live. And that coverage is easily found in other locales whose crime coverage practices would make different choices.

When reporter Annette Ramelsberger covered the initial trial of nurse Niels Högel, charged with attempted murder for an incident in 2005 in a hospital in Northern Germany, "I was obliged not to name him and called him 'Niels H.,'" she said. His crime was not yet big enough "for the history books." But under pressure from suspicious families, and healthcare workers, police examined hospital patient records where the nurse had worked in Germany, Poland, and Turkey. Then, they exhumed a number of bodies and found evidence that he was involved in many other deaths. During a second trial, running from 2014 to 2015, Högel was found guilty on two counts of murder and attempted murder. During this trial, he also confessed to a psychiatrist that he had killed 30 more people.[26] Ramelsberger noted that at this point, Högel's crime crossed the history book threshold, and most news organizations began to fully identify who he was.

"In Wolfsburg we had the case that a large number of young Muslims went to Syria to join ISIS," Hendrik Rasehorn of the *Brauchweiger Zeitung* said. "Two men—Ayoub B. and Ebrahim H.B.—later returned to Wolfsburg and were arrested. Both were convicted of membership in a terrorist group." The newspaper had access to their full names and considered publishing them because of the serious nature of their crimes and the public interest, but because Ayoub B. had several innocent family members who would have been stigmatized, the last names were withheld. On the other hand, when a police chief was accused of inappropriate conduct with female police employees, *Braunchweiger Zeitung* fully identified him in 2018. "Not only are the allegations serious and of public interest, but the accused is a public official. For a senior police officer, who is to watch over the observance of the laws, higher standards must be applied," Rasehorn said.

When Dieter Degowski was released from prison in 2018, after serving 30 years for his part in the notorious Gladbeck case, his name was not reported in German news media, despite his notoriety and a recent documentary about his crimes, because of the requirement for his resocialization.[27]

Degowski and his partner Hans-Jürgen Rösner robbed a bank, took hostages, and engaged police in a chase through Germany and the Netherlands, while journalists engaged these men for interviews, took pictures, and even televised interactions with the hostages and the hostage takers.[28] In the end, two hostages were killed, including one woman whom journalists had photographed with a gun held to her throat. Reporters were reprimanded by the German Press Council for misconduct, including interfering with police action. Michael Konken, head of Germany's largest journalists union from 2003 to 2015, the Deutschen Journalisten-Verbandes (DJV), called this incident "the darkest hour of German journalism since the end of WWII."[29]

Sometimes identities are revealed accidentally as in stories that take an odd turn. Bruning, of the Dutch Journalists Union, told the story of Hans Melchers, a billionaire head of a chemical business, whose 37-year-old daughter was kidnapped in 2005. News media had no reason to refrain from identifying the well-known and controversial family (Melchers' company had been accused of supplying banned chemicals to Iraq in the 1980s, an accusation he denied) because in this instance, they were victims and publicity could perhaps help the cause. But when the kidnappers demanded 600 pounds of cocaine as ransom, some news reports linked the kidnapping and the family to drug dealing. As the angle of the news stories shifted, hiding the family's identity became impossible. Although the speculation about drug dealing allegedly came from the police, Melchers sued both the popular tabloid *De Telegraaf* and also the Dutch news service ANP; he won a settlement and donated one million euros to a fund to help others bring legal actions against news media.[30]

Not surprisingly, the Dutch tabloid *De Telegraaf* operates outside the Netherlands Press Council and journalists union codes of ethics, and its regular readers expect it to name names. On the other hand, much of the Dutch public reacts strongly against other editors' decisions to reveal an identity. Thom Meens, who served as readers' ombudsman from 2004 to 2011 at the well-respected Dutch newspaper *De Volkskrant*, said he received numerous reader complaints that the paper reported too many details about crime and criminals, but no one ever told him that they wanted more. "I never get letters from readers that say why didn't you inform us of this or that, so they must think we give them the news they need to know," he said. Meens' experiences reflect the readers of *De Volkskrant*, which belongs to a class of newspapers Europeans call the "quality press." Those who pick up the tabloids may reflect a completely different standard. Ernst Elitz, ombudsman for the German tabloid *Bild,* reported that about half the readers he hears from want more details in the crime stories and about half wish there were fewer.

As we will explore in the next chapter, immigration—as well as populist reaction against it—puts increasing pressure on news media to change its usual practice of protecting identities, and instead to name suspects and out-line their ethnic and religious identities. Another factor we will explore is the ready availability on social media of the names and identifying features that legacy media protect in these countries. Christine Kensche, who covers crime and immigration for *Welt,* suggested that how to handle naming immigrants is an ongoing challenge for her, her own media outlet, and others in Germany. "If there is a crime, and an immigrant did it, do you name the country he came from, or not?"

Naysayers to Protectionist Policies

Not all journalists and media critics in these countries agree fully with the protectionist press policies—neither their efficacy nor their underlying aspirations. Some disagreed on practical grounds, and others found fault with aspects of the informing principles of the policies. Peter Burger, a uni-versity lecturer in the Centre for Linguistics, Journalism and New Media at Leiden University in the Netherlands, argued that such practices were of little consequence because news reporting still encouraged audiences to point fin-gers and find guilt by whipping up "moral panics" and creating the kind of "folk devils" that British academics like Stanley Cohen and others found in their country's reporting. "My take on this as a journalism scholar is [not naming] is a minor ritual, to borrow from Gaye Tuchman," Burger said. "By withholding names, [Dutch journalists] claim their actions are ethical, but they avoid the wider issue of trial by media in the way they treat parties in-volved in crime." Stories can still outline a person's background, education, class, and so on and focus a great deal of attention on crime as a singular act, sometimes connected to larger stereotypes of criminality.

Arendo Joustra of *Elsevier* magazine argued that inconsistencies in access to types of information invalidated much of the ethics policy's purpose: "If you write a letter to the editor, you can't do that anonymously, but if you kill someone, you can." When we first interviewed Joustra in 2010, he had resigned from the press council, he said, because he objected to the impo-sition of a single standard and advocated a market place of policies instead.

"I believe you should have plurality so not all newspapers should have the same rules. . . . What should be arranged is that the law should not abridge this freedom. If there is choice, the public can choose to read this paper that prints the name and not that paper that does not. . . . I say give the facts and let the people decide." And why are only Dutch citizens protected by this policy, he wondered. "It's hypocritical—to print the name of a child molester in Belgium because that is abroad. And if they kill themselves abroad, like Heath Ledger, then we can print that, too. . . . If the icon of journalism is the *New York Times*, [and they named] the killer of Theo van Gogh, what's wrong about that in journalistic terms?"

Ester Pollack, lecturer in journalism at the University of Stockholm, found hypocrisy not in journalistic practices per se, but in some Swedish journalists' self-congratulatory claim that they were motivated to protect criminals and withhold judgment of them rather than by a more practical consideration: the threat of government legislation to curb access or increase privacy. Journalists whom we spoke with did acknowledge that the Riksdag periodically threatens to limit access to information, but the press council's code of conduct and the journalism industry's willingness to self-policing of behavior has so far held the legislators at bay. Pollack, however, opined that the Riksdag's threats hold greater sway over journalistic practice than did any commitment to protect accused persons and criminals or to withhold judgment about allegations in the press.[31]

A Word About Victims

While our project focused largely on accused and convicted persons, we were often asked whether we were interested also in coverage of victims. In recent years, Protector nations have put increasing emphasis on the situations of those who, through no fault of their own, find themselves in vulnerable positions. The Dutch Press Council has been seeing greater public concern for victims, according to both Frits van Exter, who became chairman of the Netherlands Press Council in 2018, and Thomas Bruning, current head of the journalists union. Until late into the 1960s, Van Exter said, the Netherlands' major religions and the Social Democrats owned most of the newspapers, and they generally ignored crime in favor of what they saw as more "uplifting" news. Even today, crime stories are more the purview of the tabloids than the "quality" papers, although the latter do cover them. The pattern follows that outlined by Hallin and Mancini where development of press is closely linked to religious and/or political affiliation.[32] The aggressive coverage by reporters in Watchdog countries is not common among the more respected news organizations here.

Some reporters also noted a particular incident from 2010 that had heightened sensitivity to the plight of victims: Nine-year-old Ruben van Assouw became the sole survivor of a plane crash in Tripoli that killed 103 people, most of them Dutch, including his parents and brother. Photos of the badly injured boy in his hospital bed were widely disseminated by Dutch news media, including on the state television network NOS, headed by Hans Laroes at the time. A reporter for De Telegraf even spoke to the heavily sedated child when a doctor, who was unable to translate the journalist's questions into Dutch, handed Ruben the telephone. De Telegraf subsequently published photographs and headlined the fact that the boy did not yet know of his family's deaths; in contrast, all the Netherlands now did. Many news outlets later regretted what they came to see as an invasion of the boy's privacy and an exploitation of his vulnerability in a wholly tragic situation. De Telegraf apologized to its readers after it lost at least 1,000 subscribers who objected to its coverage.[33]

Bruning called a meeting of print and broadcast editors to discuss the reporting of Ruben's case, and Laroes told the group he thought there were two distinct moments of judgment. The first was when the incident occurred: Using the picture and name were legitimate then because people wanted and even needed to know. "But there is another moment after, and this goes for victims and for criminals," Bruning said, recalling Laroes' words, when the news follows a story for two or three years on the anniversary of the happening. The editors' group had invited a young man who had survived a similar plane crash in Portugal in which his parents had been killed to ask for his insights. Now 20, the young man had been 15 at the time of the crash. He told the journalists that the worst thing he experienced was being called by reporters every year on the anniversary to be asked how he was feeling. It was like being stalked, he said, and it hindered his ability to pick up and go on with his life. The editors took action, writing to news media all across Europe, asking them to take down photographs from their websites and leave the boy alone. All complied, Bruning reported, although the image remained on the Internet. On the one-year anniversary of the Tripoli crash, one NOS network affiliate did an interview with the boy's grandparents. After that, the matter was dropped, Laroes said.

Not all agreed with this course of action or the judgment behind it. Joustra argued that identifying children or even invading their privacy is not always wrong. Such strictures almost blocked the very valuable publication of *The Diary of Anne Frank*, an image of the depravity and end of innocence invoked by Hitler. "Ruben was the only person who survived, but he was standing out as a symbol of hope and that can hold the attention of all the world," said Joustra.

Being sensitive to victims introduces as much angst and disagreement as the treatment of criminals does. When a 22-year-old student went missing, Bruning said, "her bicycle was found, but she was missing. And there was a media blitz on this—where do we find her?" A regional television station set up a webcam where police were dredging the river for her body. Drones were used to show the body being brought out of the water. "And there was a lot of discussion about this—what if the family is looking at this webcam?" Those who defended the practice argued, "It's the scene of a crime, and if we aren't allowed on the ground, why can't we give the bigger picture when technology facilitates this?"

In some instances, people speak up when coverage of victims involves them or someone they know. Kerstin Dolde, ombudswoman for the regional paper *Frankenpost Neue Presse*, noted that readers complain most often about crime stories when coverage has identified them as a victim and they feel unsafe as a result of the publicity. "My editor-in-chief says I am the early warning system, and it is my job to be sensitive," she said. She encourages journalists to put themselves in others' shoes always. When younger colleagues wonder whether they should take a photo, she stresses empathy: "How would you feel about this if this were you?" she asks.

We were not surprised by the sensitivity to the plight of victims in these Protector countries because while the attitude toward accused and convicted persons is markedly different in the Watchdog countries, protection for victims is also part of journalists' crime coverage in this model. But what did surprise us was the role victims sometimes play inside the courtroom in Germany where each has their own counsel who can ask questions of the defendants. State attorneys are independent from the lawyers who represent the victims. They do not work together.[34] Thus, their stories, told in open court, can also become part of the public conversation in a manner unheard of in the other press models. In one of the most dramatic cases in recent German court history, five members of the National Socialist Underground (NSU), a far-right terror cell, were tried in connection with multiple murders, bank robberies, and various other crimes largely involving immigrants. The case began in 2013, but with about 100 victims who could speak, as well as their lawyers, a verdict was not delivered until 2018. The trial and its significance are discussed in Chapter 4.

Analysis

The readiness with which journalists and media experts in Protector countries expressed concern for the welfare of suspects and convicted criminals was unique in our research. In every interview, media professionals, press council members, and academics raised the negative impact that news coverage can have on families, an accused's presumption of innocence, and the hope for resocialization. As we have outlined, largely they were convinced that citizens in their democracies could be sufficiently well informed about the nature of a crime without causing undue harm to the suspects or the incarcerated and their families. Most cast their obligation to truth-telling as intrinsically linked to the question of what makes a "civilized or decent society," as one member of the Dutch Press Council put it.[35] Although we sometimes launched interviews with sample stories in which reporters had not followed standard protectionist policies, interview subjects quickly pointed out that such cases were exceptions. Journalists' convictions about their protectionist practices were mostly uniform and straightforward, yet the cultural and historic roots of their sentiments are complex. So is the matter of just what the practice "means" in each democratic model we considered.

Lennart Weibull of the SOM Institute told us that at one time Swedish reporters shared the beliefs held by many Watchdog reporters that they ought to explore and publish details about individuals involved with newsworthy crimes. He noted that in the 1970s and 1980s, Swedish reporters moved from an issues-oriented style of covering news to one that embraced a more personalized reporting. This change, he said, was largely due to the arrival and subsequent influence of American broadcasting in Sweden, as well as the 24-hour newscast. "And what was personalized reporting worth," he mused, "if you did not name the person? Nothing." Initially, reporters began to put victims' names and other details at the center of their stories, but the Swedish public protested. "They did not like photos about people leaving a funeral service," Weibull said, as an example of the finely tuned sense of privacy in these Protector countries. Then a journalist was raped and murdered in Stockholm and that, said Weibull, "worked as a vaccination." Once reporters could clearly identify with being in such a powerless position, they moved away from covering victims and from the more personalized American style. Weibull's anecdote suggests that, despite the global push toward the tell-all type of journalism generally followed in the United States and other Watchdog countries, journalistic practices do not transplant easily from one community or country to another. Crime coverage practices reflect the Protector countries' underlying attitudes about fairness, about what constitutes justice, and the role news media ought to play in supporting these beliefs in their democracies.

While those we interviewed did not acknowledge any particular ethical philosophy that informed their protectionist policies, we argue throughout this book that an unarticulated ethic of communitarianism, as well as a feminist ethic of care, underlies the Protector journalists' attitudes and the crime coverage choices that reflect them.[36] Offering a broad-based definition of communitarianism, David Craig, in "Communitarian Journalism(s)," suggests most adherents are united in "the view that liberalism does not sufficiently take into account the importance of community for personal identity, moral and political thinking, and judgments about our well-being in the contemporary world."[37] This approach is in sharp contrast to the underlying—and sometimes articulated—ethical beliefs expressed by the Watchdog journalists and explored in detail in the next part of this book. As Christians et al. argued in *Good News*, "the roots of Anglo-American news lie in the Enlightenment," which endowed journalists in these locales with "a pervasive individual autonomy" and left a legacy of rugged individualism, which implies a survival of the fittest, and a journalism style that sometimes sacrifices the needs of the few for the good of the many.[38] Communitarians, in contrast, would suggest that a person's sense of self stems primarily not from a rights- and justice-based perspective but rather from an acknowledgment of one's connection to others; to rephrase, humans are creatures of community, defined not by the independence favored by the Enlightenment (and Watchdogs) but rather by interdependence and connectedness. In a similar vein, Carol Gilligan argued *In a Different Voice* that traditional Western ethics approaches emphasize individual rights and the concurrent obligation to respect those rights.[39] Gilligan's ethics of care approach, in contrast, places peoples' obligations to others at the center. For her, the "justice orientation" ought to be complemented by a "responsibility orientation" where people acknowledge their relation as linked one to the next, and who see each other's histories, happenings, and stories as a part of the larger social fabric in a web of connection.[40] "This ethic, which reflects a cumulative knowledge of relationships, revolves around a central insight that the self and other are interdependent."[41] From such a perspective, as applied in the Protector countries, reporting practices focus on the broader issues of justice, else they demonize individuals and undermine citizens' moral obligations to see how their own institutions, cultural choices, and belief systems might bear some connection to, if not responsibility for, criminal behavior.

Journalism, the telling of a culture's own tales, is at the heart of how communities define themselves. Citizens' rights to undertake this ongoing conversation for social and individual discovery cannot be underestimated. This power should not be usurped either by a technology that lacks discernment or by an imposition that results from ignorance of others' storytelling practices. A community's ability to conduct its public business should not be put in jeopardy. As Carol Gilligan and then many other feminists have asserted, persons denied their own unique voice cannot undertake the work of becoming moral beings.[42] By extension, differing news reporting practices also should not readily be transplanted or imposed—even with knowledge of the differences—for two reasons: First, others' approaches are unlikely to have resonance with the public whose beliefs they purport to reflect; tone-deaf renderings could cause further alienation between citizens and their media and less participation in the democratic sphere. Second, an unthinking adaptation of a reporting style simply because the Internet and social media impose such a thing is driven by tribal or economic considerations, rather than ethical concerns. The result—a flattening of difference and a universal sameness—is not the solution.

Our data suggest that each community must undergo its own, culturally specific "moral workout."[43] Showing sensitivity to defendants by shielding them and their families by not naming in full, as is the routine or default practice for journalists in the Protector model, makes a broad statement about peoples' worth and about the degree of empathy they deserve. When seen from the perspective of an ethics of care, people are not solely individuals; rather, they are part of the social collective in which all share some responsible for their mistakes and their successes.

The idea of stories that explore life's challenges, but in the end, celebrate people's shared humanity and resilience, can be found in a tradition much older than journalism: that of the folk and fairy tale. These ancient stories, universally told and much loved in Western countries, are populated with characters who are identified generically: the milk maid, the pauper, or the king. Similarly, when reporters remove identifying information from crime stories, their tales reflect a sense that those accused or guilty of an illegal act are still members of a larger whole to which the news audience also belongs. Morgan Jerkins, an American writer and literary critic, suggests there is a paradoxical solidarity between characters and their readers when fictional characters have no name: "Nameless protagonists provide a mirror into our own souls while trying to assess their own simultaneously. And for that, the revelation is that although we have no names for the characters with whom we resonate, we know them intuitively."[44] Nameless characters ask readers to focus on their humanity rather than the specific details of how they are perceived by society, Jenkins argued. Readers perform a kind of moral workout, filling in the gaps of the narrative by projecting their own experiences onto the character.

In recent years, nameless protagonists and characters have made a resurgence and are enjoying popularity once again in the literary field. Sam Sacks, in a piece for *The New Yorker*, wrote, "The phenomenon isn't new, of course, though for a long time it was predominantly a feature of allegories: John Bunyan's Christian, for instance, or the anonymous playwright's Everyman (invoked by Philip Roth in his eponymous 2006 novel, which also has an unnamed protagonist)."[45] This kind of systematic formulation is both predictable and comforting; it reassures people that they have a place in the world, and that their experiences are shared by others around them. No one is truly alone. "Similar efforts at Everyman universality are found in fairy tales, whose characters are often kept nameless or given purely descriptive labels (Sleeping Beauty, say, or the Little Mermaid), thus facilitating projections and identifications, as Bruno Bettelheim put it."[46] These theorists and authors point to the timeless and transcendent qualities of unnamed characters to draw out readers' empathy. Stories that detail the lives of "everyhuman," like those in fairy tales, ask readers to focus not on the story's or the character's unique or personal details, but rather to access the deeper truths about human existence because the situations "are always presented as ordinary, something that could happen to you or me or the person next door when out on a walk in the woods."[47]

We argue that readers of a crime story in a German, Dutch, or Swedish newspaper where identification is usually masked, are more able to identify and sympathize with wrongdoers because criminality is not so grounded in a specific identity. Tangentially, readers might also more readily see themselves

each had their own schools, hospitals, trade unions and political parties that cut vertically through the social strata, creating parallel "pillars." The printing press became the principal tool of this pillarization process with each "pillar" urging its constituents to read particular newspapers that supported its beliefs. Even after decades of expanding secularization, the metaphor of these pillars that work together to support the moral and political temple of Dutch society still holds. The Dutch, who built a system of dikes and canals that regulate water levels and keep the country from flooding, have always worked cooperatively in practical ways. They still emphasize that the pillars are not oppositional political and religious silos: They maintain their separate identities but work together in common cause. In the 20th century, all three Protector countries adopted political models that "involved compromise and power sharing among the major organized interests of society and an expansion of the welfare state."[55] Partisan affiliations among the mass media also mellowed, yet they still affect media structures and practices. Some media professionals, including Thomas Bruning, of the Dutch journalists union, credit these historic associations with the high degree of journalistic professionalism and near consensus on professional standards. In Sweden and Germany, religious institutions, political parties, and organizational guilds and unions played a similar role in the formation of journalism ethics.

Germany, the Netherlands, and Sweden are proudly open societies, which we will explore more in the next chapter. From the time of Sweden's 1766 Press Freedom Act, all state agency documents have been open.[56] A Swedish person can trace a car license plate or look up a neighbor's salary or trust fund income. "You can see who in Gothenburg in various parishes is earning the most.... You can see what people own and what they have inherited," Weibull said. With a similar cultural impulse toward transparency, many Amsterdam houses do not have curtains on their windows. That custom holds particular intrigue for the uninitiated, but both the Dutch and Swedes emphasize that rules of decorum and opprobrium still govern social behavior. The public salary record or the unveiled window may be open for viewing, but it is generally considered impolite to look. The metaphor can be aptly applied to how journalists and citizens are expected to behave: keeping their eyes focused on the information that enhances public discourse, and not straying over to the personal and largely irrelevant prurient details.

3

Threats to and Benefits of the Protective Policies

Journalism practices in Protector countries are deeply rooted in the once largely homogenous cultures that spawned them. James Carey recognized that newsroom rituals weave and reweave a tapestry that tells the tale of what it means to be German, Swedish, or Dutch.[1] As we outlined, crime coverage practices configure a pattern of values that evolve over the years but within a larger, more stable narrative. Now, that stability is under siege. Globalization, most intensely focused on crime and immigration and the tell-all reporting style popular on the Internet and social media platforms, threatens the embedded sense of who a people are, how they treat one another, and how they ought to address the challenges of difference. In this chapter, we consider how immigrants have been framed as a threat across these nations. We examine the varying responses from news outlets, as well as press councils, about how best to outline, advance, and maintain these public conversations, and which details ought to be included and why.

Threats: Media Representations of Immigration

Kandel, Germany, December 2017: A teenage boy whose girlfriend had recently broken off their relationship used a kitchen knife to stab her inside a convenience store. She died a short time later. Within hours, German social media, coffeehouse chatter, and mainstream TV and radio obsessed over the death of Mia V. This murder traumatized the midsized town, not only because both the suspect and victim were so young but also because the boy, whom much of mainstream German media began to identify as Abdul D., was an Afghan migrant and the girl was German. Two days after the teen's death, the far-right political party, Alternative for Germany (AfD), marched through the streets of Kandel, followed by the older extremist National Democratic Party of Germany (NPD), to draw attention to what they saw

Murder in Our Midst. Romayne Smith Fullerton and Maggie Jones Patterson, Oxford University Press (2021). © Oxford University Press. DOI: 10.1093/oso/9780190863531.003.0003.

as the "problem" of immigrants and crime. Kandel's mayor lamented that ethnic tensions had propelled Mia's story into international headlines. A few weeks earlier, he said, the story of a Kandel resident who had murdered his wife and two children never made it past the local news. Reports about Abdul D. and Mia V. were a stark contrast. "Once again, the story went, a refugee had attacked a German girl. She was only 15."[2] What makes both citizens' and media's reaction to the Kandel story so surprising is that Germany and most Nordic nations normally throw a thick blanket of privacy over crime victims and perpetrators—especially when they are minors.

In Germany, it is against the law to name a minor unless the crime is "one for the history books"; in such cases, the significance of the crime is such that public need to know outweighs a juvenile's right to protection. In Sweden, journalists also routinely protect those under age 18. "We do have stories of kids killing kids and teenage girls being killed by ex-boyfriends or friends from school. Several in the past year," Martin Jönsson told us in 2010, when he was managing editor of *Svensk Dagbladet* in Stockholm. Some newspapers there had experimented with telling stories about how the murdered girls had ended up as victims. But details like drug abuse surfaced and risked further harming the victims' families, Jönsson said, and so the practice soon stopped. His paper kept both the victim and the alleged perpetrator anonymous, even though social media often spurned such conventions and offered details in full.

The aspirational journalistic commitments and concomitant press practices in these Protector countries run deep, even as they bump into challenges brought about by globalization and technology, and where information most reporters routinely hold back—like names of accused or convicted persons—is only a mouse-click away, circulated freely in neighboring nations. But in Germany, the tensions wrought by rising immigration have not only put pressure on existing protectionist policies; they have also brought about change. In 2017, the Deutscher Presserat (German Press Council) decided to implement new wording in its ethics policy that, up to then, had guided crime coverage practices firmly in the direction of anonymity; unless ethnicity was specifically relevant to the reporting of wrongdoing, it was not to be included in the copy. This earlier version, drawn up by the German Press Council, in collaboration with press associations in 2006, stated in Guideline 12.1: "When reporting crimes, it is not permissible to refer to the suspect's religious, ethnic or other minority membership unless information can be justified as being relevant to readers' understanding of the incident. In particular, it must be borne in mind that such references could stir up prejudices against minorities."[3] An example would be a crime involving the Italian mafia, pointed out Sonja Volkmann-Schluck, the German Press Council's public relations officer.

In March 2017, the code was changed. The new Guideline 12.1 "Report on Crime" stated: "When reporting on crimes, it must be ensured that any reference to a suspect's or perpetrator's membership of ethnic, religious or other minority groups does not result in a discriminatory generalisation of individual misconduct. As a rule, membership of a minority group shall not be mentioned, unless this is in the legitimate interest of the general public. In particular, it must be borne in mind that such references could stir up prejudices against minorities."[4]

"We had months of discussions" at *Süddeutsche Zeitung*, said Annette Ramelsberger, "and we decided to write [to specify ethnicity] if it's necessary to understand the story. We don't say it if a man from Bosnia sets a house on fire because he wants to get some insurance money. Then the national origin is not important. But when you have hundreds of North African boys raping women, then it would be journalistically decent to write about their origin."

Opinions on the change continued to be divided in 2018. While some criticized the revisions as a surrender to right-wing pressures, Stephan Russ-Mohl saw it differently: "German newsrooms have to be aware that one of consequences of *not* mentioning ethnicity when people would be interested in knowing [is that it] leads to the success of the populists. They—whether you want to know it or not—they are changing the rules of the game." *Süddeutsche Zeitung's* internal policy stuck with the original rule while the east German newspaper, *Sächsische Zeitung*, elected to identify all ethnicity, including German, in every crime story in order to be seen as being even-handed.

The rule change "absolutely" benefits journalists, said Cornelia Haas, spokesperson for the Deutsche Journalistinnen und Journalisten Union, one of two journalists unions in Germany and a founding organization of the press council. "We discussed it widely in our organization," she said, and with much uncertainty about how to protect minorities on the one hand and how to satisfy the public's need for information on the other hand. They studied how the Nazis smeared Jewish people and other minorities by associating them with crime. "We said it is more important to protect people against discrimination than satisfy every interest of the public. And that is why we invented the phrase 'of public interest.' And it is not curiosity—there is a big difference. We worked to make it clear that media work is not to satisfy curiosity, but it is work in the name of the public interest."

While an argument can be made that the phrase, "in the legitimate interest of the general public" ought to move coverage beyond a need to satisfy curiosity, we note that it is one that has long been deployed in Watchdog countries where it is sometimes used to justify dissemination of ethically questionable material. As we have argued elsewhere, often this defense is trotted out to explain away unwarranted invasions of privacy and can shift news reports from ones that ought to focus on information citizens need to be free and self-governing to ones that focus on the prurient and sensational; in short, "in the public interest" can protect poor press practices that serve profit-making not public ends and can demonize innocent individuals for a utilitarian good.

Given that the press code had recently been rewritten because of changes in German attitudes about the need to access information in the reporting of alleged crimes, the seemingly extreme responses to the Kandel murder were not without context. By the time that story broke, the formerly tolerant attitudes of most citizens and the protective press policies that reflected this value had already begun to shift in Germany. But the pressures for change did not originate in Kandel. A number of reporters to whom we spoke noted that the pressure on them to "tell all"—specifically, name names and ethnicity, began several years earlier in a now notorious international news event. A police document was leaked to *Süddeutsche Zeitung* and a couple of broadcasters. Its contents were then reported in the *Washington Post*. It outlined allegations that about 2,000 men assaulted 1,200 German women in various towns and cities across the country during outdoor New Year's Eve celebrations in 2015. The women said the men who attacked them appeared to be Arab or North African, but the story was not reported immediately in the mainstream German media.[5] It was a watershed moment. Right-leaning populist politicians began tying immigrants to what they claimed were rising tides of crime. They accused the German news media of colluding with Chancellor Angela Merkel to keep such stories out of the news. "Even Merkel's Bavarian coalition partner, the Christian Social Union, alleged that the media had tried to cover up the attacks in an attempt at self-censorship and in order not to threaten public support for pro-refugee policies. The general secretary of the party, Andreas Scheuer, told public radio station *Deutschlandfunk*: 'I urge everyone to report the truth. . . . Those who are in fear over how our society will evolve criticize that the published opinion partially does not reflect reality, because one [he referred to German media outlets] mistakenly thinks one must be extra careful.' "[6] In this New Year's Eve instance, then, when German news media followed their usual practice of protecting the identity of accused criminals with pixilated photos and only partial names, some German news consumers accused the journalists of hiding immigrant crime.

While the problem of when and whether to identify ethnicity is not unique to these Protector countries, decisions in Germany are particularly poignant because the memory of Hitler's genocide remains and because German journalists have been committed to guarding reputations, protecting relatives, and preserving the presumption of innocence for more than 40 years.[7] Adding to the tensions around the Kandel murder is the added consideration that the happening involved people who were not of legal age, or "the age of consent," as it is called in North America. Revealing even part of a minor's identity stirs more controversy in Protector countries than in the English-speaking, Watchdog locales (United States, England and Wales, Ireland, and Canada) where older teens can be tried and/or sentenced in adult court for serious crimes. At least Canada and the United States permit the juvenile to be identified publicly in such instances; England does not.[8] In Germany, juveniles cannot be tried as adults.[9] Nevertheless, Ernst Elitz, ombudsman for the tabloid *Bild*, said identifying Abdul D. was not unusual because he was accused of a capital offense—and because that case was con-sidered "one for the history books."[10]

The Netherlands is at a different stage of development on the issue of iden-tifying ethnicity, said Hans Laroes, past chair of the Dutch Press Council. "We had these debates 10 or 12 years ago," he said, after anti-Islam politi-cian Pim Fortuyn was assassinated in 2002 and filmmaker Theo Van Gogh in 2004. Thomas Bruning of the journalists union agreed: "We were accused then of looking away." Those accusations still stung when we first conducted interviews in the Netherlands in 2010. When we returned in 2018, however, we heard a firmer commitment to protection. The Dutch Press Council had rewritten its code in 2015 and stuck with the rule that ethnicity, religion, and other minority status should only be reported when they are necessary to the understanding of the story. "We are used to the idea that journalists are seen as leftist and siding with Islam. But whatever we do, we will be under pres-sure," Laroes said. He saw the earlier wavering by Dutch journalists reflected in the current German debates. "I know how to do journalism. I don't say that from arrogance but from professional confidence. . . . We do consider impact. It is the difference between being objective and being a professional, which goes to judgment and standards."

In Germany, the differing context led to differing decisions about handling Abdul D.'s identification. The tabloid *Bild*, which enjoys the largest daily circulation in the country, went the furthest toward "tell-all." The paper ran a front-page photograph of Abdul D., dressed in a white shirt with a black bow tie, without pixilation or the black bar that is commonly printed over a suspect's eyes in Protector countries.

Abdul D.'s story could have served as a means to tell the larger story about immigrant problems and inadequacies of the screening process, rather than a finger-pointing personal indictment. As we outline in Chapter 5, the technique of using the specifics of an individual's story as a means to dig into broader social issues is popular in Watchdog countries. But this style of reporting has a shallower history in Protector nations, where the approach can clash with desires to shield the suspect. Stephan Russ-Mohl, professor of journalism and media management at Università della Svizzera italiana, disagreed with the choice to identify and delve into the criminal's background. To illustrate his perspective, he pointed to the example of Andreas Lubitz, the Lufthansa co-pilot, who deliberately crashed a passenger plane into the Alps in 2015, killing 144 passengers and six crew members. He hid the fact that he had been treated for suicidal tendencies and declared unfit to work by his doctor; instead, Lubitz reported to work. While some German news media viewed the case as an opportunity to question the shortcomings in medical privacy rights that had allowed Lubitz to fly, Russ-Mohl and others we interviewed mistrusted this method, citing the harm to Lubitz's family. Too much emphasis on the individual, Russ-Mohl said, demonizes criminals, and in this case, might generalize too widely about mental illness. He believes too many news organizations pay excessive attention to individuals and too little to institutions and their larger systemic failings. As Lennart Weibull reported in the last chapter, Swedish journalists tried a more personal "American" style of reporting for a spell in the 1970s and 1980s but ultimately found it an ill fit with their sense of personal privacy.

A Complicated Context: Covering Immigration

Beginning in the late 20th century, the immigrant as criminal became a common meme in European politics, as well as in news coverage, especially in the tabloid press. Some Dutch news organizations would write about a "Moroccan child," even when referring to a child born in the Netherlands of Middle Eastern parents, reported Thom Meens, ombudsman at *de Volkskrant*, a Dutch national daily newspaper. Because journalists in Protector countries normally do not identify suspects or defendants, in some respects, the choice to use a first name and last initial can cause discussion in newsrooms. The effect, if not the aim, of using the first name is transparent. "If you don't write about the Moroccan guy, but you say it was Mohammad E., then everyone knows he's a Moroccan," Meens said. Some news organizations are reluctant to use the first name for just this reason, said Hans Laroes, former head of the Dutch Press Council, "and then others, like *De Telegraaf*, are eager to do this. . . . I know I have instructed the editors and journalists to be very careful about this because of the impact it can have that has nothing to do with the story at all. Of course, you do not hide the facts, but you have to bear in mind other factors."

There are times, Protector reporters and editors pointed out, when the clash between Muslims and other European cultures puts religion and ethnicity at the center of crime stories. Then, they must tell what readers or viewers need to know to understand the story; such information is then given in the public interest. For example, when filmmaker Theo van Gogh was murdered in Amsterdam in 2004, his assassin, Mohammed Bouyeri, a Dutch-Moroccan Muslim, was identified in the Dutch news media as Mohammed B., a name that signaled his ethnicity. Van Gogh had been receiving death threats ever since the release of the film *Submission*, which criticized the treatment of Muslim women and enraged many in the Dutch Muslim community. Bouyeri admitted his motives were religious, Meens said. "So, to understand the crime—if you *can* understand assassination—you need to know that he was a Muslim and that he attacked the filmmaker because he thought [Van Gogh] was big and fighting against Muslims. So, there it is of value to know [the ethnic identity]—it is part of the story."

Thomas Mattsson, editor of the Swedish tabloid *Expressen*, made a similar claim when he instructed his staff to fully identify two Kosovan brothers who were arrested for firebombing the home of Lars Vilks, a Swedish cartoonist who had drawn the head of Mohammed on a dog. Vilks received death threats after a regional Swedish newspaper, *Nerikes Allehanda*, published the cartoon, which Muslims saw as sacrilegious, to illustrate an editorial on "The right to ridicule a religion."[11] As a result, Vilks was subjected to an assassination attempt and was attacked while giving a talk at Uppsala University. An al-Qaeda front organization offered $100,000 for Vilks' murder and $50,000 for the death of *Nerikes Allehanda* editor-in-chief, Ulf Johansson.

When Vilks' home was firebombed, Mattsson was fed up. He asked the *Expressen* staff to do an in-depth profile of two alleged arsonists, Mentor Alija, 21, and his brother Mensur, 19, and identify them fully to drive home a point. "I am about freedom of expression," Mattsson said, defending himself against the backlash he received from some other Swedish journalists. "Sometimes you have a story that is more than just the news, and you want the background—who they are, how they were brought up. . . . If you make them anonymous, . . . you couldn't tell all the details, and people might not understand the background." His newspaper explored how the Alija brothers had come to Sweden from Kosovo with their parents and sister and became citizens in 2007. Neighbors described them as "nice boys," who were not deeply religious but nonetheless resented what they saw as a degradation of Islam. Mattsson's desire to tell their story echoed the sentiments expressed by American reporters we interviewed, who had probed the backgrounds of criminals as a means of exploring social issues that lay beneath their crimes. To Mattsson, the young men "were attacking the freedom of speech principle, and they knew that when they attacked this artist."

Mattsson's critics saw a different picture. They argued that his actions demonized the two young men and damaged them and their families beyond repair—exactly the problem German professor Stephan Russ-Mohl found with using individual stories, like that of Abdul D., as a means to illustrate larger social ills. In cases like the Swedish firebombing, spotlighting the young men can demonize not just them but also the entire ethnic group to which they belong. It is one way how negative stereotypes are created and perpetuated.

The recent ascent of German nationalism and populism into the political mainstream meant the press could no longer ignore the arguments of its proponents, including claims that immigrants—especially the flood of asylum seekers Germany admitted beginning in 2015—had triggered a crime spree. When Angela Merkel announced her intention to admit up to a million refugees after the Syrian crisis, the German news media had reacted positively. They said Germany needed the workers and told positive stories about refugees, Russ-Mohl recalled; even the conservative tabloid *Bild* joined the chorus. Commentators drew sympathetic parallels between the current migrants and the 750,000 East Prussians who had fled west ahead of the advancing Red Army in early 1945.[12] Ultimately, these stories may have backfired. When hopeful features about well-meaning refugees had run their course, more dramatic news—chiefly crime—took focus.[13] The 2015 New Year's Eve harassment and rape allegations shocked the world. Journalists to whom we spoke repeatedly referred to this event as the moment when sympathies for immigrants turned sour. Afterward, most German news media continued to follow the German Press Council code at the time that said to mention ethnicity in stories only when it was directly relevant to a crime. However, media readers and viewers, encouraged by a growing anti-immigrant sentiment on the right, pummeled reporters and editors with accusations that they were doing Chancellor Merkel's bidding by "hiding" the ethnicity of the accused to protect immigrants.

Christine Kensche, immigration and crime reporter for *Welt*, dug into the statistics in an effort to pull truth out of the rhetorical quagmire. Statistics can be misleading. "The crime rate for immigrants is higher but not necessarily because they are immigrants," she observed. In Germany, as in most countries, the highest crime rate is among men between the ages of 18 and 30. Many of the recent immigrants were single men in that demographic. She compared immigrants to Germans in this age group. "But then you also have to look at the kind of crime." She found lots of the crimes involved public transportation, for example, perhaps because immigrants did not speak the language or were confused about how to buy a ticket or could not afford one. Probing deeper into the accuracy of assumptions, *Welt* also looked at rape statistics "because we had the whole discussion about Cologne," Kensche said. "There is the stereotype of foreign men who rape German women because in their countries, there is not much respect for women and not the concept of equal rights." When it came to rape or sexual harassment, the number of suspects from Afghanistan and Pakistan in 2017 was the highest within the group of immigrants, she found, and so she went to rape trials of men from these countries looking for what cultural factors might be at play. In some cases, the cultural perspective that women are worth less than men did indeed play a role. Also, the fact that women in Germany go out alone at night and talk to men without meaning to signal a willingness to have sex seemed confusing for some of the suspects. She tried to explain all these things in her stories, avoiding generalizations that she knew would trigger a volume of responses, saying, "See? It's men from Arab countries who always behave like this." Although cultural differences are a factor in certain crime cases, the cases themselves were too complex to break down to a simple thesis like that. Crime statistics indicate an increasing rate of immigrants as suspects in recent years, but at the same time, there was a big influx of immigrants in Germany. The definition of the term "immigrant" and which groups and statuses of foreigners it included (e.g., asylum seekers, refugees, illegal immigrants) changed over the years and so did the laws on rape and sexual harassment. That means that statistics don't always lead to clear results; they, too, have to be interpreted, and as numbers in different years are not always comparable, there are no simple answers to questions like "are crime rates among immigrants really higher or increasing?"—which, Kensche indicated, is one of the most pressing questions from readers of *Welt*.

Reporters in the Protector countries are caught in a double bind as immigration issues flare at high temperatures. Scholars, such as Walter Fisher and Alasdair MacIntyre,[14] tell us that we are hardwired to find meaning in stories, especially when they cohere with preconceptions. Statistical evidence raises a dull sword against the power of the well-told story. Crime reporters are damned if they do identify ethnicity—by using an identifying first name or by naming a country of origin—because they both feed anti-immigrant prejudice and are condemned for doing so. But they are also damned if they don't: By concealing ethnicity, reporters stand accused of duplicity. Ethically, they must be guided by what the public needs, not wants, to know; they need the wisdom of Solomon to make that distinction.

Technology and Tabloid Threats

While fiery political disputes about immigration may color the coverage of crime, the Internet poses an even more fundamental threat to protectionist habits of journalists in these countries. One news-aggregating website in the Netherlands, for example, reruns mainstream media crime stories but adds in what journalists left out. "If I write a column about someone who is accused of committing a crime and I defend his privacy and don't use his name, they will take my column, put it on their site and fill in the full name," Liesbeth Buitink, editor at the Dutch Algemeen Nederland Persbureau (ANP) news agency, said. Similarly, when other websites link to reporters' blogs, the website's headlines show up. "We remove the names (of suspects or criminals) if we can," said Martin Jönsson of Sweden's daily *Svenska Dabladet*. Nonetheless, he added "if we decide that it's not relevant to publish the name, we don't, regardless of what *every other* publisher in Sweden may publish." He cited the example of a parking lot fight in the south of Sweden, near

Malmo, where immigrant tensions were feverish. In an angry exchange that led to punches with an elderly couple, a young Lebanese immigrant knocked down the woman, who banged her head and died. While most news media did not reveal his name, "we did have to say he was an immigrant because of the tension in society," Jönsson said. The blogs were accusing his paper and others of protecting the perpetrator because he was an immigrant, when it "was really just a row in a parking lot," he said.

The easy availability of identities on the web has had an impact on how news organizations and press councils handle these cases. "We used to deal with just the traditional media," acknowledged Froukje Santing, a Netherlands Press Council member in 2010. But with all the information readily available online, there is a global media now, said Daphne Koene, the council's general secretary. "The old borders are gone, owing to the Internet. Now people are identified beyond the boundaries of any one jurisdiction," she said. Nonetheless, when we revisited the Netherlands in 2018 to see whether attitudes had changed, many stressed their different approach from that of Germany where ethnicity is identified if it is considered "in the public interest." "We have moved a bit in the German direction," admitted Frits van Exter, current chair of the Dutch Press Council. Even before the Pim Fortuyn assassination, he said, "the left-wing parties were closing their eyes to problems related to immigrants. The police and other authorities were suppressing statistics and information, and news was seen as part of the problem by people who wanted to address this." Tagging criminals as "Dutch Moroccans" and the like became more common. But the Dutch Press Council rewrote its code in 2015 and stuck with the rule that ethnicity, religion, and other minority status should only be reported when they are necessary to the understanding of the story. Thus, the Dutch have decided that protectionism is still the best path going forward for them. In the words of ombudsman at *de Volkskrant*, Thom Meens, "People choose [to read] us because that is what we do."

Morgan Olofsson, head of news at Swedish Public Television, noted how competition often blurs an ethical focus. "It's not a moral or ethical discussion—is it right or wrong? It becomes, how would we compare with competitors if they publish and we don't?" he said, lamenting the change. Television's vast power to influence, Olofsson argued, combined with the great freedom and access to information Swedes enjoy, requires journalists to exercise restraint. "Whoever is strong must be kind as well," he said. Both Olofsson and Mats Larsson of *Dagens Nyheter* recalled a case in which a broken relationship resulted in the death of two children and the serious injury of their mother in a small Swedish town. At first, the husband was arrested. Then he was released, and his former German wife was arrested. The evening tabloids immediately identified him, then her. But Olofsson and Larsson held back. Both news outlets waited until after the conviction to identify the German woman. They had neither named nor damaged the reputation of the innocent husband. There is an advantage to following the older, more protectionist ways, Olofsson said; otherwise, you are relying solely on police suspicions. While he was attending a journalism workshop at the Poynter Institute in Florida, he said, he was shocked by the coverage of a domestic dispute on a local television station that showed the mother's mug shot and the house where the family lived. "I thought: I am a Martian. That would never happen [in Sweden]."

"In the 1960s and '70s, criminals were regarded as victims, and we needed to take care of them and educate them," said Thomas Mattsson of *Expressen*, echoing in the Swedish context the findings of British criminologist Robert Reiner about the portrayal of criminal behavior in England after the Second World War.[15] The central question at that time became, what tragic circumstances, or what social deprivation, had led to this behavior. But soon after, conservatives like Ronald Reagan and Margaret Thatcher in the 1980s reframed the issue. Their policies expelled criminals, punished them, and held out small hope for rehabilitation, Reiner said. The globalization of news through CNN, Fox, and Sky News spread that message, Mattsson said. "Then we got the Internet, and suddenly news organizations were adapting more to international press systems." Mats Larsson called the Internet "a parallel publishing system" and an extremely fast one. The new media landscape has made it difficult for the morning—broadsheet or "quality"—newspapers to continue their protective practices. The website, Flashback, Larsson believes, sprung up in the wake of mainstream media's privacy policies. A place for citizen journalism and discussion, Flashback's logo is a cartoon Sylvester-like cat with a cigarette dangling from his vicious grin. The site publishes all the specific facts about persons that Larsson's paper and others keep private, Larsson reported. And the contrast between traditional news organizations and sites like Flashback creates myths, Larsson said, "like that Muslims are more frequently involved in murder cases than blond Swedes." Sweden does not record ethnicity on criminal records, so facts can neither confirm nor negate the myth. The policy of anonymity fuels rumors, Larsson said, and the traditional media are seen as "the political 'elite' that is not really listening to the voice of the people anymore. . . . You get a media subculture growing on the net with alternative sites. It doesn't cost anything to start a blog or whatever. You can never be sure if it is true or not. But it's a fast-moving world."

Thoughts on "Belonging"

Until recent times when the European Union collapsed borders and English gained ground as the continent's *lingua franca*, many Western European peoples felt bonded by "blood and soil." Even before the Nazis poisoned that attachment with their slogan *Blut und Boden*, the idea of a people who reside in particular geographic areas with historic ties to the land and related by similar DNA was foreign to the more transient North Americans.[16] The latter moved into the wide-open spaces of the New World, driven by their sense of conquest and ownership, not by a sense of belonging, or perhaps by a sense of *not* belonging. Sections of the United States and Canada carry regional accents, but English-speaking language differences are minor compared with European dialects.

Some Germans refer to their country as *Heimat*, or homeland, a folksy notion of the connection of the people to their land and traditions before the Nazis corrupted that word, too. There is a similar term employed in Sweden—*folkhemmet*, or the people's home—a term that played an important part in the Social Democrats' shaping a corporatist welfare state, situated between capitalism and socialism and designed to diminish class lines. *Folkhemmet* implies that Swedes are supposed to care for one another. For centuries, all Swedish newborns have been registered in the *folkbokföring*, the people's book or registry, to launch their "belonging." In the 21st century, these ideas have taken on new meaning as social, political, and economic insecurities shake their very foundations. *Hygge*, an ancient Nordic word for "friendly togetherness," is now co-opted by numerous advertisements and as a T-shirt slogan. Center-left governments, which governed Sweden for most of the past 100 years, sought to fulfill that promise of *folkhemmet* with policies that met everyone's needs and left no one wanting. That commitment diminished in the 1980s when the Social Democrats introduced new free-market policies, followed by waves of economic de-regulation and the privatization of schools, electrical power, and other infrastructures during the early 1990s. Conservatives, in power from 2006 to 2014, cut income and property taxes. The number of billionaires grew rapidly, and the income gap widened.[17] Despite these setbacks, Sweden ranked first out of 152 countries on Oxfam's 2017 Commitment to Reducing Inequality Index.

But widespread immigration, both from other European Union countries and from the Middle East and North Africa, also disrupted—or at least redefined—notions of equality and belonging. Anti-immigration politicians and movements have fought to block the absorption of newcomers by constantly pointing out their alleged shortcomings. Akbar Ahmed, an Islam scholar at American University in Washington and Pakistan's former high commissioner to the United Kingdom and Ireland, accused Europe's far-right politics of exacerbating the desperation of Muslim immigrants, who are both struggling to integrate and hang onto their identity in a rapidly changing world. In his impressionistic *Journey into Europe*, Ahmed found the liberal Nordic countries and Germany harbored the strongest tribal identities and resistance to diversity. Reconciling cozy ideas of belonging with the challenges of diversification is particularly daunting, Ahmed said.[18] Here, immigration has teamed up with broader forces of globalization to loosen the once-embedded ties of religion, blood, soil, and culture.

In Sweden, a clash between diversity and equality threatens the viability of a generous welfare state. Liberals worry about what they perceive as doctrinaire Muslim religious beliefs and sexist attitudes toward women. Far-right conservatives and the liberal left agree that some aspects of Muslim immigration are pulling homegrown culture off its foundations. Thus, they find themselves on different paths to an uncomfortable common ground. The strong religious and social welfare associations that once stood as the pillars of these societies have weakened and so might the citizens' high degree of confidence in the state. Swedes trust the state, the court system, and the integrity of their police, Swedish media scholar Lennart Weibull's research found.[19] Historically, the press has supported this trust, both in its habits of practice and its story frames. Crime stories reflect a faith in the courts and the penal system. Newspapers themselves were once owned or closely associated with those pillar religious and political associations. To James Carey, and to many of our interview subjects, news organizations still reflect that history. In *Communication as Culture*, Carey detailed the way many Europeans view communication as more of a "ritual" than a mere transfer of information.[20] The ritual approach views "the original or highest manifestation of communication not in the transmission of intelligent information, but in the construction and maintenance of an ordered, meaningful cultural world that can serve as a control and container for human action."[21] This view of the communication process and its practices, products, motives, and goals encourages concern for the group—the community by preserving what they share. In Carey's definition, ritual communication "is linked to terms such as 'sharing,' 'participation,' 'association,' 'fellowship,' and 'the possession of a common faith.'"[22] It exploits "communication's ancient and common roots of the terms like 'commonness,' 'communion' and 'community.'"[23] A ritual approach to communication does not simply extend messages in space. It is more directed toward maintaining a society in time—"not just an act of imparting information but also of representing shared beliefs."[24] As we have outlined, ritual communication in the news business may not survive the forces that are pulling it apart. Yet, as some of our examples have shown, journalism can choose to keep its commitment to its fundamental missions and principles, bending without breaking, even in the face of tumultuous winds of change. Holding firm to such aspirational values is imperative to maintaining and furthering journalism's credibility and its place in the public sphere.

4

Protectors' Accountability

Democracy shifts in size and shape from nation to nation, but informed citizens always form its foundation. News, which also comes in a variety of delivery modes, holds the primary function of supplying citizens with the information they need "to be free and self-governing."[1] Overall, journalism should always be judged on how well it performs this fundamental function.[2] We use crime reporting to examine how and how well journalism reports on the criminal justice system—police and courts, key parts of the democratic process.

One option in reporting crime is to frame the story inside a fiery ring of indignation that arouses prejudices and harsh judgments. This style of reporting—used a great deal in the Watchdog countries—can serve to demonize individual perpetrators and often concentrates on the gruesome, sensational details of each crime. It shoves aside criminals as "other" or as monster and pushes them outside all bounds of decency. While such stories relieve public anxiety and provide the temporary satisfaction that "evil" has been vanquished, their long-term product is often political cynicism. Robert Reiner, emeritus professor of criminology at the London School of Economics, has examined this phenomenon.[3] This story frame rummages around in personal details but often neglects to address root causes of crime or explain why "demons" continue to surface. This style of coverage can result in harsh punitive policies that attempt to warehouse all society's folk devils but still fail to affect crime rates. Each crime is explored as a personal and individual event. Private aspects of the criminals'—and even the victims'—lives that are deemed pertinent by the press are made public. The result, political philosopher Jean Bethke Elshtain argues, is "politics is displaced, when private matters become grist for the public mill and everything public is privatized and played out in a psychodrama on a grand scale."[4] The citizen is left to judge the individual conduct and cast it all aside until the next lurid tale appears.

On the other hand, crime stories can help a community define which behaviors it finds acceptable and which lie beyond its socially constructed

Murder in Our Midst. Romayne Smith Fullerton and Maggie Jones Patterson, Oxford University Press (2021). © Oxford University Press. DOI: 10.1093/oso/9780190863531.003.0004.

and agreed-upon boundaries, legal or moral; this is Jack Katz's argument that an audience's "read" of crime offers people their "daily moral workout."[5] News stories pull audiences into a particular social conception, but in order for journalism to help build a healthy self-questioning and introspective community, the narration must reach beyond a simple demonization of each individual criminal. Stories fail to shine their light on ways the social fabric may be torn and in need of repair when they portray criminals as outside the "social relations or structures that the victims or the public are also embedded in" because they are simply "pathologically evil."[6] Such an approach, as we have argued in earlier chapters, is simplistic and undermines the public narrative.[7] Serious crimes that set people talking can, and should, signal to citizens what is happening on the moral edges of their communities. When the signal story is told inside the indignation frame, criminals are simply expelled. "Any attempt to understand, let alone any concern for their point of view or their rehabilitation, is seen as insensitive to the suffering of their victims," Reiner writes.[8] The wider frame of social, economic, educational, or cultural factors is absent, and social justice is largely ignored. Within this larger frame, the details of a particular crime can broaden beyond the private suffering of the victim and the individual perpetrator's particular wrongdoing. Instead, signal crimes reported upon as Ward suggests, offering facts, context, and stories that keep the focus firmly on institutions, and larger systems of democracy, open the opportunity for public discussion about the social ills that cause and control deviance.[9] Such stories would engage the people—not as audiences or customers—but as citizens. The public can and should hold journalism accountable for this function.

Framing: Fanning or Facilitating?

Framing is a form of interpretation. The news media focus on crime, especially signal crimes, and place the elements of those stories within a field of meaning. The process influences how the public thinks about those events.[10] Reporting on the precedent-setting trial of members of the National Socialist Underground (NSU) contains examples both of how German journalists can succeed in helping citizens sort through the implications of troubling events and how they can fail. The NSU's crime spree began in 2000 and ended in 2011 after ten murders, an explosion that injured 22, and a series of robberies. The murderers targeted members of German minorities—Turks, Kurds, and

Greeks, plus one German policewoman. Most victims were workers or small businessmen: a flower wholesaler, a kebab shop owner, a tailor, a greengrocer. The murders occurred in seven different German towns and were separated by months in some instances and even years in others. Victims were all shot with the same relatively rare gun at close range while looking at the killer, facts that, at first, led police to theorize that Turkish, mafia-style gangsters were carrying out a turf battle. Following their theory that these were gangland killings, police berated and harassed surviving family members, trying to get information on what they imagined were the criminal activities of their murdered husbands or fathers. Investigators even attempted to trick one widow into revealing her late husband's nonexistent underworld ties by making up stories of his marital infidelity to dislodge her loyalty.

In 2004, the NSU exploded a nail bomb in a Turkish section of Cologne, wounding 22 people. In 2006, one member of the German police investigative team expressed doubt about the theories of gangster warfare and suggested instead that the use of a single weapon in the shootings pointed to right-wing extremists who were trying to draw attention to themselves. Real gangsters would have hidden their identity by using different guns for the different murders, the investigator theorized. These killers wanted to connect the killings to their anti-immigrant political cause, he said. But the rest of the investigative team waved off this suggestion until, five years later, a botched bank robbery led police to the three killers and to their tell-tale gun.[11] Two of the killers committed suicide rather than submit to arrest in 2011. The third, Beate Zschäpe, appeared in a Munich courtroom in May 2013, charged with nine murders. Four men were accused of supporting the NSU and were tried with her.

In large measure, German news media spent little time reporting on how the trio had escaped police detection for so long and instead concentrated on the salacious details of their *ménage à trois* murders and Zschäpe's demeanor, hair color, and attire in the courtroom.[12] As the spectacular trial entered its fourth year, Thomas Meaney and Saskia Schäfer wrote in *The Guardian* that the case had become much bigger than the gruesome murder spree:[13] "Germany's sense of itself is also on trial. The findings of the prosecution suggest that Germany, a nation that prides itself on having confronted the dark recesses of its past with unique diligence, has left a thriving underground culture of rightwing extremism untouched."[14]

Zschäpe, born in 1975, and her NSU colleagues, came from Thuringia, a state in the east of Germany, where extremism was well established. The

NSU movement gained momentum when German Chancellor Angela Merkel promised to admit a million refugees after the 2015 crisis in Syria. The distribution of the new immigrants across the country stirred a backlash. In the 2017 elections, the vote in the former Soviet states of East Germany accounted for much of the gain made by the anti-immigrant nationalists' Alternatives for Germany (AfD) Party, which came in third overall. Voting patterns show the eastern part of the country was also responsible for much of the loss by the two moderate parties—Merkel's Christian Democratic Union and its Bavarian ally, the Christian Socialist Union.

Two of the journalists to whom we spoke were monitoring the NSU trial in Munich and also looking beyond the details of the NSU crimes and Zschäpe's outfits for clues about Germany's new search for itself. Among other things, the court's awkward embrace of almost 60 attorneys representing the families of NSU's victims intrigued Annette Ramelsberger, covering the trial for *Süddeutsche Zeitung*, and court reporter Gisela Friedrichsen, now writing for *Die Welt*. "Crime coverage is bigger than the act itself," Friedrichsen said. She sees her role, not so much as the eyes and ears of the public in the courtroom or as the voice of the defendants or prosecutors, but more as the public's voice. She turns her penetrating attention to select signal crimes in which she sees her nation's political history and social psychology coming to life and acted out in the courtroom. Through her work, she can, and does, draw attention to this larger, ongoing drama.

In the 1990s, Friedrichsen covered a case in which a Montessori kindergarten teacher was accused of sexually abusing 20 children. Writing then for *Der Spiegel*, she came under fire, especially as a woman and mother, she said, when she doubted the children's accounts of the abuse and opined that the evidence did not support the charges. Although the school's walls were glass, no adult had witnessed any of the alleged behavior. One child told a fantastic tale of the teacher grabbing a boy by his penis and swinging him in big circles above his head, Friedrichsen recalled with an incredulous roll of her eyes. Eventually, the court came to its own decision about the children's allegations: The teacher was acquitted. Friedrichsen, a highly experienced and internationally respected reporter, believed that the case reflected a kind of mass hysteria, and that the children's stories were, in fact, fantasies suggested to them by grownups, who had become fearful and agitated by tales of alleged sexual abuse in American schools.

Friedrichsen was also drawn to a case in Freiburg in 2016, where a young medical student had been found raped and drowned in the river. Prosecutors discovered that the suspect, an Afghan refugee admitted to Germany in 2015, had previously been convicted in Greece of robbing a student and pushing her off a cliff. When it turned out that he had also tossed away his identification papers and lied about his age to qualify for special benefits for juvenile asylum seekers, Friedrichsen questioned the flaws in the system.[15] According to media reports, some asylum centers were rushing migrants through the review process in just three or four days, and some of the decision-makers had received little or no training.[16]

The NSU trial intrigued Friedrichsen, in part, because of the "representation of different interests within the court." German law grants victims and their families the right to counsel, and their attorneys can even become "collateral prosecutors" in serious cases such as murder. As closing arguments began in early fall of 2017, the NSU trial had already involved five judges, almost 600 witnesses and experts, 5 defendants, 14 defense lawyers, 95 victims and their families, 60 accessory prosecutors (attorneys representing the victims), and by the start of its fifth year, it had cost sixty million euros or about one-hundred-fifty thousand euros per day.[17] Despite the time and expense, the victims' families were dissatisfied, Friedrichsen told us. While the court focused on questions of defendants' guilt or innocence, she said, the victims and their families viewed justice differently. They stood, Friedrichsen said, like a Greek chorus, voicing what ought to trouble the German conscience: They asked why their family members were chosen for execution and whether the convoluted and faulty police investigation in which the victims' moral integrity was repeatedly challenged, reflected racism embedded in the German criminal justice system. The reporting of both Friedrichsen and Ramelsberger highlighted these questions. Had German investigators simply been unwilling to see the revival of attitudes the country had so fervently sought to confront and destroy? After the verdicts, protests broke out in Munich and other parts of Germany with protestors blaming the police and the news media for the inadequate investigation and carrying banners that read: "Not the last word."[18] The families of two of the victims had filed suit against the German federal government and the states of Thuringia and Bavaria, alleging multiple investigative failures.[19]

Germany's history brings a particular poignancy to those questions, which is what Ramelsberger and Friedrichsen, whose Danish father was sent to a war-time concentration camp for helping Jews, wanted to explore as they covered the NSU trial. "[T]his process will align itself with the great historical, milestone procedures that have determined the history of the Federal

Republic," Ramelsberger wrote.[20] She compared the NSU trial to those at Nuremberg after World War II in which the Allies vowed to cleanse the moral atmosphere in Germany. "The significance of such historical processes is usually only recognized with hindsight: their role in recognition of right and wrong, their impetus for the reform of laws, their lasting impact on society. So it is with the NSU process," she wrote. The trial has forced Germany's gaze to a painful place, she said. It has countered the tendency to dismiss right-wing extremism as a minor force, limited to the unemployed in the former East, and drawn attention to the threat experienced by those "who look a bit different than the average German."[21]

While Germany has taken victims' trial rights to a new level, the widespread rise in victims' voices in the American criminal justice systems has divided experts.[22] Some see allowing an official voice for victims inside trials as a step backward to a time before the Enlightenment.[23] Victims can compromise the court's objectivity and usher in an element of personal revenge. In earlier times, criminal trials were structured like civil ones: two individual parties, the victim and the defendant, opposed each another as adversaries before the court. After the beginning of the modern age, the defendant stood trial against the state, which served as the community's collective voice, not the victim's. "As John Locke pointed out, this change was foundational to civil society, in which, 'all private judgment of every particular member being excluded, the community comes to be umpire, by settled standing rules, indifferent, and the same to all parties. Wherever people yield to public authority the judgment and punishment of crime, Locke wrote, 'there and there only is a political, or civil society.' "[24]

But some Germans argue that prosecution has remained firmly in the state's hands, and that victim representation has expanded, not contracted, the court's perspective. "The reason why I am so interested in this case," explained Ramelsberger, "is that you have all the historic involvements of Germany and the right-wing extremists regaining power." So many police and secret service were unwilling to see the Nazi resurgence in Germany, she said, that they instead imagined that some foreign mafia thugs had invaded in the form of flower merchants and kebab salesmen.

While the court weighed the fate of the defendants, the victims effectively turned the spotlight on the scales of social justice and police prejudice. Abdul Kerim Simsek, the son of the NSU's first victim, told the court he had lived under a cloud of shame since 2000 when he was just 13 years old, and when his father became the NSU's first victim. Police believed his father, a wholesale flower vendor who traveled frequently to Holland, must have been a drug courier and gangster. Nearly a dozen years later, Simsek said, he was relieved when the NSU members were indicted because that cloud of his father's guilt, and his own by association, was finally lifted.[25]

Legal systems in liberal democracies guarantee citizens equal protection under the law, but critical race theorists, like American Mari Matsuda, argue that the scales of justice tilt heavily toward preserving existing power structures.[26] Prosecutors' claims that they apply the law neutrally are inaccurate, if not impossible, Matsuda argued. Bias exists in the law itself and what it is meant to protect. To French philosopher Roland Barthes, the court system assumes its own transparency of language and of process, but it fails to recognize how its definitions of justice block alternative viewpoints.[27] As Matsuda explained, justice is clearly a legal concept, but the *interpretation* of justice is an ethical process. Journalist are not, nor should they be, bound by courtroom language and definitions, especially when covering minority peoples, who may bring different worldviews to the institutional process. The clash of two different meanings for a concept like justice creates what Jean-Francois Lyotard called *differend*. Those who belong to the subordinate culture struggle to explain their experiences to those in power, but the language itself works against them.[28] Matsuda recommended a space in the judicial system for genuine listening to minorities' stories of oppression.

From these philosophical perspectives, the Enlightenment system fails to include the minority perspective because it can confuse equality with sameness. The German system of allowing victims an official voice in the NSU trial may work toward compensating for the court's inherent bias toward the dominant culture. Sensing that possibility in this trial's unique circumstances, Friedrichsen and Ramelsberger were determined to explore its implications on behalf of the German public. In doing so, they amplified the voices of the victimized German minorities in this case, in what can be seen as an application of what Emmanuel Levinas has called "embracing the Other."[29]

For Levinas, ethics, and our obligations, begin and end with the human face. When we look into another's visage, we become aware of and moved by a personal responsibility for that person. In that moment of encounter, we ought to see a plea not to be "killed" or harmed by setting aside that other person's interests. Because the fundamental alterity of another individual manifests itself in our daily lives, we are constantly surrounded by both ethics and the web of human connections within which we live. The encounter with the Other reveals the a priori and fundamental responsibility the self, each of us, has for the Other. For Levinas, this is a primordial relationship.[30] In this relation, we see what it means to be human and what justice itself demands: consideration of the needs, wants and desires of another person—articulated or not. What is more, these concerns must be met ahead of our own. We stand in awe of the mystery of the Other and the call to justice that mystery demands.[31]

In the NSU trials, the German criminal justice system admitted an alternative view of justice into the courtroom—perhaps inadvertently. While the legal parameters of the courtroom may appear to the German public as a "natural" vessel to contain state justice against barbaric inclinations toward vengeance, Ramelsberger, Friedrichsen, and other German reporters, heard a new and different voice speaking in that courtroom. That voice spoke to the social injustices suffered by Germany's immigrant population, not only by the murderous hands of the NSU but also by the German police investigation, an institution shaped and influenced by similar prejudices.

The more common courtroom coverage that focused on the gruesome murder details and the defendant's freshly dyed hair may have attracted clicks and eyeballs and boosted the news media's bottom lines, but by itself, that coverage did little to enhance the democratic process or journalism's mission to serve the public interest. Friedrichsen and Ramelsberger, on the other hand, strove for what would pull the story above the base level of personal villainy. They wrote to address readers as citizens who can think and feel and consider what is just, not as customers who buy the product and care only about entertainment. Like the Greek chorus of victims' lawyers inside the courtroom, these reporters sought to give voice to public conscience and to connect history and contemporary facts to offer insights that could best enlighten public conversations.

Western approaches to journalism ethics, like Western legal systems, are rooted in Enlightenment ethics that are sometimes inadequate to the challenges of an ethnically complex world. Common interpretations of accepted journalistic values like fairness and equal treatment may be inadequate outside a nation's mainstream culture. These values work compatibly with ethical systems rooted in universal duties and justice, such as Kant's categorical imperative and Rawls' veil of ignorance. Such systems, however, rely on the decision-maker's ability to reason and reach objective judgment for everyone involved. They assume universality or, at least, an ability to imagine the Other's subjectivity.[32]

Barthes argues that we often accept the human-made, socially constructed aspects of our own culture as "natural" or "universal."[33] Journalists covering the courts, for example, may only be familiar with their own culture's concepts of justice in a court trial. But journalism need not be constrained by the language and rules of one country's criminal justice system or by the dominant culture's definitions of "justice." Ramelsberger, Friedrichsen, and some other German reporters covering the NSU trial showed their sensitivity to the victims' claims for justice that were not answered in the conviction by the state of the persons on trial. The victims sought to indict the state itself. Journalists will surely need to sharpen their insights and broaden their perspectives as immigration and the globalization of news increasingly present them with stories of cultures clashing and of immigrant minorities being wrongly accused and persecuted.

But journalists can be guilty not only of reflecting but also of creating and perpetuating rather than questioning these universal cultural myths. To Barthes, the word "myth" refers not to ancient stories of superhuman gods and goddesses but to fictitious or illusionary stories and ideas in which many people steadfastly believe. In *Mythologies*, he uses news articles and photographs to analyze problematic beliefs in postwar France. For example, he points to a *Match* magazine cover of an African boy wearing a beret saluting an imagined French flag. Barthes argues that the image mythologized the majesty of French colonial power. The photograph shows that the boy—and by implication his countrymen—look up to the superior French culture and honor its domination over his nativism. All racial and cultural condescension is vanquished.

In a similar manner, Melanie Verhovnik, research associate at the Catholic University Eichstäett-Ingolstadt School of Journalism, examined the way German journalists have created a myth about school shooters, which they and their publics have then come to believe. The current reporting frame— that these events are crimes that "just happen"—not only falls short of helping citizens get to the crime's root causes, according to Verhovnik, but also contributes to the problem by inadvertently encouraging copycats and wannabes. Although incidents of school violence in Germany are infrequent compared to those in the United States, worldwide media coverage connects them all, Verhovnik's research has found.[34] The first recorded school shooting happened in Poland in 1925, but after the 1999 shootings at Columbine High School in Colorado, when 400 to 500 reporters rushed in to cover the events live, the rate of shootings increased rapidly, first in the United States, then spreading to Canada and Western Europe. "Columbine was burned into the collective memory. When you research shootings in Germany, you have to start with that [one]," Verhovnik said in an interview.

German reporters use the word *Amoklauf*, or rampages, to describe school shootings. The word itself is misleading, Verhovnik argued, because it implies that these shootings are sudden outbursts, which they are for the victims, but are not for the perpetrators; many, if not all, read, consider, and plan for many months or even years. The journalists, having incorrectly typified these crimes, then follow their own word choice to look for simple, recent causes for what they have constructed as outbursts. Among the most common culprits cited in the news are the shooter's access to guns and his exposure to violent media. Both contribute to the problem, Verhovnik found, but neither offers a complete explanation nor a pathway to prevention. For example, she said, despite extremely strict gun control in Germany, shooters generally obtain legal weapons—from parents or from Shützenverein, which are local associations for huntsmen. Violent media also correlate; all school shooters have consumed violent media, but that explanation is also insufficient.

These "explanations that dominate the media reporting," Verhovnik writes in her article "School Shootings in Media Coverage," "are in contrast to the results of empirical research about school shootings from psychology, sociology, education and criminology, which emphasize the complexity of the phenomenon."[35] These academic studies show the factors that lead to these actions, and include isolation, a lack of social connections, suicidal thoughts, access to weapons, and opportune circumstances. Many of these young perpetrators interact and build their information and their plans over time. "Every perpetrator has done research on past school shootings and used violent media content," often for a year or more, Verhovnik said. Most have become part of a community online and played video games that, for example, allow them to role play as the Columbine shooters. They share media stories of previous shootings, which serve as scripts for fantasies of their being launched into a shooters' hall of fame—not in the general memory, but within these specialized, online communities of the like-minded.

"The image of a 'rampage' leaves the impression that school shootings are unpreventable and happen suddenly and are in no way recognizable," Verhovnik writes.[36] This is not the case. "It would be helpful for editors and journalists to get more information on that."[37] The problems that lead to school shootings go deep into the social structure, Verhovnik said: There are not enough teachers in the schools, for example, to notice that problems are brewing. "A lot of political things would have to change to find solutions for this," she said, but first, reporters need to help shift the conversation by shifting their coverage. The German Press Council ethics code asks reporters not to use the inaccurate and misleading term *Amoklauf*, or rampage, but the code is often ignored, Verhovnik wrote. A smart denotative reporting process that starts with the specific crime and leads to an exploration of the general social ills that underlie the crime could help. Reporters also need to recognize that they contribute to the fantasies of would-be imitators by extensive media coverage, especially by photos and videos of the perpetrators.[38]

Press Law, Press Councils, and the Public Trust

For the news media to operate effectively as a public trust, the public has to place a healthy degree of trust in its hands. A Pew Research Center study released in 2018 showed that news consumers in Protector countries do just that.[39] They think their news media do well at reporting on the most important stories (the Netherlands 89%, Sweden 86%, Germany 85%); their reporting is accurate (the Netherlands 82%, Sweden 78%, Germany 75%), and they do well at reporting on government (Netherlands 82%, Sweden 78%, Germany 77%). This faith in news correlates with a faith in government. Pew found the percentages of the public that expressed faith in their governments were almost exactly the same as those who thought news media were doing a good job.[40] Trust in public, state-sponsored media in Protector countries is especially high (90% of Swedes surveyed trust the public SVT network. Likewise, 89% of Dutch citizens trust the Dutch Broadcasting Foundation NOS (Nederlandse Omroep Stichting) and 80% of Germans trust ARD (Arbeitsgemeinschaft der öffentlich-rechtlichen Rundfunkanstalten der Bundesrepublik Deutschland). This trust is broadly shared across the political spectrum with only those citizens with populist views deviating more widely and placing less trust in news media. These public news outlets also serve as the most popular source of news and main source of information for one-third or more of the population.[41]

News organizations in Protector countries earn trust, at least in part, by opening their doors and acknowledging that the public has the right to a voice in how news is produced and presented. Since the time of John Dewey and Walter Lippmann, intellectuals and news professionals have engaged in widespread debate about what and who constitutes a public and whether such a phenomenon can even exist beyond the tugging and pulling of individual and special interests groups. But the Protector countries have acted on the idea that if you build it, they will come; that is, if you provide a forum for public voices, citizens will speak up. In doing so, they reflect what Dewey and James Carey assert: The "public" may be indistinguishable from the process that creates it. This line of argument differs from much of postmodern thought that sees communication as a rhetorical battle for hegemony.

All three Protector countries argue instead in support of public communication that builds bridges toward consensus and citizenship. Germany, Sweden, and the Netherlands house imperfect but sturdy press councils, where citizens can bring complaints against a news organization that they feel has wronged them. A social responsibility model of the press governs the press council thinking. In contrast to the libertarian model, which holds that people should be exposed to a wide range of information to be allowed to judge for themselves, the social responsibility model holds that the news media have a duty toward the common good of the community or the nation.[42] "The Dutch Press Council asks itself: 'What is the role of the press in a decent society?'" press council member Froukje Santing said. The code itself outlines that it is the "core task" of the council to "provide a framework for self-regulation" and that its guidelines "describe which requirements journalism must meet and as such clarify to all—both inside and outside of the profession—what can be expected of proper journalists and proper journalism."[43] Despite what several senior journalists told us in follow-up interviews in 2018, that the Internet is adding more pressure to name names because that information is widely available online, most of the respected news outlets continue to follow their protective traditions. Huub Evers, an ethics scholar, journalism educator, and ombudsman for *De Limburger*, said, "The tradition is the same. It's not changing. The policy of newspapers is still the same: they try to protect the privacy of suspects and so on, and it's right that they do so." In the Netherlands and Sweden, any persons directly affected by a story have the right to file a complaint. In Germany, the process is open to everyone, regardless of involvement. Press council hearing boards are made up of some combination of journalists, lawyers, and representatives of the public. They weigh journalists' behavior against the council's code of ethics. Complaints brought are handled in a number of ways. The majority are dismissed, most often because the complainant's claim was found to be outweighed by public interest or because the news medium had already issued a correction. If the council finds the news organization in serious violation of that code, the strictest sanction is to ask it to publish the press complaints commission's findings. While this judgment publicly embarrasses the news outlet, it almost always satisfies the complainant and makes libel or privacy lawsuits relatively rare.

Journalists unions in all three countries provide legal representation for members who are sued for libel. The Netherlands union would help any journalist who was a member or not, General Secretary and spokesperson for the union Thomas Bruning said. As traditional news organizations cut back on full-time reporters, between half and 80% of these unions' membership are freelancers, whose income and protection are particularly vulnerable. Petra Reski, a German freelancer who lives in Italy and reports on the mafia, published a story in Der Freitag, accusing a German businessman of being affiliated with the Italian mafia. He sued successfully on the grounds that his right to personality had been violated. Jakob Augstein, the magazine's publisher, refused to take responsibility for the article. Reski's union, the Deutsche Journalisten Union (DJU) did not help her because of a technicality (she had hired her own lawyer first, but they ask members to contact the union first), and thus she was forced to use crowdsourcing to help with her costs.[44]

The press councils in all three countries increasingly tackle issues raised by digital news media, including the ethics of hyperlinks, citizen journalism, anonymous comments on web stories, and definitions of who or what is a journalist. In the Protector countries, publishing or broadcasting the name of a person accused or convicted of a crime can be considered a violation of privacy, and, in Germany it can also be against the law. But when persons object to coverage, they are less likely to file a complaint with the courts than with the press council, a process that is usually free. Few people in Europe can afford to bring suit. Lawyers do not generally work on a contingency basis as they often do in the United States (i.e., plaintiff's lawyers charge no fee if the case is lost but take a percentage of the settlement if they win; in addition, in England, the loser pays costs), and the costs can be enormous.

By pulling together to work through the press councils despite their differences, news organizations in these countries have also succeeded, for the most part, in keeping legislative or judicial restrictions on the press at bay. No journalists in the Netherlands expressed concern about the law as a potential impediment to reporting, at least not in crime coverage. The Swedish journalists did worry that the government might step in and impose rules to protect defendants or narrow access to now publicly available information if the press did not govern itself. The German Press Council's purpose, as stated in its articles of association, is to preserve the independence of the German press and preserve its reputation.[45] While media in these countries may benefit from state subsidies, state intrusions upon media content and conduct are strictly controlled. In general, journalists in Protector countries enjoy wide access to information, but—unlike some reporters in Watchdog countries—they do not think that the public nature of information means the public has an automatic right or a need to access that information through a news outlet. An individual's claims to privacy and the right to personality, for example, often take precedence. As the German Press Council code of ethics states:

> The Press shall respect the private life of a person and his/her right to self-determination about personal information. However, if a person's behaviour is of public interest, it may be discussed by the Press. In the case of identifying reporting [i.e. reporting that identified persons], the public interest in information must outweigh the interests worthy of protection of the persons involved; sensation interests alone do not justify identifying reporting. As far as anonymization is required, it must be effective.[46]

Press councils do not declare what is allowed or what is not; individual media make that determination. All complaints to the councils are decided on a case-by-case basis. In Germany, criminal courts sometimes direct how far news organizations should go in identifying defendants, but those news organizations do not always obey. Most of the press refrained from publishing the full names of three of the NSU defendants who had not previously been in the public eye. Just two were fully named, principal defendant Beate Zschäpe, and Ralf Wohleben, who is the former deputy state chairman and press spokesman in Thurringia for the National Democratic Party (NPD). But practices about naming or anonymizing are neither consistent nor uniformly followed or enforced. While *Süddeutsche Zeitung* obeyed the court's directive to name only Zschäpe and Wohleben, according to Tanjev Schultz, it published a supplemental magazine on the case, which contained many full names, including those of witnesses "who are usually very protected," Shultz noted. But as he and colleagues prepared a book on the NSU case, Schultz said, lawyers were cautioning them to take out names, even that of a police officer. In the Freiburg murder of the medical student by the illegal asylum seeker, Hussein K., the judge asked the press not to name the defendant and to pixelate any images of him. The tabloids defied that order, Schultz said, and gambled that the defendant would not sue them.[47] As Schultz and others told us in Germany—as well as in Sweden and the Netherlands—each case is looked at individually by each news organization. While a practice of protection is widely adhered to in these countries and is quite distinct from Watchdog practices, it is far from uniform and consistent.

The news media in Germany, Sweden, and the Netherlands earn the high degree of public trust they enjoy, but many believe their voluntary participation in these press councils also benefits them. Swedish Press Ombudsman Olga Sigvardsson said that membership "is a matter of trustworthiness. You show the public that you respect the ethical code."[48] The code, in turn, must be rooted in a commitment to journalism's role in the democratic process. In a democracy, citizens have an obligation to speak up against legislative errors and abuses of power, Helle Sjøvaag writes, and to do so they need a medium that will hear and amplify their voices. The press is that voice because it holds the position of Fourth Estate—a metaphor that began with Thomas Carlyle in 1841 and has been used frequently ever since.[49] In order to legitimately bear the weight of this widely recognized role in the democratic process, Sjøvaag contends, the press's social contract must include a set of moral principles that govern it and make it worthy of trust. Thus, the social contact

> further includes the professional practices and ideals with which the ethical standards and the democratic and communicative goals are upheld. . . .
> Together these ideals make up the metaphor of the social contract of the press—a metaphor on which the press as institution and journalism as profession is greatly dependent, and from which they gain privilege, power, and responsibility in democratic societies.[50]

Concluding Thoughts On The Protectors

Comparative law scholar Mary Ann Glendon writes, "Whether meant to or not, law, in addition to all the other things it does, tells stories about the culture that helped to shape it and which it in turn helps to shape: stories about who we are and where we are going."[51] Crime stories embed themselves within this larger story told by criminal justice statutes and policies. Although the press sometimes challenges that story, together the law and the press generally reflect the community's prevailing attitudes toward criminal deviance. This story gets told each time a crime is reported. It reports the facts of what happened, but it also helps the community define and maintain its moral edges, where conduct falls outside its bounds. The story's rhetorical frame also helps determine what is to be done about the criminal. A frame of moral indignation demonizes criminals, subjugates their humanity, and permanently expels them. Such frames are sometimes employed in Protector countries, but the dominant story frame, told in the law and in the press for the past half century, is one that portrays criminals as citizens who have taken a wrong turn but who deserve a second chance and a guiding hand to correct their misdirection. Crime reporting (like the law itself, to borrow from Glendon) interprets the dominant social narrative when it converts facts about crime into news stories with characters, events and motives, but reporting also constitutes that narrative when it begins "to affect ordinary language and to influence the manner in which we perceive reality."[52] The press in Sweden, the Netherlands, and Germany take voluntary action to report in ways that usually shield the criminals' families, guard suspects' presumption of innocence, and protect those found guilty in a court of law to become rehabilitated and resocialized; thus, journalists affect the public's perception of who these deviants are and how they should be treated. This reporting frame respects the humanity and dignity of criminals and, in turn, may also maintain public trust in its reporters.

When we asked reporters in Protector countries to explain the "why" behind their routine crime-reporting practices, they repeatedly told us that the aim of their country's criminal justice systems is rehabilitation and resocialization. They profess a firm belief in their institutions of justice and governance, which they see as practical, as well as humane. Their press councils hold them accountable to that way of thinking. "Rehabilitation and bringing criminals back into society has been a large objective in Dutch society," said Gerrit Jan Wolffensperger, who was serving on the Dutch Press Council in 2010. Liesbeth Buitink, an editor at the Dutch news cooperative ANP, with whom we spoke in 2010 and 2018, said that the considerations remain the same. "We do not scapegoat people before (or after) they have been judged. That is not the job of the media." German law protects both privacy and reputation to allow the resocialization process to succeed and even requires the state to take positive action to facilitate it—ranging from prison conditions to educational opportunities and help with re-entry. Nicholas Turner, president of the Vera Institute of Justice, and Jeremy Travis, president of the John Jay College of Criminal Justice, described their 2015 tour of German prisons:

The men serving time wore their own clothes, not prison uniforms. When entering their cells, they slipped out of their sneakers and into slippers. They lived one person per cell. Each cell was bright with natural light, decorated with personalized items such as wall hangings, plants, family photos and colorful linens brought from home. Each cell also had its own bathroom separate from the sleeping area and a phone to call home with. The men had access to communal kitchens, with the utensils a regular kitchen would have, where they could cook fresh food purchased with wages earned in vocational programs.

Germans, like Americans, worry about public safety, Turner and Travis write, but the former think about recidivism differently.[53] If an inmate returns to prison after release, "the prison staff members ask what *they* should have done better."[54]

Both the laws and the press codes seek to weed out prejudices from the system. Sweden and the Netherlands make no notation of religious affiliation or ethnicity in public records; press codes in all three countries suggest that crime stories not mention either unless they are intrinsic to the story or of direct public interest. The names of sex offenders, including pedophiles, are given special protection: They are held back from public view by law in all three Protector countries.

Working hand in glove much of the time, the press and the criminal justice systems perform the "ritual" of communication that James Carey found in much of European journalism. Rather than simply conveying information, crime stories ritually weave, reinforce, repair, and change the texture of the social fabric. Compared with the harsh penalties imposed in the United States, these countries err on the side of benevolence. Prosecutors can—and frequently do—dispose of less serious cases by imposing fines or a community punishment, often without a criminal conviction or a criminal record. Prison sentences are relatively short, and prisons are relatively comfortable. In Sweden, about 20% of prisoners serve their time in open prisons with no walls, fences, or guards. Closed prisons are generally small—about 50 to 100 inmates—and are used only for the most serious offenses.[55] The quality of life is high in Dutch prisons, criminologists Michael Tonry and Catrien Bijleveld found.[56] Most cells have TV and videos (at the prisoners' expense), and there are sports activities and unsupervised visits for prisoners serving long sentences.[57]

Nonetheless, all countries must contend with a criminal population deemed an ongoing danger to the public. Tonry and Bijleveld, writing about sentencing in the Netherlands, said: "Especially for violent and sexual crimes, an entrustment order (*terbeschkkingstelling*, commonly called TBS) may be given, often in combination with a prison sentence."[58] Such sentences are reserved for those who cannot be held fully responsible and require hospital care if necessary to protect people or property. The average length of time under TBS is six years, but some may be confined for the rest of their lives if treatment is unsuccessful or if the risk of recidivism remains high.

Tonry and Tapio Lappi-Seppälä found: "The Nordic penal model has its roots in a consensual and corporatist political culture, in high levels of social trust and political legitimacy, and in a strong welfare state."[59] Trust in private social institutions, the government, police, and fellow citizens is particularly high in Nordic countries.[60] Generally, crime, prosecution, and sentencing are not a major part of partisan politics. Judges and prosecutors are civil servants, valued for their objective perspective.[61] Protector countries have some of the lowest imprisonment rates in Europe. In 2018, the highest rates were in the United States at 698 per 100,000 of the population, while the rate in Germany was 78, the Netherlands 59, and Sweden 57 per 100,000.[62]

Relatively benign attitudes toward the treatment of criminal deviance is part of a larger attitude toward social welfare, Tonry and Tapio Lappi-Seppälä wrote. "Strong welfare states sustain less repressive policies by providing workable alternatives to imprisonment. Extensive and generous social service networks often function as effective crime prevention measures, even if that is not a direct motivation for them. Consensual politics also lessen controversies, produce less crisis talk, and sustain long-term policies."[63] Governments in these countries are formed by consensus and coalition among multiple political parties. Their systems have proven less vulnerable to "penal populism" than conflictual, majoritarian political cultures "in which differences are exaggerated and controversies are sharpened" by polarized politics making emotional appeals and offering short-term solutions.[64]

Globalization and immigration threaten both the posture of criminal justice systems in these countries and the protective practices of the press that reflect and reinforce those policies. For 50 years after World War II, the Netherlands was commonly portrayed as having the West's most liberal and humane criminal justice system, but at the beginning of the 21st century, it took a repressive turn and began following practices more characteristic of Great Britain. Liberal social welfare policies and absorption of immigrants from former colonies, as well as from Turkey and Morocco, had proceeded smoothly, but by the beginning of the 21st century, welfare provisions had diminished, criminal justice policies hardened, and immigrant and refugee treatment grew harsher. Right-wing, anti-immigrant politicians vocalized widespread feelings that multiculturalism policies of the past had failed.[65] Dutch imprisonment rates remain low, but they have risen even though property crime rates have fallen and violent crime has stabilized.[66]

Prison reformers in Watchdog countries, especially the United States, have looked to the Netherlands and Scandinavia for lessons as their countries began to question the high cost of overcrowded and underproductive prisons.[67] In 2011, Tonry wrote:

> Scandinavian approaches to crime and punishment offer important lessons to scholars, citizens and policy makers in other countries. Their present may be our future. More ominously, if they succumb to the xenophobic and populist political pressures that exist everywhere, ours may be theirs.[68]

Just a few years later, the growth of populist politics made the latter outcome more likely.

Not all fears raised by globalization can be attributed to economic shifts. Even as immigration rates have dropped significantly since the Syrian crisis, the political right has played on popular worries that Muslim migrants are triggering cultural shifts that will push aside historical and religious traditions. The Bavarian state government has created a ministry of *heimat* (German for homeland). While the state capital, Munich, is ethnically and economically diverse, the AfD, Germany's radical right-wing party, has gained ground in this wealthy Bavarian region.[69] In the Bavarian town of Deggendorf, crosses and crucifixes are displayed in almost every public school classroom, in the fire station, in the mayor's office, and in the room where civil marriages are performed. "Religion is in decline in Germany," Karin Bennhold wrote in the *New York Times*, "but religious symbols are making a powerful comeback as part of the simmering culture wars playing out from Berlin to rural Bavaria three years after the country opened its doors to more than a million migrants, many from predominantly Muslim countries."[70]

These culture wars have exacted a toll on the news media. Social media, the tabloid press, and rogue websites, like Geenstijl in the Netherlands and Flashback in Sweden, have fired up the populist agenda. Motivated by right-wing politics and anti-immigrant sentiments and likely influenced by the worldwide reach of Watchdog media, these outlets challenge protectionist attitudes by publishing all the information Protector mainstream media routinely choose to hold back. Pressure from the Internet works in harmony with commercial pressure that began to change the press when pillarization broke down and a shift toward commercialization and a watchdog style in the press began. Hallin and Mancini note this shift toward "a conception of the media as collective watchdog of public power and a conception of the journalist as representative of a generalized public opinion that cuts across the lines of political parties and social groups" across their three models.[71] "A global media culture is emerging, one that closely resembles the Liberal Model," which comprises North America and the British Isles in their model.[72]

Protectionist ethics policies seem vulnerable, yet they are also sturdy. Media plurality is valued here. Not all media outlets join the press councils. Not all who belong interpret the ethics codes the same way. "We have a pluriform media here," said Daphne Koene, Netherlands Press Council general secretary, "and since we don't have specific laws, only guidelines, not all media act the same way. . . . We do have media who publish the names of criminals all the time because they think there is a public interest to it. And we have other media that are very protective." The public interest is an acceptable justification, and if the affected parties disagree with the judgement, they can bring a complaint to the press council. Press councils periodically review their codes of ethics. In 2010, Koene was worried about how right-wing political movements and the intrusion of the Internet would change journalism and its ethics in the Netherlands. "There is a global media now. The old borders are gone," she said. In 2013, the council did decide to make some changes. Among them, they ensured that the chair of the council is a respected journalist, not a lawyer. They worked together with the Dutch Journalists Union, the Society of Chief-Editors, and several coordinating organizations of the printed press, as well as those of public and commercial broadcasting, to rewrite their code into less legal language to ensure that their suggested guidelines were accessible to all and largely direct journalistic moral, not legal, behavior.[73]

Globalization of media is likely to gain momentum; ethics policies will need to adjust. In a positive light, Stephen J. A. Ward, in "Philosophical Foundations for Global Journalism Ethics," sees "the evolution of journalism ethics as a progressive enlargement of the class of people that journalism is supposed to serve, from political parties and economic or social classes (such

as the middle class) to the general public."[74] While he calls for a cosmopol-
itan, global journalism ethics that pulls against "parochial values . . . to help
citizens understand the daunting global problems of poverty, environmental
degradation, technological inequalities, and political instability," substantial
economic and political forces are also pulling in the other direction.[75] Those
"parochial values" will not be easily trashed—nor should they be. Ward
recognizes—as do we—that a global journalism ethics should not trample
community standards. The press belongs to the community it both reflects
and constitutes.

PART 2

THE WATCHDOGS

The United Kingdom, Ireland, Canada, and the United States

Preface to the Watchdogs Section

These are a few of the signal crime stories that served as our starting points for our explorations and interviews in the Watchdog countries.

Bristol, England, 2010: A young landscape architect went missing; Joanna Yeates' body was found on Christmas Day. Police arrested her landlord, Christopher Jefferies, and held him for questioning. Although he had not been charged, many national newspapers labeled him a weirdo, an effeminate, and a pervert, and some made fun of his bluish comb-over hair. While the U.K.'s Contempt of Court Act of 1981 prohibits the media from publishing information that could prejudice ongoing legal cases and influence juries, this law had, until the Jefferies case, rarely been invoked.[1] If the case had gone to court, Attorney General Dominic Grieve said it would have been difficult to empanel an impartial jury. He successfully prosecuted two newspapers for contravening this Act. Jefferies, who was wholly innocent, sued and won a substantial sum and a public apology from eight papers in total.[2] Along with the scandal that began with reporters from the *News of the World* hacking missing schoolgirl Milly Dowler's phone, the behavior of the British press in the Jefferies' case was discussed at length in the *Leveson Inquiry into the Culture, Practices, and Ethics of the Press*.

North County Dublin, Ireland, 2008: Rachel O'Reilly was found bludgeoned to death in her home. A few days later, her husband, Joe, began giving tours of the house to her family and some members of the press. He pointed out where police had found various broken objects or blood splatters and repeatedly volunteered phrases like "this is what would have happened." He admitted to reporters he was a suspect. While the Irish press routinely choose not to name suspects, in part because of concern for libel laws, because O'Reilly had outed himself, journalists could name him as a suspect in their coverage, and they did. Numerous stories also revealed potentially prejudicial details about his relationship with his wife and his mistress. The unfolding of this investigation and Joe O'Reilly's subsequent trial formed a watershed; Irish reporters, editors, and academics saw the press moving from a softer Irish approach of covering the news to a more flamboyant one, influenced by British tabloids. Soon afterward, as the Irish Parliament threatened legislation to bring Irish journalism under control by law, Irish journalists joined together to block that effort by establishing a press council and national ombudsman, in part to combat this foreign style of journalism.

Woodstock, Ontario, Canada, 2009: Eight-year-old Tori Stafford went missing. After both the police and the press pointed a finger at Tori's mother, Tara McDonald, a couple—Terri-Lynne McClintic, 18, and her 28-year-old boyfriend, Michael Rafferty—were charged with kidnapping, sexual assault, and murder. Because they were tried separately, the Ontario court invoked a publication ban on any report of McClintic's trial or the grisly details of her confession to avoid tainting a potential jury pool for Rafferty's trial and damaging his right to a presumption of innocence and a fair trial. Under a publication ban, ordered at a judge's discretion, the court is open, and members of the public and the press may attend, but the circulation of information beyond the courtroom is prohibited. McClintic's guilty plea in February 2010 was not shared with the public until a part of the ban was lifted, under court review, in December of that year. Even so, the details about Tori's death were not disclosed until Rafferty's trial almost two years later. In this case, the publication ban prevented journalists from telling the community what happened to this child for nearly three years after she had disappeared.

Washington, DC, 2010: 88-year-old James von Brunn shot and killed a guard at the Holocaust Museum. Von Brunn himself was also critically wounded and died awaiting trial for first-degree murder. In the immediate aftermath of Von Brunn's attack, American journalists mined his numerous writings that demonstrated he was a white supremacist and a Holocaust denier. Some members of the media also named his son, his son's fiancé, and spoke to the alleged shooter's neighbors and former wives. Reporters told us repeatedly that digging for and making public all the details they can find about a suspect help the public understand why this crime happened. Because of the First Amendment, any and all of this material can form part of the public discussion; given the lack of legal restrictions, U.S. journalists, un-like those in Britain, Ireland, and Canada who are more constrained, focused closely on what they believe ought to be covered, and why.

5

What the Watchdogs Watch, Why, and Why Watching Matters

Irish Daily Star reporter Michael O'Toole was shocked.[1] Having completed our interview, O'Toole indicated he would like to hear about our findings in other countries. His response was emphatic when he heard that reporters in the Netherlands do not routinely name or photograph suspected or convicted criminals.

"I disagree with those Dutch reporters. I think that's a disgrace. I don't think we own the information. They own the information—the *people* own the information," he said, leaning forward with his eyes wide. "If it's public, it's the public's right to have it."

The Obligation to Tell What They See

Reporters' habits in the Watchdog countries contrast sharply with those of their counterparts in the Protector nations of Sweden, the Netherlands, and Germany. Like O'Toole, many Watchdog reporters emphasized their duty to inform the public above all other values. What they watch is institutional power, in its many guises; all said it was their duty to keep an eye on the criminal justice system writ large and to offer space for public discussions about crime, criminals, and possible wrongdoing in their communities. To this end, Watchdog reporters routinely publish extensive details about an offense, the alleged perpetrator, and the victims, painting as complete a picture of the accused as possible when the news merits. This happens at varying times in the process: Reports can surface when someone is officially named as "a person of interest" or "under investigation." Stories often focus on arrest and charge, and once an accused's case comes to trial, whatever is said in open court can be reported legally, and usually is. All these details—about the crime, the alleged perpetrator, and so on—can serve as stepping stones in a journalistic exploration of larger social issues, especially in the coverage

Murder in Our Midst. Romayne Smith Fullerton and Maggie Jones Patterson, Oxford University Press (2021). © Oxford University Press. DOI: 10.1093/oso/9780190863531.003.0005.

of signal crimes, like the ones described in this Part's Preface. However, as we will explore in the next chapter, these same stepping stones can lead to less worthy destinations, like voyeuristic sensationalism, if the reporters' main purpose—acknowledged or not—is to turn the story into click bait or better ratings or career boosts. Such stories can cast accused persons and/or criminals as folk devils and stereotype minorities and immigrants.[2] Regardless of motivation, Watchdog reporters' news stories, as well as their interview responses, rarely expressed sympathy for alleged wrongdoers—as those in Protector countries did. Instead, Watchdogs cast many accused and convicted in the role of outliers at best and, as we consider in Chapter 6, as inhuman monsters at worst.

Like their counterparts in Protector countries, Watchdog reporters believe the devil is in the story's details, but, in many ways, their ideas of where that devil lies are diametrically opposed to those of their Protector colleagues. Whereas Protector journalists largely trust their institutions and governments, Watchdogs do not. Under the latter model, most reporters consider naming a suspect in a major crime story and publishing as many facts as they can gather to be a central duty. The reasoning is that the more people know the facts, the less likely there is to be an abuse or miscarriage of justice. In contrast, most journalists in Protector countries believe that such specific and detailed exposure does unnecessary and irreparable harm to suspects' families, their right to the presumption of innocence, and—if convicted—their ability to resume a productive life once they have paid their debt to society. In Protector countries, reporters indicated that they see many—but not all—crimes as missteps performed by "one of us" who has gone astray. Such persons, they said, will need both a second chance and help to reform and rejoin the group. Watchdog reporters' stories are more likely to tell the tale of the alleged criminal as an aberration who will—or should be—punished and put away for good because such persons are viewed in this model as irredeemable.

Storytelling is at the heart of all journalistic enterprise, and this telling truthful tales is an ethical pursuit. As Walter Fisher argues in *Human Communication as Narration*, humans are storytelling animals.[3] Fisher writes, "Western philosophies tend to treat truth, knowledge and reality as the business of 'experts' only" when, in fact, he argues all of us can evaluate the rights and wrongs of human behavior through the vehicle of narrative.[4] Fisher's approach suggests that the crime tales we tell also tell a story about our underlying community values and attitudes. While all ten countries in our sample share a belief in the presumption of innocence and the public right to know, the Protector nations foreground the former consideration, while Watchdog nations elevate the latter.

Canada, Ireland, Britain, and the United States belong to Hallin and Mancini's North Atlantic liberal model: Traditionally, the press in these countries is independent of political parties and is largely privately owned. The United Kingdom was the foundation for this paradigm where mass-circulation press is dominated by various market mechanisms. In these countries, journalists have a strong sense of professionalism. Most have university degrees and have studied journalism formally, and all enjoy a relatively high degree of autonomy, particularly from state interference. The role of government is largely limited, and while public broadcasting does form a part of the fabric in all these countries, generally journalism—even publicly funded journalism—is more likely to feel pressure from economic, commercial, and, most recently, technological influences than strictly political ones. It is an irony that the First Amendment to the U.S. Constitution—"Congress shall make no law . . . abridging the freedom of speech, or of the press"— protects media from government interference but says nothing about the market forces that threaten to curtail such freedoms. One of the caveats of this model, addressed in more detail in the next chapter, is that ethical practices can be swayed, consciously or not, by economic considerations and issues like ownership, competition, globalization, and social media. All these factors can threaten what most Watchdog journalists see as their central obligation: Serve the citizenry with enough information for it to be free and self-governing.

The phrase "public right to know," or the idea that it is the ethical duty of a reporter to disseminate information obtained legally or that is available on the public record, bubbled to the surface in virtually all the interviews conducted in the Watchdog countries. In these locales, the news hound's job is to sniff out wrongdoing and alert its master, the citizens of a democracy, to possible incursions. Whether it's an individual who has committed a crime against the state, an aspect of the justice system that has gone awry, or criminal behavior that signals possible dangers to public safety or flaws in public policy, journalists were in near-universal agreement across this Watchdog model that a reporter's primary obligation is to inform the people because, as American Justice Louis Brandeis noted and many of our interview subjects paraphrased, sunlight is the best disinfectant.[5] Journalists shine their light where it's most needed. In the words of the UK's executive director of the

Society of Editors, Bob Satchwell: "Secrecy breeds suspicion and contempt, and openness breeds trust and respect." To develop and maintain credibility with audiences, journalism must be forthright about its purpose and motivation and scrupulous about passing along information without fear or favor. Journalists told us that names and specificity matter here because they form a part of the public record. Crimes are prosecuted by the state in the name of its citizens, and who did what to whom and why are integral threads that help weave the community fabric. How much detail ought to be included, or in some instances, is allowed by law to be included, varies from country to country within this Watchdog model. As these next chapters will explore, journalistic practices differed more among the exemplars of this particular approach than did those within the Protectors or the Ambivalents groups. One of the most distinctive differences is the role that the First Amendment plays in the United States. In U.S. Supreme Court cases in the latter part of the 20th century, where the right to a fair trial was pitted against that of a free press, decisions have largely favored the free press. In effect, these rulings have generally placed the onus for protecting the presumption of innocence within the purview of the courts and not the media. Thus, the First Amendment's role in the United States contrasts with the situation in other Watchdog countries where responsibility for protecting the presumption of innocence is buttressed by laws that limit journalistic freedom. But regardless of where the emphasis falls, journalists in all four Watchdog countries share a clear normative commitment to serving the public by pushing to publish information rather than withholding it.

In this model, based on principles originating in the time of the Enlightenment, people are considered rational individuals, able to think and reason for themselves, and capable, as Jürgen Habermas argued in *The Structural Transformation of the Public Sphere*, of setting aside their private concerns to debate matters of public interest.[6] The most important value to reporters in this model is their commitment to a thoughtful citizenry, and their concomitant belief that people are rational. While reporters interpret this principle widely and deeply, all believe in transparency and public access to information; journalists' faith in this guiding concept governs their ethical decision-making. One of Canada's best-known crime reporters, Christie Blatchford, stated the widespread watchdog belief: "We are the eyes and ears of the public." Deprived of these two senses, the public conversation would be greatly diminished or fall silent. The press in all liberal democracies functions as a public trust to serve citizens with sufficient information to conduct informed debates about laws, policies, and social attitudes. Our interview data demonstrated that the Watchdog journalist's attitude is one of respect for the intellect of the public and a firm belief that individuals can, and ought to, make decisions for themselves and their communities.

Journalism's Main Mission

Entelechy is the ancient Greek word Aristotle used to describe the soul of a living thing, its essential nature, or informing principle, in which its potential achieves actuality.[7] An acorn's entelechy will always be a mighty oak tree, although many fall short of that actuality. American journalism has consistently defined its *entelechy*—or in more modern lingo, its mission—as a public trust or service. Every newspaper mission statement the American Society of Newspaper Editors has on file advances a similar end.[8] Even as journalism becomes a more collaborative effort between citizens and professionals, the center holds, Kovach and Rosenstiel contend.[9] "The primary purpose of journalism is to provide citizens with the information they need to be free and self-governing."[10] The *Washington Post*'s mission, displayed in brass linotype at the entrance to its newsroom, says, in part: "The newspaper's duty is to its readers and to the public at large, and not to the private interests of its owners."[11] Following in American journalistic style, the *Post* also pledges, "The newspaper shall tell ALL the truth so far as it can learn it, concerning the important affairs of America and the world." The *New York Times*' "core purpose" states: "Producing content of the highest quality and integrity is the basis for our reputation and the means by which we fulfill the public trust and our customers' expectations."[12] At the National Press Club in Washington, a plaque entitled, "The Journalist's Creed," reads, in part:

> I believe in the profession of journalism. I believe that the public journal is a public trust; that all connected with it are, to the full measure of their responsibility, trustees for the public; that acceptance of a lesser service than public service is a betrayal of that trust.[13]

News organizations in the other English-speaking Watchdog countries voice similar commitments. The Guardian News & Media organization puts forth its ethics code in order "to protect and foster the bond of trust between GNM (in print and online) and its readers."[14] The British Broadcasting Corporation

(BBC) identifies itself as a "public service organization," whose mission is, in part, "to provide impartial news and information to help people understand and engage with the world around them."[15] The *Irish Times* articulates a set of commitments to enable its readers "to reach informed and independent judgements and to contribute more effectively to the life of the community."[16] Canada's *Globe and Mail* promises "to inspire and inform Canadians through courageous, empathetic, and honest journalism."[17] Canada's largest daily newspaper, the *Toronto Star*, says its purpose is "to keep our customers informed about what matters most to them, to help make their life, community, country and world better. Our mission is to deliver trusted news, information and content on all platforms." But the *Star* and the *Irish Times* also offer language that suggests their stance toward coverage can advance social justice causes in a manner that no mainstream American news media outlet would employ. For example, the *Star* notes: "We focus public attention on injustices of all kinds and on reforms designed to correct them. We are the news organization people turn to when they need help; when they want to see the scales balanced, wrongs righted; and when they want powerful people held to account."[18] The *Irish Times* outlines, among its principles, "the progressive achievement of social justice between people and the discouragement of discrimination of all kinds" and "the promotion of peace and tolerance and opposition to all forms of violence and hatred so that each man [*sic*] may live in harmony with his neighbor, considerate for his cultural, material and spiritual needs."[19] These, and other principles, support their constitutional democracy and contribute to readers' informed and independent judgments of facts and current affairs.

Reporters in Protector nations shared this commitment to inform their citizenry but not with the same unbridled fever for detail. Indeed, Protector reporters conveyed shock at what Watchdog reporters see as routine revelations about crimes and alleged criminals. Dutch, Swedish, and German reporters voiced with sincerity their commitment to protecting the presumption of innocence, shielding blameless family members, and assuring the possibility of the convicted criminal to be resocialized. Protectors contend the public has no *need* for the kind of detailed and sometimes personal information those reporters routinely withhold: full names and identifying features or photographs of accused persons. At the same time, some also said that they shield the accused out of fear that their countries' legislators will impose repressive legal restraints on journalists if they fail to observe self-imposed restraints. To varying degrees, Watchdog journalists—except those in the United States who are largely protected by the First Amendment and the courts' interpretations of it—share that fear of constraining legislation and deeply resent existing laws, like publication bans in Canada and super-injunctions in England, that impede their ability to "tell all." Reporters from Canada in particular noted they wished they had the latitude enjoyed by their American counterparts. This aspirational commitment to keep the sun shining on the public's business, blocks out virtually all concern for the suspect's welfare. Watchdog journalists viewed injuring, or tainting by association, innocent family members as regrettable but inevitable byproducts of decisions made not by them but by the accused. These journalists rarely mentioned the possibility of rehabilitation for those who are convicted. The presumption of innocence, as well as the allegation that highly detailed media coverage is a punishment meted out on sometimes undeserving people, goes largely ignored or is considered a court-imposed barrier to the press' ability to fully inform the public.

Watchdog journalists want few, if any, limits on transparency,[20] yet despite their sound reasoning behind this stance, and their moving articulations of their public service purposes, they often lose sight of what the citizens *need* to know; instead, they focus on beating the competition, catering to the public's prurient interest, and pursing their own career ambitions. These pressures can pull that ethical commitment to need to know off its moorings. As Patterson and Urbanski demonstrated in their analysis of the Jayson Blair case at the *New York Times* and that of Janet Cooke at the *Washington Post*, the effect of this diversion of purpose is to reshape the news into a self-serving enterprise in which citizens feel pandered to and no longer perceive their true interests at work.[21] The argument Patterson and Urbanski make is that if a reporter is guided by the principle that journalism is a public trust, then news stories will be written for the citizens' welfare or better understanding. The foremost value becomes the truth, and allegiance is owed to readers and to the public. When journalists' work is guided by the thrill of getting a good story or seen to advance an individual's career, or for the organization's commercial success, all else in the decision-making process goes awry. Stories are written to entertain or garner a payoff; beating the competition and looking good are valued more than the truth. From such a perspective, loyalties are no longer owed to the public but to individual journalists or their careers.[22]

Unless journalism's mission to serve the public guides them, Watchdog reporters can, like actual dogs, bark and bite before they fully comprehend the situation or its nuances. No ethical approach could justify the British tabloids' vicious attacks on Christopher Jefferies (described in this Part's Preface and detailed in Chapter 6), whose only crime was being a bit odd and having a fusty fondness for Victorian literature. And to be fair, none of the journalists or editors with whom we spoke defended those stories. The accusatory outburst by a handful of tabloids cost them large, undisclosed libel settlements and several contempt of court convictions. But while stopping short of such mean-spirited and, in some instances, illegal attacks, many Watchdog news professionals still champion attitudes that expel criminals. Journalists with whom we spoke routinely dismissed what some professionals called "collateral damage"—harm to family members or the taint of guilt for an accused who may be innocent—as part of the job. As we will discuss in this chapter, we found outstanding examples of reporters exploring underlying social causes brought into the spotlight by signal crimes. But while some reporters are introspective about the implications of their reporting practices, only a few looked below the surface to analyze the forces that shaped the alleged outliers they profiled.

Neither Watchdog crime reporters nor the cultures in which they are embedded truly believe the offender should be offered a pathway back into productive citizenship, as the Protector countries routinely do. As *Irish Star* reporter Michael O'Toole noted, the crime story is not complex. "The people tell us, and we tell the people. That's it. If I thought about rehabilitation and victims' families, there would be no information coming out." While O'Toole asserted an extreme view, the staunch and scrappy bulldog, tell-all attitude he espoused was common. *Pittsburgh Post-Gazette* reporter Dennis Roddy shared this stance. "I don't view [withholding information] as protection; I view it as an imposition," he said. "The law is always going to be imperfect, and the justice system is imperfect, so the best possibility we have is to open things up." Informing the public was *the* primary ethical motivation for journalists in all four Watchdog countries. These journalists see deliberately withholding legal and public information, as journalists do routinely in Protector countries, as a step too far, as an usurpation of citizens' rights and of the journalists' responsibility to use the information as they see fit. Watchdog reporters take this commitment to serving the public seriously. After foregrounding their obligation to inform, in their interviews with us, each offered modifications and teased out subtle gradations.

Seeing the Devil in the Details

The idiom "the devil is in the details" refers to a snag or mysterious element buried in the specifics. That devilish catch can collapse a project short of its goal, yet despite the negative connotation of "devil," it can also refer to the key to solving the problem, as in the older German expression: God is in the details. Interpreted in this manner, reporters feel a keen sense of need to report all the facts in case the key to understanding is among them. They themselves may not spot it, but the path toward exploration and knowledge ought to be open to everyone, not just news professionals. Watchdog reporters are committed to spelling out what they see as *all* the telling facts of crime stories, including the same details that reporters in other democratic countries believe should be kept from the public. The most responsible Watchdog journalists—that is, ones who remain attuned to journalism's main mission to work in the public interest—tell stories that spotlight faults in public policy, rips and worn spots in the social fabric, or the need for a sturdier safety net. If, however, the reporters' habit of seeking out revealing details is done merely to beat the competition or further individuals' careers, heat replaces that sunlight. Then, the news takes only prurient interest in the devilish details. Constructed in this manner, crime stories tend to assign individual blame and fail to tie the story back to the community and its responsibilities in a meaningful manner.

Defining the Moral Edges of Community

Watchdog journalists watch what is occurring at the edges of their communities and examine whether notions of the acceptable are changing or being challenged. Crime stories draw the public's attention in part because they help construct society's moral edges and raise concerns about deviants whose behavior falls beyond. Richard Poplawski poked a semi-automatic AK-47-style rifle through a second story window of his home in Pittsburgh, Pennsylvania, and killed three police officers. The act of shooting police officers arriving in response to a domestic disturbance call from Poplawski's mother clearly lay beyond the moral limit. "We have a trust with our readers that we need to convey as much as we can responsibly who this person is, what the person was doing, what their actions were, and what led up to this thing. They [members of the public] need to understand something that's affecting them," said Cindi Lash, former assistant managing editor of the *Pittsburgh Post-Gazette*. She guided the paper's 2009 coverage of Poplawski. As reporters later discovered, Poplawski espoused white supremacist positions on the Web, subscribed to views about the police as an enemy force, and believed that then-President Barack Obama intended to take away guns from private citizens.

The specifics about this shooter were important, Lash said, not because they were titillating, but because they pointed to why the killings happened. "I don't understand why [Poplawski] started shooting out the window, and my readers don't understand either, but we are trying to help them . . . to give them as much context as possible." That context, she said, illuminated a community member who held fringe beliefs and acted upon them. "Where did he get the guns?" she wondered. "Sometimes the system fails. . . . It's supposed to protect us from some person who opens his window and starts shooting. We have something that needs to be fixed." Lash called on reporters to dig for background to answer these larger questions. Dennis Roddy, who wrote for the *Post-Gazette* at the time and had studied right-wing organizations, found examples of Poplawski's hate speech online. The public needs to understand, Roddy argued in our interview, the "connections between extreme beliefs and actions." In this instance, it was important that the public know that Poplawski was entangled in the larger foment of right-wing conspiracy discussions on the Internet. As Roddy dug deeper, he found Poplawski was both a political extremist and a racist. "I thought that this was very important—essential, in fact—for how extremism informs conduct," Roddy said. For him, the public needed to know this man's background because "then we get to motive and conduct." He noted that many people may have read this story as "a novelty story, but it's about the political fringe. More and more, the fringes are influencing the center." Specifically, in the case of Poplawski, Roddy sought to show readers that conspiracy theory websites could push individuals with already fragile minds across the line into action.

The sensational aspects inherent in armed standoffs can garner criticisms like "if it bleeds, it leads," as Lash and Roddy pointed out. But to them, moving audiences to care about and understand the complexities of crime coverage is what matters. It's part of the pursuit of truth. While many people—lay and journalistic—associate the drama of this storytelling approach with exploitative sentiments and negative motivations on the part of journalists, former *Toronto Sun* reporter and editor turned writing coach Thane Burnett put a different spin on the if-it-bleeds, it-leads phrase.[23] "I always thought from my earliest days," he said, "that saying wasn't a negative thing. I thought it meant the story had to be human—no matter what you're writing on—taxes, or politics, or murder." He recalled an occasion when he realized his interpretation differed from that of most others. Burnett was scheduled to give the second of two talks at a public gathering about journalism. He listened while the first speaker, Peter Mansbridge, longtime chief correspondent of Canadian Broadcasting Corporation's Television News and well-known anchor, upbraided the phrase and the attitude he believed informed it. Poorly done journalism focuses on the sensational, Mansbridge said. Burnett had to follow this speech with his take on the aphorism. For him, "if it bleeds it leads means the story has a heartbeat, that it's human." Reinterpreted in this manner, the phrase suggests that journalists must remember to keep in focus the idea that people and community ought to be at the heart of every story. Done well, these tales offer citizens an opportunity to know their neighbors, to better understand how and perhaps even why some came to transgress laws and social boundaries, and to consider whether social conventions, policies, and institutions function as they should.

A second type of story, while not always as inherently fascinating as the details of dramatic shoot-outs or murder, carries equally pressing implications for democracy. In these narratives, the Watchdogs keep a sharp eye on the justice system itself: reports questioning police competence or the adequacy of support agencies to care for the vulnerable are two that came up. Kirk Makin, longtime justice reporter for one of Canada's two national newspapers, *The Globe and Mail*, called these "stories that push on the big door." Sometimes they ride on the currency of a signal crime; others are independent investigations. The situation between the police and the press is complicated in every country, and reporters and editors raised aspects of it in virtually every interview we did. In the Watchdog countries, journalists profess a clear and well-articulated ethical responsibility to keep a skeptical eye on the behavior and the policies of the police. As a result, the relationship is neither static nor simple. In some instances, news people over-rely on information the police provide, and this can result in a one-sided view of a person arrested or charged. In Britain, columnist for *The Guardian* Roy Greenslade noted that two aspects drove the style of coverage of the unfortunate Christopher Jefferies: cut-throat competition (explored further in the next chapter) and the behavior of the police. Greenslade told us that the most interesting thing about Jefferies case, aside from coverage itself, was the police angle. Few reporters focused on this, either during the early investigations or afterward when another man was convicted of Yeates' murder, he said. A number of British reporters and editors with whom we spoke noted that what they printed or disseminated came directly from the police. They were following the lead offered by law enforcement by implying Jefferies was likely guilty. It is perhaps easy to say in retrospect that the press should have been more critical. Greenslade noted that the police told journalists Jefferies was arrested on suspicion of murder. "It sounds like it means a lot. It legitimizes even in minds of press, who should know better [than to make assumptions], and allows them to do a headline, 'Arrested on suspicion of murder,'" said Greenslade. In the United Kingdom, however, arrest does not mean that this person will ever be charged. "But it gives you carte blanche to publish the name." Both Greenslade and Mike Norton, the editor of the local Bristol newspaper, the *Evening Post*, noted that leaks early on said police were not looking for anyone else, which suggested to the press that the police had the man responsible for Yeates' death.

To Norton, the police were, in part, trying to 'play' the media to get more information from the public. But he suggested that the police were also falling for the lure of the national tabloids. He believed some of the leaks and tabloid exclusives were coming from the police. Norton took this up with Bristol's chief constable. "My comment to him was very simple: The [Bristol] *Evening Post* is read in Bristol more than all of these other papers put together. So, if you're serious about catching this person and securing information that will lead to his capture, the paper that will get most responses is mine. If you're giving anything to the *Sun* because you're seduced by all this interest by the national and international media, then you're stupid and you could be jeopardizing the investigation."

Sadly, most of the British press was seduced by sensationalism, constructed out of Christopher Jefferies' minor quirks and oddities, which were as completely innocent as the man himself. In this instance, journalists should have maintained more distance between themselves and their police sources. Even after the real killer confessed, few news outlets apologized or offered stories about how it was that an innocent man was made to look guilty although he had not even been charged, let alone convicted—or why it took several months for police to release Jefferies from being "on bail." He remained under police prescribed conditions even after the killer, a Dutch man named Vincent Tabak, had been arrested and formally charged with Yeates' murder.[24]

Taking a broader view of the sometimes problematic imbalance between police, who have information, and the press, who want it, Daniel Nasaw said: "I do think from time to time, what if this guy [speaking generically about an accused] really didn't do it because I do assume as a reporter that he's guilty—because I am only talking to police," mused Nasaw, who wrote for *The Guardian* at the time we interviewed him. He usually cannot get in touch with the suspect, who may not even have a lawyer yet. "So, the only people I talk to are the cops ... or a piece of paper with the cop's words on it. It does occur to me that some 26-year-old patrolman can write whatever he wants or a detective can write whatever he wants." And as a result, stories can appear—and in fact are—one-sided and can impugn guilt.

As we outline in more detail in the next chapter, in the case of the kidnapping, sexual assault and murder of 8-year-old Tori Stafford, from Woodstock, Ontario, the police saw her mother, Tara McDonald, as the prime suspect, and their suspicions tainted how journalists wrote about the woman, implying that she was, as Christie Blatchford put it, "a whack job" who had something serious to hide. But equally as disturbing was the extent of largely inappropriate and cruel police behavior toward McDonald. Reporters were eventually aware of it. "They tried to entrap her," said Randy Richmond of the *London Free Press*. And he wrote about how an officer tried to befriend her. Then, in a complicated plot, officers arranged a limo ride to a hotel near the Toronto airport so McDonald could meet an anonymous benefactor. This person, whose sex is still not publicly known, offered to put up ransom money if this were requested for Tori's safe return. Richmond detailed how this person showed McDonald a lock of hair that was the same color as Tori's and told McDonald that they shared the loss of a child; this lock of hair devastated and traumatized McDonald. But the entire situation was created by the Ontario Provincial Police who were trying to elicit information from the woman. But like Christopher Jefferies, she was innocent. She had no involvement in her daughter's disappearance or death. "In retrospect," said Richmond, "I should have asked the chief investigating officer, now the chief of police [in a nearby town] whether they had learned anything from the mistakes they made in that investigation. I didn't." Follow-up stories that detail how and in what ways institutions make mistakes, or overlook some evidence in favor of following other leads, are essential if citizens are to understand whether and how their institutions, like the police, are behaving. As newsrooms shrink and the few reporters who cover such stories are under increasing pressure to write about aspects of cases that will garner large audiences, what the public needs to know can be overlooked; instead, media offer what it knows people may want.

Christie Blatchford, among others, has tried to write these larger stories, and to raise awareness about fraying social institutions and ways in which ignoring problems may have repercussions. "Terri-Lynne McClintic's life was a mess" she said, speaking of the woman convicted in the kidnapping, assault and murder of Tori Stafford. McClintic was born to a stripper who did not want her and gave her to another stripper who had lost her own children because she was deemed by the child welfare system to be an unfit mother. "I wrote about it," said Blatchford. "I did a story about her background after she was charged. Terri was sexually abused by the time she was 15, and she would have learned how to dissociate and so on. A lot of her testimony rang true because of her background."[25] Recently, when Tori's family sought coverage to protest McClintic's transfer from a medium security prison to an Indigenous healing lodge, Blatchford again addressed McClintic's troubled past, in a piece titled, "Why I can't completely share the outrage over McClintic's healing lodge transfer." In it, she made the argument that both McClintic and Tori Stafford were victims and that "Children in McClintic's entire experience were to be hurt and ruined." Blatchford's final lines of text make her position clear: "Those two little girls, the dead one and the killer, have melded in my mind somehow. One can't be saved or helped or even made half-whole. Maybe the other can be."[26] While McClintic's behavior was clearly abhorrent, it is still worth raising questions about to what extent the community that has condemned this woman failed her in its legal and ethical obligations not only for her moral development, but also her personal safety when she herself was a child. The social institutions, created and maintained at taxpayer expense that should be providing a haven for the vulnerable, are malfunctioning. Such problems need a public airing and a reckoning.

Revealing information about an alleged lawbreaker's identity, background, family ties, and history of wrongdoing can help the community understand parts of itself that might be hidden from general view. This tell-all approach allows the public to see potential threats to the general welfare— mishandling of mental health problems, for example, an issue explored in a story told by Peter Hermann, crime reporter at the *Washington Post*, and his editor, Amy Gardner. The two outlined how an elderly Chinese woman who spoke no English had—after a lengthy search by police—been apprehended in Washington, DC. She was charged with defacing monuments with green spray paint. After the story ran, Hermann received emails from readers complaining that "we called her mentally ill and [were] delving into her private business."

"It's not voyeuristic though. There's a journalistic reason for doing this," Hermann said. "How did she end up in Washington? There's more to the story on China's end or our end or on her family's end, and she ended up this way. I think it's our duty to follow that and figure that out. The overwhelming question is, how did she do it and how did she get here?" He then extrapolated from this particular story. "In the Boston bomber case, it's how did he become what he became? How did he become a terrorist?" Hermann said reporters ask probing questions to build a narrative of a suspect's life so they can tell readers who this person is and how he became who he did. And beyond the micro-level, Hermann noted another important point: "Did our *system* protect us?" Hermann's editor, Amy Gardner, concurred. "These questions are the same—'how could this have happened?'—and the public service aspect of that question: 'how did public safety fail?'" she said.

Why Watchdogs Watch and Why [Historically] It's Mattered

Lee Wilkins, an American ethics scholar who began her journalism career covering cops and crime, emphasized that these types of institutional stories fulfill journalism's paramount obligation to guard society against abuses of power. Wilkins noted journalism's ethical foundation in the United States is to monitor how the system is working "so that . . . we have a chance to change something that's not working if we can," she said. Crime coverage should be "about fairness and thoroughness," Wilkins argued. "It's not about vilifying people—not cops, not people who are busted, not neighborhoods, not families, or a whole bunch of other people." Watchdog reporters talked about both types of stories, those that focus on individuals on the moral edges of society and those that dealt with larger, systemic concerns, as well as stories that did both. The key is that reporters and editors must keep their sights on the lodestar that is meant to guide their endeavors and justify the special protections and privileges journalism enjoys in democratic societies.

Within the Watchdog countries, journalism—itself an institution—has taken a beating in recent years: It often stands accused of being biased or shallow, too easily influenced by other institutions or by the public relations industry or by media owners' drive for profit. As we discuss in various parts of this book, these are valid criticisms that do affect ethical choices journalists make when they cover crimes, but it is also worth noting two things. First, despite these seeming lapses and short falls, many of the reporters and editors with whom we spoke in other parts of the world still see the press in these Watchdog countries as exercising their enormous freedom and power for largely positive ends, and as one media lawyer in Portugal put it, working "on the side of the angels." Second, as Hallin and Mancini outline in *Comparing Media Systems*, the relationship among media, their public, and democratic institutions is informed and shaped by the specific political, economic, and social history of these countries. In Watchdog countries, particularly the United States, this history is one characterized by defiance and mistrust of authority of all types, and of extreme self-reliance and elevation, even worship, of individualism. While a detailed outline of the complexities of historical, scientific, and philosophical thought is beyond this current project, it is important to note that some of the principles that inform journalistic attitudes and practices have their roots firmly in traditions designed to support democracy.

During the Enlightenment of the mid-to late-18th century, the rational mind came to be thought of as capable of solving all problems and moral dilemmas. The ability, and the moral obligation, to think for oneself came to the fore. Indeed, these were central arguments put forth by John Milton nearly a century earlier, in his treatise for free speech, entitled, *Areopagitica*.[27] Milton saw people in a fallen world as needing a pathway to redemption; that path was constructed through making individual moral choices, between good and evil, through exposure to a marketplace of ideas. "I cannot praise a fugitive and cloistered virtue, unexercised and unbreathed, that never sallies out and sees her adversary, but slinks out of the race where that immortal garland is to be run for, not without dust and heat."[28] For Milton, it was a person's obligation to exercise his reasoning and find for oneself the truth. "Let her and Falsehood grapple; who ever knew Truth put to the worse in a free and open encounter?"[29] And in part, these ideas of a range of thoughts and opinions, fact and falsehood arrayed in a public venue, and the concomitant obligation of each of us to consider the choices, informs contemporary journalistic attitudes even in the 21st century.

In the field of Western ethics, as the divine right of kings was being replaced by the natural rights of humankind, the religious deontological basis for resolving conflicts was also being challenged; people were less interested in following the dictates of the church or political leaders without question. What was morally right or wrong was not determined by blindly following others' dictates; instead, philosophers and intellectuals considered what the consequences might be of certain choices or actions. And one of the champions of this outcome-based ethical system was John Stuart Mill. His was a philosophy of utilitarianism, an approach that embraced the greatest good for the greatest number of people.[30] It is the ethic favored by Western journalism for most of the last 150 years, in part because its principles were largely congruent with those of democracy itself. We suggest that this attitude, largely unacknowledged by our interview subjects, but present nonetheless, is manifested in several of the themes outlined in this chapter. All Watchdogs understand that by naming names of persons accused or convicted, they are also implicating members of that person's family, including wholly innocent children. When asked how concerned they were about these implications, some borrowed a term from the American military vocabulary and called persons caught in such situations (as mentioned) collateral damage. While family members, spouses, parents, children, have done nothing to bring on the unwanted spotlight of publicity, it is for the greater good that their privacy be sacrificed. In this approach, it is of paramount importance that the processes of justice that uphold democracy function in a clear, transparent, and accountable manner; this means naming names.

The same intellectual history that formed the Western collective sense of moral propriety and still influences Watchdog outlooks on journalism ethics is the same as that which granted the press freedom under the First Amendment of the U.S. Constitution.[31] The ethical responsibility of the press and the duty to serve its citizens can be understood in the context of the philosophical and political underpinnings of journalism in the United States. Licensing of the press in England ended in 1695, and the freedoms won there established and influenced the development of press laws and attitudes in its colonies.

While the emphasis on individuals and their rational abilities sits at the forefront of traditional Western ethics, people must also live together in societies—as all of us do. Communities function smoothly if people voluntarily obey the agreed-upon rules and agree to tell the truth—also a component of the social dictum.[32] In part, the arguments around the obligations of truth-telling are linked to social contract theory initially outlined by Thomas Hobbes in the *Leviathan*.[33] He argued that, at one point in our distant history, people were born with the unlimited natural right to do as they pleased, including to kill one another. But such an approach was untenable because humans are similar enough that no one would ever be safe. Life, in such a society, would be, in his most famous phrase, "solitary, poor, nasty, brutish, and short." The solution, he posited, is for humans to surrender many of their natural rights in return for a collective security. These ideas were expanded over the next century by philosophers John Locke, Jean-Jacques Rousseau, and others, but the essential outlook remained: People are, by necessity, part of a larger social group, and its survival depends on the flourishing of its individual members. One of the central questions in the creation of a government lies in where its ultimate power ought to reside. For Hobbes, who did not have a great belief in the goodness of humanity, people surrendered their natural rights irrevocably to the government. "But for Locke, ultimate political power—that is, political sovereignty—remained with the people. In Locke's view, government worked for the people, not the other way around."[34] Among the earliest supporters of the necessity of free speech and unfettered access to information in a democracy were a pair of 18th-century journalists who wrote under the pen name, Cato.[35] One of their arguments, proffered in Essay 15, suggests that if people retain the ultimate authority over their political representatives (hired governors at the time), then the people also have the right to know how well or poorly their "employees" are doing their jobs. "Cato went further, arguing that even though other principles might be violated, popular sovereignty was, in effect, trump. It was more important to keep the sovereign people informed than it was to keep people thinking highly of their governors."[36] Thus, for the American founding fathers, nothing was more important to ensure that this political power would continuously reside with the people than the guarantee of a free press—a free flow of information that the government neither owned nor controlled. While these founding and foundational arguments are of the highest aspirational value, we will explore in the next chapter whether the government and elected officials pose the greatest threat to how Watchdog journalists report about crime, wrongdoing, and wrongdoers.

6

Risks and Challenges for the Watchdogs

Competition, Demonization, and Productive Examination

Murder: It's the most high-profile crime. Virtually all reporters want to cover these stories, and almost all readers want to read them. Packed with violence, mystery, and intrigue, these tales fascinate everyone and feed the unquenchable thirst for watercooler talk. But while murder coverage attracts enormous audiences, it also attracts a great deal of criticism: It's too graphic; the details are upsetting, and the complexity of lives and histories—of both victims and accused—can be grossly simplified. Accused people can find their lives in tatters. Victims may seem unsympathetic or somehow deserving of their fate, and communities can devolve to gossip rather than undertaking public discussions about larger issues, such as the efficacy of policing, the fairness of the current justice system, and so on.[1]

In these Watchdog countries, the overwhelming push for publication of names, identifying attributes, and an inclusive list of background details, publicly circulated within the bounds of the law, has clear merit. It is soundly based in Western Enlightenment ideals: Citizens are largely entitled to know what journalists know and can decide whether and how to act on that information. Citizens are seen not as children who must be spoon-fed sanitized information but as rational beings able to function independently and discern truth from dross for themselves. John Milton articulated this perspective more than 300 years ago in *Areopagitica*, from which numerous contemporary ethics scholars have extrapolated.[2] But the challenge for Watchdog journalists in choosing specificity and naming names, remains: Are they covering crime in the public interest, or are they covering what interests the public? The biggest caveat of this model is that ethical practices can be swayed, consciously or not, by economic considerations like competition and ownership, as well as by the related issues of shrinking job markets, globalization, technology, and social media. All threaten what most Watchdog journalists articulated as their first normative obligation: serve the citizenry

Murder in Our Midst. Romayne Smith Fullerton and Maggie Jones Patterson, Oxford University Press (2021). © Oxford University Press. DOI: 10.1093/oso/9780190863531.003.0006.

with enough factual information for them to be free and self-governing. Neal Augenstein, a reporter at WTOP radio in Washington, DC, put his finger on the crux—what exactly is the "right" amount of information, given that so much is publicly and legally available in these countries? It is a subjective call, but it's not perceived by journalists as limitless. "You report stuff that's relevant," he said. "There's no expectation that you report everything you know."

Our analysis of the data gathered from the interviews suggests that crime coverage *must* be undertaken with genuine public, not prurient, interest at its core. Otherwise, the harms of the Watchdog approach—sensationalism, trial by media, and "othering" of the accused—can displace the many benefits that historically have made this reporting approach admired by many around the world who operate under more restrictive press models.[3]

This set of journalistic practices embraced by the Watchdogs is a utilitarian one that privileges the public's right to know over individuals' privacy and embraces Brandeis' belief that sunlight is the best disinfectant to potential abuses of power by those in positions of authority.[4] British ethics scholar and journalism professor Chris Frost noted where the emphasis falls in the United Kingdom, and we would add in other Watchdog countries: "If you don't feel the prime duty is to hold government and the justice system to account, then clearly the ethical issue becomes the privacy of the individuals," said Frost. "There isn't any justification for telling on people if there isn't a need to publish and to hold the courts to account." As we noted in the previous chapter, crime stories in all democracies help citizens define their communities' moral boundaries. In Watchdog countries, this function is closely aligned with a duty to hold the criminal justice system accountable for protecting public safety, as well as a demand for decency. Hallin and Mancini in *Comparing Media Systems* pointed out the historic links among capitalist systems, democracy, and a public that is rightfully critical of those who make decisions on its behalf. Watchdogs bark loudly when necessary to alert their citizens that something is amiss. They threaten to grab the powerful by the seat of their pants and hold them to account.

Our research shows that the Watchdogs' approach to crime coverage can effectively shine a light on systemic problems in public institutions that sometimes abuse power and capital, especially in instances in which routine oversight has proven inadequate. But it can also indulge prurient curiosity for the sake of profit and sacrifice the good of the one, or the few, for the many. To begin, then, we outline the "harms" of the model as they appeared in our interviews.

Competition: Being First and "Winning" Audiences by Being Sensational

As we write this chapter, the British news media have publicly named and published Facebook photographs of a nurse arrested in the deaths of at least eight babies at a hospital in Chester. In 2020, she was out on bail and the police investigation continued.

As of this writing, she has not been charged, but headlines include her full name and phrases like "arrested on suspicion of murder of eight babies."[5] In addition, the nurse's social media has been mined for photos that include shots of her wrapped around a stripper pole and drinking alcohol. Neighbors have been quoted expressing shock: She seemed like such a nice girl, maybe even a bit of a nerd. How could she be guilty? This practice of naming people before they are charged, using personal and sometimes compromising photographs from online sites, and asking acquaintances, work colleagues, family members, and so on for personal impressions of the person are part of what media critics and laypersons see as sensational and presumptive. It is also disturbingly reminiscent of the British press' now notorious treatment of the wholly innocent Christopher Jefferies, initially suspected in the death of Joanna Yeates. The national tabloids mocked his hair, accused him of pedophilia, and called him everything from a Peeping Tom to Professor Weird. Then, some mainstream news outlets picked up the storyline since the material was now in public circulation, yet Jefferies was guilty of nothing other than perhaps being an eccentric. In all the countries under consideration, journalists said they strongly believe in the right to the presumption of innocence, but the reporting practices that routinely employ this type of coverage can amount to trial by media. And worse—impugn guilt. Roy Greenslade, media commentator for *The Guardian* and a journalism professor at City University London, noted wryly: "A united feeding frenzy by the press can destroy your reputation on the thinnest of evidence." While the press may legitimately operate as a Fourth Estate by monitoring the institutions of justice, it is not to *be* a place for justice. Numerous Watchdog journalists mentioned that they generally believe that when police make an arrest, the person is most likely guilty. As we outlined in the previous chapter, however, crime reporters' stories in the earliest days of an investigation are largely based on the information given to them by the police. At that point, all allegations are unproven, but their publication lends them unwarranted legitimacy.

Reporting done early in an investigation inhabits a legal gray area, open to interpretation by lawyers and courts. Stories that threaten a person's right to a good name and to a fair trial by an impartial jury are illegal in some Watchdog countries (Canada, the United Kingdom, and Ireland) and are ethically questionable in all. Jefferies' case served as our initial starting point in England. He successfully sued eight newspapers for libel, and the U.K.'s then attorney general, Dominic Grieve, charged two under the Contempt of Court Act of 1981 and won. Jefferies' testimony formed a central part of Justice Lord Leveson's Inquiry into the Ethics and Practices of the Press in 2012, along with the testimony of other victims of the press, like the family of famous three-year-old kidnap victim Madeleine McCann. The *Daily Telegraph* called her disappearance "the most heavily reported missing person case in recent history."[6] At present, uncertainty remains in Britain about the legality of naming persons under suspicion or arrested but not yet charged. The concern is directly tied to a successful suit by British singer Sir Cliff Richard against the BBC (British Broadcasting Corporation; Britain's public broadcaster) for invasion of privacy in August 2018. The BBC had reported that Richard was being investigated in 2014 by the South Yorkshire police for allegedly sexually assaulting a 16-year-old boy in the 1980s. No charges were ever brought. It remains to be seen whether the British press will choose to curb its most worrisome and sensational behaviors or be curbed by the courts. (We will explore this question further in the next chapter.)

In Canada and the United States, most journalists name people only once a charge has been filed, which follows quickly after arrest.[7] In the United Kingdom and Ireland, reporters follow a similar practice, but a period of months may ensue after arrest before a formal charge is brought. In addition, laws in the United Kingdom prohibit almost all but the barest of details from being disseminated once a person is actually charged in order to protect the right to a fair trial by an impartial jury.[8] As a result, some British and Irish reporters told us, they use the gap between arrest and charge to cover people and their situations before they are limited to saying only a person's name, age, where they are being held, what the charges are, and a possible court date. In cases when the stories have a high enough news value, newspapers are willing to risk being sued for libel (a possibility of varying popularity in all Watchdog countries) or charged with contempt of court (in the United Kingdom and Ireland, and, in some instances, in Canada). Speaking with us, Chris Frost pointed to the practical reason for newspapers to make this choice: "Editors want to sell more and more papers, and certainly on big stories, the lawyers might say, 'It's a big story, and only a hefty fine.' But because it will help sales, they sail closer and closer to the wind." What motivates these decisions are not ethical concerns at all—it's money.

In our increasingly globalized context, journalistic approaches that protect people or protect the presumption of innocence are being challenged, or in some cases eradicated, because consumerism and ignorance, not citizenship and responsibility, are motivating publication. The Internet can drive foreign practices inside national borders. But we may be witnessing the first signs that such intrusions will be resisted. In December 2018, New Zealand's minister of justice said that Google could face prosecution under that country's contempt of court law for naming the man accused of the murder of British backpacker Grace Millane. The suspect was granted a temporary name suppression while awaiting trial. The purpose of the gag order was to protect an accused's presumption of innocence and to ensure an unbiased jury could be selected—one that had not been prejudiced by media coverage. The man has been named by numerous British news outlets, but none in New Zealand has broken the publication ban.[9] Google initially claimed ignorance about the suppression order. While the company has since geo-blocked the story so it cannot be accessed from New Zealand, it seems this is closing the barn door once the horse has left the stable.

An Australian court made a more aggressive move. When Cardinal George Pell was convicted on five counts of child sexual abuse in Melbourne in December 2018, the judge issued a gag order, blocking all publication about the conviction in order to protect the Cardinal's right to a future fair trial on separate sexual abuse charges. The judge threatened all news media, including those from other countries, with "substantial imprisonment" for breaching his orders. Australian news media obeyed and so did Reuters and the Associated Press, two of the world's largest news services, and the *New York Times,* all of which have bureaus in Australia. A Reuters spokesperson said the news service was "subject to the laws of the countries in which we operate." *Washington Post* Executive Editor Martin Baron took a defiant stance: "Freedom of the press in the world will cease to exist if a judge in one country is allowed to bar publication of information anywhere in the world." The *Washington Post, Daily Beast,* National Public Radio, and the *National Catholic Reporter* all carried the news, and the gag order did little to stop social media from penetrating Australian borders, the *Post* reported. Tweets and Facebook posts included links to sites where the news was reported.[10]

The issue is complex. To rob a culture of its journalistic or legal practices is to dig away at more deeply defined differences about crime and deviance and defendants' rights. New Zealand, Australia, or any other democracy has the right to decide what protocols and practices must be observed in the telling of its crime tales. Journalism, as the marketplace for the exchange of ideas and the locus for public education and debate, has a responsibility to define community and assist community members to know one another and themselves. Together, they ought to decide the parameters for inclusion and exclusion, and these should be reflected in the journalistic practices of each space, community, and country. Journalism is a public trust and, as such, it has a responsibility to those it purports to serve. When news rises to the level of international interest, locally defined rules can collapse. Some international ethical standards are needed to allow countries to exercise their definitions about the free flow of information without imposing those standards on others. If commercial enterprise alone makes all the rules, citizens are replaced by consumers, and no exchanges are possible except ones based on money. Overextending such an economic outlook, James Carey writes, "paints a picture of a society without community, unless one chooses to call a market a community."[11] In the contemporary context, Michael J. Sandel, in *What Money Can't Buy: The Moral Limits of Markets*, argues that people suddenly know the price of everything and the value of nothing. "As a result, without quite realizing it, without ever deciding to do so, we drifted from *having* a market economy to *being* a market society. The difference is this: A market economy is a tool—a valuable and effective tool—for organizing productive activity. A market society is a way of life in which market values seep into every aspect of human endeavor. It's a place where social relations are made over in the image of the market."[12]

Sandel's perspective aligns with that of Carey, who asserts that the metaphor of the marketplace has reached too deeply into the American mind and nudged aside countervailing representations that might better drive our thinking about the press, politics, and public life.

The manner in which crime stories are written and the amount of personal detail in much of the copy speak directly to the concern many people express—media professionals and citizens alike—that crime coverage is too sensational. Rather than form following function, form *is* function. "If it bleeds, it leads"—in its most negative, gory sense—garners hits on websites, boosts ratings on broadcasts, and incites point-of-sale purchases of newspapers at checkout counters. Criminology professor Yvonne Jewkes,

University of Bath, described the motivation behind such reporting: "It's all about a good story, about novelty and about how to make a story quirky. And in these days of massive market competition and massively dwindling sales of paper newspapers, it's all about selling the paper and circulation figures." Natalie Fenton, professor of Media and Communications, at Goldsmiths, University of London, agreed. Fenton noted another reality: While all journalism students in the United Kingdom are taught law and ethics in school, once people become employed, these tenets may feel like an abstract ideal and an impractical consideration in the "real world." Over-the-top coverage sells, and the profit motive in a cut-throat market can drive the selection of details and coverage style. "Even in the BBC, they are all tethered to a commercial model, whether tied to the public service model or not," Fenton said. The commercial pressures to be first with a story—because having a new, unique angle still drives people to your website—is ever present, regardless of the outlet or the country. Her point is clearly illustrated by the BBC's decision in 2014 to use a helicopter to film a police raid of famous singer Cliff Richard's house, which was being searched by police as part of an historic sex abuse investigation. No charges were ever laid, and Richard accepted an apology and a settlement from the South Yorkshire force. The BBC also apologized, but then met Richard in court in July 2018, where the judge ruled in Richard's favor, saying he had indeed suffered an egregious "invasion of privacy."[13] *Guardian* columnist Roy Greenslade opined that the use of a helicopter was more in the way of "American-style" coverage than that of the British public broadcaster, which is generally thought of as a flag-bearer for ethical practices. Richard's counsel argued in the trial that "part of the reason was to scoop rivals, a reminder that the modern media landscape is no different from the old: being first with the news matters."[14]

The motivation to be first with a story—both for the reporter and for the news organization—is prevalent everywhere in the Watchdog model. In the United States, an American reporter for a wire service, who asked to be anonymized because of the negative observations offered, spoke about the priority for new and unique information. "The more detail you have that others don't, the better," the reporter said. "The base motivation is to tell a story and how it impacted the nation or the city involved. There is that sense of duty. But also, there's an obsession with getting the details before everyone else." While the American Watchdogs were the ones who most emphasized their ethical obligation to provide information to serve the public's right to know, many also noted that interests other than the most honorable can animate their actions. "Pretty much anything you can get is fair game," the wire service reporter told us. "Say you have a source and the newsroom trusts it, then you'll put out whatever they tell you." In such instances, the pressure for more information is clearly coming from above, where editors make it known that they want all the details. "Sometimes you feel a little sleazy when you tell someone who is a relative of a perpetrator and they don't have anything to do with the perp, but you say, 'This is your chance to tell your story and clear your name.' But it's really their quote you want," the reporter said. These pressures are real and felt by reporters who work at some of the most respected papers in the United States. William Rashbaum, a senior reporter for the *New York Times*, noted that, from his perspective, these are not ethical decisions at all; they are simply an accepted and routine part of the practice of covering crime. If reporters did not follow these "unwritten protocols," he said, they would not be doing their jobs. "I used to say when I was younger and even less sensitive than I am now, 'Listen, I'm going to write a story about your son, and I want to make it a story that says something about him.' And I wouldn't quite say, 'this is your shot,' but that was the gist of it. And the *Times* still does this. If there is a big crime, someone will go to the victim's house. No one is *deciding* if this should be done; it's who's going to do it because it's the way the trade or the profession does it," said Rashbaum, who once worked at the tabloid the *New York Daily News*.

Social media have changed audience expectations, said Gary Emerling, who covered the Holocaust Museum shooting for the *Washington Times*. Now, everyone expects nearly instant access to events. "Where a newspaper used to chase a lead over a day," he noted, "now we need more page views and we need [the information] up now." Judy Muller, former ABC network reporter who teaches at the University of Southern California, told the *New York Times*: "I fear we have permanently entered the Age of Retraction. All the lessons of the past—from Richard Jewell [who was mistakenly accused of a 1996 bombing in Atlanta during the summer Olympics], to NPR's announcement of the death of Gabby Giffords, to CNN's erroneous report on the Supreme Court Ruling on ObamaCare—fail to inform the present. The rush to be first has so thoroughly swallowed up the principle of being right that it seems a little egg on the face is now deemed worth the risk."[15]

As mainstream media in the Watchdog countries grapple with a changed business model, the Internet offers instant and largely free gratification to citizens' most prurient interests. And those clicks offer lucrative monetization to those who create that content, regardless of accuracy.[16] While citizens in all four Watchdog countries maintain that they disapprove of tabloid-style sensationalism, click bait can and does drive coverage across news genre. A number of newsrooms, including the *Hamilton Spectator* in Canada, hang large screens all around the newsroom to display which reporters' stories are attracting the most online attention. *Spectator* editor-in-chief Paul Berton related a story about a lobster rescued from a grocery store tank as the kind that pulls in clicks and likes. Reporters themselves are competitive and want to have lead stories, but profit also motivates such cheap competition. The more stories garner likes, retweets, and other forms of integration on social media, the more money for the content provider. As the Public Policy Forum's report, *The Shattered Mirror*, outlined in 2017, "Canadian daily newspapers have seen more than half their ad revenues—about $1.5 billion—bleed away over the past decade, most of it going to Google and Facebook, which together served up more than eight out of 10 digital ads in Canada last year."[17] Clearly, cute but trite stories—even fabricated or distorted information—cost little compared to genuine journalistic fact-finding. "Whether for commercial, partisan, ideological or geopolitical reasons, it represents a direct assault on our democracy."[18]

The precarious nature of journalism employment also threatens ethical standards. In all the Watchdog countries, secure jobs with good benefits are hard to come by and hard to keep as regular workers are replaced with freelance or contract labor.[19] Initially, digital journalism was seen as a growth sector and a possible solution to the threat of the declining investigative journalism, traditionally undertaken by newspapers. In 2016, Buzzfeed founder Jonah Peretti chastised legacy media for being slow to shift to digital, and his company seemed poised for nothing but success, but by January 2019, about 2,100 jobs were lost in that sector, including about 15% of Buzzfeed's staff.[20] Social media platforms like Facebook and Google now provide most peoples' news, and the model excludes mainstream media from making money in the manner they always have. In such a climate, the pressure on individual journalists to perform and to conform is enormous. Martin Brunt, a senior crime correspondent with Sky News in London, once worked for the tabloid the *Daily Mail*. "I haven't been a reporter [at that tabloid] for twenty years, but I know the pressure my colleagues are under, and I can see how they would be persuaded to write that kind of [sensational] copy or wouldn't complain when a sub-editor rewrote it for 'topspin.'"[21] Young reporters who don't have what Natalie Fenton called "professional capital," or status in their newsrooms, are particularly vulnerable to pressure from editors, regardless of whether what's being asked is ethical, or in the case of some tabloids' requests, whether it's legal. The fact that a handful of national reporters hacked the phone of the missing and murdered English teen Milly Dowler (giving her parents false hope she was still alive) illustrates what Fenton believes is part of the problem. "It is clearly not that they [the British press] think this is in the public interest," she said. "It was a massive distortion" and "feeds sensationalism and the frenzy around it." In Canada, the *National Post*'s Christie Blatchford noted that much of the news is gathered and assembled remotely, outside the newsroom. As a result, young reporters do not rub elbows with more seasoned staff, and thus do not benefit from their mentoring about ethical decision-making and its consequences. Shrinking newsroom resources mean thinner coverage. Every reporter must do more with less. Patrik Jonsson, a senior reporter with the *Christian Science Monitor*, an American nonprofit news organization, said his output has changed dramatically in the last ten years. "I used to do one or two stories a week when we were a paper, and now I do six or seven."[22] Copy desks and fact checkers are also disappearing, another sign that shortcuts have become a necessity.

Many Irish reporters noted that the invasion of Britain's "Red Tops"—or tabloids—changed Irish crime reporting. Gerry Curran, Dublin courts' press liaison, said Irish papers began to shift from "the nosey neighbor approach" to a more mean-spirited style. As former Irish national press Ombudsman John Horgan noted, media indigenous to Ireland had expressed concern about the effects of British tabloids since the late 1980s. "They pushed sport, sex, and the cult of celebrity, and they pursued stories about the private lives of public people, something that had not been done previously in Ireland."[23] Horgan qualified this statement, adding that the Irish cultural mindset meant that its press, including these Irish editions of British tabloids, never went as far—or as frequently—down this precipitous path as those in England. Nonetheless, the Irish editions of the British tabloids surged in popularity and placed Irish papers under increasing pressure for readership.[24] In 2003, then Irish Justice Minister Michael McDowell threatened to introduce privacy legislation because of what he saw as problematic behavior on the part of the press. Like the press in many other democracies, Irish media had undergone a dramatic economic downturn and felt the fallout from new communication technologies, increasing media monopolization (and in Ireland's case, influx of foreign media ownership), and rising immigration. Head of the Irish National Union of Journalists Seamus Dooley pointed out that Ireland, being a small country, has a strong sense of community. Many "feared that sensationalism or the invasion of privacy would ultimately result in a backlash, either from advertisers or from readers," he said.

The soap opera coverage of the 2004 murder of Rachel O'Reilly—and of the subsequent investigation, trial, her accused husband, and his girlfriend—all shocked the country and illustrated the new reporting style on a large scale. *Irish Daily Star* crime reporter Michael O'Toole said the day after husband Joe O'Reilly's guilty verdict in 2007, his editor told him he could write as long a story as he liked—and he did—almost 5,000 words. To Curran and almost all the others we interviewed, the O'Reilly coverage marked "the day that Irish journalism changed. . . . You wouldn't have twenty-eight pages of coverage of a general election," Curran said emphatically. "That was the first time I'd seen that." To Curran, and to some others to whom we spoke, the change was clear: Joe O'Reilly had been tried and convicted in the press in a reporting mode taken straight from the British tabloid model.

In Ireland, as in all the Watchdog countries, suspects are not usually named by the press until they are charged. In both Ireland and the United Kingdom, the concerns are two: libel (or defamation) and contempt of court. The former charge is a civil one, and protection for a person's presumption of innocence is enshrined in the Irish Constitution and in its Press Code of Conduct, with each citizen having "a right to his or her good name." Contempt of court is intended to protect the trial process and the ability to empanel an impartial jury, should a person be charged. Since Joe O'Reilly chose to name himself as a suspect before being charged, reporters did not need to protect his identity, but many of our interview subjects also noted that the extent to which many media outlets covered aspects of the family—including their children, and Joe's and Rachel's parents—leaned far past a statement of facts. "He was tried and convicted in the popular press before he was even arrested," said Curran.

The O'Reilly case played out differently than it did for the man in England initially arrested in the murder of Joanna Yeates. For Christopher Jefferies, the sensational coverage was more extreme but also more harmful because he was innocent. The legal restrictions in Britain are similar to those of Ireland: Once a person is charged, reporters can publicize very little in order to protect the right to a fair trial. Once the case is in court, reporters are protected by privilege and can report anything said in open court in front of the jury. Some reporters we spoke with noted that the legal situation can encourage, although certainly not excuse, the reporting of juicy stories about people only suspected of a crime. Before charges are brought, the central legal concern is whether the outlet will be sued for libel.[25] If the story

is salacious enough, it appears worth the risk. But when journalists' behavior suggests they care more about making money than acting in the best
interests of the public they purport to serve, all media lose credibility in the
eyes of citizens. And individuals' reputations and lives are changed forever.
Jefferies outlined his treatment at the hands of the press in a statement to
the Leveson Inquiry. "It was clear the tabloid press had decided I was guilty
of Ms. Yeates' murder and seemed determined to persuade the public of my
guilt," he told the Inquiry.[26] He noted that the coverage was sensational and
amounted to a "witch-hunt," with long-lasting effects. "I will never fully recover from the events of last year."[27]

Canada and the United States are not free from the lure of the sensational
either. While the copy in mainstream news organizations is generally less
outrageous than in the British tabloids, especially in Canada where there are
no national tabloids and where the justice system can and does regulate to
some extent the manner of coverage, stories can still mislead, play upon unproven allegations, and suggest guilt, even when persons are not charged.[28]
Like the United Kingdom and Ireland, Canada has legislation that would
allow media to be cited for contempt of court, but *Toronto Star* media lawyer,
Bert Bruser, noted that it has largely fallen into disuse.[29] In the mid-1990s, a
couple, Paul Bernardo and Karla Homolka, kidnapped, sexually assaulted,
and then murdered two teenage girls. Because Bernardo admitted to being
a rapist before his murder trial, he had no reputation to protect, and Bruser
pointed out that several prominent columnists wrote about him before the
verdict as if he were already also guilty of murder. It marked a change of style
in writing that walked dangerously close to impugning guilt, and it's been
present (and popular) in the Canadian press ever since.

In the United States, courts have ruled in various ways in different states
about pretrial publicity, but the U.S. Supreme Court has found that it has
little effect on the defendant's ability to receive a fair trial. If local prejudices
jeopardize that right, trials can be moved or juries brought in from different
districts. Gag orders on pretrial procedures and documents are rare and
often short-lived, although a Colorado judge made one partially stick in the
case of James Holmes, who waited nearly three years for his trial in connection with killing 12 and wounding 58 others in an Aurora, Colorado, movie
theater in 2012.[30] Generally, the protection of the right to a fair trial is viewed
as the court's responsibility in the United States, and the press operates under
few legal restrictions.

The Good, the Bad, and the Monstrous Other

In the case of Tori Stafford, Canadian journalists spoke about several coverage decisions that, in retrospect, were unfair at best and more the result of speculation rather than fact. Kirk Makin, longtime justice reporter for the *Globe and Mail*, said that reporters are often eager to decide "who wears the black or white hats" in order to slot them into a narrative of good versus evil. When no one is charged, their sights can wander and perhaps land on someone innocent. During Tori's disappearance, many reporters thought they'd hit pay dirt. "Her mother was a suspicious whack-job," said Christie Blatchford, now of the *National Post*, then of the *Globe and Mail*. "She was under suspicion by police and by us, too." Tara McDonald was holding daily press conferences, trying to keep her daughter's disappearance in the media spotlight. "What I was trying to convey," explained Blatchford about her coverage at that point, "is that this parent is acting unusually." In retrospect, Blatchford is unsure what she actually communicated. "I tried to be gentle. If I pulled punches, it's good I did because I would have been wrong," she said about her copy from those odd early press conferences. "I am pretty good at reading people, but I got it wrong there." She and many of her colleagues felt something was not quite right with this mother's behavior. In fact, McDonald was guilty of something—she and her boyfriend were addicted to OxyContin. But she was not involved in her daughter's disappearance or her death.

Randy Richmond, a senior reporter for the local *London Free Press*, said that his paper decided to live-stream McDonald's daily press conferences because so much suspicion surrounded her. Besides, they were interesting—if also tawdry. Sometimes McDonald and Tori's father, Rodney Stafford, would argue in front of the cameras. The live-streaming technology shaped the story and kept it alive in the face of scarce newsroom resources. "Without the live-streaming, I would have been pulled off the story," said Richmond. "Those live-stream conferences attracted viewers to our website, and we had a chat board going at the same time. That drew in people from across Canada and the United States and kept me in Woodstock," Tori's hometown. But it also encouraged a voyeuristic public to indulge in prurient curiosity, peering at a painful and emotionally fraught time in the life of the mother and father of a missing child. What possible public interest could be served by offering, or using, such a news feed? While the trial of Michael Rafferty eventually cleared Tara McDonald's name, before that, much of the Canadian mainstream press had vilified her at a time when she was a grieving mother. "I was made to be such a wicked, wicked witch," said McDonald. "So heartless, evil and cold."[31]

Irish journalist Seamus Dooley, as well as British academics Robert Reiner, Yvonne Jewkes, and Sadie Clifford, all pointed out that sensational coverage is driven by and created to fulfill the genre of crime as entertainment rather than crime as news. The figures and events are framed to take on an air of unreality. People are villainized and resemble stock figures from fairy tales or horror movies, rather than the complex persons they are. Dooley outlined how newspapers about 20 years earlier had created seemingly cartoon nicknames for gangsters and mob bosses (e.g., the Monk, the Penguin, the General) to sidestep prosecution under Ireland's then very strict libel laws. The practice, he said, had the effect of making serious crime and criminals seem nonthreatening and innocuous. Sadie Clifford's doctoral work at Cardiff University explored news and entertainment representations of violent women. Her dissertation, titled "Expressions of Blame: Narratives of Battered Women Who Kill in the Twentieth Century *Daily Express*" used stories from the U.K. tabloid to study the relationship between fictional crime stories and factual ones over the last hundred years.[32] She found that the two types of stories tended to reinforce one another by using a similar framing. "In all the cases, the news reporting was packaged like, or told as a story, in the same way that the most popular crime entertainment of the day was told," she said. The Canadian media's treatment of the Stafford-McDonald family—specifically their casting of the mother as wicked witch—illustrated the point perfectly: In all countries in the Watchdog model, unusual and dramatic coverage sells. And technology helps push it over the top. But adopting this reporting style oversimplifies accused, convicted, and victims alike. Thus, it undermines civic and professional responsibility. Journalists must acknowledge the high personal cost to those who are unfairly represented or pre-judged. Even more importantly, they must also consider the corresponding degradation of public conversation when citizens' understanding of accused persons, criminals, and the larger nature of crime is so stunted.

Reiner and his colleagues note the social gap affected by such coverage: "Offenders are portrayed not as parts of social relations or structures that the victims or the public are also embedded in, but as pathologically evil. Any attempt to understand them, let alone any concern for their point of view or their rehabilitation, is seen as insensitive to the suffering of their victims."[33] Many Watchdog reporters to whom we spoke implied that detailing the stories of alleged perpetrators could be construed by their public as sympathizing with a wrongdoer and perhaps undermining the victims' suffering. Matt Shaer wrote a long read for *New York Magazine*, "A Monster Among the Frum: The Story Behind the Murder of Leiby Kletzky and the Trial of Levi Aron," in which he explored the disappearance of a young Jewish boy in the Hasidic community of Borough Park, New York.[34] From the beginning, Shaer wanted to explore who Aron was—his experiences and his relationships with family and community. Through speaking to two of his ex-wives, Shaer learned Aron lived both inside and outside the Hasidic community his whole life. "He was a fascinating character," Shaer said, "and the idea that he was so ostracized and he was on some level devout, but he didn't fit in." But the bigger question that informed the story—as well as which details to include—point to the zero-sum game many Watchdog reporters implied when explaining and exploring aspects of an accused person's life. "One of the things we ran into right away—and it was quite a challenge—was not to be too, well, sympathetic," explained Shaer. "He was obviously someone who suffered a crack in his psyche and in his world. . . . His crime was really savage and really bloody. It involved a really small child, and he showed no remorse. It was so horrific, but I still thought that it was worth explaining how someone got to that point," when injuries Aron had suffered built up and he snapped. "It is worth knowing about to prevent that."

When readers set criminals and their victims outside their communities' boundaries, they fail to connect the individual crime to the larger culture and social policies. They can fail to understand the long-term toll that crime takes on its victims and on the social fabric. They can fail to obtain the necessary foundation for a clear evaluation of the effectiveness of the criminal justice system. In short, they fail to understand the role of what's missing from the stories they read.

Reality, James Carey writes, "is for us a vast production, a staged creation—something humanly produced and humanly maintained. Whatever order is in the world is not given in our genes or exclusively supplied by nature."[35] We live in a symbolic reality. Communication then is the primary phenomenon of reality and not merely a reflection of something more real. To explain this, Carey describes a map drawn to help a child find her way home from school. That map is "capable of guiding behavior and simultaneously transforming undifferentiated space into configured—that is known, apprehended, understood—space."[36] Like maps, crime stories transform the horror of criminal behavior into a form we can grasp. The setting for this story is the community in which it happened. In Protector countries, the characters—victims and perpetrators—dwell within that community. Their behavior speaks to citizens and points out their failures to prevent such aberrant actions. We have discussed examples of Watchdog crime reporting that also use the individual crime cases to point to social weaknesses. But, more often, the Watchdogs' stories that are told to render deviance understandable are tales in which the individual miscreant no longer belongs in that community, if he ever did. He must be expelled and rejected lest his rot spread. Only the individual criminal, not the community, is held responsible. The community is then called upon to agree on what behavior lies outside its pale. But by turning its back on the criminal instead of seeing him as a citizen who has taken a misstep, the community denies the reality that perpetrators and victims have lived in its midst and developed who they are inside its boundaries. "Communication" thus loses part of the root it shares with "community."

Carol Gilligan argues in *In a Different Voice* that traditional approaches in Western ethics emphasize individual rights and the concurrent obligation to respect those rights.[37] In contrast, her ethics of care approach, reflected largely by the practices of the Protector countries, places peoples' obligation to others at the center. For Gilligan, the "justice orientation" ought to be complemented by a "responsibility orientation" where people acknowledge their relation as linked one to the next, and who see each other's histories, happenings, and stories as part of a larger social fabric in a web of connection. "This ethic, which reflects a cumulative knowledge of relationships, revolves around a central insight, that self and other are interdependent."[38]

Reporting choices that focus on a narrow sense of justice and demonize the perpetrator and his or her personal responsibility undermine citizens' moral obligations to see how their own institutions and cultural choices might bear some connection to, if not responsibility for, criminal behavior. Without this acknowledgment of social justice, citizens view those accused and convicted of crimes as apart from, not a part of, their own societies. Put succinctly: "They" are not "us," and "we" have no responsibility for them because they are aberrations. That this is the style of much British journalism is outlined in the work of Yvonne Jewkes and Chris Greer, who argued British tabloids regularly serve up a spectrum of deviant others to be feared and loathed.[39] Jewkes told us in an interview that even some of the mainstream, respected newspapers follow the tabloids' lead because, the papers argue, the material is now in the public domain. Reiner found that the British press portrays accused persons "not as parts of social relations or structures that the victims or the public are also embedded in, but as pathologically evil."[40]

Crime reporting engages in a process of signification that can generate moral indignation on the one hand or constructive problem-solving on the other. In addition, social reactions "may include either a retreat from public space by members of the community, or alternatively, the instigation of informal or formal social controls to deal with the perceived causes of the deviance."[41] Our examination of crime coverage shows that most Watchdog reporters do the former by addressing how the accused or the criminal deviates. But as Carey suggested, reporters appear to be caught up in a transmission view of communication that focuses almost exclusively on the concrete here and now, rather than a ritual form that reinforces community.[42] Stories such as the *Washington Post's* coverage of the elderly Chinese woman who spray-painted monuments or the *Pittsburgh Post-Gazette's* reporting on the young man who shot three police officers from a bedroom window introduce a broader discussion of why and in what ways communities themselves might be implicated. But much of crime journalism misses an opportunity to encourage citizens to shoulder the ethical responsibility of being a part of a community that discusses, debates, and defines its own boundaries.

Collateral Damage and Other Inconvenient Truths

A commitment to identifying abuses of power comes with the warrant to publish in these democracies. Watchdogs and, in fact, journalists across all three of our media models, believe that it is their duty to expose wrongdoing by public officials in the execution of office. In such cases, innocent family members who might inadvertently be negatively affected by such a calling out are seen by journalists as justifiable collateral damage. Numerous persons with whom we spoke across all four Watchdog countries used this phrase, or a version of it, to express the same sentiment. David Stout of the *New York Times* considered an example that illustrated whether there was a choice about what to publish: "Donald Manes [16th Borough President of Queens, NYC] was involved in scandal and took a lot of public money, and it was interesting and important. He had a wife and teenaged son or daughter. I personally felt sorry for that teenager, but what was the alternative?" The alternative, to protect the identity of a public figure turned criminal, was inconceivable to Stout and one he saw as a great injustice to the public interest.

Chris Frost pointed to the lack of confidence in those in positions of authority in the British Isles, and the idea that regardless of potential harm caused by publication to either an innocent accused or that person's family, the scale must tip in favor of disclosure, not secrecy. "I think it's much more important that we're aware who's been arrested, why they were arrested, and that we see that justice is done, than if any one person is hurt in the process," Frost said. "It's imperative that we know who authorities are bringing through the system." Tom Kent, an editor at the Associated Press for more than 40 years and an adjunct professor at Columbia School of Journalism, concurred. He noted that Americans, as descendants of the British justice system who had their own set of skirmishes with those authorities over the last 250 years, share the lack of trust articulated by the Brits. "We feel our overwhelming responsibility is to hold governments accountable, so when police are arresting people, that's news as far as we're concerned, and the police publish the tales of arrests, press releases, and mug shots and so on, on social media, and the information would still be out if we didn't publish it," Kent told us. "In this country, with our traditions, we are nervous about people being grabbed off the street and locked up. The government is a coercive force—they can arrest people, lock them up, and watching those government people is a high responsibility." Our data suggest the public's right to know as much relevant and detailed information as possible is an ethical cornerstone in American and in Watchdog practice writ large. While this commitment to exposing wrongdoing of elected officials is justified and even considered honorable across all the models, the practice takes on a different hue when a private citizen is accused of a crime. The distinction for the Watchdogs is, as we illustrated through the coverage decisions in the cases of Christopher Jefferies or Tara McDonald, and some others, that they create collateral damage in virtually all crime coverage.

Journalism as Practice

Walter Fisher, acknowledging Alasdair MacIntyre, notes that there are two sites where community can be built: in interpersonal relationships (like those between citizens who see themselves as part of a larger whole) and in what MacIntyre calls "practices"—medicine, law, scholarship, sport, and, we would contend, journalism. "Each of these sites is the home of a set of values that constitutes a community, specifying norms of character, role performance, interaction, and ideal aspiration. Put another way, a community is at bottom an ethical construction."[43] The practices can become corrupt, however, when practitioners pursue values that are external to the practice: "When doctors or lawyers pursue money, power, and prestige to the detriment of health and justice, their professions suffer and so do their characters."[44] As we will discuss in the next chapter, Ireland's journalists found their own answer to this: a mediator, in the form of a national press ombudsperson and press council to unite media voices and speak for all. As our data have demonstrated, competition, technology, and self-interest can drive reporters to act in ways that demean journalism's honorable and aspirational practice. Reporting the news with these lesser values undermines contextual and factual discussions that the public ought to hold. In the current context of market economies that underlie and underline journalistic practices in this model, it can become expedient to say that acting ethically is too complicated; thus, anything goes.

7

Accountability

Resistance and Reconciliation

*Our standards matter more now because how do you differentiate
yourself when so much of the content you have, others have, too? The
way you reassure your audience and cultivate a larger one is you demonstrate you're serious about your standards, and seriousness includes
a willingness to listen to criticism and act upon it and have a mech-
anism that works with that.*

—Kirk LaPointe, Ombudsman,
Canadian Broadcasting Corporation, 2011–2013

In an era of ubiquitous information, public confidence in mainstream journalism in all countries under consideration is undergoing a slight uptick,
while trust in social media is declining. In part, these gains appear to be
arising out of citizens' concerns about the weaponization of fake news and
mis- or dis-information most prevalent on social media platforms.[1] It is a
time when legacy journalism might be able to build on its sometimes bruised
and battered credibility. The Watchdog's Enlightenment attitudes, largely
embraced and unquestioned by North American and U.K. news people, are
well rooted in paradigms and epistemologies that can confuse equality with
sameness and go hand in hand with news practices that encourage citizens to
view the accused, their families, victims, and crime in general, as apart from,
not a part of, daily democratic life. Such journalistic reporting approaches
that focus largely on individuals and their choices and imply an exclusively
personal responsibility for their own fate can lead to a style of coverage that
tramples the humanity of anyone caught in the news' sights. Some results
of this approach were explored and evaluated in Chapter 6 when considering specifically the coverage of Christopher Jefferies and Tara McDonald,
and the tangentially related notion expressed by many journalists that any

Murder in Our Midst. Romayne Smith Fullerton and Maggie Jones Patterson, Oxford University Press (2021). © Oxford
University Press. DOI: 10.1093/oso/9780190863531.003.0007.

harm to the families of an accused is regrettable but necessary "collateral damage." Routine practices of crime reporting have, as our data demonstrate, varied widely even within and among the countries of Western Europe and North America that share similar histories, cultures, and democratic institutions. Those variations are under threat in an increasingly globalized age. To consider what may be lost or gained and to define what is at stake, this chapter details some of the threats to preserving cultural difference by respecting those differences when practicing journalism. Then, we suggest each Watchdog country consider borrowing aspects of Ireland's approach as one possible way to "talk back" as a profession against government threats of legislation and business incursions or profit motivations, and, most importantly, to counter, in ways unique to each country, others' influence on coverage. All of these forces threaten best practices, and each Watchdog country faces a need to shore up public faith that someone is watching the watchdogs.

Hallin and Mancini outlined three central criteria to measure the professionalism of journalism across their media systems: autonomy, agreement on professional norms, and a strong commitment to public service.[2] The existence and efficacy of codes of ethics and accountability structures like press councils and ombudspersons play an important part in the evaluative process in whether and how well journalism serves democracy. Theoretical work on press and media systems abounds, and virtually all scholarly undertakings have similarly placed these criteria as central.[3] Most agree that the United States led the way historically. Michael Schudson points out, in *Why Democracies Need an Unlovable Press*, professionalization was constructed as the antidote to the scandalous behavior of the Yellow Press more than a century ago.[4] After debates about how best to "manage" unethical press practices and garner audience trust, Americans set up professional standards and were the earliest adopters in the Watchdog countries of ethics codes, the concept of reporting fact-based information, and the style of objectivity. They also invested in education, as exemplified by the establishment of the University of Missouri and Columbia University Schools of Journalism, which taught professional skills and valued the concept of journalism as a higher calling and a public service. This approach led to generally ethically sound and quality journalism in the United States over the last hundred years. However, new developments are challenging journalism: The recent increase in public relations personnel and the proliferation of digital media that has undermined the notion of an achievable objectivity, as well as the impact of Donald Trump and politically aligned cable news have all contributed. These factors are leading journalists to look for new ways to maintain audience share and their position of public influence. Stephen Ward points out in *Ethical Journalism in a Populist Age: The Democratically Engaged Journalist* that democracy can be defined differently. The established measure of "thin" democracy generally means one having minimal characteristics, like the existence of free and fair elections. A "thick" democracy can be evaluated by variables in the norms of political culture or the ability of a government to function effectively. Whether thick or thin criteria apply, however, journalism professionals consistently hold primary responsibility for initiating and carrying on public conversations that respect and value the institutions of democracy and maintain belief in them.[5] Using the data gleaned from our interviews and close readings of relevant codes, we suggest that the efficacy of the press's role in a democracy and its public service orientation can be assessed, in large measure, by examining its media accountability systems.

Hallin and Mancini argue that in their North Atlantic liberal model, which includes our Watchdog countries, informal self-regulation of the press is common and effective to some degree. We suggest, along with numerous scholars, that other industry interests are undermining the efficacy of these informal structures. The weakening of self-regulation has, in turn, eroded public trust and citizens' belief that the media can, in fact, police themselves.[6] It is difficult to imagine that this situation will change without a genuine rethink of this media model's paradigms and the influence of profit motive that powers it. As we have argued throughout this Watchdog section, when journalism loses sight of its public service mission, it floats adrift of its ethical moorings. Sensationalism, career advancement, profit, and other less worthy goals supersede. While some of these goals may have value, the quality of the public conversation suffers if they are placed before public service. In each of our Watchdog countries, systems of press self-regulation and accountability differ. As such, we will use each country as an exemplar of one of the challenges we address in this chapter, but there is also overlap, and many more examples exist beyond the few we have chosen.

Britain, under weighty public pressure, occasional governmental threats of legislation, and the recommendations of the Leveson Inquiry, chose to establish, by Royal Charter, the requirement for an independent press regulator and offered strong incentives to all media to join. Now, the United Kingdom has two regulators—IPSO (the Independent Press Standards Organisation) and IMPRESS (the Independent Monitor for the Press). Both are vying for top spot, although in terms of sheer number of members, the former leads by a solid margin and has maintained most of its media membership (as well as staff) from its much-criticized predecessor, the Press Complaints Commission (PCC). IMPRESS, the first officially sanctioned regulator, enjoys the support of celebrities who have been maligned by British tabloids, like J. K. Rowling, Hugh Grant, and Max Mosely, but it has attracted no high-profile or mainstream media members. In addition, several of Britain's largest newspapers refuse to participate in voluntary regulation and have refused to join either regulator. For a while, there was even a possibility that the British Parliament might enact press legislation to curb journalistic excesses, but that time appears to have passed.

In the United States, despite the continued attacks by President Donald Trump on "fake news" and his calling journalists "the enemy of the people," for now, the tradition of the protection of the First Amendment is strong. While the country has a robust offering of media criticism, journalism think tanks, and reputable, active professional organizations that represent journalists, to date the press councils and ombudspersons have enjoyed less enthusiastic support. The Washington News Council, the last of its kind in that country, closed its doors in May 2013. Its executive director and chair, John Hamer, outlined why the decision was made. "We had a great 15-year-run, and we helped a lot of people who were damaged by media malpractice," he told the Poynter Institute. "But the news media have changed tectonically since we began. The eruption of online digital news and information made our mission of promoting high standards in journalism more difficult, if not impossible. How can anyone oversee a cyber-tsunami?"[7] But in June 2019, the *Columbia Journalism Review,* lamenting that National Public Radio was the only major American media outlet to retain an ombudsperson, appointed four new watchdogs to oversee coverage in the *New York Times, Washington Post,* CNN, and MSNBC. In announcing these appointments, *Columbia Journalism* Review editor Kyle Pope said the "flameout" of public editors in American media "is the most visible sign of the growing distance between news organizations and the people they serve." A "defensive huddle" is not the right answer to the threats that face American media, he said. "I am convinced we are about to enter one of the most important chapters in the history of American journalism. We have to get it right."[8]

In Canada in 2015, three regional press councils amalgamated to create the National NewsMedia Council (NNC).[9] As in other Watchdog countries, its creation was, in part, a response to the growing challenges of the Internet and globalization of news, as well as rising costs of litigation and threats of government interference. Kathy English, public editor for the *Toronto Star* and a member of the committee that created the NNC, hailed it as a positive development for both readers and media credibility. She echoed concerns about the current state of journalism in other countries when she said: "The cross-country scope of the news organizations that have signed on to the national council recognizes the digital media reality that news now has no geographic boundaries. And, as one former newspaper editor so aptly put it on Twitter this week, 'neither should the watchdog.'"[10]

Against this mixed backdrop of media accountability across the Watchdog countries, a new regulatory model has emerged: In 2008, under threat of possible legislation and in a push-back attempt against draconian libel laws, Ireland created a legislatively recognized and wholly independent national press council and ombudsperson. The autonomy of journalists was strengthened by defining clearly journalism's role in, and obligations to, the public, and by establishing Irish-specific industry standards that support a unified professional voice. After considering the various challenges raised in the other three countries in the Watchdog model, we proffer the Irish model as a possible framework for exploring how best to restore citizens' faith that media are fair and accountable, to push back against pressures from economic interests or possible threat of legislation or control, and to maintain journalistic practices that best reflect the concerns and values of the individual communities, and specific countries, of which they are a part.

Resistance to Change Across the Watchdog Model

The United Kingdom

We conducted interviews in England immediately before and then six years after the *Leveson Inquiry into the Ethics and Practices of the Press*, which held hearings beginning in November 2011 and continued well into the next year; its report was made public in November 2012.[11] In some instances, our interview subjects' attitudes, and even whether they would grant us interviews, were starkly different between 2011 and 2017. For example, when we first visited England, we had a lengthy and detailed discussion with the then chair of the Crime Reporters Association (CRA),[12] John Twomey, a reporter for the national middle-market tabloid the *Daily Express*. He outlined the

history and original purpose of the CRA, how relations between the police and reporters evolved, and how the close connection with cops meant
that reporters gained access to stories that otherwise might go untold. The
Association began in 1945, and in those early years, CRA members enjoyed a
lot of cooperation with police. "They were the ones the police officers trusted,
and they'd give you information based on the idea that you'd not publish it, or
attribute it," he said. This unofficial arrangement meant that reporters had tips
that could lead to stories about the force, and it offered one way to keep an eye
on the inner workings of the police. In terms of the sensational and libelous
coverage of Christopher Jefferies, Twomey made no excuses. "All of us know
the law." He also soundly condemned the too-close-for-comfort relationship
between some *News of the World* (NOTW) executives and the Metropolitan
Police (the Met) that in part gave rise to the Leveson Inquiry. "It's a dangerous
time for us and for newspapers," Twomey said. "And they [newspapers] have
to confront some of the skeletons in their own closet as well." The informal relationship meant police felt it possible to leak to journalists with whom they
had trusted relationships. Formalizing transparency did not seem the best
way forward when possible wrongdoing or abuses of police power turned up,
according to Twomey and others to whom we spoke.

When we returned to England in 2017 to conduct follow-up interviews,
the head of the CRA (not Twomey), said he did not feel comfortable speaking
on the record with us. Other reporters suggested he declined because he
works for a tabloid and likely feared possible repercussions from his em-
ployer.[13] CRA Vice Chair Simon Israel, a senior home affairs TV reporter
for Channel 4 News, agreed to speak with us. When we observed that there
seemed to be a pervasive fear in the United Kingdom in the wake of Leveson,
he agreed. He said the situation among papers is particularly fraught. The
head of CRA "belongs to the Mail Newspaper group. Newspapers are different; there's a much tighter rein." Israel suggested his situation was different
for two reasons: He works in television and noted he is nearing retirement.
"If I didn't want to talk with you, I wouldn't meet," he said wryly. He also
noted that the newspaper industry in Britain is small, and that reporters, including the current chair of the CRA, generally don't speak out against their
employers. While we were not raising questions about the *Mail* in our current
work, perhaps the risk was too great. "The *Daily Mail*," Israel said, "is ruth-
less." He shared numerous observations about how the scandal with NOTW,
the Met, and then the fallout from the Leveson Inquiry had all affected crime
reporters' relationships with police.

The College of Policing put out revised guidelines, "Engagement and Communication: Media Relations," in 2017.[14] As Twomey had predicted in 2011, the document now requires that all meetings between press and police are recorded by senior officers as having taken place with notes about what was discussed.[15] According to the College's website, the new recommendations take into account the Leveson Inquiry's suggestions.[16] The preamble highlights the need for police "to recognize the role the media discharge on behalf of the public in ensuring we [the police] are account-able." Its Code of Ethics clearly stipulates that openness and transparency are "essential to maintaining and enhancing a positive relationship between the policing profession and the community."[17] This all sounds reasonable and positive: ensuring that the public will learn about police practices and thus be able to hold them to account. But further into the document, the con-cern that Twomey raised on behalf of the CRA, and journalists generally, is laid bare. Under a section titled "Recording contact with the media," the new guidelines stipulate, "Chief officers should record all their contact with the media where policing matters are discussed. This record should be publicly available." Further down, it notes: "Where another officer or member of staff meets with a media representative, takes part in an interview, or provides in-formation verbally or in writing for a matter for which they are responsible, it is good practice for a similar (unpublished) record to be kept."[18] The College also firmly states the term "off the record" is to be avoided.

In response to questions about these changes, Israel said, "It's hard for crime reporters to do their jobs, and if you think about the nature of how you do your job, it's your contacts over time [that assist you in holding power to account]. You're no more specialist than anyone else without them." Like many other journalists with whom we spoke, he said that it is now very diffi-cult to keep an eye on what police are doing because no one on the inside can tell the press if there are possible improprieties within the force. "Leveson went beyond . . . and it scared people, so now you don't get leaks," said Israel.

One central observation that emerged from our interviews in Britain was that ethical concerns did not take center stage.[19] British reporters' concerns focused more on what the laws allow than on what ethical choices exist. Regulation, broadly defined, was their central preoccupation both in the early interviews and in the later ones; only the emphasis was changed. In the earlier discussions, in the context of the Jefferies case, focus generally fell on the rarely used Contempt of Court Act 1981, which has strict liability rules. If a media outlet breaches this Act, as several did in their stories about Jefferies, they are liable for the consequences. The Act states the press may not publish anything that might create "a substantial risk that the course of justice in the proceedings in question will be seriously impeded"—in short, that a jury would be prejudiced by the information and thus a person's right to a fair trial would be undermined.[20] Our initial interviews occurred just after Britain's then Attorney General Dominic Grieve had successfully prosecuted two tabloids for breaching the Contempt of Court Act in their coverage of Jefferies. The case was on many reporters' and editors' minds. No one justified the excesses perpetrated in the Jefferies coverage. As the Leveson Inquiry was about to get underway, the possibility of further government regulation was hanging over their heads.[21] "Our journalists are amongst the most regulated in the world in terms of legal restrictions placed on them," said Tony Johnston, who spent 25 years as a reporter and then began assisting media in understanding evolving legal situations and implications, first for the Press Association (a national news agency for the United Kingdom and Ireland) and then as an independent consultant. "It's a complex legal mine field. Our primary concerns are defamation, libel, and contempt of court."

In November 2012, Lord Justice Brian Leveson published his report. It recommended that newspapers continue to be self-regulated, as they had been by the PCC, but that there should also be a press standards body created by industry and underpinned by legislation that would incorporate a new code of conduct for newspapers.[22] In October 2013, a Royal Charter on press regulation was granted, and it set up key recommendations, allowing for one or more independent self-regulatory bodies to be established for the press and overseen by the Press Recognition Panel (PRP).[23] Publishers who joined a recognized body could expect kinder treatment if action were taken against them in court. As we have noted, two regulators came into existence. Most newspapers signed up with IPSO, which has publicly stated it has no intention of applying for recognition by the PRP. A few small publications joined IMPRESS, which is "Leveson-compliant." But both *The Guardian* and *The Observer* have resisted joining either regulator and instead appointed an internal ombudsperson.[24] In our 2017 interviews, many of our subjects spoke at length about the change in climate after Leveson. Keith Perch, an IPSO board member, head of the School of Journalism at University of Derby, and former editor for the *Leicester Mercury*, emphasized the difference between regional papers' beliefs and behaviors and those of the tabloids. The Inquiry did not make any distinction. "Leveson said almost nothing about the serious press," he said, "and then wanted blanket legislation." Perch and numerous other reporters and editors who worked for regional papers said they felt Leveson's report tarred everyone with the same brush. "I wrote the PCC Code of Conduct into all my employment contracts," Perch said, to demonstrate how important following the ethics guidelines was at the *Leicester Mercury*. "If you breach this, you breach your contract of employment."

Tony Johnston acknowledged the turmoil in the current system, but he saw ways that the British situation has improved since Leveson. "One of the most significant changes is the seriousness with which the Editors' Code is now treated compared to pre-Leveson," he said. "It is embedded into the working practices of journalists now." Before a story is even started, he said, editors and reporters discuss any potential for breach of the Editors' Code. "Previously, we would have published, and then tried to align our ducks to show why it was not a breach. Now we say, 'What are our risks?'" and discuss whether the story and the risks are in the public interest.

As we outlined in Chapter 6, the U.K.'s chair of the National Union of Journalists' (NUJ) Ethics Council Chris Frost believes the financial pressures account for a greater measure of the press' climate change than do the fears of regulation. "There has been a massive decline in standards of crime reporting, with a few exceptions," he said. "The main reason is reporters are overworked. People are eager to follow the code of ethics, but there's no time, and no investigative reporting. Everyone is doing more stories with fewer people." Frost's perspective is not new; critics have long argued that media are subservient to business interests, advertisers, and largely focused on sensational aspects of stories to sell papers and attract viewers. In this regard, commercial media often neglect their responsibility to the public.[25] In the spring of 2018, the British Parliament was again raising the specter of another public inquiry into press practices in the form of an amendment to the data protection bill.[26]

The British media's lack of agreement about a way forward and the ongoing unease in newsrooms march on. "The press is on a path to self-destruction, and they are parallel paths—government regulation and economic pressure," said Frost. "They're not inevitable, but it's going in that direction." We are not suggesting that British media need to be monolithic in their support for a way to be accountable and to push back against the economic model that is driving some of the ethically bad behavior. But if a clear system of self-regulation were supported by members of the press and the public believed such a system to be effective, the government would back off its continuous threats. British press resistance to genuine change is baffling. According to

Frost, "The NUJ feels that if self-regulation does not happen, [regulation] will be imposed on them."

United States

Crime stories play a key role in how a nation's values are discussed, challenged, and perhaps reaffirmed. While geography once contained this "daily moral workout" within the reach of news distribution, the Internet shows no respect for boundaries.[27] Instead, it annihilates borders that contain laws that define crime, as well as journalistic practices that reflect each culture's attitudes to privacy and dignity. The story of Dominique Strauss-Kahn, broken by the American press and picked up internationally, demonstrated this collapse.[28] In New York in May 2011, the managing director of the International Monetary Fund, Strauss-Kahn was paraded in front of television cameras and photographers by police for what is commonly known in that country as "the perp walk." He was charged with various offenses, including sexual assault and forcible confinement, in an alleged attack on a hotel maid. He appeared publicly and against his will, dragged from his hotel room, shamed and embarrassed. At this point, Strauss-Kahn had been neither tried nor convicted; he was legally presumed innocent. And yet, the intention of the perp walk is clearly to humiliate the accused. Defenders of the practice note that it offers the American people the opportunity to see the beginnings of its justice system in action, and one cornerstone of that system is its openness and transparency. Publicity is also seen as a deterrent. Some of the journalists we interviewed in the United States argued the perp walk is indicative of the United States' attitude about equality: All persons, regardless of stature, can be made to face the public. The fact that this was a man held in high regard in his own country, France, does not matter. He, too, can be seen to be held to account; no one is above the law. The photographs and video of Strauss-Kahn in handcuffs, escorted by members of the New York Police Department, were widely circulated around the globe.

French television stations ran the footage, despite a law, implemented in 2000, that forbids the publication or circulation of images depicting handcuffed criminal suspects. The law reflects French beliefs that such visuals can undermine the presumption of innocence. In France, the reaction from commentators and politicians was swift and furious: How dare American media impose its values beyond its borders. Former Justice

Minister Elisabeth Guigou found the images of a handcuffed Strauss-Kahn led by several police officers "to be brutal, violent and cruel."[29] "France's media is struggling to reconcile strict privacy laws with the age of twitter and the internet," the French international radio station, reported.[30] Celebrities there were safe from public intrusion, but after the arrest in New York, Strauss-Kahn and his wife, Anne Sinclair, "were regularly snapped around Paris and numerous stories about the state of their marriage were published," Angela Diffley at Radio France Internationale (RFI) later said.[31] In some parts of Northern and Central Europe, the arrest might have been ignored if it had happened on their soil because the alleged crime was not directly related to Strauss-Kahn's performance in office. Interestingly, several French newspapers chose to run the name of the alleged victim of the assault, something that American, Canadian, and even British papers would rarely do. While the charges against Strauss-Kahn were eventually dropped because of inconsistencies in the complainant's story and lack of physical evidence, the damage to Strauss-Kahn's reputation was permanent.

For the French, the story was a social catalyst, but one that was injected into their culture and politics by another country with different values about privacy, relevance to public office, and so on. Depending on one's perspective, the American tell-all style of crime coverage and its routine dissemination of the perp-walk photos either opened a much-needed conversation about predatory sexual behavior in France or it cost that nation the leadership of a valued economist and politician. Regardless, what was clear is that the Internet had disrupted French law and reporting custom, and few American reporters knew or cared. Through our interviews, it became clear that only about 20% of reporters or editors are aware that their reporting norms and routines, and the stories that result from them, can be out of step with those in the far corners to which their news stories travel. Moreover, few considered how or whether these differences might be understood, and with what effect, in other locales. For Americans, Strauss-Kahn's arrest in New York fit into a larger narrative they had been exploring for decades about powerful men taking advantage of women. From Gary Hart to Bill Clinton, John Edwards, and Anthony Weiner, sexual scandals became as much about arrogance and character as they were about sexuality. For Americans, bringing down great men might be seen as an exercise to prove their fallibility. They represent America's post-Vietnam and Watergate loss of faith in its leaders and political processes. They function as "dramatic articulations of popular fears about the seeming encroachment of the forces of disorder, drawing upon diffuse and inchoate existential anxieties about the state of contemporary society."[32] The alleged Strauss-Kahn crime reflected the qualities of a "signal crime." It received widespread coverage about the alleged crime itself and about how the story was reported. Violence against women, an issue once hidden behind a curtain of privacy and relegated to the private sphere, had been propelled into a worldwide spotlight by a series of signal crimes.

In addition to the Strauss-Kahn case, two high-profile suicides of Canadian teenage girls in the wake of online bullying and sexual harassment, and in one case of rape and circulation of photos on the Internet, as well as a series of gang rapes in India; the shooting of Malala Yousafzai in Pakistan; the National Football League's suspension of Baltimore running back Ray Rice for beating his fiancé; Canadian CBC radio host Jian Ghomeshi's alleged choking and beating of women before, during, or after sexual encounters; and the conviction against comedian Bill Cosby on charges of drugging and rape. In the wake of #MeToo and the conviction of movie mogul Harvey Weinstein, the list continues to grow. As technology conflates geography and removes or redraws national and international boundaries, countries are losing the legal and moral ability to control and contain the definitions and conversations that once defined them. As a result, creating and establishing meaningful intercultural communication is one of the greatest challenges facing scholars, journalists, and newsrooms today.

A Way Forward

Reconciliation in Ireland and Canada

"I have to take this call," Ireland's Press Ombudsman John Horgan said, turning his attention from our questions to the voice on the other end of the telephone. "Hello, Father," Horgan began. A parish priest was on the line, asking the ombudsman to protect the privacy of a family being targeted by a media scrum after a high-profile domestic situation.

"In circumstances like these," Horgan said after he hung up, "if I think that there is a serious risk that press activities may amount to a breach of Principle 5 of our code on privacy, I send an advisory note around to editors and pass along the family's request for privacy to them.[33] Generally, they do pull the dogs off, once they know everyone else is going to as well, so they are not so pressured by competition." Such a request has no bearing on any future complaint the family—or anyone else—might bring to the Irish Press Council, Horgan said. "But prevention is so much better than cure."

As we discussed in the previous chapter, the British tabloid style of reporting the murder of Rachel O'Reilly and subsequent trial of her husband, Joe, moved coverage in a direction literally foreign to many of Ireland's journalists. In response, they wanted to push back against press practices that could be detrimental to creating conversations that were Irish in nature, not British.

This anecdote of John Horgan's phone call illustrates that it is possible for a country to implement an approach to covering crime informed by its own cultural values and beliefs, told in the voices of its people. This is true, despite living in the shadow of a much bigger and more influential country, the United Kingdom, whose competitive news institutions are traversing the Irish Sea and bringing with them the tell-all style of crime coverage that respects little beyond the pursuit of audience share and, implicitly, money. Horgan, retired, was the first to hold the ombudsman position in 2007 when the Press Council of Ireland and the Office of the Press Ombudsman was founded.[34] The Irish arrangement is modeled in part after the Swedish one, and, to some extent, ironically, that of the United Kingdom. At that time, the Irish Parliament, or Dáil Éireann, threatened the news industry with restrictive measures, but because Irish journalists took the initiative, Parliament backed off. Ireland still ranks higher on the "Reporters Without Borders" world press freedom index than its English-language counterparts in Canada, the United Kingdom, and the United States.[35]

In "Policing the Press: The Institutionalisation of Independent Press Regulation in a Liberal/North Atlantic Media System," Stephen Dunne argues that all self-regulating press councils in Hallin and Mancini's North Atlantic system failed to enforce their mandates and to hold journalists accountable for ethical breaches.[36] The Irish, however, set out to establish something different. In conjunction with the government, editors, publishers, and the National Union of Journalists created an independent, legislatively underpinned and incentivized national press council and an office of the press ombudsman. The arrangement has legal recognition, and this has resulted in the codification of a widely accepted and agreed-upon set of professional journalistic norms. Its unique features are its structural independence from both the state and the industry, and it boasts more lay members on its council than journalism practitioners. Dunne outlined some criticisms of the Press Council of Ireland (PCI): Its procedures could be slow, and sometimes council findings are not published prominently, or sibling papers may not publish findings against others within their conglomerates at all. But largely, the Irish model has many merits and supporters.[37] "Setting up, running and maintaining a system of press regulation is a difficult task," writes Dunne. "During this time [2007–2017], it has received virtually no significant criticisms from any of the main stakeholders."[38]

Canada Follows Suit in Its Own Way

In September 2015, Canada stepped in a similar direction to Ireland by founding the NNC for newspapers, magazines, and digital publications. While several provinces previously had regional press councils, lack of interest and inadequate funding had rendered most obsolete. As in Ireland, increasing threats of possible government press regulation, the costs of litigation, and the need to boost public trust with press self-regulation, informed the creation of this new council. Its website outlines its main aims: to function as a forum for complaints and to promote ethical practices within news media. In addition, "when appropriate, [the council] represents the public and the media in matters concerning the democratic rights of freedom of speech and freedom of the media." John Fraser, an experienced journalist and former educator, was the founding president and in 2020 was the NNC's executive chair.[39] Since 2017, he has unrolled an ambitious mandate. In addition to hearing public concerns about the behavior of its nearly 600 member media organizations, he and his staff, like their Irish counterparts, offer community outreach in the form of educational talks to schools, colleges, and community groups.[40] Initially, Fraser hoped the NNC would offer insights into the news business and become a thoughtful, unified media advocate to combat threats to press freedom and the public right to know. The council is still a young organization, but Fraser cited a number of successes to date: Several position papers, available on the NNC site, outline the council's position on topics varying from the need for wire services to become press council members (Canadian Press, the country's national news co-operative, has since joined) to the importance of partnering with nonprofits and universities to achieve shared objectives like co-sponsoring journalism events, co-signing statements about media, and presenting media ethics courses for journalism students.[41] One of its biggest projects is working to educate Canadian media about threats to current journalistic practices, such as the concept of the right to be forgotten, which has wide acceptance in the European Union.

In the early days of the NNC's existence, Fraser pointed out that one of the motivations to establish this national council came from abroad, specifically from the United Kingdom, where the PCC failed to manage press behavior effectively. This failure, he said, "produced Leveson, and that produced IPSO. That's a press council out of every publisher's nightmare." IPSO has been widely criticized by both the British public and members of the media. While Canada lacks the sensational tabloids that precipitated the British imposition on press freedom, "nevertheless, the specter of government intervention is tangible now," Fraser said in 2015, because Canadian publishers can see how restrictive press legislation can happen. It is the current reality in England. Effective and voluntary self-regulation by the media is a better way forward. "The council got started because we wanted to show we could police our own mistakes," he said. "That's even more important for digital news sites now." He is aware that foreign news outlets have a presence in Canada, that outlets like the *New York Times* and the BBC are increasing audience share on Canadian soil, and that their practices may diverge from those of Canadian media. At present, broadcast digital news is completely unregulated in Canada. These outlets may get complaints, and if they were to join the NNC, citizens would have a route to raise such concerns.

Concluding Thoughts On The Watchdogs

Our data suggest that the more protective crime coverage practices of two of the Watchdog countries, Ireland and Canada, remain under threat by two bigger dogs, the United Kingdom and the United States. At stake is the moral right of the smaller countries to tell their own stories and to maintain their unique press practices and legal restrictions. The borderless nature of the Internet means citizens can access whatever information they choose. And journalists, without knowledge of others' laws or cultural practices, disseminate information based on their own standards. The Irish and Canadian responses to practicing journalism in the shadow of a mastiff are specific to their countries, but the manifestation of their experiences suggests some shared considerations about the importance of ethics, community, independence, and voice. For Ireland, this threat from the United Kingdom meant creating its own national press council and ombudsperson position and undergirding them with legislation. For Canada, which is geographically enormous and has a relatively small but highly diverse population, it meant something different. While the NNC Executive Director Pat Perkel acknowledged the council's debt to the Irish model that speaks for both its media and the public, she noted challenges specific to Canada. "We are a big and diverse country, and it's harder to figure out, but that's certainly the goal, offering a unified Canadian voice," she said. "The Irish are right—it's the highest level to aim for: When information is available, and you decide as a *culture* what you need, and you decide what is the right thing to do without having [legislative] rules around it."

The other specifically Canadian aspect to the press council that is unlike all other counterparts we considered is that the NNC does not endorse one single ethics code. "It's at the behest of our members," Perkel explained, "because I believe their view is they have their own codes, so to avoid [the council] being regulatory—and if we are trying to avoid government regulation, then why would we be regulatory ourselves?" Instead, the NNC asks its members to uphold their own media organizations' codes or a widely accepted code like that of the Canadian Association of Journalists. "Given Canada's diversity and breadth, and our regional cultures, that seemed a reasonable thing. Being Canadian is a loose federation in that regard," said Perkel. Despite that looseness, the various Canadian codes say similar things about the need for accuracy, fairness, balance, respect for victims and families, special treatment for minors, identifying sources, self-identification of journalists, and so on.

While the Irish solution differs from its Canadian counterpart, both countries share the struggle against the powerful shadow of their neighboring giants' economic muscle and the devolution of their own ethical standards in the face of the popularity of American and British tabloid-style coverage. American journalism practices have transgressed local laws about what can and cannot be publicly disseminated about persons charged with a crime or crime victims in several cases in Canada, as well as in New Zealand and Australia in 2018.[42] As financial and social pressures to "tell-all" continue, both Ireland and Canada have developed a national approach that they created and that, at present, is enjoying success. The same cannot be said for the United Kingdom, where IMPRESS and IPSO continue to divide journalists and public alike. And the United States stands apart from the perspective of its media practitioners, if not from that of ordinary citizens—many of whom see their press as biased, opinionated, and acting in ethically questionable ways. "Through most of the last century the professional approach to news-paper journalism in the US has produced high quality, ethically sound, re-porting," writes Richard Sambrook, in his comparison of accountability mechanisms in England and the United States, but the perception, if not the product, has changed. "Critics would say it has been less innovative or crea-tive than British journalism, and has not protected US journalism from some of its own scandals (e.g. Jayson Blair at the *New York Times*). In addition, the digital age has undermined the value of such professional norms as objec-tivity which, in the US more than the UK is now widely discredited as an im-possible and therefore unhelpful standard to which to aspire."[43]

Underlying these discussions and observations, however, is the centrality of creating and maintaining community—that's where the work of defining self and group members must take place. When community boundaries—broadly defined as encompassing towns or cities, territories, or even countries—are breached by others' ways of representing values, the status quo is challenged. In some respects, this can function as a healthy oppor-tunity. Consider the tell-all coverage of Strauss-Kahn that spilled over into the previously highly protective French media. Because of this incursion, public conversations raised new questions: How ought the relationship be-tween men and women, often in unequal positions, be represented in media? What constitutes public versus private for persons who hold public office or head powerful institutions? And are the nuances of feminism playing a role in these discussions? Ought they to?

It is not up to members of the press to answer these questions; they must be put to members of the public. John Dewey notes there is no community if people are not participating in public discussions, conjointly and cooper-atively. "Democracy is not an alternative to other patterns of associated life. It is the idea of community itself."[44] The storytelling function, the public as-pect of this telling, is central to encouraging people to work out together how best to live a shared existence. The ethics, in this instance, are inherent in the narrative: "Regardless of form, discursive or non-discursive texts are meant to give order to life by inducing others to dwell in them to establish ways of living in common, in intellectual and spiritual communities in which there is confirmation for the story that constitutes one's life."[45] Therefore, news serves not only as a way for individuals to define themselves but also as a means for defining themselves as a people. Defining themselves, however, is chal-lenging in an environment where others' media ethics and differing media or cultural attitudes overshadow.

Beyond the codes of ethics, journalism has a *telos*, an inherent end, which lies in public service. In order for the practice of journalism to be ethical, it has to serve that end, the end it is always meant to reach. In *Journalism as Practice*, Sandra Borden suggests locating this virtue in the pursuit of good appropriate to journalism's purpose can save it from the ways that money and other external goods threaten that pursuit. But Borden argues that journalism can only save itself from the moral challenges of commodification by developing a robust and shared professional identity.[46] Ireland found its own answer to this: A mediator who could unite the voices and speak for all. As the anecdote about the phone call from the parish priest illustrates, competition can drive reporters to act in ways that demean journalism's aspirational values and honorable practice. When Ombudsman Horgan reminded the journalists of those ideals and reassured them he would maintain the level playing field—no one would bother the grieving family and there would be no scoops—they "agreed to pull off the dogs."

At the heart of journalistic enterprise lies the telling of true tales, and this undertaking is inherently ethical. As Fisher argues in *Human Communication as Narration*, humans are storytelling animals, and the tales they tell about themselves and each other reflect and shape their communities.[47] But when others usurp their storytelling power, a community's ability to conduct its public business is in jeopardy; as Carol Gilligan initially, and then many other feminists, asserted, persons being denied their own voice cannot undertake the individual or communal task of becoming moral beings.[48] Such denial or repression of voice is an attack on identity. Ireland is seeding new ground to emerge from the British shadow and reassert control over how it tells its own tales and manages its media behavior. It has become the first English-speaking country in Europe and North America to create the national ombudsperson position and form a self-governing press council—a system that has real power to influence press behavior, unlike its then British counterpart, the PCC, which lacked teeth because it lacked respect.[49] The Irish system works, we contend, not because it is set in law, but because it is an Irish solution that reflects Irish values. This approach, which predates the British Leveson Inquiry into the Culture, Practice, and Ethics of the Press, was prompted by threats of existing privacy and defamation laws and by possible statutory legislation when the Irish Parliament felt journalists were disregarding privacy and indulging prurient interests.[50]

If countries cannot maintain their own distinct voice, crime coverage is at risk of devolving to lowest forms and motives of the "tell-all" American or British style that is synonymous with the technology of the Internet: the everything-goes attitude that ensnared Strauss-Kahn, and thus his country, in details their journalists, their storytellers, may have chosen to leave out of the public eye. The no-holds-barred style clearly privileges the public's right to know over an individual's privacy. In some instances, that is a reasonable tip of the scale, but not when it merely indulges prurient curiosity for the sake of profit and undermines a community's legitimate right to define itself, set its own standards, police its own moral boundaries, and tell its own stories.

PART 3
THE AMBIVALENTS
Portugal, Spain, and Italy

Preface to the Ambivalents Section

These are a few of the signal crime stories that served as starting points for our explorations and interviews in the Ambivalent countries.

Lisbon, Portugal, November 2014: The cameras of Correio da Manhã TV (CMTV) were rolling when former Prime Minister José Sócrates disembarked from a flight from Paris. He was immediately placed under arrest. The television station, generally known for its favorable coverage of the police, had advanced notice of the event. All other news outlets were left in the dark, and they remained in darkness for the next ten months while Sócrates was imprisoned as a suspect in an unspecified crime. While the former prime minister remained detained, police leaked select details about the investigation almost exclusively to Correio da Manhã TV and its sister newspaper, *Correio da Manhã*, forcing all competing news outlets to follow their lead and use their material. Little else was available.

Barcelona, Catalonia, Spain, October 2013: Late on a Saturday, reporter Guillem Sánchez Marín was alone on the news desk at the Agència Catalana de Notícies (ACN, Catalonia News Agency) when a tip came in from the El Raval neighborhood: Police had badly beaten a homeless man on the street, the source told him. Police confirmed that a man of no fixed address had been brought in and later died at the end of the night while in custody. Then on Monday, a police spokesperson said the man had cocaine in his system and died of a heart attack while being handcuffed at the scene. Sánchez knocked on doors in El Raval, a central, historic but also somewhat run-down neighborhood. Three neighbors said they had witnessed a fight with police officers repeatedly kicking and punching the man, who cried for help at first and then went silent. The story ACN put out contained these different versions of what had happened from the neighbors and the police, and much of the Spanish news media ran the story. But Sánchez's colleagues in other news media criticized him for questioning the police account. He could spoil their good—and interdependent—relationship with the cops, they warned. The reaction disheartened Sánchez, who felt that he had done the right thing. Then two weeks later, a cell phone video of the incident turned up that confirmed what Sánchez had heard from neighbors. "In that video, you can see some police officers are punching, and the man is crying out," Sánchez said. His colleagues called him to apologize. "You were right," they said. "Sorry."

Brembate di Sopra, Italy, November 2010: A number of Italian reporters referred to one sensational murder story of Yara Gambirasio, then age 13. The girl had disappeared from a small river town, one hour north of Milan. Four months later, her partially decomposed body was discovered in a field of weeds, and small amounts of a suspect's DNA were retrieved. Local police then launched the most complex investigation in Italian history. Over four years, Italians were mesmerized by the story's complex twists and turns, as police tested the DNA of 18,000 local men, exhumed a man's body whose DNA was a partial match with the suspect's, uncovered that man's decades-old extramarital affair, and began to suspect a child born from that affair, named Massimo Bossetti. In a spectacular ploy to obtain Bossetti's DNA and match it to that found with the girl's body, police set up a roadblock and faked a breathalyzer test to obtain Bossetti's saliva. An exact match pinned him to the murder. Because of the intense and prolonged publicity around the case, the Italian home secretary announced Bossetti's arrest, using the suspect's full name. That gave the Italian news media a greenlight to also name him, explore his background, and even run a photo taken of him with his children.

8

Ambivalent Behavior in Portugal, Spain, and Italy

The Commitment to Maybe

When former Portuguese Prime Minister José Sócrates stepped off a plane arriving in Lisbon from Paris and into the hands of police who were waiting to arrest him, only one television outlet, Correio da Manhã TV, had its cameras rolling on the tarmac to record the event. Portuguese reporters assumed police had tipped off the station. The next day, Portugal's general prosecutor's office named Sócrates as an *arguido*, or formal suspect. He was imprisoned and questioned about suspicious banking activities and money transfers, and his apartment was searched. No further details were released, not even whether the allegations stemmed from Sócrates' time as prime minister, from March 2005 to June 2011 when he was an elected public official leading a democracy.[1] He remained in prison without being charged for the next ten months, until the following September when he was released. Portuguese law allows suspects to be kept in preventive detention for close to a year without formal charges.

In the three countries that make up our Ambivalent model—Italy, Spain, and Portugal—police may or may not choose to inform crime reporters when a suspect has been arrested. The prosecutor in charge of the investigation oversees official police actions. Arrest records may not become public until official charges are filed and the prosecutor/judge determines that the suspect will, in fact, be held for trial. This relatively closed approach to justice is meant to protect both the integrity of the police investigation and the suspect's right to the presumption of innocence, but unofficial actions reflect a lack of commitment to those stated purposes. Law and practice are far from uniform across the three countries we group into the Ambivalent model. In Spain, for example, famous persons—from politicians to celebrities—have a diminished right to protect their reputation, privacy, or image. In Portugal, however, when the crime itself or the prominence of the suspect

Murder in Our Midst. Romayne Smith Fullerton and Maggie Jones Patterson, Oxford University Press (2021). © Oxford University Press. DOI: 10.1093/oso/9780190863531.003.0008.

make the story newsworthy, as in the case of Prime Minister Sócrates, official records can be sealed, although that seal can spring leaks. Then, police and prosecutors dole out details about the accused or the alleged crime to the press—but they often do so selectively, favoring only certain reporters or news outlets whose coverage they like. Reporters, in turn, court police for such favors, and that courtship can flavor the stories they write or broadcast. If police are not forthcoming, reporters often seek out details from possibly unreliable witnesses and hope police are willing to confirm what they find.

During the former prime minister's long detention, the Portuguese media operated in darkness. Reporters had no access to official records and received few definitive statements about the nature of the investigation.[2] But information continued to be handed out informally. Despite the official and legally sanctioned secrecy, ongoing leaks—almost exclusively to the privately owned CMTV and its sister newspaper, Correio da Manhã—allowed the Portuguese public to learn a few details of what was happening to their former prime minister. Other news outlets were unable to source original content. They could only pick up what the two Correio da Manhã news outlets reported and carry secondhand stories about what police and prosecutors had leaked through their favored channels. Prosecutors said little publicly. In this sense, Portugal's criminal justice practices retain a few elements of an emerging or transitional democracy, although Portugal is generally "considered as a case of successful democratic consolidation,"[3] following the successful end of dictatorship in 1974: Free and fair elections are held, democratic institutions are in place, but government bureaucracies often function poorly. Portuguese scholar Luis de Sousa describes his country as one that fully embraces democratic government and the rule of law, as well as the ethical values that undergird them—"equality, transparency, accountability, impartiality and integrity—as found in most other mature Western European democracies."[4] But he also points to an exception: "The coexistence of modern/rational and pre-modern/family-based relations between citizens and the public administration."[5] He outlines a system of clientelism, the academic name for those "premodern/family-based relations" of trading favors to get what is desired.

Two years after his release, Sócrates was formally charged in October 2017 with 31 counts of receiving bribes, money laundering, falsifying documents, and tax fraud. Nineteen corporate and banking officials were also arrested, and nine companies were named in the largest corruption case in Portuguese modern history.[6] Finally, at this point, official records totaling 4,000 pages became public.[7]

Police and prosecutors in Italy, Portugal, and Spain sometimes operate behind a translucent veil of secrecy. Although justice officials are accountable within the court system, they may keep arrest and pretrial records from public view to protect the suspect's presumption of innocence and the integrity of the investigation until it is complete and formal charges are rendered. But the law exerts a weak hold on news media behavior. Journalists in these countries routinely obtain leaks of so-called protected information from police and prosecutors, who slip select facts to favored news outlets, which, in turn, request exclusives and often give police positive publicity as payback. The legal structures restrict public—and thus journalistic—access, and ethics codes similarly suggest that reporters follow both the laws that protect identities of accused and the moral imperative to respect the presumption of innocence. In our interviews, crime reporters generally professed faith in the legitimacy of the law's protection of the defendant and protecting the integrity of the police investigation, both of which are values embedded in ethics codes. But their inconsistent journalistic behavior speaks to other values and concerns. We found instances where, on the one hand, some accused persons were identified only by their initials or by first name and last initial, and thus shielded from public condemnation. On the other hand, we saw examples where an accused was not only fully identified but also labeled unambiguously as guilty long before the case had gone to court. One Spanish newspaper, for example, ran a photograph of a man from the Canary Islands—who turned out to be innocent—with his name and the prejudicial caption, "the face of the murderer of a 3-year-old girl."[8] The behavior and practices of journalists in these countries are inconsistent, and our data suggest no overriding ethic governs decisions. Reporters voice little concern for how their ambivalence might undermine the public's belief that media outlets and, by extension, the justice system itself treat all citizens fairly. This defamatory treatment of accused persons is often worse when suspects are immigrants or from a marginalized population. Marco Deriu, who teaches media ethics at the Catholic University of the Sacred Heart in Milan, notes that Italian journalists use suspects' full names more often when they are not native born. That type of coverage, he said, implies that immigrants come to Italy to commit crimes, a dangerous and inaccurate perception.

In this chapter, we consider how the term "in the public interest" is used in this model. We outline instances of ambivalent media practices that illustrate contradictory journalistic impulses. Then, we discuss the effects on democracy and its institutions of what we call Ambivalent journalists' "commitment to maybe": One that professes to see value in the norms of privacy and protection for both the investigative process and presumed innocence of accused persons, but which simultaneously breaks that protective "rule" if the public is interested (enough) or the story might advance their own journalistic careers.

In the Public Interest

For a variety of reasons (especially the widespread distribution of American entertainment media), journalists in these Ambivalent countries were at least passingly familiar with press practices in the United States, and some told us they covet the openness they believe their U.S. counterparts enjoy, both their access to arrest records (which are public in the United States) and freedom to disseminate information (with constitutional protection from the First Amendment). Like journalists in the United States, journalists in Spain, Italy, and Portugal employ the term "the public interest" to justify releasing an accused person's full name along with details of the alleged crime. But the Ambivalents mean something quite different by "public interest" from the Watchdog or Protector interpretation of the phrase. Codes of ethics in the Ambivalent countries explicitly state that journalism should operate in the public interest and supply sufficient information for citizens to make informed decisions in their lives and at the ballot box. In our interviews, however, journalists in the Ambivalent countries used the term most often to refer to what the public finds interesting, and in the news value of telling a "good" or entertaining story. Ana Terradillos Azpiroz is a TV and radio reporter for media outlets owned by Promostora de Informaciones, S.A., commonly referred to as PRISA. She pointed out crime stories are incredibly popular in Spain. "In TV, I have one hour for politics and then two hours for crime because there is a lot of public interest in this." The comment is telling. It suggests that journalists like Terradillos, who is well-respected and admired by her professional colleagues, gauge what needs to be told by how popular the story will be. Watchdog and Protector journalists used the same expression but modified it with concern for what the public *needs*—not just *wants*—to know. In our interviews in Spain, Italy, and Portugal, journalists rarely suggested that their decisions about what details to include in crime stories bore any relation to journalism's role as a public trust. Only a small fraction of the reporters saw themselves as acting on behalf of citizens to inform them about the institutions and processes of justice.

From a legal perspective also, public interest can be interpreted differently in these countries. It was at least in part what initially kept the Sócrates investigation under wraps. The Segredo de Justiça (Secret of Justice) Act in Portugal, for example, permits authorities to tighten the seal on any or all parts of an investigation, even documents that will be admitted at trial, and the need for protection of an accused's presumption of innocence is greater when the public curiosity about a crime climbs particularly high. The Act's purpose, according to Francisco Teixeira da Mota, legal counsel for the Portuguese newspaper *Público*, is to put an extra layer of protection over both the police inquiry and the accused's presumption of innocence. While Portuguese prosecutors invoke the Act infrequently, they may employ it when police fear the suspect could interfere or tamper with evidence or when the accused person's presumption of innocence might be particularly compromised by press attention. From this vantage, public interest is viewed as a legal justification—not for releasing information as in the Watchdog or Protector countries—but rather for withholding it, explained Teixeira da Mota. But in actual practice, he conceded, information that is supposed to be protected by law still leaks out to favored reporters, even when the Segredo Act is imposed. Police and prosecutors can selectively disclose information as a way of pulling strings with reporters and affecting public opinion, but, in some instances, even the most basic information is completely withheld.

When a crime story piques their interest, journalists in the three Ambivalent countries scramble for information in what can be a challengingly dry desert. Many take pride in piercing routine police secrecy, and they calibrate the success of their journalistic careers by their ability to do so. In this sense, they resemble reporters everywhere who revel in the ability to reveal what authorities often want kept quiet. But the atmosphere differs in the Ambivalent locales. Hallin and Mancini point to a relatively low level of professional development in these Mediterranean regions, and we suggest that this is reflected in how crime news is reported and how reporters gauge their professional accomplishments.[9] Journalists with whom we spoke rarely cited any underlying ethical conviction or motivation behind their desire to inform the public about a crime, nor did they express awareness of journalism's role in the democratic process—both sentiments that we heard readily, if differently, expressed by reporters in Watchdog and Protector countries. In advanced liberal democracies, like those included in our Protector and

Watchdog models, both law and custom demand that details about arrests be made available to the public. If the material is public, then reporters in the Watchdog countries especially see its dissemination not only as an option but also as a central professional obligation. Matters of public interest belong to citizens. Transparency and accountability, held in high regard normatively if not always in practice, ought to flourish. While journalists in Protector countries (Sweden, the Netherlands, and Germany) may choose to hold back from reporting some matters they consider private, including the identity of persons arrested, they do have access to that information. They would rarely, if ever, fail to disclose that a public official like José Sócrates had been detained by police—especially if the arrest was for a crime involving his performance in office. As Lennart Weibull suggests in his diagram of what is usually made public in Sweden (outlined in detail in Chapter 2), public officials accused of committing crimes while holding elected office would almost certainly be publicly named.

The Mediterranean countries employ an inquisitorial approach to trials rather than the adversarial approach common in the Watchdog and Protector models.[10] Like those in Northern Europe and North America, Ambivalent countries value both the public's right to see justice done and the defendant's right to a fair trial. But in each country, history and geography shape how these values are prioritized in their criminal justice systems and in the legal and ethical regulation of the press. What stood out in our interviews about crime coverage in the Ambivalent countries were the wide-ranging and often worrisome interactions of reporters with the police and prosecutors. While definitions of democracy vary, one informing principle of this system of governance is that it aspires to offer equal access to citizens in all aspects of democratic life. But the anecdote about Portugal's former prime minister illustrates a couple of key issues: Not all persons are considered equal before the law if the Segredo de Justiça Act gives the famous person an extra layer of protection, not enjoyed by the common person; and it makes clear that citizens do not always have access to a wide and varying range of information because only one news outlet was tipped off about the impending arrest and other details of the investigation. Cofina group, which owns Correio da Manhã TV, the newspaper of the same name, and a sports publication, held a near monopoly on the news of this situation throughout the ten months of Sócrates' detention. Other outlets had access only to what Cofina news outlets reported. As Manning wrote, "if we want to assess the health of the public sphere(s) and its (their) capacity to serve the democratic good in contemporary capitalist societies, we must consider issues of access" granted to the news media.[11] While we found nuanced differences among the three Ambivalent countries, the similarities in Spanish, Portuguese, and Italian reporters' practices were striking in their consistent inconsistency and their heavy reliance on personal judicial or police sources for information. These crime coverage practices contrasted to those in the United States, Canada, Great Britain, Ireland, the Netherlands, Sweden, and Germany, where arrest records are public and the relationship between police sources and reporters was—at least to some degree—more independent.[12]

Reporting Practices: Consistently Inconsistent

In Italy, Spain, and Portugal, the law and journalistic ethics dictate that a suspect's right to the presumption of innocence is paramount, but the behavior of law enforcement officials and reporters often makes a counter statement about what is truly valued. Journalistic habits of practice are hard to pin down in all three Ambivalent countries where the most consistent pattern is inconsistency. One habit (like naming an accused person) and its opposite (not naming or employing first name and last initial) simultaneously hold true. Ethical commitments are weak. Situations and circumstances sway decisions about media coverage. "The Italian press is full of anomalies," observed Angela Giuffrida, a British citizen who worked in Rome for *The Local*, a pan-European, English-language news source. Indeed, contradictory behavior is frequent, acknowledged Jacopo Barigazzi, Italian correspondent for *Politico Europe*. The Italian news media might withhold the name of a suspect, but then call him a killer. "Not an alleged killer, but a killer," he said, emphasizing the implied difference. Members of the press often identify a native of Italy only by initials if the person is arrested at home, but they will publish the full identity of a person if an Italian is accused of a crime abroad, Rose Scammell of *The Local* noted. She pointed to the case of Italian citizen Saverio Bellante, whom the Italian news media fully identified when he was found not guilty by reason of insanity of the murder of his landlord, Tom O'Gorman, in Ireland in 2014.

The Italian Parliament has passed legislation that prohibits showing a suspect in handcuffs because such photographs imply guilt.[13] "Italy's culture is very visual," Barigazzi said. He noted Italians (like the French, whom we discuss in Chapter 7) were deeply shocked when American news showed a handcuffed and disheveled International Monetary Fund President Dominique Strauss-Kahn being paraded in front of cameras after his arrest in New York City in May 2011; however, Barigazzi added, despite the law, the Italian news media also employ coverage that shows the perp walk when cuffs are placed on a mafia figure's wrists.

Paolo Colonnello, crime reporter for *La Stampa* in Milan, distinguished the reporting on business wrongdoing from the more sensational coverage of murders. Newsworthy white-collar crime often involves public institutions and has an impact on taxpayers, he said. With *persone pubbliche*, public persons, "you have to worry less about privacy" and more about public interest, he said, using the term in the broader sense used by Watchdog and Protector reporters. Yes, you risk that white-collar suspects are innocent when you publish their names, but you can do little about it. He recalled the case of an innocent man who was exonerated after three years in prison, during which time his son died of cancer. Colonnello later befriended the man when their children played sports together. He saw firsthand the devastating toll publicity had taken on the family. "Journalism is like war," Colonnello said ruefully. "It has side effects."

Murder stories are different. While mafia murders play in the press like ongoing war coverage, the inherent shock and sensation of private family murders comes through in the style of the copy, Colonnello said. Journalists employ what Fabrizio Tonello, a Padua University political scientist who studies Italian media, calls a "soap opera style." In prose strewn with "rhetorical flowers" (by which Tonello means emotionally laden language and a lot of adjectives), they describe all murders as "barbaric" and all alleged perpetrators as "Satan." In a qualitative study of murder stories, Elisa Giomi and Tonello found women victims were most often idealized as one of three rhetorical constructs: a "Daddy's girl," a "Mother," or an "Angelic Woman."[14] As we have argued elsewhere, such reductive portraits undermine the public's ability to have thoughtful discussions about the factors that inform the commission of a crime.[15] Moreover, painting the accused or convicted as satanic and without nuance encourages citizens to see those who transgress laws as monsters. The style undermines a public consideration of what role community might play in crime.[16] Rose Scammell of *The Local* agreed that language choice and narrative style can skew the public's perception of wrongdoing. To illustrate, she compared a hypothetical text of an Italian crime saga to one covered in the more staid and matter-of-fact manner of a British broadsheet. While the English (non-tabloid) news media, she said, might report, " 'A three-year-old child was killed in Calabria after being shot in the head today,' the Italians would set a scene: 'They were driving to the beach when a thug came by and shot this beautiful child.' " Italian reporters also connect the dots between events and imply connections that may, or may not, be factual. And they conjecture about possible causes. " 'Oh, he lost his job' or 'there was a rift in the family'—theorizing on what the motive was or what happened in the room," she said.

Italian reporters hit the jackpot when the story unfolds with the "Three S Formula": *sesso, sangue, soldi*—sex, blood, money—elements used to tell passionate tales of lust, shame, and greed in a dark reflection of the culture's decadence, Colonnello said. Suspects and their families get swept up into the drama, he added. "We forget the humanity of the actual people involved."

To illustrate this soap opera style, many Italian interview subjects pointed to the story of Massimo Giuseppe Bossetti, who had been arrested in the widely publicized murder of Yara Gambirasio, age 13, which we outlined at the beginning of this chapter.[17] In 2010, the girl had disappeared in the small river town of Brembate di Sopra in the north of Italy. Four months later, when her partially decomposed body was found in a field of weeds, police retrieved small amounts of the suspect's DNA. Local and national law enforcement then launched what turned out to be the most complex investigation in Italian history. For four years, Italians fixated on the amazing twists and turns of the plot, which included tens of thousands of DNA tests, an exhumation, the public revelations of a secret extramarital affair, and adult twins who had resulted from that liaison.[18] With the mysteries all seemingly resolved, the Italian home secretary himself announced that police had arrested Massimo Bossetti, the male twin. Given that authorities had clearly greenlighted the identification of the suspect, Italian news media ran photos that showed not only Bossetti but also his pets and his children.[19] Implicating the innocent family members in this instance particularly disturbed Barigazzi. We told him that reporters in Protector countries routinely withhold identification of suspects and that the primary reason they gave for this practice was to protect innocent family members. Barigazzi shook his head. "We don't care at all for the families of the accused," he said dolefully. Colonnello agreed. Bossetti's children "cannot be charged with their father's guilt, but all the family together with the murderer have their lives completely ruined," he lamented. When Colonnello speaks to journalism students, he tells them to keep their humanity alive, be empathetic, and don't become cynical. "Protect the person from the commercialization of news," he said. "Everything that you do impacts people's lives, even parts you do not know. They [defendants] have private lives. They are not a bad person one hundred percent. . . . Every time I cover this news, I suffer because of the impact I can have on these people's lives."

Showing Bosetti's children was unusual. By law, ethics policy, and popular public sentiment, children are given special consideration in Southern Europe under all circumstances[20]—whether they become implicated because a parent is accused, they are the victims of a crime, or they are the perpetrators of wrongdoing. Mayka Navarro, reporter for *El Periódico* in Barcelona, had just started on a meditative walk along Spain's famous El Camino de Santiago in April 2015 when she received text messages about a Barcelona schoolboy who had killed one of his teachers and wounded four others, using a crossbow and knives. Calling contacts on her cell phone from the trail, she gathered enough information to file the breaking story. She also reached the teacher who had talked the boy down from his frenzy, and she recorded an interview with him on her phone. Navarro agreed not to ask about the boy's personal problems or mental health history. Because of the story's sensitivity, Navarro also agreed to send the teacher the story before it was published. When they spoke again, the teacher asked her to turn off the recorder and told her what he had held back in the first interview. The story made a big splash and, with the additional information, might have made a bigger one, but Navarro kept the teacher's confidence despite some pressures from her editor. "For me, the most important image was the teacher asking the boy to take everything out of his pockets and give up the arrows. They had had a close relationship before, and he loved that student," Navarro said. "The boy was just a small kid. . . . He was ill. He said that he heard voices," she said. She never published those details out of respect for the child and her pledge of confidence to the teacher. The day after her second interview with the teacher, Navarro's boss asked her to find out the psychiatric information from the hospital where the boy was being held. She refused. She did not believe the public needed to know those details in order to be informed about what had transpired at the school.

Effects of the Commitment to Maybe

Both the widespread concern for children and Navarro's emphasis on the public's need to know were exceptions; many reporters in Spain, Italy, and

Portugal persistently emphasized their careers over any shared public or professional values. Their behaviors that we describe here are hardly unique to the countries of Southern Europe, but that emphasis on career ambition differed distinctly from the ways Watchdog or Protector reporters framed reporting practices. The responses from the Ambivalent reporters are indicative of a weak awareness of the connection between journalists' habits of practice and their service in support of democratic institutions and public conversations about them. Particular cases and anecdotes serve to illustrate dangers in these reporting practices, including risks to democracy they might pose. Reporters' and experts' testimonies—as well as our own readings of crime coverage—told us that inconsistency was the chief characteristic of journalistic behavior. Reporters everywhere break their own ethics rules, but the measure of professionalism lies in their reasons for doing so. A lack of commitment to ethical practice is unlikely to inspire public trust. When crime reporters skirted legal and ethical rules meant to protect the integrity of an investigation and the presumption of innocence of those accused, they did so chiefly for commercial or career reasons, even while they professed to believe in the principle behind the rules. At times, the unintended consequence was a volatile tangle of leaks, rumors, and unreliable eyewitness accounts, exacerbated by a fiercely competitive and unrestrained news media, one that still bears the mark of its highly partisan past.

In all three Ambivalent countries, urban police departments send out daily press releases on arrests with additional details posted on their websites, but police and prosecutors decide whether and what information to release. Usually these official releases give only the first name and last initial of a suspect, maybe age, and a few details, including nationality and past criminal records, but never—or very rarely—the full name. But as we have outlined, both the legal system that allows law enforcement to screen the initial information about crime and the system of leaks and rumors that reporters use to pull aside that screen have repercussions. These habits have side effects and influence how the public views crime and criminals.

The Favoritism Side Effect

Most reporters we spoke with in these Mediterranean nations said they agreed that both defendants and their families should be protected from the damage of publicity while the investigation is ongoing. After all, the person might not be guilty, and media coverage can suggest otherwise. Nevertheless, our interview subjects also identified big fault lines in the practical implementation of the reporting practices because people within the justice system decide what is news. "Police arrest hundreds of people but only send an email to reporters when they deem it important. I cannot go to the police station and see a record of who was arrested," Antonio Baquero of Spain's *El Periódico*, said. "Every journalist gets the minimum information," ABC reporter in Madrid Pablo Muñoz said. Police then decide who gets more. They reward reporters for being accurate and responsible, he said, but their judgment is not always objective. In an effort to curry favor and get tip-offs to potentially big news stories, reporters become reluctant to write negative information about police or prosecutors. As Alberto Pozas, crime reporter at Cadena Ser Radio Station in Madrid, said: "Police take information and send it to certain media. That is the way they make it public. That is a danger because it is voluntary. Police are not forced to tell." Baquero in Barcelona echoed the sentiments of many in the news business when he said: "The work of a police reporter is difficult because it depends on police. The investigation takes time. If you have to write a story today, it is very hard if you don't have a relation with police—at an official and unofficial level."

"You get burned; it's exhausting," said Álvaro de Cózar, a journalist for Spain's *El País*. In a voice heavy with irony, he added that he found covering the invasion of Iraq easier than jockeying for sources on the police beat. "Yes, you might get killed when you are in Baghdad or Afghanistan, but it is easy to get stories."

Manuella D'Alessandro, court reporter for the Italian news agency AGI, said La Guardi di Finanza, the Italian financial police, work more cooperatively with reporters than the Carabinieri, the military police, or the local Polizia. La Gardi di Finanza "hold press conferences and give out press kits about investigations, but the kind of further details you get from them depends on your ongoing relationship with them." Police can and do leak information at any stage of an investigation, she said. In Italy, the reporter is usually legally safe to publish once the suspect has been notified, she said, but legally risky stories have come out before that point.

Likely someone from the prosecutor's office or the police leaked Prime Minister Sócrates' impending 2014 arrest exclusively to CMTV. Later, that outlet and its sister newspaper established a corner on leaks in the case. Both news outlets belong to the Portuguese media conglomerate Cofina, which leans to the right politically. Other reporters and journalism academics describe the crime and political reporting of Cofina outlets as a tabloid style that highlights the prosecution's version of events. Cofina's deputy director petitioned the court and obtained status as a "legal assistant to the process," that is, as a party that has an established interest in the outcome of the case. Cofina acquired this special status by arguing in court for public interest in the case but also by saying that *Correio da Manhã* was defending itself against two lawsuits that Sócrates had filed against them, one of which was asking for over a million euros. This legal status gave the TV station and newspaper access to investigation records not open to their competitors.

With this special access to court-protected information, *Correio da Manhã* published a series of disclosures begrudgingly picked up by various news outlets, which had no other way to get the information. These revelations included accounts about the spending habits of Sócrates' family members. Sócrates accused the newspaper of invading his privacy, and in October 2015, *Correio da Manhã*'s fortunes were reversed when a judge ordered that the entire Cofina media empire cease publication of *any* stories about the Sócrates case. The day Sócrates was released from police custody in September 2015, the prosecution allowed the defense access to the investigation's evidence. In October, the judge lifted the Secret of Justice order, and the investigation ended without official charges until the end of the much larger investigation that led to formal charges against Sócrates in 2017 on a long list of fraud and corruption crimes. The specifics of this example point out the challenges for Portugal, and indeed all media in the Ambivalent countries, when information can be selectively given to one or two outlets, on whom all other journalists must rely. Prosecutors show little concern for all citizens when they grant only selective access to information that would be considered public in Watchdog and Protector countries.

While the tangles and complications of the Sócrates' case were extreme, police and prosecutors in these countries control access to facts and details to an extent that shocks crime reporters in Northern Europe and North America, where laws and customs, as well as cultural expectations, differ about what information is—and should be—public. In the Ambivalent countries, the self-interests of media and the justice systems are linked, said Guido Romeo, a data and business journalist in Milan. "The media need the justice system because we need the lawyers and judges to pass papers, transcripts, etc." And the dependence cuts both ways. "Prosecutors need the media to get visibility, to have a career, and become famous," Romeo argued. He recalled when former Italian Prime Minister Silvio Berlusconi was on trial for a variety of charges in 2005. Romeo had been sailing off the coast of Sicily. At every port, he said, the crew would hop ashore to grab the papers from the newsstands. The coverage in *Corriere della Sera*, thought of as the *New York Times* of Italy, was more scandalous, like a tabloid, he said. "It was all there, and it was coming from the prosecutors." *Politico Europe*'s Jacopo Barigazzi called Southern Europe's court systems "byzantine." The investigatory process is extremely well documented in Italy, but when those documents become public is regulated. "Judges and lawyers use newspapers to conduct battles for popularity or particular interpretations of events by leaking documents," Barigazzi said. Fabrizio Tonello, of the University of Padova, agreed. "Editors and reporters forge links with prosecutors without realizing the price they are paying in lack of autonomy and independence."

Some reporters in these three countries saw this interdependency in a somewhat different light. "Journalism is a PR job," said Colonnello. "You have to cultivate your sources. The more trustworthy and serious you are, the better quality of news you will get from sources." Leo Sisti, founder of Investigative Reports Project Italy (IRPI), author, and longtime reporter for *L'Espresso* magazine, concurred: "When a person is arrested, his attorneys receive the arrest warrant. The problem [for reporters] is how to get a hold of the arrest warrants. It depends on the attorneys you know and on what, in that precise moment, you can report on the documents."

Even after the public notification that an investigation is under way, in a document called *informazione di garanzia*, usually issued when prosecutors press formal charges, reporters in Italy are not necessarily free to report all that those documents contain, as they would be in most Watchdog countries. "Many people are mentioned in the arrest warrant," Sisti explained. For example, perhaps "a wire-tapping [transcript] is included in the arrest warrant." Not all the information in those transcripts pertains to the case. Reporters have to be careful how they use such information because publishing material about persons not directly involved in the alleged crime can land reporters in court on libel or invasion of privacy charges.

In Italy, Spain, and Portugal, the favor-trading behavior between reporters and police and/or prosecutors builds on a much larger and more deeply rooted system of favor-trading in these countries that we mentioned earlier, commonly referred to as "clientelism."[21] Hallin and Papathanassopoulos define clientelism as a relationship in which access to information (or other resources and favors) is controlled by patrons and provided to "clients" in exchange for "deference and various kinds of support. It is a particularistic and asymmetrical form of social organization, and is typically contrasted with forms of citizenship in which access to resources is based on universalistic criteria and formal equity before the law."[22] With no official requirement to make public that an arrest has been made, law enforcement agencies in Italy, Spain, and Portugal have developed a practice that makes reporters dependent on official sources. When and what those officials release shapes a highly selective crime coverage. The system is not transparent, and journalism cannot function effectively as a check on power or its abuse when it is so reliant on those official sources for information. "Clientelism increases the importance of particularistic ties among social actors," Hallin and Mancini write.[23] Reporters attest to that. Despite some awareness of the problems for democracy inherent in this favor-trading system with the police and prosecutors, most we spoke with measured their careers by their skill at favor-trading and dismissed the consequences for the public with a shrug. "That's Italy [or Spain or Portugal]."

Heavy Reliance on Unofficial and/or Questionable Sources

Journalists worth their professional salt can always find information somewhere, many of our interview subjects in the Ambivalent countries argued. The police might issue a three-line statement while an editor wants the story to fill a page, said Alberto Pozas, a Spanish radio reporter. If the public record is unavailable, reporters hustle to get information elsewhere. Police may agree to confirm reporters' independent findings, but journalists can make mistakes when deadline and commercial pressures override verification, a situation that reporters told us happens frequently. And one of the central reasons that citizens question or lose faith in media credibility is that journalists make mistakes.[24] Some more experienced colleagues have better sources than he has as a relative newcomer, Pozas added. He has been forced to fish among people whose witness status was questionable. Sometimes "you get good information, and sometimes you get offal," he admitted. In fact, relying on unofficial sources because of the vacuum caused by official silence ranked second in frequency and emphasis in the list of concerns or drawbacks that emerged from our interviews in these Ambivalent countries, right behind the effects of favoritism.

As an illustration, several reporters cited a recent case in Spain: The Spanish press nicknamed Bruno Fernández the "Majadahonda Ripper" after he allegedly murdered and dismembered Adriana Gioiosa, who lived in the Majadahonda neighborhood of Madrid in the spring of 2015. Speculation mounted that Fernández could be a serial killer. "There was very little info about this case at first," said Alberto Pozas. Under pressure to get more, some reporters cobbled material from police and neighbors to construct fantastic, but false, stories about the Ripper: He had used a chopping machine to dismember bodies, he was learning to speak Basque (the official language in the Spanish territory of the same name, which has been blamed for terrorism), he killed his aunt to get her money, and he slaughtered animals. As Mavi Doñate of Spanish public television network RTVE said, problems—like the Majadahonda Ripper exaggerations—arise when police give out too little information. "Journalists make mistakes because nonofficial sources are not reliable." No official sources claimed Fernández was a serial killer, she said, but reporters trusted unreliable sources and imagined more than was factual. Fed up with the fantastical coverage, police finally held a press conference to straighten out the story. The unverified information should not have become public, Pozas said. "If you ask people if they saw a polar bear, some will say yes," he noted. But journalists should not disseminate information until they verify it; spreading false rumors helps no one.

Discussion

While Italians may love the melodrama of a good crime story, journalists' crime coverage lacks emotional restraint, political science professor Fabrizio Tonello noted. And, even more importantly, in democracies where citizens need to understand what factors contribute to crime, the coverage also lacks context, like actual crime data and statistics. In this manner, it creates "the impression that crime is going up when the opposite is true," Tonello said. "We are a very safe country. We have a lower homicide rate than Denmark. We have a lot of pickpockets, but not many bank holdups. Violent crime has gone down to a level below which it is difficult to go. Less than four hundred murders in a population of sixty million is very low."[25] Sensational media coverage fuels moral panics in Italy, Tonello said. The manner of reporting fuels much of the worry, and vitriol is directed toward immigrants, he said, a tendency exacerbated recently by increased migration and populism. The partisan and competitive nature of Italy's press fans those fears, creating a journalistic model that Tonello would describe as "opportunistic." "The

Italian press tends to describe criminals—except white-collar criminals, of course—as an absolute evil, using hysterical tones even when the facts are not clear-cut and responsibilities are murky. People accused of child abuse are routinely described as *monsters* even if there are only vague accusations."

In the early days of 13-year-old Yara Gambirasio's murder case, for example, police executed hundreds of wiretaps, which led to false accusations. A police interpreter overheard a Moroccan native, who had been working nearby at the time of the murder, say: "Forgive me God, I didn't kill her." Police became further convinced he was the murderer when they found a blood-stained mattress in the van he had been using. Italian authorities intercepted a ship heading for Tangiers to arrest this man. But the man was subsequently cleared of all wrongdoing in this case. The phrase heard on the wiretap had been misinterpreted, and the blood was unrelated.[26] Blaming a foreigner, especially when the victim is female, is a common meme in Italy that reflects prevailing stereotypes but does not correlate with the realities of crime.[27]

Gaye Tuchman was the first to argue that news is a social construction in her 1978 book, *Making News*.[28] After her groundbreaking work, theorists rarely argue that journalism offers a direct correlation with the "truth" of the external events it records, represents, and disseminates. But this is not to suggest that journalism has no responsibility to offer citizens accurate, credible facts and information in context, which best equip them to participate in public discussions about matters that affect their lives, including crime—its root causes, its frequency and type, and policies or procedures created by governments to assist in human flourishing.

The sensational and sentimental style of reporting crime in these countries can further push reporters to uncover salacious details—and publish them ahead of the competition. All crime reporters we spoke with in the Ambivalent countries accepted some element of double dealing with police and prosecutors to get what they wanted for their stories. On the one hand, they said they embraced their professional ethics codes and legal systems, which in Spain and Portugal dictate that police actions, including arrests, can stay out of the public eye for days, weeks, or even close to a year while prosecutors detain a suspect and determine whether the evidence warrants official charges. In Italy, defendants must be arraigned within five days of arrest, but the journalism ethics codes still prescribe that the defendant's identity be protected, regardless.[29] No reporter or journalism organization in any of these countries expressed a desire to fight the protective system or the

prevailing processes of secrecy. Journalists held up the protection of innocence as an important value and noted it in their discussions with us. But
they routinely—and often proudly—published police and prosecutor leaks
of information to which they had no legal (or in some cases moral) claim if
the story had a high enough public appeal. Reporters also conducted their
own investigations and interviews with witnesses, during the period of official secrecy, and they leaned on police for confirmation of information and
for further tips. In return for receiving favored treatment, reporters sometimes allowed police and prosecutors to call back favors. Few reporters
complained about this system of clientelism or about their lack of access to
public records. In fact, some bragged about their abilities to dodge the system
by strategically using their sources.[30]

   Hallin and Mancini's research finds that clientelism, as we have described
it, has a long history and a widespread practice in many parts of the culture
and politics of Southern Europe.[31] The relationship developed as feudal
institutions broke down and then persisted because of "the weakness of the
universalistic forms of social organization associated with liberalism—the
market, the bureaucratic state, and representative democracy."[32] Clientelism
hurts the "horizontal" forms of organization like mass parties and voluntary
organization. More recent economic growth in this region and the effects
of European integration have diminished but not eliminated its influence.
"Clientelism is also connected with a political culture that is relatively cynical about the notion of a general public interest transcending particular
interests."[33] This attitude was clearly reflected in our interview data. In fact,
such cynicism undermines "the notion of a transcendent 'public interest.'"[34]
Mario Calabresi, former editor of La Repubblica writing about "The Trust
Issue in Italy," noted that the problem of credibility in journalism is particularly serious; "in recent years a deep divide has been created between legacy
[or traditional] media and an important part of public opinion."[35] He asked a
selection of media professionals to weigh in on what he sees as a crisis of trust
in journalism, as well as offered surveys that studied the issue. What emerged,
he concluded, was a number of editorial challenges Italian journalism must
take on if it is to rebuild a trusting relationship with its public: change the reporting agenda; pay less attention to power and more to problems of citizens;
reduce rhetoric; write clearly and in a manner that is "less self-centered."[36]

   The modern and rational Portuguese political system is held back by a
premodern system of clientelism, a disparity that Luis de Sousa describes in
his aptly named article, "'I Don't Bribe, I Just Pull Strings.'"[37] These older

relationships pervade crime reporting practices, he agreed in our interview with him. "There is lots of collusion between [reporters and] the staff of the attorney general's office" that handles criminal investigations, he said. Over time, regular exchanges include not just information but also gift giving and hospitality. Eventually, boundaries blur. And when they do, the possibility diminishes that journalists can act as an impartial eye on those in positions of power (like the police) or offer factual accounts of a crime. "Then neither side is acting impartially. . . . The granting of special information to a journalist might be part of a political agenda," he said. Politicians can have friends in the prosecutor's office, so can businessmen who want to push their business agenda, de Sousa argued. In the young democracies of Spain and Portugal, journalists form another wing of this difficult-to-end interaction and thus risk becoming entwined participants in unequal processes with unclear outcomes, instead of independent observers and reporters of the public business to their citizens.

Katrin Voltmer in her book, *Media in Transitioning Democracies*, makes the point that journalistic professionalism in a democracy manifests itself through three main characteristics: Journalists must subscribe to a set of norms that guide their activities and set standards for what is regarded as "good" journalism; they must differentiate between differing roles like offering opinion or commentary and writing straight news; and they must have autonomy, "which safeguards journalists from interference from actors outside the profession."[38] Journalists in the Ambivalent countries operate on the edge of all three. While they say that they subscribe to norms that protect the integrity of investigations and the presumption of innocence of those accused, our interview data clearly suggest they often act in ways that contradict these stated values. We posit that these inconsistencies are not escaping public notice. In an international survey of 37 countries, published by the Reuters Institute at the University of Oxford in 2018, Portugal ranked highest for citizens' trust in news, but "almost half [surveyed] say they have seen examples of bad journalism in the previous week, and 38% say they have seen content which has been manipulated to suit a specific agenda."[39] When citizens cease to trust their media or believe journalists can be influenced by politicians or big business or those who offer them news tips in exchange for favorable coverage, then the institutions that constitute democracy are implicated and thus put at risk.

While we note that few, if any, of those to whom we spoke suggested the journalism profession as a whole might push back against a system that denies them autonomy, journalists alone cannot instigate a radical rear-rangement of the relationship among the police, the prosecutors, the press, and the public. But as our next two chapters suggest and explore, perhaps journalists might begin a conversation among themselves, their organiza-tions, and their publics—one that foregrounds the importance of supporting both the processes and institutions of democracy itself. The upshot of such a discussion could articulate how the Ambivalents might borrow elements of journalistic practice from the Protectors, whose normative practice is to shield individual privacy, while outlining public issues, and the best behavior of the Watchdogs, who try to balance yielding individual privacy in the name of what they see as a greater public interest.

9

Threats, Harms, and Benefits

At a Crossroads or in a Crossfire?

Journalists in the Ambivalent countries of Portugal, Spain, and Italy are at a crossroads. Crime reporting practices in these locales, where democratic institutions are younger and have less ethical or professional precedent than those in the Protector or Watchdog countries, raise questions about the way journalism is evolving. As we outlined in Chapter 8, current reporting practices are ambivalent and often point in contradictory directions. Professional practice dicta and reporters' words suggest one thing (e.g., respect for protection of accused and police investigations), but their actual behaviors suggest another (e.g., offer names and details of crimes when professional stakes are high). Under a system in which prosecutors keep some information about arrests and crimes from journalists and the public for the stated purpose of protecting the integrity of the investigation and the accused's presumption of innocence, journalists often seek or accept leaks from inside the criminal justice system, or they pound the pavement to gather accounts from sometimes unreliable witnesses. These "tell-more," if not "tell-all," reporting practices might indicate they are leaning toward Watchdog thinking and values; that is, Portuguese, Spanish, and Italian journalists are coming to see their primary professional duty as informing the public and keeping a wary eye on the criminal justice system, which can act unfairly or abuse institutional power. Select examples of reporters' occasional willingness to expose police misconduct point in that direction, as does the nascent development of tough-minded and independent investigative reporting. But at the same time, reporters' professed faith in the merits of protecting accused persons' presumption of innocence by shielding their identities and employing first name and initial, or initials only, signals their sympathy with the codes of behavior usually followed in the Protector countries.

These Ambivalent journalists must now choose. They have an opportunity to break a new path for their democracies by embracing aspects of *both* Watchdog and Protector value systems and creating something unique, but

Murder in Our Midst. Romayne Smith Fullerton and Maggie Jones Patterson, Oxford University Press (2021). © Oxford University Press. DOI: 10.1093/oso/9780190863531.003.0009.

history may stand in the way. News practices in these nations are still deeply rooted in a past that offered little independence to journalists. As Katrin Voltmer notes in *Media in Transitioning Democracies*, "the transformation of journalism after the demise of authoritarianism combines different streams of meanings and practices that originate from the role journalists had under the previous regime, the constraints of the post-authoritarian environment, cultural norms and the perception of Western role models."[1] In the process of such transitions, hybrid forms of democracy can emerge with a range of journalism models that reflect diverse political, economic, and social realities. While the commitment to democracy itself may vary, support for the free press and its oversight of democratic institutions remains paramount for any democracy to grow and thrive.[2]

Journalistic autonomy is necessary for media professionals to function as representatives of the people and to ensure citizens can access factual, contextual information to facilitate their participation in the public sphere. But recent market realities have exerted pressure on evolving practices and standards. Autonomy is receding further as layoffs and newsroom closings make employment in the news business more precarious. In this environment, the Internet is a mixed blessing. On one hand, it has undermined news media's traditional economic foundation. It weakens professional development by pushing competition, rushing deadlines, and lowering ethical standards. Both legacy media, as well as new and experimental news ventures, wobble on unsteady financial footing. They risk losing sight of what might be good for citizens and public discussion because they rely too much on how reporting choices affect the bottom line. When that happens, journalists push aside noble values to accommodate the more instrumental goals of the market. But on the other hand, we can cite examples where the Internet has opened opportunities that broaden journalism's reach and influence practices in constructive ways, both inside and beyond national boundaries.

While many of these cross currents buffet the press everywhere in the world, news traditions in the Ambivalent countries are less firmly established. Journalism's ethical commitments have shallow roots. In this chapter, we explore the links among Protector, Watchdog, and Ambivalent practices and build on the discussion initiated in the last chapter about the effects, intended or otherwise, of favoritism and clientelism. We then reaffirm the need for a journalism that puts its commitment to democracy front and center and

provides oversight of political institutions, regardless of any country's definition of democracy.

Watchdog Leanings and Protector Beliefs

Catalonian News Agency (ACN) reporter Guillem Sánchez Marín got to a
tip from a woman in the El Raval neighborhood of Barcelona that police had
badly beaten a man on the street. The reporter immediately checked with
police. As we outlined at the beginning of the section on Ambivalents, a police spokesman confirmed only that they had fought with a homeless man
who had died while in custody. Police released no further details, so Sánchez
knocked on doors in the neighborhood, and found three neighbors who
had witnessed police officers kicking and punching a man, even after he was
down. They reported that the man had cried for help at first and then gone
silent. An ambulance picked him up. One witness agreed to tell his story
to Sánchez on camera, but police denied this version of events and other
neighbors' accounts. The dead man was Juan Andrés Benítez, 50, who had
once owned a series of clothing stores but had fallen on hard times. A police
spokesman told a different story: The police had gotten into an altercation
with the man. Officers tried to subdue Benítez. He had cocaine in his body
and suffered a heart attack as he was being handcuffed. (They had originally
said he died at the end of the night in prison.) His death was unrelated to his
detention by police, the spokesman said.

As we recounted earlier, the story ACN put out contained these conflicting
versions (from neighbors and police) of what had happened, and much of the
Spanish news media ran with it. But Sánchez's colleagues in other news media
criticized him for questioning the police account. They were concerned that
by offering the views of the neighbors, Sánchez could spoil their good—and
interdependent—relationship with the cops. The reaction disheartened
Sánchez, who felt that he had done the right thing by offering the account of
the neighbors, not just the official version of the police. Then, two weeks later,
El País, Spain's largest newspaper, published a cell phone video of the incident, turned over to them by an El Raval witness. "In that video, you can see
some police officers are punching, and the man is crying out," Sánchez said.
The kicking continues after the man is down and submissive. The truth, in
this instance, came out. It was a case of alleged police brutality, but it was only
caught because of the cell phone video.

"Normally, when there is a homicide here," said Antonio Baquero, deputy editor at the world desk at *El Periódico* in Barcelona, "the Catalonian police issue a brief statement . . . but police did not send any statement, so we did not know" about it until Sánchez's report. After the video confirmed what witnesses had said, the Watchdog instinct to bark loudly at a possible abuse of power kicked in. His paper went hard after the story, Baquero said, "because we realized that the police were lying to us." For him, the El Raval case was "like a bomb between us and the police." Because each reporter's success often depends on the goodwill of the officers to dole out information, they generally tried to nurture good relations. But after this story, police accused reporters of having no idea how difficult it was to restrain a suspect hopped up on drugs. Baquero, in turn, tried to assure his police contacts that the decision to run the eyewitness video and air the implications that the police were at fault, was not personal. "It is my job," he said. In November 2013, one month after Benítez's death, eight Barcelona police officers were indicted for aggressive behavior. They were also accused of covering up evidence after an autopsy revealed Benítez's heart attack was brought on, in part, by police blows to his head. The officers involved were suspended from the force. Ultimately, six of them were suspended without pay for two years and placed on probation for five years for "failing to comply" with police protocols and for taking "disproportionate" action, which had lasted up to 12 minutes.[3]

The El Raval case, as it became known throughout Spain, illustrates a problem that is not unique to Catalonia or even to the Ambivalent countries: Police have tremendous power and are not always held accountable for their actions. As has been true in numerous police actions in the United States, only the credible evidence of citizen-shot cell phone videos has broken through police denials of misconduct. Such incidents illustrate clearly the benefits of technology to aid in truth and its public dissemination. But the thin records of day-to-day arrests in Spain, Portugal, and Italy can make reporters exceptionally dependent on police as sources for any and all information. Reporters are reluctant to challenge them for fear of burning their contacts, as evidenced by the initial reaction of Sánchez's colleagues.

As the details of this incident show, the journalistic situation is complex. Sometimes, reporters told us, they will burn their sources if the public interest—by which they mean, in this instance, when there is a risk to the public—is compelling enough. *El Mundo* staff writer Pablo Herráiz outlined an instance where three women were crushed in a stampede at the Madrid Arena in 2012. He wrote that the police chief had filed a false report about the arena's safety to protect politicians trying to keep their seats in City Hall. Herráiz's negative but accurate report cost him a friend and a good source who no longer talks to him. Reporting on police behavior is not routine in Spain. As a result, some officers do not recognize it as a part of the reporter's job and cast their interactions with reporters as more personal than professional. The police chief shut Herráiz off after his exposé, he said, and he had to search for other sources for information when crime stories occurred.

Perhaps no incident better illustrates the dangers brought on by the ambivalent and compromised state of journalistic independence than the 2004 Madrid train bombings. After this horrific violence, the government tried to use members of the press to spread misinformation for its own benefit. The bombings occurred three days before Spain's general elections. Most Spanish media initially published a claim put out by the party in power, the Partido Popular (PP), that the Basque separatist group Euskadi Ta Askatasuna (ETA) was responsible for the attacks. It is now widely accepted that then Prime Minister José María Aznar himself called a number of journalists to plant that story. An estimated 11 million Spaniards poured onto the streets to express sympathy for the victims. But the police investigators almost immediately began looking at Islamic militants, not Basque separatists. Members of al-Qaeda were arrested on March 13, while the PP continued to blame the Basques. The PP allegedly worried that the public would link an Islamic attack with the PP government's support of the U.S.- and U.K.-led invasion of Iraq in 2003. Linking the bombing to that already unpopular war could cost them the March 14 election. While some partisan news media remained complicit with the lie that Basques had planted the bomb, other news outlets associated with the opposition Socialist Party (PSOE) quickly launched an historic communication campaign to counter the misinformation. Street demonstrations turned angry as people sought the truth. The PP suffered a resounding and unforeseen defeat at the polls on March 14. For years afterward, some news media sympathetic to the PP were still looking for a Basque connection to the bombings.[4]

Whether journalists are led astray by politics, competition, or the challenges of a criminal justice system that guards information, publishing falsehoods causes harm. Talking about the mistakes journalists made in the Majadahonda Ripper case (in which the press published speculation by neighbors that the suspect in a murder case was a serial killer and was hacking up bodies in his garage), Alberto Pozas of Cadena Ser Radio Station shook his head. "You have a family that is suffering because someone died," he said. "And you are giving them a lot of misinformation."

In the long run, *ABC* newspaper reporter Pablo Muñoz of Madrid believes police reporting in Spain is transparent, albeit not necessarily timely. Truth, seen from this perspective, is a process rather than a discrete product. More important to him and others is that their justice and their media systems are meant to protect an accused's presumption of innocence, so even when journalists choose to identify a person, they rarely mention family members. Muñoz sees the Watchdog model of assuming all arrest records should be made public as hurtful to suspects and their families and, therefore, problematic. When he first took on the police beat, Muñoz recalled, his boss warned him to be careful "because we are dealing with people's honor and once it's lost, it is lost." Coverage of a simple accusation in the United States or the United Kingdom can, as we have detailed in the Watchdog section, ruin people's reputations—even if they are later found not guilty. News audiences often assume where there's smoke, there's fire, regardless of the outcome of an investigation or even a court case. They know a not-guilty verdict is not a declaration of innocence. Reporters in all three Ambivalent countries generally support the court's protection of the presumption of innocence by keeping arrest records under wraps, even though for a variety of reasons, they often violate their own ethics codes and legal restrictions to skirt the norm.

Spanish police scramble their radio calls, thereby blocking another means journalists might use to monitor their day-to-day activity. Ambivalents reporters' attitudes about information can closely resemble those of the Watchdog journalists: More access and greater transparency lead to more public accountability and result in better stories for citizens—stories grounded in fact and context that offer substance to public conversations.

But access to verifiable information remains a structural challenge. The main difficulty for reporters, said Herráiz, is that "we are taught in universities that you must have proof of everything you publish and, if possible, have documents or some sources that you identify. But for me, that is impossible because no one—the police, the lawyers, the civil servants—is allowed to talk to the press." They all defer to the press office. To get the information he needs, Herráiz said, he has resorted to tactics that sounded like film noir. "I must talk to people in very strange places. I knew three police who would say go to these two streets and we'll pass in a black car, and then you get in." They gave him information as they rode around and insisted on remaining anonymous. With no documents to check against, he must have faith that his sources are reliable or opt not to publish.

Prosecutorial Bias and Misleading Coverage

In a democracy where equitable access is paramount, Justice is pictured as blindfolded to ensure impartiality as she wields a set of scales in one hand and a sword in the other. Journalism, by contrast, requires open-eyed vision. "Being impartial or neutral is not a core principle of journalism," Kovach and Rosenstiel repeatedly stress in *The Elements of Journalism*.[5] But journalists must keep off the path of propaganda and be steered instead by the principles of truth and verification. Journalism is defined by these principles, they say, and by "an allegiance to citizens and community at large, and informing rather than manipulating."[6] Stephen Ward, in *Democracy in a Populist Age*, notes that truth-telling is the prime directive in democracies. Anything that pulls a journalist away from a "democratically engaged" and "egalitarian democracy" is putting citizens' freedoms at risk.[7] Crime reporters in the Ambivalent countries unwittingly bend toward a prosecutorial perspective—and away from independence—by depending heavily on sources who weigh in on one side of the justice scale. "Journalists in Italy tend to follow the opinion of the prosecutor instead of looking for the truth," said Lanfranco Vaccari, an Italian reporter and foreign correspondent since 1968 who teaches journalism in Milan. "In Spain, we call it the '*pena de telediario*,' punishment of the television bulletin," said Antonio Baquero of *El Periódico*, lamenting that journalists too often take a prosecutorial and judgmental perspective. Sometimes when handing out sentences, judges consider whether a politician "has already been punished [for corruption] by the '*pena*' [pain] of the news." This perspective of seeing media coverage as a form of punishment is reminiscent of the situation in the Netherlands, outlined in Chapter 2, where a judge reduced jail time for a businessman, Jan-Dirk Paarlberg, convicted of fraud, because the judge felt the man had suffered from the adverse, but also accurate, publicity.

In a similarly misleading and problematic fashion, journalists' predilection for framing murder stories in a soap opera style often pitches a larger-than-life evil "folk devil" perpetrator against an angelic victim, according to numerous reporters to whom we spoke. The most egregious coverage happens when reporters become swept up in the drama and suspend their own skepticism to follow police finger pointing at suspects who readily fit a cultural stereotype. In many instances, those fingers point to immigrants. As we noted in the last chapter, in Italy, a Moroccan man was initially arrested for the murder of 13-year-old Yara. "People liked him as the guilty party because he was foreign," Magistrate Letizia Ruggeri, who later presided over the investigation, told *The Guardian*.[8] "Liking" foreign suspects in cases of violence against girls and women applies to news reporters as well, according to the study "Moral Panic: The Issue of Women and Crime in Italian Evening News," by Elisa Giomi and Fabrizio Tonnello.[9] They found news broadcasts about high-profile cases stirred moral panic by focusing obsessively over immigrants as posing a danger to Italian women. Broadcasters repeated police accusations against immigrants even when there was no evidence, and this was the case even after the actual killer had been identified as Italian. Looking at murders of women in Italy in 2006, Giomi and Tonello found that only 4% were committed by men unknown to the women or their families. By contrast, almost 62% of the women were killed by their partners or ex-partners.[10] Yet, murders committed by strangers received far more media coverage. Stories about murders of women by foreigners boosted the coverage numbers even higher. Although Italians were responsible for 86.4% of the female murders in 2006, murders committed by people who were not native-born Italian were the subject of one-quarter of the news coverage. The authors tied their findings to the particulars of Italian news media. "No moral panic is independent from the role of the media in framing the issues, assessing the threat, and proposing solutions. The very conditions in which the media operate (ownership, competition, standardised processes) are a key factor in the production of moral panic."[11]

Melodramatic murder stories also blur the ethical distinction between what material draws audiences for prurient reasons as opposed to what citizens actually need to know about crime and the criminal justice system to make reasoned decisions about whom to elect and whether the state of their justice system is good. Lost in the dramatic story telling, said Fabrizio Tonello in an interview, is the context that the Italian murder rate dropped precipitously from about 2,000 in 1992 to under 468 in 2014, following a widespread clampdown on organized crime. With a population of 60 million, Italy's murder rate has fallen to .9%, placing it among the world's lowest. Murder rates in Spain and Portugal are even lower.[12] But the theatrical reporting style common in all three countries can warp this picture and stir fears. Lorenzo Bagnoli, reporter at *Terre di Mezzo* magazine in Milan and board member of the Investigative Reporting Project Italy (IRPI), lamented that as long as salacious murder stories pull eyes and ears to a news outlet, and in turn, draw advertisers who pay the bills, news organizations will cover them heavily. And the public's perceptions, or misperceptions, of crime will continue.

Beyond journalism per se, a variety of television shows in all three countries feature real crimes and hover in a space between news and entertainment. These shows further exploit audiences' prurient tastes. In Spain, talk shows invite families of victims and even accused murderers to appear as guests. Show hosts then press them for details that have not yet come out in court. Javier Galán Gamero of the Madrid Press Association described one case of a boy who had been convicted of raping and killing a girl with mental deficiencies. The boy was not incarcerated because of his age, but he granted interviews on television talk shows, appearing with his mother and girlfriend. "It's not journalism," Galán lamented. But entertainment programs are not bound by the same ethical standards. Unfortunately, Galán said, "the public does not see the distinction," and journalism's reputation for dealing with more legitimate material takes a beating.

Another manifestation of reporters' prosecutorial bias came to light in our interviews in Ambivalent countries: reporters' willingness to set aside their journalistic impartiality and compromise their commitment to truth to help police pursue a criminal. Ana Terradillos Azpiroz, of Madrid's Cadena Ser Radio and Telecinco TV, recounted a story that followed the rape of four children in Madrid 2014. The prime suspect had gone missing for seven months until police discovered him hiding in a relative's house in the northern Spanish region of Cantabria. Although reporters also had this information, they reported that police remained baffled about the suspect's whereabouts in order to convince him that he was safe until police could close in and apprehend him. "Ordinarily, I would not go along with [misleading the public to help police], but I did this because of the children involved," Terradillos said. In another Spanish case, three children disappeared while in a park with their father Manuel M. M., whose full name was not used in the reports. The children had been removed from their family home by social services, and the father's visit was being supervised by a psychologist, who was fetching coffee and treats when the children vanished. Although both police and the press knew the most likely explanation was that the mother had been hiding nearby and the parents had collaborated on a plan to repossess the children, reporters filed stories that implicated only the father to confuse the family and facilitate the police investigation, as well as the recovery of the children.

Such cooperation with police could put press credibility at risk, admitted Terradillos, but the public almost never finds out she said, and reporters owe police sources on whom they lean heavily for leaks and favors in numerous situations. She generally protects victims and the accused's presumption of innocence by not revealing their identities. "But when the victim is a minor and some data can only be provided by the police, you need to rely on your police contacts," she said.

"There is a natural tendency for reporters to side with their sources, and their sources are more often prosecutors than defense lawyers," said Fabrizio Tonello. This can have advantages, he added. Prosecutors work outside the Italian political system, which allowed them to work with partisan newspapers when former Italian Prime Minister Silvio Berlusconi was in political and legal trouble. Together, the opposition press and prosecutors made a powerful coalition. "Not powerful enough to block Berlusconi at the polls," Tonello said, "but powerful enough to use political scandals in a politically effective way" and eventually to rob Berlusconi of power through a series of court cases and reports of his wrongdoing.

When Álvaro de Cózar of Madrid's *El País* began working on a corruption investigation involving government contracts, he chose to share his findings with law enforcement while he was still working on the story. "The case had to do with government corruption. It was called *caso Aneri* de formación, or training courses." De Cózar's investigation uncovered evidence of individuals and organizations taking government money to train workers but never teaching them anything. "There were fake contracts and fake courses. I found lots of information the police did not have. I went to police and gave them a USB [drive] with information that was useful to their case," de Cózar said. "And they started to work with us. It was the best time I had working on an investigation because I could confirm everything [with police]. My relationship with the police was not one of friendship, but workers doing the same job." The joint investigation resulted in arrests and trials of those perpetrating the corruption, an outcome both de Cózar and the police desired.

The picture here is not simple. While most reporters in Watchdog and Protector countries would see working this closely with law enforcement as a compromise of journalistic integrity, police in Ambivalent countries can punish reporters by withholding or refusing to verify information that might be considered a matter of public record elsewhere in the world. Such a system of structural inequities of access and dependence on police and prosecutors as sources is especially challenging for investigative reporters in Ambivalent countries, where government corruption is generally assumed to be higher than in the Protector and Watchdog nations.[13]

Blocked Paths for Investigative Reporters:
Ineffective Legislation

Lorenzo Bagnoli said Italian open records laws were supposed to give reporters more access to material relevant to the public, but the legislation simply does not work well. "We are one of the countries with the most laws and the least compliance," he said with a shrug of resignation. António Granado, former managing editor and online editor for the Lisbon newspaper *Público*, fought for years for access to presidential documents. He confirms that reporters in Portugal, too, are often stonewalled, despite the open public records laws there. In Spain, the situation is similar.

"There is a formal way of asking for documents—the way you do in the U.K.," Guido Romeo, data and business editor for *Wired* magazine in Milan, told a British friend, who was covering the Amanda Knox murder trial in Perugia for the BBC. "But nobody goes through that road," he said.[14] When his friend, who was fluent in Italian, asked a judge for trial documents, the judge looked at her: "What are you talking about? Get out of here." The Italian way of getting what you need is to befriend one of the prosecutors or defense lawyers and ask them to pass documents over to you, Romeo said. Otherwise, the story's news value could wilt before any documents come through more formal channels. To cover corruption in Italy, a reporter must be as well connected as any crime reporter but also must be well versed in the mechanisms of corrupt finance, said Paolo Colonnello, who reported on white-collar crime for *La Stampa* in Milan. Corrupt money can move from one company to another, he said, in the form of favors or bribes or services—anything that can be traded to get something back.

Journalists who report for the Investigative Reporters Project Italy (IRPI) follow corruption along far-reaching, international pathways. In doing so, they offer a bright light and a way forward for the Ambivalent countries. Founded in 2013, IRPI's investigative reporters write in English about transnational corruption that few Italian papers follow. "Some of the police work on organized crime turns up in the police-issued press releases," said IRPI reporter Giulio Rubino, "but neither newspapers nor ANSA, the state news agency, pick up on it. The news is there, but it would still require some legwork. . . . The directors of the newspapers want to keep their strong ties with their political powers, so they don't want to be differentiated by the content of their news but by some much less harmful aspects, like appearance and info graphics." The partisan nature of Italian journalism and news outlets' limited budgets tamp down editors' willingness to rock the boat, said IRPI reporter Cecilia Anesi of Rome. "We [IRPI reporters] have six months to work on stories, and we can decide when an investigation is in-depth enough to report." Reporters for the daily press can be limited to a week on such an assignment, she said. IRPI's stories are all placed on its website in English. They are picked up more often by foreign news organizations than by those in Italy. The 34% of Italians who speak some English might access the coverage on IRPI's website. Otherwise, the IRPI's investigations and their potential contribution to Italian political conversation is largely lost.[15]

Leo Sisti, who has been reporting for the Italian newsweekly L'Espresso for 30 years and is also a contributor to the daily Il Fatto Quatidiano, helped launch IRPI and serves as one of its senior writers and editors. He began his career reporting on the Italian "Clean Hands" movement, a six-year legal investigation that sought to stamp out corruption in Italy. He uncovered funds from an offshore company owned by Silvio Berlusconi's family that were used to bribe the late Prime Minister Bettino Craxi, and he has written seven books on scandals in the Vatican, Italian soccer, Cosa Nostra ties to Berlusconi, and the Italian trial process. He has been a part of seven cross-border investigations with the International Consortium of Investigative Journalists (ICIJ), including the Pulitzer Prize–winning Panama Papers.[16] The habit of milking sources inside the legal system for information during the Clean Hands investigation continues to prove useful, Sisti found. "The first thing a journalist must know is how to cultivate a source: drinking coffee, having lunch or dinner and so on. . . . I exploited my sources just so I could have documents before the other newspapers."

Funded by a mix of foundations' monies, grants from other journalists, sales of stories to Italian and international media outlets, and crowdfunding initiatives, IRPI calls itself a "watchdog on democracy" with an Italian soul and a global reach. The mafia may have wormed its way into Italy's soul, Sisti said, but its reach is no longer contained within the country. This is precisely the message that IRPI disseminates. If it's a difficult story for Italian media to tell in Italy, then it's a story that can be told beyond its borders. Since organized crime is not confined to this country, journalism writ large must follow. "'Ndrangheta [an organized crime group with roots in the Calabria region], for example, is no longer old guys. The younger guys are educated, sophisticated, and know foreign languages. They have ties with Colombia, Venezuela, Mexico. 'Ndrangheta are the drug dealers, working with Zetas in Venezuela and Colombia. They can swing elections and then get money for public contracts on construction," he said. Nigerian organized crime within Italy is like a subcontractor for the older mafia organizations. Camorra, the Naples-based mafia, controls large segments of the drug market but keeps a safe distance from the actual trade. They rent out the docks where illegal imports are brought in and take a cut. They control where drugs are sold and by whom through subcontracting systems, but "they don't risk getting arrested for importing drugs."

Italian crime organizations have also moved into Rotterdam and Brussels, said IRPI reporter Giulio Rubino, but local journalists there are unprepared to cover them. They are short staffed and often unaware of the context and background of such criminal organizations—realities that the IRPI is more able to manage. "The Cosa Nostra is operating like an international company, intercepting EU structural funds, by using proxies." The distribution of agriculture subsidies in Italy is now private. "We cannot find out what farmers are getting in support. Cosa Nostra is getting a lot of those agricultural subsidies, but we cannot prove it," Rubino said in 2014. While not intended to protect illegal activities or persons who are breaking national or international laws, Europe's privacy laws, especially in Germany, provide shelter for organized crime, IRPI reporters said. Accused criminals have little fear that phone or bank records will be seized, which is a routine investigative tool in the United States since the days of Chicago gangster Al Capone. In most of Europe, such information is protected by privacy legislation.

Journalists who undertake investigative work are not seen uniformly as heroic defenders of democracy; all are under threat, physically and legally. Alberto Spampinato founded Ossigno per L'Informazion to record and scrutinize threats to Italian reporters after his journalist brother was murdered in 1972 while investigating the mafia. He believes Italian journalism lacks a sense of common cause and any genuine dedication to public service—aspects that are more common in Protector and Watchdog countries. Instead, fear and partisanship pervade the Italian media, he said. Reporters rarely support one another or concern themselves with challenges faced by investigative reporters, he asserted. That challenge is not one that infects journalism alone; its endemic and systemic to institutions and to culture itself. "The problem is that you live in a country where people—not only journalists—do not speak about what they really see," Spampinato said, invoking a metaphor. "People come into a room where there is a corpse," but no one speaks of it. At last, one journalist points out the corpse and asks why no one is mentioning it. "The other reporters are made uncomfortable. He has switched the light on. Embarrassed, they deny seeing the body and accuse the investigative reporter of putting them all in danger," Spampinato said. His organization has studied this dynamic and puts the blame on the Italian news media's political divisions, that is, partisanship. "If [that reporter] is not of your party, if you do not agree with him, you are not used to giving solidarity."

Investigative reporters endure two types of intimidation, Spampinato said. The first is violence or the threat of violence, which may come as a form of "advice" given to the reporter or a family member. The other is what Spampinato called "an abuse of rights," a threat of legal action as an instrument of intimidation. "In Italy, you can accuse me of defamation even if everything I wrote is absolutely correct because the law is very old and has many holes." To move forward to a place where journalists can tell the truth in a nuanced context, and without fear for their positions and, in some instances, their lives, citizens must push for changes in the transparency and accountability of their democracies; and they must see value in the role a free and independent press can play in the evolution.

Discussion

In this chapter, we detailed a variety of inconsistent practices and statements: journalists nurturing and massaging sources, largely for the benefit of their own careers; journalists ignoring legal and ethical dicta about identification of accused persons; officials ignoring laws meant to increase public access to information; outlets embellishing stories for prurient rather than public interest; and implied or direct threats to journalists, to name but a few. While these factors post roadblocks along the path forward, some journalists in the Ambivalent countries are beginning to embrace the greater and more responsible role they are poised to play in these democracies. This group includes those involved in investigative initiatives like the IRPI and the International Consortium of Independent Journalists, who put together the Panama Papers. Collaborative projects like these draw together highly knowledgeable reporters from different countries, who are aware of the shortcomings in both their own countries' journalistic practices and their criminal justice systems. Collaboration replaces competition. They share a desire across borders to improve conditions for journalists, for citizens, and for democracy itself. Working together, these journalists foster a shared sense of professionalism and determine what ought to be emphasized in their coverage. They transcend parochialism. Their new approaches to practice provide concrete examples of routines and products that benefit citizens under democratic rule.

IRPI makes the goal of bettering the common good paramount. They proclaim it first under the heading "What we do": "Our work seeks to inform our readers on all sorts of wrongdoings, with a special focus on topics of public interest."[17] As we noted in Chapter 8, the term "public interest" was deployed in many of our interviews in the Ambivalent countries to mean stories that attracted an audience. IRPI embraces another meaning, one more predominant in Watchdog and Protector interviews: News in the public interest provides audiences with what they need to know to be informed citizens. In the former definition, audiences are seen as consumers. In the latter, they are viewed as citizens. While entertaining material can offer audiences some welcome relief from serious or disturbing stories, entertainment cannot be the sole, or even the primary, impetus behind disseminating news. Journalists in every kind of democracy must accept that they operate as a public trust, gathering factual information that enriches civic discussion about the common good and encourages policies that best achieve that end.

Younger professionals in these Ambivalent countries are instigating new ideas about journalism and ethics. Sofia Branco, a young reporter at *Público*, had just been elected as the new president of the Portuguese Union of Journalists when we met with her in 2015; that she continues to enjoy colleagues' support is suggested by her re-election in 2018. Branco brought a fresh outlook that set her apart from her predecessors. The union president had been closely affiliated with the Portuguese Socialist Party. Branco was aiming to be politically independent. Belonging to a union is an individual choice in Portugal, and faith in the unions' efficacy is low, she said. Only about a quarter of all journalists belong. To better understand the current concerns of journalists in the field and to familiarize them with her group's revised agenda, she and her executive officers were traveling across the country to initiate informal conversations. "We see two main actions" for the union, Branco said. "One is labor: [We need to address] wages, layoffs, and in Portugal we have a lot of that. The other is ethics, and this is also important." Many of our interview subjects highlighted connections between these two issues. When jobs are precarious, discussing best practices is difficult for those who might question the status quo. Branco was also organizing the first Portuguese journalists' conference in 17 years to provide a place for journalists to meet, to "think about the profession itself," and ultimately to speak in a unified voice, she said.

While younger journalists, like her, are not yet inured to news practices that undermine a consistent ethic, Branco said, she put a disturbing caveat on her optimism: "The new people who come to the job, if they want to stay, won't be doing anything about ethics," largely because they are not in positions to challenge current practices. Old newsroom cultures persist, despite these new employees, she said. Journalists who remember what reporting was like under the dictator are fast disappearing, she said. As a result, newsrooms are losing both their institutional memory of that problematic past and the mentors who know the value of press freedoms.[18]

There are glimmers of change and bright spots that shine—or at least reflect—the values shared by all liberal democracies, such as equality for all, justice that can be seen to be done, respect for diversity and minority views, and respect for the rule of law. Yet, complex factors make success less certain in these Ambivalent countries. They stand poised at a crossroads. They themselves must decide about the best way forward and consider what media's role ought to be in the future. They must ask how journalists can affirm their commitment to democracy by both supporting and overseeing its institutions. Such considerations must become and remain paramount. In the next chapter, we will examine journalism's accountability to the public and its emerging—or perhaps retreating—role.

10

Is There a Way Forward for Ambivalent Journalists?

Yes, No, and Maybe

In the previous two chapters detailing Ambivalent journalists' crime coverage practices, we have argued that the inconsistent behaviors coupled with more positive developments suggest that an overarching ethic of public service could take root and grow in these countries. Those positive developments include new access-to-information laws, journalists unions with reinvigorated goals that support democracy, and the creation of fledgling investigative consortia. Viewed in the most positive light, journalism in Spain, Italy, and Portugal may be heading in a direction that blends the best practices of the Watchdog and Protector models and could inspire a new, more mature journalistic approach. In this chapter, we employ Kohlberg, Perry, Belenky et al., and Gilligan to critique current attitudes and to suggest ways forward to better serve these fledgling democracies.[1]

A Cautionary Tale: The Reporting About Aitana

In November 2009, an injured three-year-old girl named Aitana was brought to a hospital in Aronain, Tenerife, in the Spanish Canary Islands. A medical examination revealed multiple traumas, including injuries to the vagina and anus that implied physical abuse. When Aitana died a few days later, her mother's partner, Diego Pastrana, was arrested for murder. Journalists en masse condemned the accused. Pastrana, whose name appeared in a slew of stories, was repeatedly shown in handcuffs by multiple news sources. One newspaper, *ABC*, ran a headline identifying Pastrana as "Boyfriend, babysitter and murderer," while an editorial called for the death penalty. Some news outlets covered the story as if it were a melodramatic soap opera, an approach the Spanish call "chronicle" reporting. Maciá-Barber and

Murder in Our Midst. Romayne Smith Fullerton and Maggie Jones Patterson, Oxford University Press (2021). © Oxford University Press. DOI: 10.1093/oso/9780190863531.003.0010.

Galván-Arias pointed out in their case study of the Aitana coverage that reporters use this style to describe details of the alleged murder and speculate on the suspect's motives. They also suggest that this type of writing creates "a mere effect [illusion] of reality" in the public's mind, by which they mean readers come to think of the narrative as factual, when it may be largely speculative. The upshot is that such erroneous or misleading accounts are not easily erased from public memory.[2]

In fact, the reporters covering Aitana's "murder" were erroneous: An autopsy concluded that her injuries, including a head trauma, had resulted from a playground fall. Pastrana was released from jail and admitted to the hospital, suffering from depression. He left the Canary Islands some days later. News media immediately began painting Pastrana anew, this time as a victim. They blurred or hid his face in photos, even though they had shown his full image when initially portraying him as a child murderer. Some members of the media—a minority—publicly examined their own behavior and a few even apologized.[3] In addition, Pastrana was awarded €60,000 from *ABC* and €50,000 from *La Opinión de Tenerife* in 2017 for their failure to respect his presumption of innocence.[4]

Spain's Law of Criminal Procedure stipulates that harm to suspects and their reputations should be minimized when police arrest and remand a suspect to custody. Showing the alleged individual in handcuffs—as mentioned, a common media trope in the United States where it is popularly referred to as the "perp walk"—is frowned upon by Spanish courts, which believe that such photographs damage the suspect's reputation. The Tribunal Constitucional (TC), Spain's constitutional court, stresses that the presumption of innocence should be one of the central criteria used as a check on a journalist's diligence in verifying facts. The European Court of Human Rights places a similar obligation on journalists.[5] In addition, the Spanish Commission of Arbitration, Complaints, and Deontology of Journalism ethics code prescribes that "every person is innocent until proven otherwise."[6] The code cautions journalists to minimize harm to suspects and their families.[7] But as our previous two chapters have shown in detail, crime coverage choices and the resulting patterns of behavior in these regions are, at best, ambivalent. These edicts, our data also revealed, are frequently violated.

Spanish, Italian, and Portuguese crime reporters offered numerous anecdotes that highlighted their preference for Watchdog aggression over the more cautious deference spelled out in their countries' legal and ethics codes. As their illustrative examples demonstrate, most journalists to whom we spoke would first talk about their desire to draw public attention to any perceived wrongdoing or a person accused of breaking the law; yet, the protective laws and ethics were not always abandoned. Instead, they remain a part of their journalistic approaches, and reporters profess respect for the principles of protection. Considered from this perspective, in the Aitana case, the Watchdog instinct meant journalists patrolled society's moral edges by coming down hard against the abuse of a helpless child. However, in this case, the dog barked prematurely and damaged a person's reputation, unrestrained by an obligation to qualify claims and verify speculations, despite how legislation and ethics codes emphasize their importance.

Maciá-Barber and Galván-Arias argue that Aitana is "a typical case" of the reporting methods employed by a representative segment of the Spanish press, indicative of a "widespread journalistic madness" evident in a range of Spanish newspapers.[8] Intense and inflamed competition drove these journalists' erratic action, Maciá told us in an interview. Similar competitive pressures warped ethical judgment in other countries examined in this study, including those within Watchdog and Protector models. But the relatively young and immature free press in the Ambivalent countries renders journalism particularly vulnerable to the temptation to over-dramatize and sensationalize stories, especially at times when little information can be gleaned in a transparent, legal manner.

Overlapping social factors embedded in the history and politics of the countries in the Ambivalent model help explain their approach to reporting: a widespread system of clientelism; a partisan and competitive news media in a tight job market; weak journalistic professionalism; and a definition of "public interest" at variance with Watchdog and Protector nations' interpretations. These factors intersect to form the crossroads where journalism finds itself poised to retreat or move forward. At this particularly turbulent moment, economic and technological crosswinds threaten to carry journalists off a forward, progressive course.

Open-ended interviews—such as those we conducted with crime reporters, editors, and media experts—sometimes reveal as much by what is not said, as what is. Comparison shines a helpful light into these silences. Subjects in the Ambivalent countries rarely mentioned concepts of journalism's moral mission or its role in shaping an informed citizenry. Their counterparts in Watchdog and Protector countries, on the one hand, often volunteered without prompting their sense of professional, ethical duty and framed that responsibility within journalism's broad mission in democratic processes. Reporters in the Ambivalent countries, on the other hand, focused their ethical concerns on a more particular level, that is, concern for matters of taste or consideration of the families of victims or perpetrators. Awareness that news coverage might compromise the presumption of innocence was the one broader principle they frequently cited, but that was sometimes only in the context of how their country's laws intersected with their practice. Similarly, many mentioned the protection of youths, especially perpetrators, who are also protected by law. Even when we encouraged media professionals to articulate some sense of public mission, their responses were generally passive and negligible. Formal codes of ethics in these countries embed journalism within a sense of civic purpose, but reporters themselves did not indicate that they had internalized that mission or that it genuinely informed their practice.

The explanation for the Ambivalent model's distinctiveness lies in the region's history, which contrasts sharply with our other models. Not only was much of the press in this region owned by political parties or interests until just a few decades ago, but also those parties weaponized their affiliate newspapers in ideological battles and used them as tools in political mobilization.[9] Newspapers and television networks still bear that mark. They feel free to display strong political leanings, and their bias is often built into the reporting, as reporters themselves attest. Political interests and even politicians align closely with media control. Silvio Berlusconi serves as one outstanding example. Pioneering commercial television in Italy in the 1980s, he used it to forge his Forza Italia Party and amass political power that carried him through nine years as Italy's prime minister during four different governments. He continues to wield influence despite being convicted of tax fraud and banned by the courts from holding public office.

In *Comparing Media Systems*, Hallin and Mancini argue that the countries falling into their Polarized Pluralist model, including the three Ambivalent countries on which we focus, are characterized by a high level of politicization: The state and political parties intervene strongly in domestic institutions and social life, and much of the population is strongly loyal to widely varying political ideologies.[10] Such loyalty is an intrinsic part of the widespread cynicism about a concept of the "common good" that would unite them, and a relative absence of agreed-upon rules or norms. "The news media are similarly characterized by a high degree of external pluralism, in which media are seen as champions of diverse political ideologies, and commitment to these ideologies tends to outweigh commitment to a common professional culture."[11] Thus, while fewer of today's news media are directly affiliated with political parties, a distinct political perspective still holds sway at many news organizations, and ties remain between journalists and politicians; the state continues to intervene in the media sector. Hallin and Mancini further argue that in the Polarized Pluralist system, there is unequal consumption of public information and a clear division between those who are politically active and those who consume little political information.

Offering a nuanced view of these principles in practice, Christians et al. write that in the Pluralist model, the press's duty to monitor power—of the police, those elected to public office, or those who administer justice—must be carried out from a specific political perspective, with different media presenting different viewpoints.[12] In such a system, according to Christians et al., individual media offer channels for different political groups.[13] But as many of our case studies demonstrated, this diversity is normative and often remains unrealized. In the Aitana instance, almost all media initially condemned Pastrana; there was little range of interpretation or differing analysis. In the case of former Prime Minister Sócrates, such diversity of reporting and of opinion was virtually impossible because all information was filtered through a single media owner—Cofina media group, whose newspaper, *Correio da Manhã*, and broadcast outlet, CMTV, share one political perspective. All other outlets had to rely solely on Cofina's version because the information was structurally inaccessible. Ideally, journalists in this model report events and offer a unique interpretation of the world. Distinct political views are largely maintained within each media outlet. A diversity of views is thus offered across various outlets. Under this model, reporting in a neutral fashion is not the norm. "Journalism reflects the antagonisms of the society, and there is little chance for neutral, objective reporting. By contrast, under conditions of liberal or moderate pluralism, without sharp conflicts of ideas, we are more likely to find internal forms of media pluralism."[14] As a result, informing the public in the Watchdog or the Protector countries can take the form of neutral and objective reporting, and media also offer separate commentaries that reflect different allegiances or perspectives.

The legacy of the Ambivalent region's partisan media history prevents journalists from readily reaching common ground across political divides. As Hallin and Mancini note in *Comparing Media Systems*, "commitment to particular interests is stronger and the notion of the common good weaker" in the Ambivalent region than it is in the countries that comprise our other two models.[15] In Watchdog and Protector countries, professionalism—by which we mean the sense that journalists are working on behalf of the public—is high, and many mainstream news professionals align their newsgathering practices and motivations, at least on an aspirational level, with democratic processes.

What Moral Development Offers to the Discussion

In their study of journalists in the United States, Renita Coleman and Lee Wilkins determined that the recognition of such responsibility requires a level of moral maturity, at least to the "conventional" level found in Lawrence Kohlberg's hierarchical stages of moral reasoning.[16] On this level, thinkers embrace a willingness to obey laws and professional practices. They do so because obedience is expected of them, and they grow to realize that civil laws and professional rules are necessary for maintaining social order. That level of reasoning emerged in our interviews with reporters in the Ambivalent countries, but it was easy to see how competition, clientelism, and contrary political interests were blocking broader commitments that could lead to moral growth.

The journalists we spoke with in Spain, Italy, and Portugal often mentioned their belief in the laws that protect the presumption of innocence and reflected that belief in some of their reporting practices. Acting voluntarily on that commitment constitutes behavior at Kohlberg's highest "post-conventional" level, where ethical reasoning and the decisions themselves are governed by principles of social good and justice. But Ambivalent reporters also frequently violated that commitment. When they did so, they rarely situated their justification in a moral principle that outweighed the presumption of innocence in the particular circumstance. Instead, they frequently displayed reasoning at a lower level—at Kohlberg's "pre-conventional" platform where self-interest—such as career advancement—determined whether rules were obeyed. Such habitual self-focus, and even self-absorption, makes it unlikely that individuals or professions will ask themselves questions about a broader social welfare. Nor is it likely that journalists, as a profession, will write crime stories in ways that promote ethical maturity and higher order reasoning about social justice.

Theories of moral maturity that identify a hierarchy of ethical and intellectual reasoning can be usefully applied to the way in which journalists talk about, and practice, their craft.[17] Although the roots of these theories reach back to classical philosophical ethics, psychologists only began to study moral maturity during the first part of the 20th century when Jean Piaget watched Swiss boys playing marbles. While two-year-olds just put the marbles in their mouths, by the time the boys were seven or eight, they were moving toward more cooperative play and agreeing on rules of the game. A series of four studies done by Harvard scholars later refined these concepts of moral development. Lawrence Kohlberg and William Perry conducted their research with only male subjects, mostly Harvard undergraduates.[18] Kohlberg's and Perry's studies were each countered respectively by Carol Gilligan and Mary Field Belenky et al. who argued that the earlier studies of males were hampered by sexism and class distinction.[19] These feminist scholars questioned female subjects and drew participants from broader socioeconomic backgrounds. All four research projects developed hierarchies of moral reasoning, based on what study respondents told them. All four found that some, but by no means all, persons progress morally from a child-like recognition of what behavior results in reward or in punishment. The lowest level of intellectual development was marked by a simple belief in knowledge as true and fixed; however, even advanced thinkers might use different levels of reasoning for different situations. All four hierarchies reach a peak in which individuals engage in more sophisticated thinking about responsibility to others and social justice for all. Reasoning on these highest levels requires reaching beyond the individual self and one's immediate allegiances, taking a leap of faith, and committing to abstract principles, like social justice and responsibility. When we framed our findings within these moral theories, it seemed to us that most of the Ambivalent journalists to whom we spoke had not yet reached the level where their concerns were for others and for a greater public good.

Scholars have widened the application of these hierarchies beyond their intended relevance to individual moral development. In their study involving 249 subjects, Wilkins and Coleman found journalists in the United States were sophisticated moral thinkers, reasoning well about general moral dilemmas and profession-specific questions.[20] Their complex thinking incorporated elements—duty, character, and veracity—that classical philosophers would recognize, and these interview subjects appeared to have internalized these principles.[21] Wilkins and Coleman's findings suggested "thinking like a journalist involved moral reflection, done both dynamically and at a level that in most instances equals or exceeds the members of the other learned professions."[22] Calling upon these principles requires journalists to move beyond self-focus, which in turn affects how issues are framed in the press and in political forums. "Moving the values of journalism and the tone of public discussion toward a more communitarian and universalist end is compatible with more mature intellectual and ethical orientations," Patterson and Hall wrote in an analysis of journalism and the abortion debate.[23] By contrast, a polarizing black-or-white rhetorical frame freezes discussion politically and ethically on an immature level.

Moral maturity does not always come with age, but it rarely comes without it, and democratic institutions—including a free press—are young in these Mediterranean countries. Serious reforms that ground journalism in a more universal set of values that benefit citizens are springing up in Southern Europe. These new endeavors articulate an agreed-upon commitment to a public mission that sees journalists as serving those citizens. The new direction of the Portuguese Union of Journalists and the fledgling consortia of investigative journalists, like IRPI (Investigative Reporters Project Italy), are examples. But both journalists individually and organizations broadly must battle political, economic, and cultural forces that can block their forward motion to a practice that offers consistent support of democracy, its institutions, and its principles.

While we have outlined the numerous disadvantages to the clientelist practices of police and reporters in these countries, a more positive interpretation can be made: Many journalists in these Ambivalent countries are prompted by a drive that seems akin to the Watchdog instinct to push past official secrecy to inform citizens about matters critical to a healthy democracy. Certainly, that instinct propelled coverage of the *Mani puliti*, or Clean Hands movement in Italy, discussed in Chapter 9, when *L'Espresso* reporter Leo Sisti was a reporter writing about bribes to public officials for government contracts. *Mani puliti* began in the 1990s in Milan where Sisti works. It became a nationwide judicial investigation into political corruption in Italy and led to the collapse of several political parties and the indictment of half of the members of the Italian Parliament.

Journalists unions and government regulatory agencies pave another path to reform in Southern Europe. As we outlined in the last chapter, the Portuguese Union of Journalists elected a new, young board of officers in 2015 with Sofia Branco as president. This board has steered the union away from its close affiliation with the Socialist Party and toward broader advocacy for political transparency and professional development. "I do not think we have a culture of transparency yet," Branco said, speaking of Portugal as a whole. "We do not ask for accountability here. We find another way to say this person is corrupt, and we do not confront publicly." In 2017, the union, along with two other journalism organizations, called the first national Conference of Journalists since 1998 to discuss some of these concepts, and the severe economic conditions that were threatening press freedoms. The Observatório da Comunicacão (Communication Observatory) found that about 20% of the Portuguese media workers had lost or left their jobs between 2007 and 2014. Since then, many publications have closed, and a study by João Miranda, a journalism researcher at Universidade de Coimbra, found that more than half of working journalists were making under €1,000 per month and almost 15% were paid below minimum wage. Branco made clear that journalism's independence and autonomy are strained under such conditions.[24]

The Portuguese regulatory agency ERC (Entidade Reguladora para a Communicação Social or Regulating Entity for Social Communication), unlike its more political predecessor AACS (Alta Autoridade para a Communicação Social or Higher Authority for Social Communication), has a dual mission: to protect the public from the media's power, and to protect the media's autonomy and freedom from external pressures, according to Tânia Soares, head of Media Analysis at ERC. Created in 2006, ERC hears citizens' complaints, but it also monitors and defends the media. "It is our duty to preserve the right to be informed," although, Soares cautioned, the public does not need to know everything. But ERC has yet to prove its worth. Journalists whom we interviewed were skeptical about its abilities to speak for them. In addition, Alberto Arons de Carvalho, ERC's vice president, admitted the Portuguese public is largely unaware of its function. Professor Luis de Sousa of the University of Aveiro shrugged off ERC's claim that it protects the news media. "There have been cases in the past when we [media] were defrauded by regulators' stance," he said. The first day that the courts slapped a gag order on the *Correio da Manhã* and the Cofina media group in the Sócrates' case, ERC should have been protesting, he said.[25] Instead, they remained silent.[26]

In Italy, AGCOM (Autorità per le Garanzie nelle Comunicazioni or Communications Guarantor Authority) is the main regulatory body for all media industries and is responsible for ensuring fair competitive conditions and pluralism in the news. AGCOM is an independent agency but is accountable to Parliament. The board president is appointed by the president of Italy upon the advice of the government; two of the board's four members are elected by the Senate and two by the House of Deputies. Critics have noted that this system, which in practice results in political appointments based on party affiliation, is an impediment to AGCOM's neutrality.[27]

Italy's first freedom of information act was approved by the Council of Ministers in 2017 and went into effect in December of that year. An independent monitoring system has been tasked with overseeing the operation. Although the Act allows the government wide exemptions (for information that may compromise state secrets, public order, national defense, international relations, the state's economic and financial stability, or ongoing criminal investigations), civic groups have applauded the law's approval.[28]

Pressure for change also comes from outside these countries: the European Council, the Council of Europe, and the United Nations have all brought their prescriptive policies about press freedoms to bear.[29] In 2013, UN Special Rapporteur Frank La Rue urged Italy to democratize the media by allocating broadcasting frequencies more fairly, breaking up media monopolies, ensuring transparency in the election of regulatory boards, making public television independent of government, and decriminalizing defamation laws.[30] Italy's leading newspaper, *Il Corriere della Sera*, strongly supported the last recommendation, noting that harsh punishment for journalists had earned Italy a number of rebukes in international tribunals.[31] As of May 2020, the Italian Parliament had removed "insult" from the list of defamations that could be punished as a crime, but proposals to limit criminal charges and possible imprisonment for other forms of defamation were still being considered.[32]

As we have noted throughout discussions about all our media models, the term "public interest" has different definitions in differing contexts. In the British Isles, Canada, and the United States, law, ethics codes, and custom would all facilitate media coverage of an arrest and detention like that of former prime minister of Portugal José Sócrates. Because of his elected position and the concomitant expectations of both transparency and accountability under this democratic model, key details of the alleged crimes would be made public almost automatically. Sócrates would have had virtually no "right" to privacy, and the (hypothetical) Watchdog coverage would have been undertaken in the interest of informing the public, in whose interests he was supposed to be administering the affairs of the country. In contrast, we noted that it was public interest, as defined by the Portuguese, that placed the case beyond the reach of their journalists. While arrest records are never public, the Segredo de Justiça Act can be invoked to create an extra veil of secrecy when public interest is high. From this perspective, public interest is viewed as a justification for withholding information rather than a compelling reason to release it.[33] In the Anglo-Saxon tradition, the public interest is served by opening the process to public scrutiny, beginning with arrest. From this latter perspective, the practice of arresting and detaining people in secret is seen as an invitation to corruption, especially in countries like Italy, Portugal, and Spain, with political dictatorships in their recent histories.[34]

Watchdog reporters—at least when they are at their best—consider various factors connected to what they broadly define as "newsworthiness," as well as weighing the public's need to know in covering crime. In their judgment, public figures score high on both counts, and little besides legal constraints holds back criminal coverage. Protector journalists however have greater regard for privacy. They especially guard private persons and family members but would be unlikely to shield a former prime minister or president under investigation. In Ambivalent countries, the public figure receives the greatest protection both by law and through journalistic practice. While such practices in these Southern European countries include nascent elements of both Watchdog and Protector thinking, this practice of protecting someone like Sócrates shows more deference for power than protection for the vulnerable. Katrin Voltmer writes that journalism under post-authoritarian rule "combines different streams of meanings and practices that originate from the role journalist had under the previous regime, the constraints of the post-authoritarian environment, cultural norms and the perception of Western role models."[35]

Gabriela Bravo, member and spokesperson for Consejo General del Poder Judicial (General Council of the Judiciary), Spain's supreme judiciary body, lamented that in the Aitana case, outlined at the outset of this chapter, an innocent man had been publicly condemned without evidence, while famous politicians accused in corruption cases are given more generous consideration and have their honor and image protected and respected. In this way, she said, Spanish society creates first- and second-class citizens.[36] The accused in the Aitana case was shown in handcuffs, which, jurist Alberto Jabonero wrote, not only caused him to appear guilty in the public, but also trivialized the criminal justice process by implying a disbelief in the benefits of the presumption of innocence.[37] This kind of "trial by media," as such publicity is often called, not only creates a scandal that damages the life of the suspect, but it also creates a harmful paradigm, he said.[38] Building on this assertion, we would add that when citizens cease to believe in the fairness of their democratic institutions, as in this case, the justice system, then the larger system of democracy itself is put at risk. As Ward argues in *Ethical Journalism in a Populist Age*, democracy is often being slowly and almost imperceptibly undermined from within countries or cultures, rather than being attacked from the outside.[39]

Gregorio Saravia, law and ethics lecturer at Madrid's Carlos III University, described Spain as a "low-intensity democracy"; that is, one in which elections and other democratic institutions are in place, but not the concurrent civil liberties that allow citizens to see and assess that the exercise of power is fair and equitable. In clientelist systems like those of the Ambivalent countries, Luis de Sousa of the University of Lisbon said, information is treated as a private resource, not shared publicly (as evidenced by the lack of public records). This lack of faith in, or concern for, a common right of access to information is pointed out as one reason independent journalism has been slow to develop in the region.

Concluding Thoughts On The Ambivalents

Our research on crime reporting indicates that Ambivalent media have transitioned from earlier models of a largely partisan press tied to political parties to one that is now influenced by both commerce and politically motivated owners. But hints on the horizon point to an autonomous journalism that initiates its own inquiries and accepts responsibility for shaping an informed electorate. This analysis leads into the murky territory of the "proper" role and task of journalism that Christians et al. explored. While all "democracies promise rule by the people" and almost all pledge themselves to equality and liberty, their forms and means vary.[40] So, too, do the forms of media, as *Normative Theories of the Media* makes clear.[41] The role of journalism in democracy is so central that it was largely taken for granted until it began to be transformed by information technology in a globalized economy. "The issue is not only what is the role of journalism in society but also above all, what *should* it be. Such a perspective of the media's mission in democracy leads us to a normative level—beyond factual landscapes toward values and objectives."[42] The authors cite Blumler and Gurevitch in saying that "citizens have needs for material to support their political beliefs; guidance in making choices, basic information about events, conditions, and policies; and affective satisfactions to promote engagement in politics."[43] On this, Christians et al. offer an apparent consensus about what journalism should provide.

Voltmer and Hallin and Mancini set out similar characteristics for journalistic professionalism across borders.[44] These include a broad set of norms and standards agreed upon by practitioners in each locale about what constitutes "good" journalism: autonomy, without which journalists could not follow the norms or ethical standards they have set out, and a separation of journalistic expressions of opinion from factual reporting of news.[45] Hallin and Mancini applaud the concept of journalistic independence articulated by an editor who wrote about the need to be "an honest witness" and tell "the story of the present" as the reporter perceives it to be.[46] In this manner, the reporter "serves the public; and this is why journalistic autonomy matters—to preserve not neutrality, but the integrity of this process of social judgment."[47] This idea contrasts with so-called objectivity, a value often claimed—and debated—by journalists in the Watchdog model.[48] The authors suggest that such a coherent view of the journalist's social role can allow for professionalism and political parallelism to exist side by side.

Interviews conducted for this project normally centered on "signal" crimes, the kind of events that set everyone talking. We chose these cases because we believe they give an accurate measure of how well journalism is informing the public about issues around society's moral edges. One side effect of this methodology in the Ambivalent countries is that these are also the crimes most likely to trigger the clientelist practices among police, prosecutors, and reporters. By their newsworthy nature, these cases demonstrate the strong inclination toward Watchdog-style exposés. What they may mask, reporters were often at pains to tell us, is the more Protectionist approaches of crime coverage in these Ambivalent countries. In less exceptional crime cases, these journalists do routinely show respect for the presumption of innocence beyond lip service, and they fiercely defend privacy for young offenders, who are also protected by law.

Watchdog ethics reflect the Enlightenment's faith in the value of each individual and upright person. Its ideals of a social contract with free speech and free press rights took strong hold in Great Britain and the United States beginning in the 18th century. But Professor Gregorio Saravia of Madrid's Carlos III University said this ethical and political approach had relatively little effect in Spain. Enlightenment values align with those found by Kohlberg in his study of moral reasoning in boys and men. At the top of

Kohlberg's hierarchy, the principle of justice, based on fairness and equity, is used to determine moral permissibility and prohibition. It requires "detachment, which is the mark of mature moral judgment in the justice perspective."[49] But at the same time, detachment becomes the moral problem in the care perspective—that is, caring about and caring for others—because it fails to attend to particular needs.[50] The reasoning found in our interviews with journalists and experts in Protector countries contained more elements of an ethics of care perspective in moral judgment than any of the other countries we considered. Carol Gilligan identified care as the chief moral determinant in girls and women in her 1982 breakthrough book, *In a Different Voice*.[51] Attention to the particular needs and circumstances of individuals, the mark of mature moral judgment in the care perspective, becomes the moral problem in the justice perspective, that is, failure to treat others fairly, as equals.[52] Nona Lyons provided a comparison of Kohlberg's and Gilligan's models.[53] In Kohlberg's morality of justice, individuals are defined as separate from one another; all relationships are grounded in reciprocity; impartial rules are employed to resolve conflicts; and judgments are based in equal treatment. Within a morality of care, individuals are defined within their connections to one another; relationships are grounded in response to others on their terms. Moral problems are issues of relationship and responsibility, and the best moral outcomes maintain and restore relationships.[54] Gilligan and Attanucci found men and women used both modes of reasoning, but not equally.[55] In her original work, Gilligan denied that these modes of reasoning are inherently gendered or that they are incompatible. In fact, she argued that they are complementary: Both function fully in the morally mature individual. We concur. While attitudes of individualism or caring can be attributed more to the masculine gender in the former and the feminine in the latter, such attitudes are embedded in cultures that are themselves gendered and encourage boys and girls along these differing lines.

William Perry notes that being able to hold onto complexity and ambiguity is a mark of ethical and intellectual maturity.[56] It appears then that the real hierarchy of moral decision-making rests in the ability to hold onto reasoning based on justice and rights, on the one hand, and on care and responsibility, on the other, and not lose sight of either. Gilligan and Attanucci describe this possibility at the end of their article "Two Moral Orientations":

> If moral maturity consists in the ability to sustain concerns about justice
> and care . . . then the encounter with orientation difference can tend to

offset errors in moral perception. Like the moment when the ambiguous figure shifts from a vase to two faces, the recognition that there is another way to look at a problem may expand moral understanding.[57]

And in this possibility lies the pathway opening to journalists at the crossroads in the Ambivalent model, as their democracies and their journalisms mature and benefit from the lessons globalization can bring.

11

Conclusion

What Comparison Lets Us See

Murder stories—from domestic disputes to massive hate killings—rivet public attention as they play out on the furthest fringes of human behavior. Because all cultures hold that human life is sacred,[1] murder ignites the imagination and shocks audiences by demonstrating the human capacity for ruthlessness. However, while news coverage attracts attention, murder stories also provoke complaints from people: the details are too graphic, the material is overwhelming, sympathies are misplaced, or complex lives and histories are overly simplified or distorted. Crimes of a sexual nature, and even many lesser trespasses, evoke similar reactions. Reporters and editors puzzle over where to draw lines about what to include and what to exclude. No wonder. Culture, which in large part determines the limits of taste, is a shapeshifter in motion with the times, the place, the media outlet, the generation, and even the individual.

At the beginning of this book, we questioned whether crime coverage practices in various capitalist democracies could be identified and what they might suggest about deeper, underlying cultural values like public, private, public right to know, and justice. We believe we have indeed demonstrated that while differing journalistic practices exist, there are enough similarities among reporting habits and the underlying attitudes that inform them to enable grouping our ten countries into three media models: (1) The Protectors (Sweden, the Netherlands, Germany), where reporters' default is to shelter those accused of crimes out of concern for innocent family members, the presumption of innocence, and the success of rehabilitation and reintegration; (2) the Watchdogs (the United Kingdom, Ireland, Canada, and the United States), where reporters give highly specific details of crimes and criminals (within legal boundaries), and the concern to keep an eye on the authorities outweighs consideration for the accused; and (3) the Ambivalents (Spain, Portugal, and Italy), where journalists usually follow strict privacy dicta set out in law and in ethics codes about naming an accused, but they also break

Murder in Our Midst. Romayne Smith Fullerton and Maggie Jones Patterson, Oxford University Press (2021). © Oxford University Press. DOI: 10.1093/oso/9780190863531.003.0011.

these rules when the stories are big or the persons involved are sufficiently newsworthy and sales-worthy.

Our comparative approach allowed us to explore our own and others' conceptual definitions of key concepts, but it also forced us to consider the limits of their application. Terms' definitions differ in subtle and sometimes overt ways, not just among models but sometimes between countries within those designations. They can also change and evolve over time. Because they are a part of culture, words and their applications are not static. Still, comparison sensitizes us to variation and similarity, urging journalists and citizens everywhere, in a gesture of both personal and public self-reflection, to think about how and why we make the choices we do. Further, we can, and in fact, we *ought* to, consider whether these practices are congruent to the values we hold as members of a community, a country, a nation. We can opt to revise them if they cease to match our democratic goals. Throughout this project, we were intensely aware that such work can be ethnocentric, and we have endeavored not to impose our beliefs about which systems are "best," but rather to consider whether each democracy, individually defined and constituted, is well served by the type of crime coverage being offered. The point of the comparison was not to create a hierarchy, but to demonstrate how different considerations become paramount in each model—care, responsibility, rights, and justice. And there are different ways that reporters might achieve "good" ends: ones that sustain or build on aspects of a shared democratic life. We posit that crime coverage served as an effective lens to compare various practices and to offer an evaluation of the ways in which a range of democratic values are upheld, sustained, or undermined by choices reporters make on a daily basis. As Hallin and Mancini point out in *Comparing Media Systems*, "Comparative analysis makes it possible to notice things we did not notice and therefore had not conceptualized, and it also forces us to clarify the scope and applicability of the concepts we do employ."[2]

Comparing Murder in Our Midst

Murder always tells an intimate story of loss, grief, betrayal, and violation. In this sense, it can seem personal and even private. While it deeply affects those directly involved, it is, always and everywhere, a crime against the state, and therefore, a public concern. Journalism bridges the gap between the horror of the private act and public nature of the crime. Reporters use storytelling to drive audiences across that bridge. A wrong turn, and the story can tumble over the brink. The job is demanding, and it's not without risks.

All crime can be examined as a form of social betrayal, but for what larger purpose? No one method of telling crime stories will work for all audiences, not even for those within one country, much less across national borders. Still, we have argued in this book that placing different reporting choices side by side in countries similar enough to bear comparison lets us see why some crime stories strike a balance between what is private and what must be subjected to public discussion, while others miss the mark. Comparison lifts the blinders that cause journalists to assume that their particular practice is the right—or even the only—one. It shows us differences and similarities, shared values, and varying preferences. Most importantly, it makes visible journalism's mission, shared across these developed democracies, and tells us what that mission suggests about the "right" and "wrong" ways to report the news.

Why Reporting Practices Differ

Within the borders of each of the ten countries in our sample, reporters, editors, media experts, and academics were remarkably uniform in describing normative journalistic ethics and practice. This consistency also applied, albeit more loosely, to the three models we created, despite a few particular practices that differed more within these models than between them.[3] We chose our sample countries from the three models Hallin and Mancini identify. We sought to discover whether journalism ethics and practice follow a pattern similar to what they found. Since the publication of *Comparing Media Systems* in 2004, Hallin and Mancini's findings have been both criticized and reaffirmed by scholars, including Hallin and Mancini themselves.[4] As we have outlined, our findings show that journalistic ethics and practice do indeed conform to Hallin and Mancini's original models. In each country, they look at the news media's shared history, its professionalism, economic foundations, and political relationship to government, but the first of these factors was primary. "Our approach to social theory is an historical one," Hallin and Mancini wrote in a 2012 response to their critics.[5] Given their historical approach, it is not surprising that our results traced a similar configuration to the ones they drew. Ethical values and newsroom practices are shaped by history and exist in the larger historical, economic, and political context.

In reviewing the models in *Comparing Media Systems*, scholars have questioned, for example, whether Britain's strong public broadcasting and politically polarized press make it incompatible with Hallin and Mancini's Liberal model, which the United Kingdom shares with Canada, Ireland, and the United States. Similarly, some suggest Portugal's news media may have moved too far away from the political parallelism (where outlets are aligned with particular political parties or interests) that, in part, placed that country in the same category as Spain and Italy. And Germany, with its strong public broadcasting, absence of press subsidies,[6] and high level of political parallelism in the press, arguably shares more with the United Kingdom than with the Nordic countries with which it was grouped in Hallin and Mancini's Democratic Corporatist model.[7] These are all valid questions, but they ignore that the press is a form of communication and conversation through which a society affirms its history and creates its present. As James Carey wrote:

> We must . . . discard the view of language as reference, correspondence, and representation and the parallel view that the function of language is primarily to express assertions about the world. Then we must substitute the view that language—communication—is a form of action—or, better, interaction—that not merely represents or describes but actually molds or constitutes the world.[8]

In this passage, as elsewhere, Carey displays a penchant for dichotomies. He sets up a similar opposition in his theory of the ritual vs. transmission models of communication. He posits that continental Europe adheres to the ritual communication form and North America to a transmission model, but we would counter with a more nuanced portrait. European journalists do envision their mission as one of transmitting accurate information, as well as reinforcing the culture. Their concerns for protecting both the families of those accused of crime and the presumption of innocence embrace an ethic of care for persons affected by crime coverage as an intrinsic part of the community. Such concerns are largely absent among reporters in the Watchdog countries, where the accused are mostly expelled from the community. At the same time, however, Jack Katz characterizes citizens reading, viewing, or listening to American crime coverage as a "daily moral workout," a practice that allows them continually to define and redefine their community's moral boundaries. Reading crime coverage is a function that seeks to bind people together, to create community, and, therefore, holds more closely to a ritual model rather than one based purely on transmission.

Until relatively recently, citizens consumed news within geographic boundaries as small as a village and rarely larger than a nation. News production both reflected and shaped a shared cultural identity. Hallin and Mancini's three models, and our three, contain countries that share common linguistic roots. The Watchdogs speak English; the Protectors' tongues are Germanic; and the Ambivalents all speak Romance languages. These groups of nations are strongly bound by history and geography. Historically, they traded ideas, as well as goods. They shared attitudes and beliefs that influenced the development of their cultures and institutions. Journalism, too, both reflects and creates the culture in which it is embedded. Given its freedom and independence from coercion within a democratic model, the practice of journalism is likely to assume the shape that history and culture have bestowed upon it. It is likely to mirror the underlying cultural values that it has both emanated from and reflected back to its citizens.

All ten countries in our sample are capitalist democracies, and they share some of their history and many of their ideals: equal treatment before the law, the right to the presumption of innocence, the right to fair trial, a free press, and a public right to know. When these ideals clash—as they inevitably do—priorities must be determined by those who live in each locale. This exercise of prioritization reflects each nation's particular history, culture, and value system. Once in place, the exercise becomes habit. A resulting attitude permeates newsrooms such that news practices become routinized and nearly invisible to those who perform them. This is one of the reasons we could not simply ask journalists in various parts of the world, "So tell us: How do you cover crime, and what values do you think those choices suggest you and your fellow citizens hold?" Instead, it was important to start with the practices themselves and to allow our interview subjects to talk about why they made the choices they did (and do). When Karst Tates launched his failed and fatal attempt to assassinate Queen Beatrix in the Netherlands, ANP, the Dutch national news service, referred to him only as Karst T. "to protect his family," editor Liesbeth Buitink told us. She put her hand over her mouth and gasped when she heard what American reporters often publish about much more run-of-the-mill criminals. "Why would you do that to someone? What if he had children?" she asked. In contrast, when a white supremacist shot and killed a guard in Washington's Holocaust Museum, reporters for the U.S. national news service sought out his neighbors, his children, even his former wife, used all their names, and publicly exposed whatever they could uncover about the shooter. Watchdog reporters were surprised when we told them about the habits of their Protector counterparts. While some found

Protector practices thought-provoking or even admirable, many echoed the emphatic response of Irish crime reporter Michael O'Toole: "I think it's a disgrace." To the Watchdogs, the public's business belongs in the public light, even though many admit that competition often leads their pursuits beyond what can be justified through an appeal to the public right to know.

Sharing the Primacy of Public Trust

Journalism practiced within a democracy has to hold the public trust if it is to sustain what we argue is its primary mission: providing citizens with the information they need for reasoned public discussion and genuine self-determination. As Ward noted, "While journalism can (and does) exist without democracy, no form of democracy worth having can exist without a journalism dedicated to democratic principles."[9] Central, then, is the idea of a public trust that holds two congruent and equally applicable interpretations. First, that members of the public—citizens—place their trust in what the press reports. They see journalists as gathering and disseminating information vital to the health of their communities and countries. In part, too, journalism provides both the facts for that discussion and the public space in which citizens can participate. For their part, journalists must search earnestly for the truth, offering facts in context and publicly pronouncing that they work in the public interest. Only in this way can the public come to understand journalism's practices, appreciate that the profession is one shaped by ethics, and thus trust its credibility. Second, the press acts in trust for the public's right to know when it serves as the public's eyes and ears, supporting, monitoring, and, when necessary, critiquing the performance of its democratic institutions.

We have focused on the coverage of crime and the criminal justice system in order to compare differing choices reporters and media institutions make. Within this frame, we can evaluate—or at least begin to evaluate—how well each model serves the public trust and with what ethical considerations. This is not to imply a hierarchy, but rather to see how different ethical considerations are foregrounded or minimized in various situations. To organize and summarize what we have been exploring throughout this book, we have created a matrix (Figure 11.1) . This figure adapts and blends two previously published illustrations: (1) Lennart Weibull's model of how the Swedish press approaches its treatment of the private vs. public person in the private vs. public sphere,[10] and (2) the matrix of Self in Domain published by Maggie Patterson and Megan Hall in an analysis of the American abortion debate.[11]

[1]	[3]
CARE	*RESPONSIBILITY*
Private person Private event	Private person Private event
[2]	[4]
RIGHTS	*JUSTICE*
Private person Private event	Private person Private event

Figure 11.1 Self in Domain

In this Self in Domain matrix, each quadrant represents a set of roles, contexts, and activities that influence the ways people often frame ethical considerations.

To garner and keep the public trust, the press must weigh—and show that it weighs—the public's need (not want) to know against the harm that coverage and publicity can cause. The process of weighing requires putting long-term credibility ahead of short-term ratings boosts and forces journalists to make difficult decisions. Readers and viewers may bite on stories that appeal to their prurient interests, but most people are not fooled, regardless of country. Many know that they are being baited to feed a media outlet's hunger to beat the competition, to garner profit, or to advance individual careers. While ratings and readership may follow exploitative stories, resentment—not trust—is never far behind.[12] Public reaction displayed at the Leveson Inquiry in England, for example, laid bare the British people's antipathy for the tabloids' abuses, even while many continued to consume them.

Quadrant [1], the private person in the private event, describes a crime that is committed by a person not generally known in the public sphere. The crime may be minor or major, but with little consequence beyond the immediate family and intimate community. Such stories may only be newsworthy in small markets or when the event itself is highly unusual or indicative of shifting norms. In this first quadrant, individual concerns—as opposed to the common good—are paramount. The ethic of care should be shown for the welfare of the persons involved, and, in such instances, privacy claims commonly outweigh the public's need to know. Reporters in Protector countries generally show this care when they choose not to cover such events, and if they do (perhaps the story is highly unusual, for example), they voluntarily hide the identities of those involved because they are not germane to the public conversation. The Ambivalent reporters often do the same, but their actions are not always voluntary and, therefore, are not wholly done out of the journalists' sense of care. The Ambivalent reporters may not be alerted that such an event has taken place because the accused, at least initially, is being shielded from public scrutiny by law. As we have outlined, legal restraints on crime coverage vary from one country to the next within the Watchdog model. Watchdog reporters often consider any legal restrictions as a violation of the public's right to information and an invitation to police and prosecutorial corruption.[13] When free to act and to report, Watchdog reporters often follow their nose for news and disregard potential harm to the persons involved—those accused as well as wholly innocent family members.

A domestic incident involving persons who are not public figures would fit into Quadrant [1]. Family murder-suicides, for example, might be seen as private events, but they are routine stories in the Watchdog countries of the United Kingdom, Ireland, Canada, and the United States. In Ireland, the press has shrugged off much of the influence of the British press that had invaded Dublin. A 2008 reform, led by journalists and the Irish media industry, created a new national press council that encourages adherence to its code of ethics. Ireland's first press ombudsman, John Horgan, while we were in his office, fielded a call from a village priest asking for help. A pestering press scrum was gathering outside the home of a family who were in shock after a murder-suicide. Horgan successfully appealed to reporters at the scene to put compassion and cooperation in front of competition, and the press backed off. "Sometimes you have to be proactive about these things because prevention is better than the cure," Horgan said. The Irish looked to Sweden as a model for their reform, and Swedish reporters and editors almost always conclude that the ethic of care for persons involved outweighs a public interest in such instances.

Decisions about how news coverage should play out in Quadrant [2], when a private person is involved in a public event, vary widely within and among the three models. While there may be little doubt about the public nature of the crime, the alleged perpetrators in these instances are previously unknown to the public. Therefore, concern for the individual remains prominent, and conflicts of rights come into play. The nature of the crime may place it within the public sphere, but violation of the privacy rights of suspects and their families may not be warranted. Open democracy demands that the public be informed, but its right to know the identity of suspects or perpetrators can be disputed and weighed against harm to defendants and their families. Privacy rights are not the only consideration here. The right to preserve reputation or to a fair trial and an unbiased jury may also outweigh the public's right to know.[14]

After Karst Tates killed several people, and inadvertently himself, while trying to assassinate the queen, a number of Dutch news outlets not only used his full name but also ran a graphic photograph of him in his crashed car. To the dismay of some in the Dutch press and the public, the photo won a national news award that year. But the Dutch national news service, ANP (Algemeen Nederlands Persbureau), withheld Tates' surname, even after he died, and his family granted ANP an exclusive interview. The Dutch news media agreed this case occupies a moral edge, and varying decisions about the "right" way to cover it were legitimate. Similarly, most Swedish news outlets broke with their usual protective practices and named the man accused of assassinating Anna Lindh, minister of foreign affairs, in 2003. Reporters gave complicated reasons for this anomaly and situated those reasons in how they best served the public interest. In this instance, the public's right to know superseded care for the suspect's individual welfare, as well as his right to privacy.

In England, the maligning of Christopher Jefferies, who was initially arrested (but never charged) in the murder of Joanna Yeates, was an extreme case of abuse of privacy by the British tabloids. Yeates' mysterious disappearance was already in the national spotlight before her body was found, and the police and then the press pounced on the retired schoolteacher. One of the tabloids' tactics was to mine online comments from Jefferies' adolescent students and put a malevolent spin on any negative ones. In his statement to the Leveson Inquiry, Jefferies maintained he never fully regained his reputation, despite a public acknowledgment of his innocence and the substantial settlements he won against the offending newspapers. Whether suspects are ultimately proven to be guilty, no public need justifies demonizing them and exposing their families to public shame. When reporters' stories portray accused persons, and even convicted criminals, as one-dimensional bad folks, they rob citizens of what they need to consider; that is, what crime can illuminate about their community's ills. The intense individual focus of such stories may provide some temporary satisfaction that singular justice has been served, but these tales fail to initiate debate about the roots of crimes' causes. Under these circumstances, such discussions usually do not, and perhaps cannot, even occur. What ought to be paramount is the right of citizens to information about the health of their communities.

Two cases in Pittsburgh, however, paint an alternative picture with the same Watchdog brush. After Richard Poplawski's horrific crime of killing three police officers who were arriving at his home in response to his mother's call about a domestic dispute, reporters for the *Pittsburgh Post-Gazette* dug into his past. They connected his outburst to his mental health history and his consumption of conspiracy websites that convinced him the police were coming to confiscate his guns. Almost a decade later, the same newspaper won a Pulitzer Prize for Breaking News for the staff's coverage of the mass shooting during services at the Tree of Life Synagogue. Again, the newspaper documented the psychological profile of the killer, Robert Bowers, as a loner obsessed with paranoid conspiracy theories. He kept a shotgun by his door and worried that United Nations "blue hats" might come to get him.[15] Like Poplawski, Bowers, too, became a follower of "aggressive online provocateurs of the right wing's fringe,"[16] *Post-Gazette* reporter Rich Lord's article told readers. He wrote, "According to experts who study extremism, the Internet and social media have created new pathways for strident ideology to radicalism."[17]

By exploring this issue in their articles, Lord and other reporters in the United States and elsewhere are waking the public to what might be seen as the moral and legal edges of free speech rights. They point to a connection between actual violent actions and the conspiracy echo chambers on the Internet that urge such aggression. The public can weigh the similarity of this connection to yelling "fire!" in a crowded theater, the classic limit to free speech in U.S. legal history.[18] In the two *Post-Gazette* examples, defendants are portrayed as complicated persons, neither demonized nor sacrificed on the altar of profits and competition but held up as indicators of wider social threats. Guided by responsibility, journalistic decisions can both explore the individual's background and emphasize the common good.

In Quadrant [3], a public person involved in a private event, the differences in journalistic practice are stark and surprising. We are not arguing here whether such events should be a part of the public record; that is a matter of law and beyond our current consideration. The question within journalism ethics is whether such events should be the subject of media coverage. The Associated Press' photograph of Dominique Strauss-Kahn's perp walk in New York shocked the French, not only because showing such a degrading and prejudicial moment is illegal in France, but also because the allegation of sexual misconduct against him might well be considered a private matter in

France and many other countries. In Sweden, for example, Lennart Weibull told us, a public figure is still considered entitled to a private life. Such an approach opens that entitlement, and its limits, to interpretation. Only those matters that pertain to the subject's performance in public office are considered legitimate public business. But this line is contestable.

A similar entitlement once prevailed in the United States. White House photographers turned their lenses away from President Franklin D. Roosevelt's wheelchair and legs hobbled by polio. And reporters ignored sexual peccadilloes in the White House as recently as the John F. Kennedy administration, from 1961 to 1963. In parts of Europe, particularly in the Protector countries, the press continues to draw a line of privacy between what actions do or do not pertain to the official's performance in office. That line has faded in most Watchdog countries. Now, public officials have virtually no claim to privacy under the law or in commonly accepted ethical practice. After revelations of President Richard Nixon's underhanded behavior were uncovered in the Watergate scandal, the American press and the public went searching for ways to measure the character of candidates for public office. For a time, sexual fidelity became that yard stick, but its efficacy was short-lived. President Bill Clinton's fling with White House intern Monica Lewinsky was laid bare in excruciating detail, but he remained in office. At the time, ethicists debated whether public officials had the right to guard their privacy. Swedish-born American ethicist Sissela Bok considered both Clinton's conduct and his right to lie to the public about it:

> People disagree about boundaries between conduct in the White House that is of genuine public concern and what is purely private. . . . In public as in private life, everyone has reason to consider to what extent their actions erode or help restore this social good of trust. But public servants, doctors, clergy, lawyers, bankers, journalists and other professionals have a special responsibility in this regard, given the privileges they have been granted. Public officials, above all, can have a uniquely deleterious effect on trust. When they act so as to undermine trust, this cuts at the roots of democracy.[19]

A lie about an affair would be justified, professor of law and philosophy Anita L. Allen suggested, if, for example, a public official were working to rebuild a marriage, because making the mistake may have been done in private, but so might its correction.[20] The tensions between whether public concerns or private ones ought to be paramount are clear in Bok's and Allen's statements. In more recent times, numerous allegations of sexual misconduct by President Donald Trump have cropped up. They have become a battleground between members of the #MeToo movement, who see the possible truth of these allegations as indicators of aggressive disdain for women, and Trump's faithful supporters, who appear to shrug them off as purely private matters. Patrick L. Plaisance, in *Media Ethics: Key Principles for Responsible Practice*, points out that privacy's value and its importance lie in how it facilitates association *with* people, not independence *from* them.[21] This more public purpose for privacy becomes especially poignant in matters concerning public officials. Journalists' ethical focus must be on whether any invasion of privacy is conducted in the interest of the public's need to know information that might serve one or more of the functions of democracy.

Quadrant [4] designates happenings concerning a public person and a public event; these are considered the public's business by journalists in all our sample countries. As we outlined in Part 3 on the Ambivalents, in the case of former Prime Minister José Sócrates of Portugal, the state may think otherwise about what should be public and move to keep any and all information under wraps and out of the public eye, at least during the investigation. But crime-reporting practices in Portugal, Spain, and Italy, such as seeking extra-legal leaks to access such information, point toward a desire for increased access to information and a wider interpretation of the public's right to information. In stories that fall within this quadrant, justice must be served, and be seen to be served, but how and when these matters are seen by the public are open to interpretation within different democratic structures; however, under this ethic of justice, the public interest is generally seen as paramount.

In Canada, conflicting perspectives arose when two media outlets alleged that then Toronto mayor Rob Ford had smoked crack cocaine. The story was broken first on the American website Gawker and then on the front pages of Canada's largest metropolitan daily, the *Toronto Star*. The stories were based on a granular cell phone video that *Star* reporters had seen but not copied. The video appeared to show an incoherent Ford lighting the bottom of a pipe and making slurred homophobic and racist remarks. While many members of the media felt strongly that this information was necessary because of Ford's position, many citizens expressed dismay at what they considered unwarranted invasions of Ford's privacy. In fact, Ford's case sits on the edge between a private and public event. An elected executive of a major city—as opposed to an official serving in the legislative or judicial parts of government—is always on call in case of an emergency. Therefore, this reasoning held, evidence that he was incapacitated and, therefore, unable to perform his office, put his conduct in the public realm.[22]

Transnational Commitment to Democracy

As one reporter told us, in the context of whether journalists need to be popular to do their jobs: "If you need a friend, get a dog."[23] Journalists cannot avoid criticism, and it is not their role to please people, or to be liked; instead, news professionals must justify their decision-making about crime coverage, and all coverage, by considering what is best done in the public interest. As Ward, Christians, and Kovach and Rosenstiel have argued, reporting should not take a neutral stand in defending democracy and its institutions. In *Ethical Journalism in a Populist Age*, Ward wrote, "Democratically engaged journalism must not be a neutral spectator or a channel of information that merely repeats peoples' alleged facts. Critical evaluation and informed interpretation motivated by a clear notion of the goal of democratic media are essential."[24]

This is not to suggest that responsible, thoughtful, and ethical journalism can't be executed in a variety of ways in different democracies that define the public interest in a manner unique to each locale; in fact, we have argued throughout this book that it can. Consider the Protectors' default reporting practice of not naming persons accused of a crime. Under this model, what the reporters consider to be important to the public are the details of the crime, not the specifics of the person or persons involved. Naming the person who is accused is not something, from their perspective, that citizens always need to know to understand the crime. In fact, they might argue stories that employ such a focus on the life and details of an accused person can lead citizens to develop a prurient interest in crime, to fixate on ways in which someone is not "like them." Then, it becomes a simple matter to distance society's responsibility for the underlying causes of crime: poverty, lack of education, lack of equal opportunity, and so on.

The Winds of Change

Data collection for this book spanned nearly ten years. We began our initial study with a consideration of the media coverage of Karst Tates and the

Queensday incident in the Netherlands in 2009, and we completed our final set of interviews with reporters, editors, and news professionals in Germany in 2018. Throughout that time, and beginning even earlier, there were two significant developments that affected and shaped crime coverage and will continue to do so for the foreseeable future. The first is the widespread popularity and use of social media in reporting crime (building on Internet usage generally). Initially, social media's influence was downplayed by many of our interview subjects, but in our most recent interviews, concerns about Twitter or Facebook and the manner in which information can be disclosed and circulated, without regard for laws or ethics, sometimes took center stage in our discussions. As we outlined earlier, people working for legacy media in the Netherlands, with whom we did follow-up interviews in 2018, are standing firm in their protectionist policies and are resistant to populist accusations that they are throwing a blanket over immigrant crime. In contrast, material gathered from interviews in Germany conducted during the same year (2018) suggested that many mainstream papers, and the German Press Council itself, made changes to their ethics policies because of pressure from social media and accusations that journalists and their protectionist approaches were instruments of the German government.

The second development that is buffeting routine crime coverage practices everywhere is the massive worldwide migration of people. Within the countries in our sample, immigration as a news item hit a crescendo in 2015 with Angela Merkel's welcoming nearly a million migrants and asylum seekers as part of Germany's "*Willkommenskultur*," or culture of welcoming.[25] But the volatile discussions certainly have not ended there: In Canada in 2019, racism and anti-immigrant sentiment was growing across the country, and politicians and media commentators employed partisan and sometimes misleading terms when describing the world's most vulnerable: asylum seekers.[26] As we have outlined throughout this book, these phenomena—technology and migration—not only challenge ethics policies but also threaten the very existence of differing journalistic crime coverage practices employed in each country. Hallin and Mancini predicted, in the conclusion to *Comparing Media Systems*, that the North Atlantic Liberal model, with its standards and norms, would eventually prevail, and journalistic practices innate to that system would become the default in the other models as well. We would add a slightly nuanced, additional observation: It's possible that if we do not speak up for respecting others' practices, that journalism may default to an even more extreme tell-all style than what's accepted at present in the United States, the United Kingdom, Canada, or any of the countries of the North Atlantic model. The reason is this: Technology has no ethic, and populism's code is questionable at best. If journalists want to preserve their unique media practices, they need to educate themselves and their audiences about the reasoning behind these practices and the ways they reflect cultural values. Then, they must defend crime coverage approaches that best match each democracy's beliefs about what's public, private, and what constitutes justice. An educated public discussion about what is at stake is much needed. As we noted earlier in this book, the Dutch Press Council recently rewrote its code and stuck with the rule that ethnicity, religion, and other minority status should only be reported when they are necessary to the understanding of the story.[27] The press council first wrote this policy after the news media came under fire when anti-Islam politician Pim Fortuyn was assassinated in 2002 and filmmaker Theo Van Gogh in 2004. "We were accused then of looking away," said Thomas Bruning, head of the journalists' union. "We are used to the idea that journalists are seen as leftist and siding with Islam, but whatever we do, we will be under pressure," Hans Laroes, former head of the press council, said. "I know how to do journalism. I don't say that from arrogance but from professional confidence. . . . We do consider impact. It is the difference between being objective and being a professional, which goes to judgment and standards."

As we have noted, many to whom we spoke throughout this project expressed genuine surprise that the way *they* covered crime—naming or not naming an accused person, or when to name someone, for example— was not the way that *everyone* covered crime. Today, journalists' work can be disseminated around the world without any consideration of whether what's being told (or how) might dissolve cultural differences or undermine each community's right to set its own reporting standards. These standards should—and usually do—reflect the values of that community's citizens. Adding another layer of complication, technology itself can emphasize some elements of a story and minimize others, but an ethic of technology has never been seriously addressed. Clifford Christians, in his *Media Ethics and Global Justice in the Digital Age*, takes on the challenge: He posits we ought to have an ethics that considers specifically the physical characteristics of any transmission medium. Borrowing from Christians, we suggest that the medium of the Internet, with few rules and no single entity in charge, inclines toward a tell-absolutely-everything style. This bias inherent in the technology threatens the protective behaviors of countries in all three models, as well as some other countries beyond this study whose laws or ethics policies some-times favor withholding information about crimes, including the name of the accused. Canadian communications scholar Marshall McLuhan was prophetic in warning about technologies' impact. He was deeply concerned about the effects of television when it became widely used in the early 1960s, and he feared that many did not consider how different kinds of transmission affected people in unpredictable and unique ways. He wrote, "The medium is the message. This is merely to say that the personal and social consequences of any medium—that is, of any extension of ourselves—result from the new scale that is introduced into our affairs by each extension of ourselves, or by any new technology."[28] While he was not an ethics scholar, his inflection is implicit: We ought to pay attention to the global impact of a medium—think about how its inherent characteristics change society for better or worse, rather than focus exclusively on content. In short, the Internet has a social ef-fect and social consequences. Harold Innis, from whom McLuhan borrowed many ideas, urged people to consider how "changes in communication technology affected culture by altering the structure of interests (the things thought about) by changing the character of symbols (the things thought with), and by changing the nature of community (the arena in which thought developed)."[29] Innis is suggesting that every communication technology—the phonetic alphabet, the printing press, a contemporary magazine, a com-puter, and today, the Internet and social media—creates, shapes and (re) produces the attitudes, values, and character of its culture(s) or public(s). But in the context of our current consideration of crime-reporting practices, the question becomes: Given how this technology operates, will coverage de-volve to a single style, a "tell-everything" that's close to—but goes beyond—the routine in the United States, for example, but is not the norm in the Netherlands? If it does, a great deal will be lost.

Conclusion: Murder in Our Midst

Our research foregrounds two types of ethical issues. The first is not new: Old and tired ways of reporting crime are failing citizens. Ethically told crime stories—especially signal crime stories—need to take news readers and viewers beyond the personal and into the issues that crime reveals about an unraveling around the edges of the social fabric. The second type of ethical issue is a relatively new problem brought on by Internet sites, bloggers, and ordinary people on social media, who bypass national codes of ethics by putting information online that mainstream journalists have decided to withhold. Web blogs, such as Gawker in the United States, Flashback in Sweden, and GeenStijl in the Netherlands, operate inside the countries where they are distributed but outside the institutions and ethical codes of journalism. They splash information across social media that journalists have not yet verified or have concluded would cause more harm than benefit. Historically, tabloids played a similar role. Once the news is in the public realm, all journalists are forced to either ignore it or follow suit with coverage. At the same time, the web now carries crime stories across geographic boundaries, and many of those stories are written and edited by journalists who have little or no knowledge of ethical or legal codes that govern their counterparts in other countries. While these stories may be considered ethical in the countries in which they were produced, they often violate the norms elsewhere. Solutions to these problems are not easy, but what must guide them is clear.

As the simple truism goes: Crime, like sex, sells. When selling becomes the primary goal, however, news stories lure audiences with shock and horror. A good-versus-evil frame paints perpetrators as fearsome and loathsome outliers and outsiders, not like the rest of us. Although most crimes and those involved in them are often all part of one region, this story frame creates a distance from, not connection to, the community. British tabloids, for example, regularly serve up a spectrum of such deviants, Jewkes and Greer write.[30] By extension, these publications encourage any number of "oppositional classificatory systems: 'insider' and 'outsiders,' 'us' and 'them,' men and women, black and white, 'normal' and 'deviant.'"[31] We would add "native born and immigrant" to that list. Crime reporting that engages in such a process of signification can generate moral indignation. Instead of coming together to address problems, communities can react by retreating from public space, which citizens come to perceive as a "mean" place where personal danger and exploitation threaten.[32] In countries like the United States, this "othering" of accused and convicted persons has contributed to extreme criminal justice policies that have extracted the "others" from the community's midst and warehoused them in prisons under long, mandatory sentences. Thus, justice is seen to be done; the cancer is excised, but with little or no examination of its causes or possible prevention that might benefit society in the future. Because crime stories drive powerful fear into communities, news professionals need to include more contextual information, including showing how violence is rare, predictable, and largely, preventable.

Alternative forms of crime reporting can pull communities together toward constructive problem-solving. The remedy Coleman and Thorson offer is for journalists to cover crime as a public health issue.[33] Reporters can then apply an ethic of care, so that alleged criminals are seen as a part of the community, and that community can then better understand the causes, motivations, situations, and implications of the crime. In this way, conversations can implicate the group's, as well as the individual's, responsibility and address the challenges of violence in its midst. There is precedent for such methods of cooperative problem-solving. The causes of violent crime, like the causes of traffic fatalities, are well-known. Addressing automobile fatalities as a public health issue in the United States (and elsewhere) led to the institution of multiple mandatory safety features, most notably seatbelts in 1968. As a result of such measures, traffic fatalities continue to fall steadily, despite an increase in cars on the road.[34] With a similar alternative framing, crime stories can signal physical and social disorders that point to a need for protective action. They can also instigate means of dealing with the perceived causes of the deviance and its violent results.[35]

To do this, journalism needs to evolve in the way it frames crime stories and conceptualizes crime and its causes. David Simon, former *Baltimore Sun* police reporter and script writer for the television series *The Wire* and *Treme*, believes journalism generally needs to take a broader, more sociological approach. He has criticized the news beat system, which he sees as boxing reporters into what the *Columbia Journalism Review* calls a "rifle-shot approach." Such approaches fail to connect malfunctioning social systems like criminal justice, schools, politics, and journalism, which often work together to reinforce poverty and criminal behavior, he says.[36] Truth and justice, which sit at the heart of journalism's mission, should lead reporters to explore whether democratic institutions are upholding their goals and standards, and if not, tell citizens what prevents them from doing so. Journalism's range of exploration needs not be restricted by a beat system or by the walls of any one institution. Court reporters, for example, are not limited by legal definitions of justice when they cover trials and the court system. Rather than simply conveying information, crime stories with farsighted perspectives can weave, reinforce, repair, and change the texture of the social fabric.

For example, the German court system—and most reporters in the courtroom—focused on the guilt or innocence of five members of the terrorist organization, National Socialist Underground, during their five-year trial from 2013 to 2018. But at least two German reporters, Annette

Ramelsberger for *Süddeutsche Zeitung* and Gisela Friedrichsen for *Die Welt*, listened to what Friedrichsen described as the Greek chorus in the courtroom. As we recounted in Chapter 4, lawyers representing the victims—mostly all small business owners with roots in Turkey and other Middle Eastern countries—raised a warning voice to the German people about an evil in their midst. Why, the victims' lawyers asked, were police so insistent that a "Turkish mafia" was behind the series of killings? The investigators' premise blinded the ten-year investigation to a nightmarish racism rearing up in Germany and prevented police from solving the crime. The victims' lawyers spoke to the social injustices suffered by Germany's immigrant population, not only by the murderous hands of the NSU, but also by the German police, an institution that was shaped and influenced by similar prejudices. The German criminal justice system admitted the victims' alternative view of justice into the courtroom. The court tried and sentenced the defendants, but reporters Friedrichsen and Ramelsberger brought the victims' voices to the German people, to the public beyond the courtroom, and wrote about the larger, unmet issues of justice that the investigation of the NSU crimes signaled.

Friedrichsen's and Ramelsberger's coverage was situated specifically within Germany's history and the country's sensitive and self-conscious sense of itself. The case reminds us that the word "communication" and "community" share the same root in the Latin word *communis*, or "common." The community is defined by, and takes its shape in, the communication process. As technology conflates geography and removes or redraws national and international boundaries, countries are losing the legal and moral ability to control and contain the conversations that delineate and define them. A consideration of the impact technology is having on journalism is particularly relevant when considering crime stories because these texts define the edges of a society by exploring what behaviors fall outside a culture's pale, how deviants should be treated, and what larger social ills are nascent. Thus, a comparison of crime-reporting practices across advanced industrialized capitalist societies serves as a telling exemplar of how the Internet disrupts the cultural integrity of these practices. In addition, it shows why and how newsrooms, in the Age of the Internet, ought to operate to respect more sensitive intercultural realities. The realities are now both inside their national borders and beyond those borders when the stories they produce have news value in other countries. Creating and establishing meaningful intercultural communication is one of the greatest challenges facing scholars, journalists, and newsrooms today.

Emmanuel Levinas argues that all human institutions that allow us to function day to day—mass media, law, government, and politics—should be grounded in the primal ethical obligation to tend to the other's needs. If not, human beings risk detaching themselves from their ethical anchors. Journalism runs such a risk if it fails to come to terms with its penetration into cultures far beyond its traditional circulation area. Before all other obligations, Levinas asserts, we must first heed the primal plea of every interpersonal encounter: *Please don't kill me. Help me instead.* Levinas turns the pronouns of the Golden Rule in a way that speaks to the challenges of his Holocaust experience and continues to speak to our age of globalization. "Do unto others as they would have you do unto them."[37] The Internet can broaden knowledge and knock down the confines of parochialism, but it can also run roughshod over Levinas' ethical tenets by "killing" the other with cultural imperialism. Journalists now have an outsized obligation to deal with diversity inside their own countries and to gain awareness of whether their way of doing their job travels abroad. Reporters, editors, and media academics would do well to keep in mind a famous quote by anthropologist Wade Davis: "The world in which you were born is just one model of reality. Other cultures are not failed attempts at being you; they are unique manifestations of the human spirit."[38] Imposition of one culture's version of reality upon another may be inadvertent, but it is most often motivated by a desire for dominance by technology, profit, or power. If so, it is not serving democracy; it functions as imperialism and is a form of cultural murder.

Throughout this book, we have explored how journalists cover criminal events that resonate in their communities and signal to citizens that norms are being violated and public safety threatened. Comparison has allowed us to identify what each country's reporting style suggests about its underlying values, its attitudes toward deviance, and its philosophy of criminal justice. We looked behind the differing crime coverage practices to discover how they connect to public conversations, politics, history, and culture. Form does indeed follow function. The way reporters sculpt the story's details reflects public attitudes and actions. These stories play a central role in how a nation's values are discussed, reaffirmed, and changed. They define the behavioral borders of a society and influence the ways those borders shift over time. We have found that each country's practices and the ethic behind them are often so habitual that reporters hardly recognize their presence; yet, the practices may be considered odd, alien, and even unethical elsewhere.

What then, should journalists and policymakers do about the Internet's threat to flatten these differences and impose what may be foreign and wrong for a people? And what ought citizens expect or even demand of coverage? The process of addressing the Internet's power and effects on journalism—and on democracy—begins with awareness. Journalists everywhere have much to learn about themselves from understanding what others do. Comparison forces self-examination, and building on our approach, more could be done. One possibility for future exploration would be to consider the same topic in every country in each model; for example, researchers could look specifically at how media have, and are, covering pedophilia and abuse by Catholic priests. While in this book we used different signal crimes as starting points for discussion in each of our locales, taking an approach that employed a standard case might offer additional nuance among what kinds of choices reporters make and why. We also have not delved deeply into the idea that photographs, video, and other types of visuals are a kind of naming. It would be possible to enlarge our data to consider the photograph selection and composition that accompanied the stories, or perhaps even consider what kinds of video were offered. And while we have been resistant to making an exploration of how the choices around naming are playing out on social media—largely because we chose to deal with institutions and their requisite frameworks that encourage adherence to ethics codes and laws—such an undertaking might yield different and thought-provoking possibilities. It may be, as scholars consider the role publics ought to play in constructing the conversations of their communities, that citizens themselves are utilizing language choices or making choices that challenge or confirm our findings about mainstream media.

Beyond these ruminations, we hope that we have demonstrated how important particular practices are to the countries where they reside. We have listened in each country to what journalists, their stories, their codes of practice, and the experts who study them said about journalistic habits of practice and what those habits mean to that country. We hope we have conveyed the value of what these voices tell us about that most fundamental tenet of democratic thinking—the core value of self-determination. Another idea for future research might include an exploration of how citizens themselves see journalistic practices and whether they wish to see them preserved or challenged.

At the heart of all journalistic enterprise lies the telling of true tales, an ethical pursuit. By reporting the news, journalists provide the raw material for building community. But when a community loses control of its own voice, when others usurp its storytelling power, that community's ability to conduct its public business is in jeopardy. Persons being denied their own voice cannot undertake the individual or communal task of becoming citizens and moral beings. News serves as a means for societal definition—for a people to define themselves. Technology is not neutral. Larger, louder voices are threatening to drown out smaller ones. Although this may be happening inadvertently or sometimes out of ignorance, the effect jeopardizes people's right to govern themselves. Conversations and education are key. While journalists' judgment can never be perfect, discussions about why they choose the details they do and how best this aligns with underlying ideas about public, private, and justice itself, are paramount. These discussions must happen—across professions, citizenry, and national and international boundaries. We hope this book provides a first step.

List of Interview Subjects

Note: Interview subjects are identified with the position they held at the time of the interview.

Canada

Ammerata, Carla. City and business editor, the *Hamilton Spectator*, March 19, 2014.

Appleby, Timothy. Reporter and former foreign correspondent, the *Globe and Mail*, August 1, 2012.

Benedetti, Paul. Former reporter and columnist, the *Hamilton Spectator*; lecturer in journalism, the University of Western Ontario, March 19, 2014.

Berton, Paul. Editor-in-chief, the *Hamilton Spectator*, May 5, 2014.

Blatchford, Christie. Reporter and columnist, the *National Post*, and previously of the *Globe and Mail*, November 1, 2012.

Bruser, Bert. In-house counsel, the *Toronto Star*, August 2, 2012.

Burnett, Thane. Recently retired reporter, columnist and editor, the *Toronto Sun* (and the Sun newspaper chain), March 17, 2014.

Butler, Colin. Reporter, Canadian Broadcasting Corporation, November 1, 2012.

Clairmont, Susan. Crime reporter, the *Hamilton Spectator*, March 21, 2014.

Cornies, Larry. Former editor, the *London Free Press* and the *Globe and Mail*, March 14, 2014.

Dubinsky, Kate. Reporter. Reporter, the *London Free Press*, March 21, 2014.

Edwards, Peter. Crime reporter, the *Toronto Star*, July 31, 2012.

English, Kathy. Public editor, the *Toronto Star*, July 31, 2012.

Fraser, John. Founding president and executive chair of the National NewsMedia Council, February 15, 2019.

Jones, Alison. Reporter, Canadian Press (CP) national news agency, November 1, 2012.

La Pointe, Kirk. Ombudsman, Canadian Broadcasting Corporation, July 25, 2012.

Macintyre, Linden. Investigative reporter and host, Canadian Broadcasting Corporation's "The Fifth Estate", October 31, 2012.

Macintyre, Nicole. Reporter, the *Hamilton Spectator*, March 19, 2014.

Makin, Kirk. Justice reporter, the *Globe and Mail*, November 1, 2012.

O'Brien, Jennifer. Reporter, the *London Free Press*, March 25, 2014.

Perkel, Pat. Executive director, National NewsMedia Council, February 15, 2019.

Richmond, Randy. Reporter, the *London Free Press*, March 25, 2014, and February 20, 2019.

Ruscitti, Joe. Editor-in-chief, the *London Free Press*, March 12, 2014.

Seglins, Dave. Reporter, Canadian Broadcasting Corporation, November 1, 2012.

Stead, Sylvia. Public editor, the *Globe and Mail*, August 1, 2012.

England

Brock, George. Professor and journalism department head, City University of London, February 28, 2012.

Brown, Jonathan. Senior lecturer in journalism, University of Teesside, formerly with the *Independent,* March 7, 2017.

Brunt, Martin. Crime correspondent, Sky News, February 27, 2012.

Campbell, Andy. Editor, *Daily Post* (N. Wales), March 9, 2017.

Clifford, Sadie. Researcher, specialist on women and trial coverage, June 26, 2011.

Coleman, Amanda. Head of Corporate Communications, Greater Manchester Police, March 13, 2017.

Fenton, Natalie. Professor of Media and Communications, Department of Media, Communications and Cultural Studies, Goldsmiths, University of London. March 7, 2017.

Frost, Chris. Former head of journalism, John Moores University, Liverpool, and chairman of the National Union of Journalists Ethics Council, August 7, 2009 (in Boston); June 24, 2011 and March 13, 2017 (in England).

Greenslade, Roy. Emeritus professor of journalism, City University, London, and media commentator for *The Guardian* and other publications, June 23, 2011.

Israel, Simon. Home affairs correspondent, ITN Channel 4 News; vice chair, Crime Reporters Association, March 13, 2017.

Jempsen, Mike. Director, MediaWise, Bristol, June 24, 2011.

Jewkes, Yvonne. Professor of criminology, Leicester University, June 27, 2011.

Johnston, Tony. Engage Media Training, former head of training for the Press Association and *Trinity Mirror,* March 7, 2017.

Norton, Mike. Editor, the *Bristol Post,* August 2, 2011 (interview conducted by Mike Jempsen).

Perch, Keith. Head of journalism, University of Derby, director of Independent Press Standards Organisation (IPSO); former editor, *Derby Telegraph, South Wales Echo, Leicester Mercury,* March 8, 2017.

Reiner, Robert. Professor of criminology, London School of Economics, June 22, 2011.

Satchwell, Bob. Executive director, Society of Editors, June 28, 2011.

Simmons, Kier. UK editor, ITV News; June 28, 2011.

Thomas, Joe. Crime and courts reporter, *Liverpool Echo,* March 9, 2017.

Twomey, John. Crime reporter, *Daily Express,* chair, Crime Reporters Association, February 29, 2012.

Walker, Chris. Group managing editor, *Trinity Mirror* regionals, March 9, 2017.

Wright, Roy. Recently retired editor, *Huddersfield Examiner,* March 10, 2017.

Wykes, Maggie. Senior lecturer, School of Law, Sheffield University, June 27, 2011.

Two subjects interviewed in 2017 who wished to be anonymized:

A former regional newspaper editor and reporter based in England.

A former reporter for a city daily in England.

Germany

Dolde, Kerstin. Ombudsman, *Frankenpost Neue Presse,* April 12, 2018.

Ernst, Elitz. Ombudsman, *Bild Zeitung,* April 17, 2018.

Friedrichsen, Gisela. Court reporter, *Die Welt*, formerly with *der Spiegel*, April 9, 2018.
Hass, Cornelia. Director of the German Journalists Union (DJU), April 12, 2018.
Kensche, Christine. Crime and immigration reporter, *Die Welt*, April 11, 2018.
Klehm, Michael. International representative for DJV (Deutscher Journalisten-Verband), the German journalists association, April 16, 2018.
Krützfeld, Alexander. Crime reporter, freelancer for *der Spiegel*, Leipzig, April 10, 2018.
Radulovic, Jens. Complaints officer, German Press Council, April 9, 2018.
Ramelsberger, Annette. Crime reporter, *Süddeutche Zeitung*, April 13, 2018.
Rasehorn, Hendrik. Crime reporter for several regional newspapers, April 16, 2018.
Resti, Petra. Former freelance German correspondent and mafia reporter in Italy, residing in Venice and writing thriller novels, April 10, 2018.
Reuter, Dirk. Reporter, RTL West TV, April 11, 2018.
Russ-Mohl, Stephan. Professor of journalism and media management at the Faculty of Communication Sciences, Università della Svizzera italiana, Lugano, and director of the European Journalism Observatory, April 8, 2018.
Sahlender, Anton. Ombudsman, *Mainpost*, Würzburg, April 16, 2018.
Schultz, Tanjev. Professor of Principles and Strategies of Journalism, Department of Journalism & Communications, Johannes Gutenberg Universität Mainz, and reporter for *Süddeutche Zeigtung*, April 13, 2018.
Verhovnik, Melanie. School of Journalism, Catholic University of Eichstätt-Ingolstadt and police consultant on violence and young offenders, April 15, 2018.
Volkmann-Schluck, Sonja. Public relations officer, German Press Council, April 9, 2018.
Zörner, Hendrik. Spokesman for the DJV (Deutscher Journalisten-Verband), the German journalists association, April 16, 2018.

Ireland

Curran, Gerry. Media relations adviser for Dublin courts, June 30, 2011, March 1, 2012.
Dooley, Seamus. General secretary, National Union of Journalists, June 30, 2011.
Doyle, Mike. Crime reporter, *Irish Daily Sun,* March 3, 2012.
Horgan, John. National press ombudsman, March 2, 2012.
O'Toole, Michael. Crime reporter, *Irish Daily Star*, March 3, 2012.
Phelan, Shane. Investigations editor, *Irish Independent*, March 1, 2012.
Sheridan, Kathy. Court and features writer, *Irish Times*, March 2, 2012.

Italy

Anesi, Cecilia. Reporter, Investigative Reporters Project Italy (IRPI), June 27, 2014.
Bagnoli, Lorenzo. Organized crime reporter, *Terre di Mezzo* magazine and board member of Investigative Reporters Project Italy (IRPI), July 2, 2014.
Barigazzi, Jacopo. Freelance columnist at Abu Dhabi's *The National* and contributor at *Il Sole 24 Ore,* Reuters, and *Newsweek,* former deputy editor at Rome-based journalism laboratory pagina99, July 1, 2014.
Bolzoni, Attilio. Palermo correspondent, *La Repubblica*, July 6, 2014.
Colonnello, Paolo. Crime reporter, *La Stampa*, June 30, 2014.

D'Alessandro, Manuella. Court reporter, Reuters and AGI Wire Service, July 2, 2014.

Deriu, Marco. Lecturer, Catholic University of the Sacred Heart, July 2, 2014.

Giuffrida, Angela. Founding editor at Italian edition of *The Local*, English-language website, June 26, 2014.

Iacopino, Enzo. President of National Order of Journalists, June 25, 2014.

Randacio Emilio. Crime reporter, *La Repubblica*, July 1, 2014.

Romeo, Guido. Data and business editor, *Wired* magazine and Investigative Reporters Project Italy (IRPI), July 3, 2014.

Rubino, Guilio. Reporter, Investigative Reporters Project Italy (IRPI), June 27, 2014.

Scammell, Rosie. Reporter, *The Local*, June 26, 2014.

Sisti, Leo. Organized crime reporter, *L'Espresso* magazine and founding editor of Investigative Reporters Project Italy (IRPI), July 3, 2014.

Spampinato, Alberto. Councilor for Ossigno per L'Informazione, June 25, 2014.

Tonello, Fabrizio. Professor of political science, University of Padua, June 28, 2014.

Vaccari, Lanfrana. Former third-world correspondent for *Il Corriere Della Sera*, July 1, 2014.

The Netherlands

Awad, Isabel. Associate professor, Erasmus University School of History, Culture, and Communication in Rotterdam, June 10, 2010.

Brouwers, Bart. Editorial chief at Dichtbij.nl, Hyperlocal Online Media TMG at Telegraaf Media Nederland, June 15, 2010.

Bruning, Thomas L. W. General secretary, NVJ or the Dutch Association of Journalists, June 10, 2010 and April 18, 2018.

Buitink, Liesbeth. International editor for crime, Algemeen Nederlands Persbureau (ANP), June 14, 2010 and April 19, 2018.

Burger, J. Peter. Lecturer, Centre for Linguistics, Journalism and New Media at Leiden University, June 16, 2010.

Evers, Huub. Independent researcher and media expert in the field of media ethics, and board member, Netherlands Press Council, April 18, 2018.

Halkema, Fleur. Reporter, Algemeen Nederlands Persbureau (ANP), June 14, 2010.

Joustra, Arendo. Editor-in-chief, *Elsevier* weekly magazine, former chair of the Dutch Society of Editors-in-Chief, June 15, 2010.

Kester, Bernadette. Associate professor, School of History, Culture, and Communication in Rotterdam, Erasmus University, June 15, 2010.

Koene, Daphne. General secretary (and lawyer), Netherlands Press Council, June 11, 2010 and April 19, 2018.

Laroes, Hans. Former chair, Netherlands Press Council (2013–2015), and editor-in-chief of Nederlandse Omroep Stichting (NOS), one of the broadcasting organizations comprising Nederlandse Publieke Omroep (NPO) or Dutch Public Broadcaster (2006–2011), April 18, 2018.

Meens, Thom. Ombudsman, *de Volkskrant,* June 10, 2010.

Overdiek, Tim. Presenter at NOS Radio 1 Journal, former deputy editor at NOS Dutch Public TV and radio, June 14, 2010.

Santing, Froukje. Member, Netherlands Press Council, June 11, 2010.

Streefkerk, Kees. Member, Netherlands Press Council, June 11, 2010.

Van Exter, Fritz. Chair, Netherlands Press Council, April 20, 2018.
Wolffensperger, Gerrit Jan. Member, Netherlands Press Council, June 11, 2010.

Portugal

Arons de Carvalho, Alberto. Former editor, *Republic*; faculty member, the New University of Lisbon; vice chairman of the Board of the Regulatory Authority for the Media (ERC), November 3, 2015.

Branco, Sofia. Reporter, *Público*; president of Union of Journalists, November 3, 2015.

Calado, Vanda. Research analyst, the Board of the Regulatory Authority for the Media (ERC), October 28, 2015.

Coelho, Pedro. Assistant professor, Faculty of Social and Human Sciences of New University of Lisbon; collaborator with the Center for Media and Journalism Investigation; reporter, TV SIC, November 3, 2015.

Godinho, Jacinto. Assistant professor of media, Faculty of Social and Human Sciences of New University of Lisbon; head of the Comissão da Carteira Profissional do Jornalista (Commission for the Professional Journalist License), which issues licenses to practice journalism, November 2, 2015.

Granado, António. Assistant professor, Faculty of Social and Human Sciences of New University of Lisbon; former managing editor and online editor, *Público*; multimedia editor, RTP cable channel, October 28, 2015.

Marôpo, Lídia. Adjunct professor, Department of Communication Science and Language, Polytechnic Institute of Setúbal, October 30, 2015.

Martins, Paulo. Assistant professor, Social and Political Sciences Superior Institute; former editor, *Jornal de Notícias* newspaper, October 28, 2015.

Pereira, Eulália. Media analyst and researcher, the Board of the Regulatory Authority for the Media (ERC), October 28, 2015.

Prata, António. Assistant news director, TVI, November 2, 2015.

Rosenbusch, Cláudia. Society and justice reporter, TVI, October 30, 2015.

Soares, Tânia. Head of the Media Analysis Department, the Board of the Regulatory Authority for the Media (ERC), October 28, 2015.

Sousa, Luis de. Research fellow, political and social science, University of Lisbon, November 5, 2015.

Teixeira da Mota, Francisco. Lawyer, *Público*, November 5, 2015.

Torres da Silva, Marisa. Assistant professor of communication, New University of Lisbon, former *Público* journalist, November 3, 2015.

Spain

Baquero, Antonio. Reporter, *El Periódico*, June 4, 2015.

Campo, Jesús Díaz, del. Media ethics professor, Universidad Internacional de la Rioja, June 9, 2015.

Carmen Fuente Cobo, Maria, del. Professor, Centro Universitario Villanueva, University Complutense, June 10, 2015.

Carranco, Rebeca. Crime reporter at the Barcelona newsroom of *El País*, via Skype, June 17, 2015.

Cózar Palma, Álvaro, de. Reporter, *El País,* June 8, 2015.
Doñate, Mavi. Deputy director, Society Department, RTVE Spanish Public Television, June 16, 2015.
Fernández, Roger. Director, Information Council of Catalunya (FCIC) and columnist, *La Vanguardia*, June 4, 2015.
Flores, Carmen. Director, Catalunya Press, June 3, 2015.
Galán Gamero, Javier. Representative, Press Association; Professor of Journalism, Carlos III University of Madrid, June 15, 2015.
García-Alonso Montoya, Pedro. Professor, Journalism Department, University Complutense of Madrid, June 9, 2015.
Herráiz, Pablo. Reporter, *El Mundo*, June 10, 2015.
Herrero Curiel, Eva. Professor, Carlos III University of Madrid, June 8, 2015.
Maciá-Barber, Carlos. Professor, Carlos III University of Madrid, June 15, 2015.
Marcos, Rubén. Reporter, Agencia EFE, Spainish news agency, June 16, 2015
Muñoz, Pablo. Reporter, *ABC* newspaper, June 16, 2015.
Navarro, Mayka. Reporter, *El Periódico*, June 5, 2015.
Ojea, Luis Alfonso. Courts and crime reporter, Cadena Ser Radio, June 15, 2015.
Pozas, Alberto. Crime reporter, Cadena Ser Radio, June 11, 2015.
Ruiz, Roberto. Reporter, *El Confidencial-News* digital newspaper, June 12, 2015.
Sánchez Marín, Guillem. Reporter, Catalonia News Agency, June 3, 2015.
Santamaría Marcos, Rubén. Director, El Economista, June 16, 2015.
Saravia Méndez, Gregorio. Professor, philosophy and law, Carlos III University of Madrid, June 15, 2015.
Terradillos Azpiroz, Ana. Reporter, Cadena Ser Radio Station and Telecinco TV, June 11, 2015.
Urbaneja, Fernando González. Former president, Federación de Asociaciones de Periodistas de España (FAPE) or the Press Association of Spain, June 12, 2015.

Sweden

Gieretta, Helena. Editor and publisher, *Journalisten*, June 21, 2010.
Jönsson, Martin. Managing editor, *Svenska Dagbladet,* June 22, 2010.
Larsson, Mats Johan. Political reporter and news editor, *Dagens Nyheter,* June 21, 2010.
Mattsson, Thomas. Editor-in-chief, *Expressen,* June 22, 2010.
Olofsson, Morgan. Correspondent and program manager, Sveriges TV, June 22, 2010.
Pollack, Ester. Associate professor, Journalism, Media and Communication Studies Department, Stockholm University, June 18, 2010.
Weibull, Lennart. Professor, Department of Journalism, Media, and Communication; senior researcher at the SOM Research Institute, University of Gothenborg, June 17, 2010.

United States

Augenstein, Neil. Reporter, WTOP radio, Washington, DC, August 8, 2013.
Bauder, Bob. Reporter, *Pittsburgh Tribune Review,* October 24, 2013.
Clark, Mike. Anchor, WTAE News, Pittsburgh ABC affiliate, October 24, 2013.

Emerling, Gary. Reporter on the Holocaust Museum shooting for the *Washington Times*; August 8, 2013.

Fuoco, Mike. Crime reporter, *Pittsburgh Post-Gazette*, October 25, 2013.

Gardner, Amy. Crime and courts editor, Washington and Baltimore for the *Washington Post*, August 8, 2013.

Gest, Ted. Board member, Criminal Justice Journalists, author of *Crime and Politics*, August 9, 2013.

Gottlieb, Frank. Retired news director, KQV radio, Pittsburgh, October 26, 2013.

Hermann, Peter. Police reporter, *Washington Post*, August 8, 2013.

Jonsson, Patrick. Atlanta correspondent, *Christian Science Monitor*, August 8, 2013.

Kent, Tom. Standards editor, Associated Press (2008-2016), August 9, 2013.

Kerlik, Bob. Court reporter, *Pittsburgh Tribune Review*, October 24, 2013.

Knowlton, Brian. U.S. editor and correspondent, *International New York Times*, August 5, 2013.

Lash, Cindy. Former reporter and editor, *Pittsburgh Post-Gazette*, October 24, 2013.

Nasaw, Daniel. Correspondent, *The Guardian*, based in Washington, DC, August 6, 2013.

Nathan-Kazis, Josh. Reporter, *The Forward*, New York, March 6, 2014.

Nootbaar, Mark. Reporter, WESA-FM, Pittsburgh National Public Radio affiliate, October 25, 2013.

Orr, Bob. Terrorism reporter, CBS News, Washington, DC, August 6, 2013.

Plaisance, Patrick. Professor, Colorado State University, August 10, 2013.

Rashbaum, William. Law enforcement reporter, *New York Times*, March 6, 2014.

Roddy, Dennis. Former reporter and columnist, *Pittsburgh Post-Gazette*, October 25, 2013.

Shaer, Matt. Feature writer, *New York Magazine*, March 7, 2014.

Stockey, Andrew. Reporter, WTAE-TV, Pittsburgh, October 24, 2013.

Stout, David. Reporter, *New York Times*, Washington bureau, August 5, 2013.

Tapinsh, Alex. Reporter, Thomson Reuters and Agence-France Press in Latvia, interviewed in Pittsburgh, October 26, 2013.

Triay, Andy. Producer, CBS News, Washington, DC, August 6, 2013.

Wilkins, Lee. Former crime reporter; professor of journalism, University of Missouri, August 8, 2013.

Zeveloff, Naomi. Former Middle East correspondent and deputy culture editor, *The Forward*, New York, March 6, 2014.

One of the subjects interviewed in 2013 wished to be anonymized:

A former reporter for a news service, based in Washington, DC.

Notes

Chapter 1

1. The *Columbia Journalism Review* studied peoples' preferences in news. Since the beginning of the new millennium, their choices have remained largely static, with war and terrorism at the top of the list, followed by human and natural disasters. In third place is crime and health news, which can sometimes be related. See: Curtis Brainard, "What Kind of News Do People Really Want?," *Columbia Journalism Review*, 31 August 2007, https://archives.cjr.org/behind_the_news/what_kind_of_news_do_people_re.php.

2. Nicholas Carr in *The Shallows: What the Internet Is Doing to Our Brains,* builds on the tradition of McLuhan and Innis to suggest that technology has an ethic and shapes how humans gather, process, and disseminate information. Its ethic is one of the industrialist, where speed and efficiency are valued. Humans are not becoming deeper or more conscientious thinkers; instead, we are losing our capacity to contemplate, reflect, and concentrate. See: Nicholas Carr, *The Shallows: What the Internet Is Doing to Our Brains* (New York: W. W. Norton, 2011).

3. Tuchman called these often-unexamined news practices "rituals" because they are performed regularly, almost religiously, but without an acknowledged awareness of what informs them. Gaye Tuchman, *Making News* (New York: Free Press, 1978).

4. For example, the following media organizations cite ANP as their source and employ the "Karst T." moniker: Nieuwsblad Staff, "Motief Karst T. ook voor zijn ouders een raadsel," *Nieuwsblad*, 7 May 2009, https://www.nieuwsblad.be/cnt/dmf20090507_075; Omroep Gelderland Staff, "Ouders Karst T.: geen idee motief," *Omroep Gelderland*, 7 May 2009, https://www.omroepgelderland.nl/nieuws/266111/Ouders-Karst-T-geen-idee-motief;Sanoma Digital Staff, "Motief Karst T. voor zijn ouders ook een raadsel," *Sanoma Digital*, 7 May 2009, https://www.nu.nl/algemeen/1960782/motief-karst-t-voor-zijn-ouders-ook-een-raadsel.html; Het Parool Staff, "Psychiatrisch onderzoek voor dode Karst T," *Het Parool*, 22 June 2009, https://www.parool.nl/binnenland/psychiatrisch-onderzoek-voor-dode-karst-t~a249479/.

5. Martin Innes and Nigel Fielding, "From Community to Communicative Policing: 'Signal Crimes' and the Problem of Public Reassurance," *Sociological Research Online* 7, no. 2 (2002): 1–12.

6. Innes and Fielding, "From Community to Communicative Policing," 2.

7. Martin Innes, "'Signal Crimes': Detective Work, Mass Media and Constructing Collective Memory," in *Criminal Visions: Media Representations of Crime and Justice*, ed. Paul Mason (Cullompton, Devon, U.K.: Willan, 2003), 52.

8. The notion of civil strife, and journalism's role in documenting it, is not new. Sociologist Herbert Gans pointed out that inherently dramatic stories with negative implications for citizens and nations are particularly upsetting because they threaten the status quo. Gans outlined four types of "disorder" stories—natural, technological, social, and moral—and suggested that crime coverage falls into an index of "moral disorder." See Herbert J. Gans, *Deciding What's News: A Study CBS Evening News, NBC Nightly News, Newsweek and Time* (New York: Pantheon Books, 1979).

9. Innes, "'Signal Crimes,'" 51.

10. Richard V. Ericson, Patricia M. Baranek, and Janet B. L. Chan, *Representing Order: Crime, Law, and Justice in the News Media* (Milton Keynes, U.K.: Open University Press, 1991), 239.

11. There are some excellent books that focus exclusively on journalism's role in democracies and offered us differing definitions of democracy and helped situate crime coverage specifically within this system: Robert A. Dahl, *On Democracy* (New Haven, CT: Yale University Press, 2008); C. Edwin Baker, *Media Concentration and Democracy: Why Ownership Matters* (Cambridge, U.K.: Cambridge University Press, 2006); Clifford G. Christians, Theodore Glasser, Denis McQuail, Kaarle Nordenstreng, and Robert A. White, *Normative Theories of the Media: Journalism in Democratic Societies* (Urbana and Champaign: University of Illinois Press, 2010); Leonardo Morlino, *Changes for Democracy: Actors, Structures, Processes* (Oxford: Oxford University Press, 2012); Katrin Voltmer, *The Media in Transitional Democracies* (Hoboken, NJ: John Wiley & Sons, 2013).

12. Daniel C. Hallin and Paolo Mancini, *Comparing Media Systems: Three Models of Media and Politics* (Cambridge, U.K.: Cambridge University Press, 2004).

13. About 20% of our interview subjects were aware that how they covered crime was not how everyone covers crime. Those who had knowledge of difference(s) were almost all foreign correspondents or people who had worked as journalists or editors in other countries.

14. The Freedom of the Press Index for 2017 ranked the press as "free" in all the countries in our sample, except for Italy, which it ranked as "partly free." The Index is compiled by Freedom House, which describes itself as "an independent watchdog organization dedicated to the expansion of freedom and democracy around the world." See: Freedom House, "About Freedom House," Freedom House, n.d., https://freedomhouse.org/about-us.

15. Christians et al., *Normative Theories of the Media*; Voltmer, *Media in Transitional Democracies*; Stephen Ward, *Radical Media Ethics: A Global Approach* (Hoboken, NJ: John Wiley & Sons, 2015).

16. We are frequently asked what effect these reporting practices and the cultural attitudes about criminal justice that they reflect have on crime and recidivism rates. Such comparison lies beyond our current study because definitions of what constitutes crime differ from one country to the next. While homicide rates can be measured, they offer little insight because so many factors affect these rates. Similarly, recidivism rates cannot be contrasted for many reasons, including broad differences in incarceration rates, definitions of crime, and methods of data collection.

17. Hallin and Mancini, *Comparing Media Systems*.

18. In fact, application of their theories to journalistic practice is something Hallin and Mancini suggest for future research. See their Introduction in *Comparing Media Systems* for more.

19. We would note that *Comparing Media Systems* has created a great deal of discussion since its publication in 2004: Fengler et al. take issue with the divisions and some of Hallin and Mancini's findings. See: Susanne Fengler, Tobias Eberwein, Gianpietro Mazzoleni, Colin Porlezza, and Stephan Russ Mohl, *Journalists and Media Accountability: An International Study of News People in the Digital Age* (New York: Peter Lang, 2014).There are those whose own studies largely support Hallin and Mancini, like that of Michael Brüggemann et al. See: Michael Brüggemann, Sven Engesser, Florin Büchel, Edda Humprecht, and Laia Castro, "Hallin and Mancini Revisited: Four Empirical Types of Western Media Systems," *Journal of Communication* 64, no. 6 (2014): 1037–1065. They write, "The study at hand is, to the best of our knowledge, the first to comprehensively validate the original dimensions and models using aggregated data from the same sample of Western countries" (1037). There are also others who walk a middle line, like Pippa Norris. See: Norris, "Comparative Political Communications: Common Frameworks or Babelian Confusion?," *Government and Opposition* 44, no. 3 (2009): 321–340. Finally, Hallin and Mancini themselves have answered some of their critics: Daniel C. Hallin and Paolo Mancini, "Comparing Media Systems: A Response to Critics," *Media and Journalism* 17, no. 9 (2010), 52–67; and more recently in Daniel C. Hallin and Paolo Mancini, "Ten Years After Comparing Media Systems: What Have We Learned?," *Political Communication* 34, no. 2 (2017): 155–171.

20. Our study is focused on news about crime, and the analysis is focused primarily on print news, words that are said in broadcasts, and text that is disseminated via Internet news websites. While we note that accompanying visuals can function as a kind of "naming" or identifying, we interviewed few journalists who commented specifically on these practices, and the broadcast reporters to whom we spoke were not questioned deeply about ethical choices and considerations related to visuals or images. An inquiry into how and in what ways visuals can function to identify persons accused would make an interesting future study.

21. Jack Katz, "What Makes Crime 'News'?," *Media, Culture & Society* 9, no. 1 (1987): 47–75.

22. Katz, "What Makes Crime 'News'?," 70.

23. In recent years, the number of freelancers working for large media institutions skyrocketed while the number of journalists with permanent contracts went down. As they are often paid a pittance (as low as three dollars for an article), they are constantly overworked and tempted to ignore ethics codes.

24. We averaged close to 20 interviews in each country, and, in some instances, we spoke with people more than once over the eight-year period of this project.

25. Ernst Elitz, the ombudsman for the tabloid *Bild*, in Berlin; *Irish Daily Star* reporter, Michael O'Toole; and *Toronto Sun*'s Thane Burnett were exceptions and were generous with their insights.

26. A full list of persons interviewed appears in the Appendix.

27. Barney G. Glaser and Anselm L. Strauss, *The Discovery of Grounded Theory* (Hawthorne, NY: Aldine, 1967).

28. Walter R. Fisher, *Human Communication as Narration: Toward a Philosophy of Reason, Value, and Action* (Columbia: University of South Carolina Press, 1989).

29. Grant McCracken, *The Long Interview* (Newbury, CA: Sage, 1988), 9.

30. Al Tompkins. "Cynics Might Call the Perp Walk the Crime Reporter's Red Carpet': How We Justify Images of Accused IMF Chief in Handcuffs," *Poynter*, 17 May 2011, https://www.poynter.org/reporting-editing/2011/is-it-ethical-to-use-perp-walk-images-of-dominique-strauss-kahn-imf-chief-accused-of-attempted-rape/.

31. Stephen Ward, *Ethical Journalism in a Populist Age: The Democratically Engaged Journalist* (Lanham, MD: Rowman & Littlefield, 2018).

32. Ward, *Ethical Journalism in a Populist Age*, 15.

33. And here, Ward is also building on the arguments he put forward in *Radical Media Ethics*.

34. Ward, *Ethical Journalism in a Populist Age*, 23.

35. Ward, *Ethical Journalism in a Populist Age*, 183.

36. Bill Kovach and Tom Rosenstiel, *The Elements of Journalism: What Newspeople Should Know and the Public Should Expect* (New York: Three Rivers Press, 2014), 12.

37. Ward, *Ethical Journalism in a Populist Age*, 17.

38. James W. Carey, *Communication as Culture: Essays on Media and Society* (London: Routledge, 2008).

39. G. Stuart Adam, "Foreword," in *Communication as Culture: Essays on Media and Society*, ed. James W. Carey (London: Routledge, 2008), xiii.

40. Carey, *Communication as Culture*.

41. Carey, *Communication as Culture*, 15.

42. Carey, *Communication as Culture*, 15.

43. Carey, quoted in Kovach and Rosenstiel, *The Elements of Journalism*, 12.

44. Walter R. Fisher, "Narration, Reason, Community," in *Writing the Social Text: Poetics and Politics in Social Science Discourse*, ed. Richard Brown (New York: Routledge, 2017), 29–31.

45. Carol Gilligan, *Mapping the Moral Domain: A Contribution of Women's Thinking to Psychological Theory and Education* (Cambridge, MA: Harvard University Press, 1988).

46. Fisher, "Narration, Reason, Community."

47. Dewey, quoted in Fisher, "Narration, Reason, Community," 308.

48. Fisher, "Narration, Reason, Community," 314.

49. This can be confusing. In Italy, for example, there are three steps: the prosecutor files charges, a judge (*Tribunale del riesame*) decides if the arrest warrants are justified, and finally another judge (*Giudice delle indagini preliminari*) decides about dropping the charges or validating a deal (*patteggiamento*). This explanation was provided to us by Fabrizio Tonello.

Chapter 2

1. James McAuley and Rick Noack, "What You Need to Know About Germany's Immigration Crisis," *Washington Post*, 3 July 2018, https://www.washingtonpost.com/news/worldviews/wp/2018/07/03/what-you-need-to-know-about-germanys-immigration-crisis/?utm_term=.09ffd1f25fef.

2. Lennart Weibull and Britt Börjesson, "The Swedish Media Accountability System: A Research Perspective," *European Journal of Communication* 7, no. 1 (1992): 123. In 1765, the Swedish government undertook a complete revision of their constitution. A priest was instrumental in one of the pleas submitted to parliament in support of freedom of the press. In his work, he concluded, "No evidence should be needed that a certain freedom of writing and printing is the backbone of a free organisation of the state." See: Swedish Institute, "20 Milestones of Swedish Press Freedom," *Swedish Institute*, 1 October 2018, https://sweden.se/society/20-milestones-of-swedish-press-freedom/.

3. ANP is the primary news agency in the Netherlands. It began as a cooperative in 1934, and currently it provides information to a number of newspapers, radio, and television programs, internet sites, and mobile apps such as SMS, MMS, Wap, and I-Mode. It works closely with international news agencies like Reuters, Deutsche Presse Agentur (Germany), Agence France-Presse (France), and Belga (Belgium).

4. Raad voor de Journalistiek, "Guidelines of the Netherlands Press Council," *Raad voor de Journalistiek*, 1 June 2018, https://www.rvdj.nl/english/guidelines.

5. Several passages from the 2018 Guidelines of the Netherlands Press Council are relevant: Under Section C.1. "Privacy": "Journalists must prevent information or images from being published as a result of which suspects and convicted persons can be easily identified and traced by the public at large. Journalists are not obliged to observe this rule if the name forms a vital part of the report, if omission of the name on account of the general reputation of the person involved does not serve any purpose, if omission of the name can cause confusion with others who can be expected to be harmed as a result of that, if the name is mentioned within the framework of issuing appeals or if the person involved goes public him or herself" (pp. 7–8). Three iterations of the ethics guidelines are available for comparison (2010, 2015, and 2018), and all include a very similar section to the one from 2018 quoted here. For more, see: Raad voor de Journalistiek, "Guidelines of the Netherlands Press Council," *Raad voor de Journalistiek*, 2010, 2015, and 2018, https://www.rvdj.nl/english/guidelines.

6. The 2010 Ethics Guidelines of the Netherlands Press Council made specific reference to this, but the initial sentence disappears in the 2015 edition of the Code: 2.4.6. "A journalist prevents himself from publishing details in pictures and text as a result of which suspects and accused can be easily identified and traced by persons other than the circle of people that already know about them.

   A journalist does not have to observe this rule when:

   - the name forms an important part of the report;
   - not mentioning the name because of the general reputation of the person involved does not serve any purpose;

- not mentioning the name could cause a mix-up with others who can be predictably harmed as a result of that;
- the name is mentioned within the framework of investigative reporting;
- the person himself seeks publicity." See: Raad voor de Journalistiek, "Guidelines of the Netherlands Press Council."

7. Evening tabloids are most often criticized by the Swedish Press Council. See: Weibull and Börjesson, "The Swedish Media Accountability System."

8. For more about *De Telegraaf*, see: Amsterdam Info Staff, "Amsterdam Newspapers," *Amsterdam Info*, n.d., https://www.amsterdam.info/newspapers/; Expatica Staff, "Media in the Netherlands: Expat guide to The Netherlands," *Expatica*, 15 November 2018, https://www.expatica.com/nl/living/telecommunications/media-in-the-netherlands-106958/; Press Reference Staff, "Netherlands Press," *Press Reference*, n.d., http://www.pressreference.com/Ma-No/Netherlands.html#ixzz5dl9feTuj. While we did request interviews with journalists and editors at *De Telegraaf*, no one agreed to speak with us on the record.

9. In libel proceedings in Sweden, jury trials are required; they are an exception to the usual system of judge only. See: Weibull and Börjesson, "The Swedish Media Accountability System."

10. Weibull and Börjesson, "The Swedish Media Accountability System," 137.

11. Weibull and Börjesson, "The Swedish Media Accountability System," 137.

12. The vast majority of privacy laws in the Netherlands, Sweden, and Germany follow the directives of the European Union and relate to the protection of personal data and privacy on line. Germany does, however, have some specific laws that limit when a media organization can disseminate information about a convicted person.

13. For more information, see: Taylor Wessing Staff, "German Personality Rights in 2012," *Taylor Wessing LLP*, 1 February 2013, https://www.taylorwessing.com/download/article_germanpersonalityrights.html#.XIfWUC0ZPUo. The site also outlines that under this legislation, German courts consider three "spheres" where privacy can be infringed upon: "core," which covers all aspects of an individual's private life. If content affects this sphere, German law does not balance the interest against factors like freedom of expression. Instead, there is absolute protection of private life. "Private," which covers aspects of a person's life like family. It can be balanced against all interests involved. "Social," which includes business and social life and is less protected than the previous two spheres. A number of reporters to whom we spoke mentioned that they were careful to observe the "right to personality" laws in Germany as well as the guidelines of their press council.

14. This story, from the Dutch newspaper, *De Volkskrant*, offers the following [translated from Dutch]: "In the end, it became less than half a year because of all the 'negative publicity' that Paarlberg received. That has damaged him both professionally and personally, the judges believe." Merijn Rengers and John Schoorl, "'Verbijsterde' Paarlberg on Appeal," *de Volkskrant*, 8 June 2010, https://www.volkskrant.nl/economie/verbijsterde-paarlberg-in-hoger-beroep~b4948088/.

15. For ways in which resocialization is both a practical—i.e., a community concern—and also a moral one, see: Christine Morgenstern, "Judicial Rehabilitation in

Germany—The Use of Criminal Records and the Removal of Recorded Convictions," *European Journal of Probation* 3, no. 1 (2011): 22.

16. Germans prefer the term "resocialization." Historically, "rehabilitation" has referred to revocation of illegitimate legal judgments rendered under the Third Reich or during the German Democratic Republic (Soviet East Germany between 1945 and 1990).

17. Laws in most countries recognize some form of personality rights, generally referred to as privacy rights in the English-speaking world. These laws usually protect the commercial appropriation of one's name or image. In German legal precedent, it has come to mean a right to honor (based in a more fundamental right to dignity) and of reintegration into society, both of which place limits on the press. Dieter Dörr and Eve Aernecke, "A Never Ending Story: Caroline v Germany," in *The Right to Privacy in the Light of Media Convergence*, ed. Dieter Dörr and Russell L. Weaver (Berlin: De Gruyter, 2012), 114–124.

18. Public interest is not specifically defined in the German Press Council code, but Section 1 of the code does state: "Respect for the truth, preservation of human dignity, and accurate informing of the public are the overriding principles of the Press." See: Deutscher Presserat, *German Press Code: Guidelines for Journalistic Work as Recommended by the German Press Council* (Berlin: Deutscher Presserat, 2017). This passage suggests that the Germans do not see any incompatibility between conveying truth and protecting a person's dignity; in other words, truth can be conveyed as it must to the public to serve its democratic interests but not at the expense of an individual. This is a contrast to how Watchdog countries see naming names and the public interest.

19. Morgenstern, "Judicial Rehabilitation in Germany"; Ronald J. Krotoszynski Jr, *The First Amendment in Cross-Cultural Perspective: A Comparative Legal Analysis of the Freedom of Speech* (New York: New York University Press, 2006).

20. The decision by the Bundesverfassungsgericht of the German Federal Constitutional Court quoted here is taken from Morgenstern, "Judicial Rehabilitation in Germany."

21. Lennart Weibull drew this diagram for us; it does not exist in published form in English. He has, however, published a version of it in Swedish. It can be found in Lennart Weibull and Britt Börjesson, *Publicistiska seder: Svensk pressetik I teori och praktik 1900–1994* [Publishing Traditions. Swedish press ethics in theory and practice]. (Stockholm: Tidens förlag, 1995).

22. American ethics scholar Lou Hodges argued that journalists should publish private information about public officials, even against the officials' will, if the private activity might reasonably have a significant effect on their official performances. In a democracy, the activities of those whom citizens elect need to be made visible to all; transparency is key both for the role journalists play and for the politicians themselves. See: Lou Hodges, "Privacy and the Press," in *The Handbook of Mass Media Ethics*, ed. Lee Wilkins and Clifford Christians (New York: Routledge, 2009), 282.

23. Several people used this phrase or a close variation: crime researcher and academic Melanie Verhovnik; crime and courts reporter Annette Ramelsberger.

24. Juveniles are protected by law in Germany, Canada, Ireland, and England. There are exceptions, however. In Germany, Verhovnik pointed out that some school shooters, usually in their late teens, are named, because these cases are ones "for the history books." When children are tried as adults, as has happened in several cases in Canada and England, they can be named by the press. Juvenile records are generally not public in the United States, and the press usually abides by that protection. U.S. trials of juveniles in adult court are public.

25. Verhovnik has studied school shootings in Germany (and compared them to elsewhere). Melanie Verhovnik, "School Shootings in Media Coverage: Why Media Play an Important Role in the Genesis of School Shootings," *The International Journal of Interdisciplinary Studies in Communication* 10, no. 3 (2015): 31–46.

26. BBC Staff, "German Nurse 'Admits Killing 30' with Fatal Overdoses," 8 January 2015, https://www.bbc.com/news/world-30732841.

27. The Gladbeck hostage crisis or hostage drama occurred in August 1988 after an armed bank robbery in Gladbeck, North Rhine-Westphalia, West Germany. The robbers were Dieter Degowski and Hans-Jürgen Rösner, both with previous criminal records. They took hostages and went on the run. In part, though, the story is referred to because a number of German reporters conducted interviews with the hostage takers and some assisted them in various ways. This story was relayed by Tanjev Schultz, an academic educated in Germany and the United States, and who has also worked as a journalist for *Tagesspiegel*, as well as *Süddeutsche Zeitung*, mainly on topics of internal security and terrorism, with a focus on the trials of the National Socialist Underground (NSU). With colleagues, he is writing a book about this.

28. One reporter, who later became editor in chief of *Bild*, allegedly even hopped in the hostages' car and gave them directions around Cologne to avoid police.

29. Michael Marek and Marie Todeskino, "German Hostage Drama: The Day the Press Became the Story," *Deutsche Welle*, 16 August 2018, https://www.dw.com/en/german-hostage-drama-the-day-the-press-became-the-story/a-17025034.

30. For details, see two articles from the newspaper *De Volkskrant*. De Volkskrant Staff, "Hans Melchers Establishes Press Victims Foundation," *de Volkskrant*, 21 October 2006, https://www.volkskrant.nl/nieuws-achtergrond/hans-melchers-richt-stichting-slachtoffers-pers-op~b82912ad/; Willem Beusekamp, "Suspicious Abduction Melchers Dissatisfied," *de Volkskrant*, 14 August 2006, https://www.volkskrant.nl/nieuws-achtergrond/verdachte-ontvoering-melchers-ontevreden~bedd340e/.

31. Periodically, legislatures consider laws that journalists and media freedom advocates raise concern about. The most recent proposal was an espionage act (2017) that if passed, would have affected both the Fundamental Law on Freedom of Expression (1991) and its much older counterpart, the Freedom of the Press Act (1766). The op-ed piece suggests that the vague wording might mean that a reporter investigating Swedish wrongdoing in the context of something like a UN operation, would be risking four years of imprisonment if convicted. See the full article: Ole von Uexkull, "Opinion: Proposed Law Change Threatens to Erode Sweden's Press Freedom," *The Local Sweden*, 13 March 2018, https://www.thelocal.se/20180313/opinion-proposed-law-change-threatens-to-erode-swedens-press-freedom.

32. Daniel C. Hallin and Paolo Mancini, *Comparing Media Systems: Three Models of Media and Politics* (Cambridge, U.K.: Cambridge University Press, 2004).

33. See Sydney Smith's article, "Where Is the Outrage? Dutch Newspaper Interviews 9-year-old Plane Crash Survivor from His Hospital Bed," iMediaEthics, 10 May 2010, https://www.imediaethics.org/wheres-the-outrage-dutch-newspaper-interviews-9-year-old-plane-crash-survivor-from-his-hospital-bed/.

34. Tanjev Schultz noted that state attorneys are independent from the lawyers who represent the victims; they do not work together.

35. Froukje Santing (member, Netherlands Press Council) in discussion with the authors, 11 June 2010.

36. Communitarianism was much discussed in the late 1990s, and several respected ethicists have written about the term, its definition, and its application to the practice of journalism. See: David A. Craig, "Communitarian Journalism(s): Clearing Conceptual Landscapes," *Journal of Mass Media Ethics* 11, no. 2 (1996): 107–118; Clifford G. Christians, John P. Ferré, and P. Mark Fackler, *Good News: Social Ethics and the Press* (Oxford: Oxford University Press, 1993).

37. Bell quoted in Craig, "Communitarian Journalism(s)," 108. Also see: Daniel Bell, *Communitarianism and Its Critics* (Oxford: Clarendon Press, 1993).

38. Christians et al., *Good News*, 21.

39. Carol Gilligan, *In a Different Voice* (Cambridge, MA: Harvard University Press, 1993).

40. Gilligan, *In a Different Voice*, 101.

41. Gilligan, *In a Different Voice*, 101.

42. Gilligan, *In a Different Voice*.

43. Katz, "What Makes Crime 'News'?"

44. Morgan Jerkins, "The Genius Behind Nameless Protagonists," *Book Riot*, 14 March 2015, https://bookriot.com/2015/03/14/critical-linking-march-14-2015/.

45. Sam Sacks, "The Rise of the Nameless Narrator," *The New Yorker*, 3 March 2015, https://www.newyorker.com/books/page-turner/the-rise-of-the-nameless-narrator.

46. Bettelheim quoted in Sacks, "The Rise of the Nameless Narrator."

47. Bruno Bettelheim, *The Uses of Enchantment: The Meaning and Importance of Fairy Tales* (New York: Vintage, 2010), 37.

48. Bettelheim, *The Uses of Enchantment*, 5.

49. James W. Carey, "A Cultural Approach to Communication," in *Communication as Culture: Essays on Media and Society* (London: Routledge, 2008), 23.

50. Carey, "A Cultural Approach to Communication," 23.

51. Carey, *Communication as Culture*, 15.

52. Carey, *Communication as Culture*, 15.

53. Hallin and Mancini, *Comparing Media Systems*.

54. Hallin and Mancini, *Comparing Media Systems*, 144.

55. Hallin and Mancini, *Comparing Media Systems*, 144.

56. Lennart Weibull, "Press Law of 1766, Sweden," in *Encyclopedia of Political Communication*, ed. Lynda Lee Kaid and Christina Holtz-Bacha (Thousand Oaks, CA: SAGE, 2007), 645–646.

Chapter 3

1. James W. Carey, *Communication as Culture: Essays on Media and Society* (London: Routledge, 2008).

2. Katrin Bennhold, "Grappling with Death in a Small German Town," *New York Times*, 17 January 2018, https://www.nytimes.com/2018/01/17/insider/kandel-germany-mia-v-murder.html.

3. German Press Council Guidelines for Journalistic Work. Section 12.1, as of 2006. Accountable Journalism, https://accountablejournalism.org/ethics-codes/Germany-Press-Council.

4. German Press Council Guidelines for Journalistic Work. Section 12.1, as of 2017. Presserat (German Press Council), https://www.presserat.de/files/presserat/dokumente/download/Press%20Code.pdf.

5. Rick Noack, "Leaked Document Says 2,000 Men Allegedly Assaulted 1,200 German Women on New Year's Eve," *Washington Post*, 11 July 2016, https://www.washingtonpost.com/news/worldviews/wp/2016/07/10/leaked-document-says-2000-men-allegedly-assaulted-1200-german-women-on-new-years-eve/?noredirect=on&utm_term=.6aa3be390ffc.

6. Rick Noack, "Sexual Assaults Challenge Germany's Welcoming Attitude Toward Refugees," *Washington Post*, 6 January 2016, https://www.washingtonpost.com/news/worldviews/wp/2016/01/06/sexual-assaults-challenge-germanys-welcoming-attitude-toward-refugees/?utm_term=.4fd111e72dd5.

7. The previous iteration of the Deutscher Presserat Code, used until March 2017, was presented to Federal President Gustave W. Heinmann on December 12, 1973, in Bonn, Germany.

8. Nicole Scialabba, "Should Juveniles Be Charged as Adults in the Criminal Justice System?," American Bar Association, 3 October 2016, https://www.americanbar.org/groups/litigation/committees/childrens-rights/articles/2016/should-juveniles-be-charged-as-adults/; Youth Justice Legal Centre Staff, "Which Court?," Youth Justice Legal Centre, 20 January 2015, https://yjlc.uk/which-court/; Citizens Information Staff, "Children and the Criminal Justice System," *Citizens Information*, 3 May 2017, https://www.citizensinformation.ie/en/justice/children_and_young_offenders/children_and_the_criminal_justice_system_in_ireland.html; Chinta Puxley, "A Look at How Canadian Courts Handle Young People Charged with Murder," *The Canadian Press*, 26 January 2016, https://globalnews.ca/news/2476202/a-look-at-how-courts-handle-youth-murder-suspects/; Department of Justice, "Publication Bans," Government of Canada, 5 March 2015, https://www.justice.gc.ca/eng/cj-jp/yj-jj/tools-outils/sheets-feuillets/publi-publi.html; Anthony Hooper, David C. Ormerod, and Duncan Atkinson, "Section F19 Inferences from Silence and the Non-production of Evidence," in *Blackstone's Criminal Practice 2012* (Oxford: Oxford University Press, 2012), 2709.

9. Sibella Matthews, Vincent Schiraldi, and Lael Chester, "Youth Justice in Europe: Experience of Germany, the Netherlands, and Croatia in Providing Developmentally Appropriate Responses to Emerging Adults in the Criminal Justice System," *Justice Evaluation Journal* 1, no. 1 (2018): 59–81.

10. Several people we interviewed used this phrase or a close variation: e.g., crime researcher and academic Melanie Verhovnik; crime and courts reporter Annette Ramelsberger. When stories reach a subjective point where they are so (in)famous, then reporters can use names; this includes the names of minors, as has sometimes been done in the cases of school shootings.

11. Lorenz Langer, *Religious Offence and Human Rights: The Implications of Defamation of Religions*. (Cambridge: Cambridge University Press, 2014), 33.

12. Corinna da Fonseca-Wollheim, "750,000 Germans Fled East Prussia in 1945: A Novelist Imagines One Family's Exodus," *New York Times*, 25 May 2018, https://www.nytimes.com/2018/05/25/books/review/walter-kempowski-all-for-nothing.html.

13. David Abadi, Leen d'Haenens, Keith Roe, and Joyce Koeman, "Leitkultur and Discourse Hegemonies: German Mainstream Media Coverage on the Integration Debate Between 2009 and 2014," *International Communication Gazette* 78, no. 6 (2016): 561.

14. Walter R. Fisher, *Human Communication as Narration: Toward a Philosophy of Reason, Value, and Action* (Columbia: University of South Carolina Press, 1989); Alasdair MacIntyre, *After Virtue* (South Bend, IN: University of Notre Dame Press, 1984).

15. Robert Reiner, "Crime and Control in Britain," *Sociology* 34, no. 1 (2000): 71–94.

16. Despite this, some American right-wing, anti-immigrant organizations have tried to adopt the "blood and soil" notion.

17. David Crouch, "The New 'People's Home': How Sweden Is Waging War on Inequality," *The Guardian*, 17 July 2017, https://www.theguardian.com/inequality/2017/jul/17/peoples-home-sweden-waged-war-inequality-rich-poor-gothenburg.

18. Akbar Ahmed, *Journey into Europe: Islam, Immigration, and Identity* (Washington, DC: Brookings Institution Press, 2018).

19. Prof. Lennart Weibull is senior researcher at the SOM Institute at the University of Gothenburg, which collects survey and other data on "Swedes' habits, behavior, opinions and values with respect to society, politics and media, https://som.gu.se/som_institute/about-som.

20. Carey, *Communication as Culture*.

21. Carey, *Communication as Culture*, 15.

22. Carey, *Communication as Culture*, 18.

23. Carey, *Communication as Culture*, 18.

24. Carey, *Communication as Culture*, 18.

Chapter 4

1. Bill Kovach and Tom Rosenstiel, *The Elements of Journalism: What Newspeople Should Know and the Public Should Expect* (New York: Three Rivers Press, 2014), 17.

2. Journalism has secondary functions: to entertain, amuse, or educate, for example. Journalism as a whole, not every article, has an obligation to fulfill this basic mission.

3. Robert Reiner, "Media Made Criminality: The Representation of Crime in the Mass Media," in *The Oxford Handbook of Criminology*, ed. Mike Maguire, Rodney Morgan, and Robert Reiner (New York: Oxford University Press, 2002), 302–340. Reiner writes "not unambiguous decline in the quality of life" by which he means a decline of shared communal outlooks and values (xxxviii). Reiner also argues, in "What's Left? The Prospects for Social Democratic Criminology," that the social democratic conceptions of crime and criminality were displaced in the 1970s with the law-and-order outlook closely associated with neoliberalism. See: Robert Reiner, "What's Left? The Prospects for Social Democratic Criminology," *Crime, Media, Culture* 8, no. 2 (2012): 135–150.

4. Jean Bethke Elshtain, *Public Man, Private Woman: Women in Social and Political Thought* (Princeton, NJ: Princeton University Press, 1993), 38.

5. Jack Katz, "What Makes Crime 'News'?," *Media, Culture & Society* 9, no. 1 (1987): 47–75.

6. Robert Reiner, Sonia Livingstone, and Jessica Allen, "From Law and Order to Lynch Mobs: Crime News Since the Second World War," in *Criminal Visions: Media Representations of Crime and Justice*, ed. Paul Mason (Cullompton, Devon, U.K.: Willan, 2003), 31.

7. See also: Romayne Smith Fullerton and Maggie Jones Patterson, "Murder in Our Midst: Expanding Coverage to Include Care and Responsibility," *Journal of Mass Media Ethics* 21, no. 4 (2006): 304–321.

8. Reiner et al., "From Law and Order to Lynch Mobs," 31.

9. Stephen Ward, *Ethical Journalism in a Populist Age: The Democratically Engaged Journalist* (Lanham, MD: Rowman & Littlefield, 2018).

10. Robert Entman writes: "To frame is to select some aspects of a perceived reality and make them more salient in a communicating text, in such a way as to promote a particular problem definition, causal interpretation, moral evaluation, and/or treatment recommendation for the item described." Robert M. Entman, "Framing: Toward Clarification of a Fractured Paradigm," *Journal of Communication* 43, no. 4 (1993): 52.

11. Katrin Bennhold, "German Intelligence Agency Says It Will Track Members of Far-Right Party," *New York Times*, 16 January 2019, https://www.nytimes.com/2019/01/15/world/europe/alternative-for-germany-investigation.html. Bennhold writes: "It eventually emerged that paid informers of the intelligence service helped hide the group's leaders and build up its network. The case has become a byword for the failure of Germany's post-war security apparatus to monitor and control far-right extremism."

12. Spiegel Staff, "Neo-Nazi Evil Has an Ordinary Face," *Spiegel*, 7 May 2013, https://www.spiegel.de/international/germany/german-press-reaction-to-start-of-nsu-neo-nazi-trial-a-898557.html.

13. Thomas Meaney and Saskia Schäfer, "The Neo-Nazi Murder Trial Revealing Germany's Darkest Secrets," *The Guardian*, 15 December 2016, https://www.theguardian.com/world/2016/dec/15/neo-nazi-murders-revealing-germanys-darkest-secrets.

14. Meaney and Schäfer, "The Neo-Nazi Murder Trial Revealing Germany's Darkest Secrets."

15. Gisela Friedrichsen, "Fast alles, was Hussein K. erzählt hat, war gelogen" [Almost everything that Hussein K. said was a lie], *Welt*, 3 February 2018, https://www.welt.de/vermischtes/plus174127866/Vergewaltigung-in-Freiburg-Fast-alles-was-Hussein-K-erzaehlt-hat-war-gelogen.html.

16. Asylum Information Database, "Overview of the Main Changes Since the Previous Report Update," Asylum Information Database, 1 March 2018, http://www.asylumineurope.org/reports/country/germany/overview-main-changes-previous-report-update.

17. Felix Hansen and Sebastian Schneider, "Facts & Figures About the NSU Trial—An Overview," NSU Watch, 23 September 2017, https://www.nsu-watch.info/2017/09/facts-figures-about-the-nsu-trial/; Annette Ramelsberger, "Eine schrecklich normale Entwicklung" [A terribly normal development], *Süddeutsche Zeitung*, 6 May 2018, https://www.sueddeutsche.de/politik/nsu-prozess-wo-es-wehtut-1.3966494.

18. Die Welt News Staff, "Germany's NSU Neo-Nazi Trial Verdict Sparks Protests, Calls for Investigation, *Die Welt*, 11 July 2018, https://p.dw.com/p/31JDB.

19. Rebecca Staudenmaier (with DPA, Tagesschau), "NSU Victims' Families Sue Government over Investigation Errors," *Die Welt*, 18 June 2017, https://p.dw.com/p/2etKY.

20. Ramelsberger, "Eine schrecklich normale Entwicklung" [A terribly normal development].

21. Ramelsberger, "Eine schrecklich normale Entwicklung" [A terribly normal development].

22. The rise of the victims' rights movement began with American conservative and lawyer Frank G. Carrington in 1966 when he founded Americans for Effective Law Enforcement to push back against a series of court decisions in the early and mid-1960s that protected the rights of defendants. He also wrote a book, titled *The Victims*, published in 1975 that popularized his ideas. See: Frank Carrington, *The Victims* (New Rochelle, NY: Arlington House, 1975).

23. Former district court judge from Massachusetts Nancy Gertner; former prosecutor Scott Sundby, who studies capital juries; and Raphael Ginsberg, who runs a prison-education program through the University of North Carolina. All are quoted in American historian Jill Lepore's article, "The Rise of the Victims'-Rights Movement," *The New Yorker*, 14 May 2018, https://www.newyorker.com/magazine/2018/05/21/the-rise-of-the-victims-rights-movement.

24. Lepore, "The Rise of the Victims'-Rights Movement."

25. Beate Zschäpe, 43, was sentenced to life in prison on July 11, 2018, for the murder of ten persons, two bombings, and several attempted murders and robberies between 2000 and 2007. Ralf Wohlbeben, who supplied the murder weapon, was sentenced to ten years. The other three defendants, who had aided the group in various ways, received lesser sentences.

26. Mari Matsuda, "Critical Race Theory and Critical Legal Studies: Contestation and Coalition," in *Critical Race Theory: The Key Writings that Formed the Movement*, ed. Neil Gotanda and Garry Peller (New York: New Press 1995), 62–79.

27. Roland Barthes, "Dominici, or the Triumph of Literature," in *Mythologies*, trans. Annette Lavers (New York: Hill and Wang 1972), 43–46.

28. Jean-Francois Lyotard, *The Differend: Phrases in Dispute*, trans. G. Van Den Abbeele (Minneapolis: University of Minnesota Press, 1988).

29. Emmanuel Levinas, *Ethics and Infinity*, trans. Richard Cohen (Pittsburgh: Duquesne University Press, 1985).

30. Levinas, *Ethics and Infinity*.

31. Levinas, *Ethics and Infinity*.

32. Romayne Smith Fullerton and Maggie Jones Patterson, "'Killing' the True Story of First Nations: The Ethics of Constructing a Culture Apart," *Journal of Mass Media Ethics* 23, no. 3 (2008): 203.

33. Roland Barthes, *Mythologies*, trans. Annette Lavers (New York: Hill and Wang, 1972).

34. Melanie Verhovnik, "School Shootings in Media Coverage: Why Media Play an Important Role in the Genesis of School Shootings," *The International Journal of Interdisciplinary Studies in Communication* 10, no. 3 (2015): 31–46.

35. Verhovnik wrote in her article "School Shootings in Media Coverage . . . are in contrast to the results of empirical research about school shootings from psychology, sociology, education and criminology, which emphasize the complexity of the phenomenon" (42–43).

36. Verhovnik, "School Shootings in Media Coverage," 39.

37. Verhovnik, "School Shootings in Media Coverage," 43.

38. Verhovnik, "School Shootings in Media Coverage," 43.

39. Amy Mitchell, Katie Simmons, Katerina Eva Matsa, and Laura Silver, "Global Publics Want Politically Balanced News, but Do Not Think Their News Media Are Doing Very Well in This Area," Pew Research Center, 11 January 2018, https://www.pewglobal.org/2018/01/11/publics-globally-want-unbiased-news-coverage-but-are-divided-on-whether-their-news-media-deliver/.

40. Mitchell et al., "Global Publics Want Politically Balanced News."

41. Katerina Eva Matsa, "Across Western Europe Public News Media Are Widely Used and Trusted Sources of News," Pew Research Center, 8 June 2018, https://www.pewresearch.org/fact-tank/2018/06/08/western-europe-public-news-media-widely-used-and-trusted/.

42. Mark Wollacott, "Differences Between Libertarian & Social Responsibility Models of the Press," *Bizfluent*, 26 September 2017, https://bizfluent.com/info-8109528-differences-social-responsibility-theories-press.html.

43. Raad voor de Journalistiek, "Guidelines of the Netherlands Press Council," Raad voor de Journalistiek, 1 June 2018, https://www.rvdj.nl/english/guidelines.

44. European Federation of Journalists Staff, "Freelance Journalist Facing Alone Lawsuits After Publication of Articles on Italian Businessman," European Federation of Journalists, 21 April 2017, https://europeanjournalists.org/blog/2017/04/21/freelance-journalist-facing-alone-lawsuits-after-publication-of-articles-on-italian-businessman/; Andreas Rossmann, "Learning from the Mafia Means Learning to Be Silent," European Centre for Press and Media Freedom, 3 May 2017, https://ecpmf.eu/news/ecpmf/learning-from-the-mafia-means-learning-to-be-silent.

45. Daphne C. Koene, *Press Councils in Western Europe* (Diemen, The Netherlands: AMB, 2009), 88.

46. Deutscher Presserat, "Section 8: Protection of Personality," in German Press Code (Berlin: Deutscher Presserat, 2013).

47. To date, he has not.

48. Quoted in Lara Fielden, *Regulating the Press: A Comparative Study of International Press Councils* (Oxford: Reuters Institute for the Study of Journalism, 2012), 40.

49. Thomas Carlyle, *On Heroes, Hero-Worship, and the Heroic in History* (Oakland: University of California Press, 1993).

50. Helle Sjøvaag, "The Reciprocity of Journalism's Social Contract: The Political-Philosophical Foundations of Journalistic Ideology," *Journalism Studies* 11, no. 6 (2010): 880–881.

51. Mary Ann Glendon, *Abortion and Divorce in Western Law* (Cambridge, MA: Harvard University Press, 1987), 8.

52. Glendon, *Abortion and Divorce in Western Law*, 9.

53. Nicholas Turner and Jeremy Travis, "What We Learned from German Prisons," *New York Times*, 6 August 2015, https://www.nytimes.com/2015/08/07/opinion/what-we-learned-from-german-prisons.html.

54. Turner and Travis, "What We Learned from German Prisons."

55. Michael Tonry, "Preface," in *Crime and Justice in Scandinavia*, ed. Michael Tonry and Tapio Lappi-Seppälä (Chicago: University of Chicago Press, 2011). These facts prompt questions about how recidivism rates compare. Daniel Nagin, Teresa and H. John Heinz III professor of Public Policy and Statistics at Carnegie Mellon University, cautioned us against making any cross-border comparisons. Variations in definitions of crime and record keeping make comparisons of crime and recidivism rates generally unreliable, he said.

56. Michael Tonry and Catrien Bijleveld, "Crime, Criminal Justice, and Criminology in the Netherlands," in *Crime and Justice in the Netherlands*, ed. Michael Tonry and Catrien Bijleveld, (Chicago: University of Chicago Press, 2007), 1–30.

57. Tonry and Bijleveld, "Crime, Criminal Justice, and Criminology in the Netherlands," 10.

58. Tonry and Bijleveld, "Crime, Criminal Justice, and Criminology in the Netherlands," 10.

59. Michael Tonry and Tapio Lappi-Seppälä, "Crime, Criminal Justice, and Criminology in the Nordic Countries," in *Crime and Justice in Scandinavia*, ed. Michael Tonry and Tapio Lappi-Seppälä (Chicago: University of Chicago Press, 2011), 8.

60. Tonry and Lappi-Seppälä, "Crime, Criminal Justice, and Criminology in the Nordic Countries," 5.

61. Tonry and Lappi-Seppälä, "Crime, Criminal Justice, and Criminology in the Nordic Countries," 8.

62. Peter Wagner and Wendy Sawyer, "States of Incarceration: The Global Context 2018," Prison Policy Initiative, 1 June 2018, https://www.prisonpolicy.org/global/2018.html.

63. Tonry and Lappi-Seppälä, "Crime, Criminal Justice, and Criminology in the Nordic Countries," 8–9.

64. Tonry and Lappi-Seppälä, "Crime, Criminal Justice, and Criminology in the Nordic Countries," 9.

65. Tonry and Lappi-Seppälä, "Crime, Criminal Justice, and Criminology in the Nordic Countries," 1–2.

66. Tonry and Lappi-Seppälä, "Crime, Criminal Justice, and Criminology in the Nordic Countries," 23.

67. See for example the idealization of the Norwegian prison system in Michael Moore, dir., *Where to Invade Next*, (2015; United States; Dog Eat Dog Films and IMG Films), film.

68. Tonry, "Preface," in *Crime and Justice in Scandinavia*, ix.

69. Katrin Bennhold, "Bavaria: Affluent, Picturesque—and Angry," *New York Times*, 30 June 2018, https://www.nytimes.com/2018/06/30/world/europe/bavaria-immigration-afd-munich.html.

70. Katrin Bennhold, "Crosses Go up in Public Offices: It's Culture, Bavaria Says, Not Religion," *New York Times*, 30 May 2018, https://www.nytimes.com/2018/05/30/world/europe/bavaria-germany-crucifix-migrants.html.

71. Daniel C. Hallin and Paolo Mancini, *Comparing Media Systems: Three Models of Media and Politics* (Cambridge, U.K.: Cambridge University Press, 2004), 271.

72. Hallin and Mancini, *Comparing Media Systems*, 294.

73. Such stipulations are outlined here: Raad voor de Journalistiek, "Developments," Raad voor de Journalistiek, n.d., https://www.rvdj.nl/english. They were also outlined to us by the current chair of the Netherlands Press Council, Fritz Von Exter.

74. Stephen Ward, "Philosophical Foundations for Global Journalism Ethics," *Journal of Mass Media Ethics* 20, no. 1 (2005): 4.

75. Ward, "Philosophical Foundations for Global Journalism Ethics," 5.

Part 2

1. For a bit of history, see: Nicola Laver, "Contempt of Court Act 1981," *Inbrief*, n.d., https://www.inbrief.co.uk/legal-system/contempt-of-court-act/; Roy Greenslade, "See You in Court—Dominic Grieve Lays Down Law on Contempt," *Evening Standard*, 30 November 2011, https://www.standard.co.uk/business/media/see-you-in-court-dominic-grieve-lays-down-law-on-contempt-6373540.html.

2. Joel Gunter, "Chris Jefferies Wins 'Substantial' Libel Damages from Newspapers," Journalism.co.uk, 29 July 2011, https://www.journalism.co.uk/news/chris-jefferies-wins-substantial-libel-damages-from-newspapers/s2/a545392/.

Chapter 5

1. We had little success in garnering interviews with tabloid reporters. Michael O'Toole was one exception. His colleagues noted that he was the best crime reporter in Ireland.

2. Moral panic was a concept first developed in the United Kingdom in the 1960s largely by Stanley Cohen. Working from his dissertation, Cohen published *Moral Panics*

(1973), which analyzed the definition of a social reaction to youth subcultures, focusing on the clash between the Mods and the Rockers. He wrote, "Societies appear to be subject, every now and then, to periods of moral panic. A condition, episode, person or group of persons emerges to become defined as a threat to societal values and interests; its nature is presented in a stylized and stereotypical fashion by the mass media; the moral barricades are manned by editors, bishops, politicians, and other right-thinking people; socially accredited experts pronounce their diagnoses and solutions; ways of coping are evolved or (more often) resorted to; the condition then disappears, submerges, or deteriorates and becomes more visible. Sometimes the object of panic is quite novel and at other times it is something which has been in existence long enough, but suddenly appears in the limelight. Sometimes the panic passes over and is forgotten, except in folk-lore and collective memory; at other times, it has more serious and long-lasting repercussions and might produce such changes as those in legal and social policy or even in the way society conceives itself." Stanley Cohen, *Folk Devils and Moral Panics* (London: Psychology Press, 2002 [1972]), 9.

3. Walter R. Fisher, *Human Communication as Narration: Toward a Philosophy of Reason, Value, and Action* (Columbia: University of South Carolina Press, 1989).

4. Fisher, *Human Communication as Narration*, 17.

5. Brandeis University Staff, "Louis D. Brandeis Legacy Fund for Social Justice," *Brandeis University*, n.d., https://www.brandeis.edu/legacyfund/bio.html.

6. Jürgen Habermas, *The Structural Transformation of the Public Sphere*, trans. Thomas Burger and Frederick Lawrence (Cambridge, UK: Polity, [1962] 1989).

7. Lesley Brown, *The New Shorter Oxford English Dictionary on Historical Principles* (Oxford: Oxford University Press, 1993).

8. Bill Kovach and Tom Rosenstiel, *The Elements of Journalism: What Newspeople Should Know and the Public Should Expect* (New York: Three Rivers Press, 2014), 10.

9. Kovach and Rosenstiel, *The Elements of Journalism*, 10.

10. Kovach and Rosenstiel, *The Elements of Journalism*, 17.

11. Washington Post Staff, "Policies and Standards," *Washington Post*, 1 January 2016, https://www.washingtonpost.com/news/ask-the-post/wp/2016/01/01/policies-and-standards/?utm_term=.522f55ae655e.

12. New York Times Staff, "Standards and Ethics," *New York Times*, n.d., https://www.nytco.com/who-we-are/culture/standards-and-ethics/.

13. Jay Rosen, *What Are Journalists For?* (New Haven, CT: Yale University Press, 1999), 1.

14. The Guardian Staff, "The Guardian's Editorial Code," *The Guardian*, 5 August 2015, https://www.theguardian.com/info/2015/aug/05/the-guardians-editorial-code.

15. BBC Staff, "Mission, Values and Public Purposes," BBC, n.d., https://www.bbc.com/aboutthebbc/governance/mission.

16. Irish Times Staff, "About the Irish Times," *Irish Times*, n.d., https://www.irishtimes.com/about-us/the-irish-times-trust.

17. The Globe and Mail Staff, "About Us," *The Globe and Mail*, n.d., https://www.theglobeandmail.com/about/.

18. Toronto Star, "About the Star," *Toronto Star*, 27 November 2018, https://www.thestar.com/about/aboutus.html#c.

19. Irish Times Staff, "About the Irish Times."

20. In Canada and in the United Kingdom, there are statutory publication bans on the names of complainants in sexual assault cases, as well as on accused persons under the age of 18. While court is open and the broad outlines of the stories can be reported, no identifying characteristics or photographs can be disseminated. Britain also has a gag order, usually requested by wealthy or powerful people when there are allegations of misbehavior until a decision is made about whether the information invades a person's privacy. These are called super-injunctions, and they cover not only information about the case but also the fact that a case is before the courts at all. In Ireland, the names of persons accused of sexual assault are not released unless they are convicted.

21. Maggie Jones Patterson and Steve Urbanski, "What Jayson Blair and Janet Cooke Say About the Press and the Erosion of Public Trust," *Journalism Studies* 7, no. 6 (2006): 828–850.

22. Patterson and Urbanski, "What Jayson Blair and Janet Cooke Say About the Press and the Erosion of Public Trust."

23. One of a handful of interviews we procured at a tabloid newspaper.

24. Interestingly, while all U.K. media named Tabak and published photos of him and his girlfriend from their Facebook accounts, the Dutch press largely withheld all identifying information, referring to him as Vincent T. or not naming him at all.

25. Canadian Press (CP) reporter Allison Jones wrote similar pieces for the news co-operative.

26. Christie Blatchford, "Christie Blatchford: Why I Can't Completely Share the Outrage over McClintic's Healing Lodge Transfer," *National Post*, 1 October 2018, https://nationalpost.com/opinion/christie-blatchford-why-i-cant-completely-share-the-outrage-over-mcclintics-healing-lodge-transfer.

27. John Milton nearly a century earlier, in his treatise for free speech, entitled, *Areopagitica*. John Milton, "Areopagitica," in *The Complete Poetry and Essential Prose of John Milton*, ed. William Kerrigan, John Rumrich, and Stephen M. Fallon (New York: Modern Library, 2007), 923–966.

28. Milton, "Areopagitica," 939.

29. Milton, "Areopagitica," 961.

30. See: John Stuart Mill, "Utilitarianism," in *Seven Masterpieces of Philosophy*, ed. Steven M. Cahn (New York: Routledge, 2016), 337–383.

31. Freedom of speech and freedom of the press are also enshrined in the Canadian Constitution Act, 1982. In Britain, there is a long tradition of a free press, but it is not a constitutional right.

32. See: Sissela Bok, *Lying: Moral Choice in Public and Private Life* (New York: Vintage, 1999).

33. See: Thomas Hobbes, *Leviathan*, ed. G. A. J. Rogers and Karl Schuhmann (London: Continuum, 2006).

34. Steven Knowlton and Bill Reader, *Moral Reasoning for Journalists* (Westport, CT: Praeger, 2008), 16.

35. Knowlton and Reader, *Moral Reasoning for Journalists*, 17–18. These journalists were John Trenchard and Thomas Gordon, who wrote a weekly column for several London newspapers beginning in 1720. Cato was the name of a Roman statesman known for his integrity and honesty.
36. Knowlton and Reader, *Moral Reasoning for Journalists*, 18.

Chapter 6

1. For more, see: Romayne Smith Fullerton and Maggie Jones Patterson, "Murder in Our Midst: Expanding Coverage to Include Care and Responsibility," *Journal of Mass Media Ethics* 21, no. 4 (2006): 304–321.
2. John Milton, "Areopagitica," in *The Complete Poetry and Essential Prose of John Milton*, ed. William Kerrigan, John Rumrich, and Stephen M. Fallon (New York: Modern Library, 2007).
3. It's worth mentioning that in virtually every country we visited, some of our interview subjects would note with envy the protection afforded American journalists under their First Amendment.
4. Brandeis University Staff, "Louis D. Brandeis Legacy Fund for Social Justice," Brandeis University, n.d., https://www.brandeis.edu/legacyfund/bio.html.
5. The naming of the nurse and use of numerous photographs is not the sole purview of tabloids. While *The Sun* wrote, "Who is [Full Name]? Countess of Chester Hospital nurse arrested on suspicion of murdering eight babies," *The Independent* chose a similar focus: "[Full Name]: Police search home of nurse after arresting health care worker on suspicion of murdering eight babies." See: Jay Akbar and Sofia Petkar, "Who Is [Full Name]? Countess of Chester Hospital Nurse Arrested on Suspicion of Murdering Eight Babies," *The Sun*, 8 July 2018, https://www.thesun.co.uk/news/6688782/lucy-letby-nurse-arrested-murder-eight-babies-hospital/; Samuel Osborne, "[Full Name]: Police Search Home of Nurse After Arresting Health Care Worker on Suspicion of Murdering Eight Babies," *The Independent*, 4 July 2018, https://www.independent.co.uk/news/uk/crime/lucy-letby-baby-murders-countess-cheshire-hospital-neo-natal-unit-arrest-police-a8430196.html. *The Guardian* ran a large headshot of the woman, taken from Facebook, directly under the headline, "Nurse arrested over Cheshire baby deaths released on bail" and the cutline above the photograph said, "[Full Name], 28, had been held on suspicion of murder of eight infants at Chester hospital." See: Nazia Parveen, "Nurse Arrested over Cheshire Baby Deaths Released on Bail," *The Guardian*, 6 July 2018, https://www.theguardian.com/uk-news/2018/jul/06/nurse-arrested-over-cheshire-baby-deaths-released-on-bail-lucy-letby.
6. "Master of Media Circus for Madeleine McCann," *Daily Telegraph,* 24 April 2008, https://www.telegraph.co.uk/news/1902515/Master-of-media-circus-for-Madeleine-McCann.html.
7. In Canada, *News Writing and Reporting* and, the older but well-established, the *Canadian Reporter* both suggest this approach. See: Bruce Gillespie, *News Writing and Reporting: An Introduction to Skills and Theory* (Oxford: Oxford University Press,

2018); Catherine McKercher and Carman Cumming, *The Canadian Reporter: News Writing and Reporting* (Scarborough, ON: Nelson Thompson Learning, 1998). U.S. journalists generally wait until charges are filed, rather than publish the name of a "person of interest." But there are a few notorious exceptions, such as the slander of Richard Jewell, who underwent "trial by media" despite never being charged in connection with a bomb planted at the 1996 Summer Olympics in Atlanta.

8. In addition to the possibility of being sued for libel, reporters risk violating the Contempt of Court Act 1981, which prohibits publication or dissemination of information that carries "substantial risk of serious prejudice" to the person charged. The right to a fair trial is a cornerstone of the justice system in England, and it's protected by both the European Convention on Human Rights and the Human Rights Act 1998. The latter states that a court will weigh the right to a fair trial (Article 6) against the right to freedom of expression, including media freedom (Article 10). Many media critics and practitioners, however, refer to the case that Cliff Richard won against the BBC for invasion of privacy in 2018 as a landmark indication of how that balance of freedoms will be weighed by jurists.

9. For more, see: Kate Lyons, "Grace Millane Murder: New Zealand Rebukes Google for Emailing out Suspect's Name," *The Guardian*, 19 December 2018, https://www.theguardian.com/world/2018/dec/19/grace-millane-new-zealand-rebukes-google-for-emailing-out-suspects-name; BBC News Staff, "Grace Millane: New Zealand Anger over Google Naming Murder Suspect," *BBC News*, 13 December 2018, https://www.bbc.com/news/world-asia-46548574. The *New York Times*, however, chose not to name the person but did outline the discussion about the inefficacy of laws designed before the Internet.

10. Paul Farhi, "An Australian Court's Gag Order Is No Match for the Internet, as Word Gets Out About Prominent Cardinal's Conviction," *Washington Post*, 13 December 2018, https://www.washingtonpost.com/lifestyle/style/an-australian-courts-gag-order-is-no-match-for-the-internet-as-word-gets-out-about-prominent-cardinals-conviction/2018/12/13/5137005c-fef5-11e8-83c0-b06139e540e5_story.html?utm_term=.a0da49bcf32c.

11. James W. Carey, *Communication as Culture: Essays on Media and Society* (London: Routledge, 2008), 6.

12. Michael J. Sandel, *What Money Can't Buy: The Moral Limits of Markets* (London: Macmillan, 2012), 10.

13. For the story about the high court ruling, see: Roy Greenslade, "Why Cliff Richard's Case Against the BBC Should Worry Us All," *The Guardian*, 17 April 2018, https://www.theguardian.com/commentisfree/2018/apr/17/cliff-richard-bbc-court-case-police-press-media.

14. See Greenslade's column about the case: "Why Cliff Richard's Case Against the BBC Should Worry Us All." In July 2018, Richard won a £210,000 settlement against the BBC for invasion of privacy. The BBC said it would appeal the decision. Jim Waterson, "Cliff Richard Wins £210,000 over BBC Privacy Case,"18 July 2018, *The Guardian*, https://www.theguardian.com/music/2018/jul/18/cliff-richard-wins-damages-from-bbc-over-police-raid-footage.

15. Muller was speaking in the context of the many media mistakes made after the 2013 bombing of the Boston Marathon. Bill Carter, "The F.B.I. Criticizes the News Media After Several Mistaken Reports of an Arrest," *New York Times*, 17 April 2013, https://www.nytimes.com/2013/04/18/business/media/fbi-criticizes-false-reports-of-a-bombing-arrest.html.

16. Consider how fake news sites during the 2016 American election incentivized the production of sensational, misleading, and wholly false information. Craig Silverman and Lawrence Alexander detailed how teenagers in the Balkans were creating outrageous stories—the more extreme, the more hits, and thus the more lucrative—not for political reasons, but to make money. To these teens in Macedonia, "a US Facebook user is worth about four times a user outside the US. The fraction-of-a-penny-per-click of US display advertising—a declining market for American publishers—goes a long way in Veles," wrote Silverman and Alexander. Craig Silverman and Lawrence Alexander, "How Teens in the Balkans Are Duping Trump Supporters with Fake News," *Buzzfeed News*, 3 November 2016.

17. Bob Cox, Jerry Dias and Edward Greenspon, "In a 'Fake News' Era, We Must Support Real News Reporting," *Winnipeg Free Press*, 9 September 2017, https://www.winnipegfreepress.com/opinion/analysis/in-a-fake-news-era-we-must-support-real-news-reporting-444478753.html. This op-ed offers a succinct summary of the detailed arguments about the links between the decline of journalism and the efficacy of democracy set forth by Edward Greenspon in *The Shattered Mirror: News, Democracy and Trust in the Digital Age* (Ottawa, ON: Public Policy Forum), 2017.

18. Cox, Dias and Greenspon, "In a 'Fake News' Era."

19. In the United States, for example, newsroom employment dropped nearly 25% between 2008 and 2017, with the greatest decline in newspapers, whose number of jobs dropped by 45% during this period, according to the Pew Research Center. See: Elizabeth Grieco, "Newsroom Employment Dropped Nearly a Quarter in Less Than 10 Years, with Greatest Decline at Newspapers," Pew Research Center, 30 July 2018, https://www.pewresearch.org/fact-tank/2018/07/30/newsroom-employment-dropped-nearly-a-quarter-in-less-than-10-years-with-greatest-decline-at-newspapers/. In Canada, the numbers are a bit less clear, but figures from Statistics Canada show that as a proportion of all working Canadians, the relative share of journalists is down by 20%. See: Chad Skelton, "There Are Fewer Journalists in Canada Than 15 Years Ago—But Not as Few as You Might Think," *J-Source*, 4 May 2018, https://j-source.ca/article/canadian-journalists-statistics/.

20. Emily Bell, "What 2,000 Job Cuts Tell Us: The Free Market Kills Digital Journalism," *The Guardian*, 2 February 2019, https://www.theguardian.com/media/2019/feb/02/what-2000-job-cuts-tell-us-the-free-market-kills-digital-journalism.

21. By "topspin," he means a kind of excessive gloss, done intentionally to sell more papers.

22. The *Christian Science Monitor* was the first American newspaper to switch to an all-digital format and update its stories throughout the day. The change occurred in April 2009. See: David Cook, "Monitor Shifts from Print to Web-Based Strategy," *Christian Science Monitor*, 29 October 2008, https://www.csmonitor.com/USA/2008/1029/p25s01-usgn.html.

23. John Horgan, *Irish Media: A Critical History Since 1922* (London: Routledge, 2001), 45.

24. Horgan, *Irish Media*.

25. In Ireland, defamation laws previously considered "draconian" by people like Seamus Dooley, head of the journalists union, were changed when the press and the government came to an agreement about establishing a press council and ombudsman. Consequently, if the organization is a member in good standing of the press council, they can use this as part of their defense if they were sued. Up to that point in Ireland, according to courts' press liaison Gerry Curran, juries had also awarded some enormous sums of money to parties that were far from innocent. In England, Christopher Jefferies successfully sued eight tabloids for libel, and reportedly won a substantial settlement, although the amount is not publicly available. See: Roy Greenslade, "Eight Newspapers Pay Libel Damages to Christopher Jefferies," *The Guardian*, 29 July 2011, https://www.theguardian.com/media/greenslade/2011/jul/29/joanna-yeates-national-newspapers.

26. Withness Statement of Christopher Jefferies to The Leveson Inquiry, 4 November 2011, 4, https://www.yumpu.com/en/document/read/35565190/witness-statement-of-christopher-jefferies.

27. Withness Statement of Christopher Jefferies to The Leveson Inquiry, 16.

28. Neither Canada nor the United States has the kind of national tabloid found in the United Kingdom, which has four national tabloids—*The Sun*, the *Daily Mail*, the *Daily Express*, and the *Daily Mirror*. According to the Audit Bureau of Circulation, *The Sun* is the most popular paper in the country, enjoying a daily circulation of nearly a million-and-a-half readers. For comparison, the most popular broadsheet, *The Times*, has a circulation of just under half a million.

29. Bruser noted that before 1982, when Canada's Constitution was repatriated and the Charter of Rights and Freedoms enshrined freedom of the press, the country followed common law and journalism practices very similar to that of England and Ireland. In this earlier period, when the right to a fair trial was pitted against the freedom of the press, the balance fell in favor of the former. In practice, this meant that once someone was charged, journalists were careful not to impugn guilt and trials were reported in a hard news manner, with no columnists in attendance. But once freedom of the press was enshrined as a constitutional right, a case referred to as *CBC v. Dagenais* was decided in favor of public dissemination, journalists in Canada moved toward a more American, tell-all style that leans on a push for publication.

30. "Pretrial Publicity Has Little Effect on the Right to a Fair Trial," Reporters Committee on Freedom of the Press, n.d. https://www.rcfp.org/journals/pretrial-publicitys-limited/.

31. Randy Richmond, "More Than Six Years After Her Child Was Slain, Tara McDonald Is Helping Bring New Life to Others," *London Free Press*, 30 July 2015, https://lfpress.com/2015/07/30/more-than-six-years-after-her-child-was-slain-tara-mcdonald-is-helping-bring-new-life-to-others/wcm/4922a06a-58a4-6d8b-99ed-e57190cc2b0c.

32. J. Sadie Clifford, "Expressions of Blame: Narratives of Battered Women Who Kill in the Twentieth Century *Daily Express*." Ph.D. thesis, Cardiff University, 2009.

33. Robert Reiner, Sonia Livingstone, and Jessica Allen, "From Law and Order to Lynch Mobs: Crime News Since the Second World War," in *Criminal Visions: Media Representations of Crime and Justice*, ed. Paul Mason (Cullompton, Devon, U.K.: Willan, 2003), 31.

34. Matt Shaer, "A Monster Among the Frum," *New York Magazine*, 2 December 2011, http://nymag.com/news/features/levi-aron-2011-12/.

35. James W. Carey, *Communication as Culture Essays on Media and Society* (Boston, MA: Unwin Hyman, 1988), 26.

36. Carey, *Communication as Culture*, 27.

37. Carol Gilligan, *In a Different Voice* (Cambridge, MA: Harvard University Press, 1993).

38. Gilligan, *In a Different Voice*, 101.

39. Chris Greer and Yvonne Jewkes, "Extremes of Otherness: Media Images of Social Exclusion," *Social Justice* 32, no. 1 (2005): 20.

40. Robert Reiner, *Policing, Popular Culture and Political Economy: Towards a Social Democratic Criminology* (New York: Routledge, 2017), 249.

41. Martin Innes, *Investigating Murder: Detective Work and the Police Response to Criminal Homicide* (Oxford: Oxford University Press, 2003), 53.

42. Carey, *Communication as Culture*.

43. Walter R. Fisher, "Narration, Reason, Community," in *Writing the Social Text: Poetics and Politics in Social Science Discourse*, ed. Richard Brown (New York: Routledge, 2017), 212.

44. Fisher, "Narration, Reason, Community," 212.

Chapter 7

1. Edelman communications conducted an online survey of over 33,000 people in 27 countries: https://www.edelman.com/sites/g/files/aatuss191/files/2019-02/2019_Edelman_Trust_Barometer_Global_Report_2.pdf?utm_source=website&utm_medium=global_report&utm_campaign=downloads.

2. Daniel C. Hallin and Paolo Mancini, *Comparing Media Systems: Three Models of Media and Politics* (Cambridge, U.K.: Cambridge University Press, 2004).

3. See, for example: Claude-Jean Bertrand, *Media Ethics and Accountability Systems* (London: Transaction, 2000); Denis McQuail, *McQuail's Mass Communication Theory* (Thousand Oaks, CA: Sage, 2010); Fred Siebert, Theodore Peterson, and Wilbur Schramm, *Four Theories of the Press: The Authoritarian, Libertarian, Social Responsibility, and Soviet Communist Concepts of What the Press Should Be and Do* (Champaign and Urbana: University of Illinois Press, 1956); J. Herbert Altschull, *Agents of Power: The Role of the News Media in Human Affairs* (Harlow, U.K.: Longman, 1984); John Calhoun Merrill, *The Imperative of Freedom: A Philosophy of Journalistic Autonomy* (New York: Hastings House, 1974); Jürgen Habermas, *The Structural Transformation of the Public Sphere*, trans. Thomas Burger and Frederick Lawrence (Cambridge, UK: Polity, [1962] 1989).

4. Michael Schudson, *Why Democracies Need an Unlovable Press* (Cambridge, UK: Polity, 2008).

5. Stephen Ward, *Ethical Journalism in a Populist Age: The Democratically Engaged Journalist* (Lanham, MD: Rowman & Littlefield, 2018), 14–16.

6. In Canada, see: David Hemmings Pritchard, ed. *Holding the Media Accountable: Citizens, Ethics, and the Law* (Bloomington: Indiana University Press, 2000). In the United States, see: Erik Ugland and Jack Breslin, "Minnesota News Council: Principles, Precedent, and Moral Authority," *Journal of Mass Media Ethics* 15, no. 4 (2000): 232–247; Erik Ugland, "The Legitimacy and Moral Authority of the National News Council," *Journalism* 9, no. 3 (2008): 285–308. In the United Kingdom, see: Tom O'Malley and Clive Soley, *Regulating the Press* (London: Pluto Press, 2000), as well as in England, see specifically: Chris Frost, *Journalism Ethics and Regulation* (Essex: Pearson, 2000); Chris Frost, "The Press Complaints Commission: A Study of Ten Years of Adjudications on Press Complaints," *Journalism Studies* 5, no. 1 (2004): 101–114; and Chris Frost, "A Crisis of Ethics: Breaking the Cycle of Newspaper Irresponsibility," in *The State in Transition: Essays in Honour of John Horgan,* ed. Kevin Rafter and Mark O'Brien (Dublin: New Island Press, 2015), 78–100.

7. Craig Silverman, "Last Press Council in U.S. Will Close Next Month," *Poynter,* 10 April 2014, https://www.poynter.org/reporting-editing/2014/last-press-council-in-u-s-will-close-next-month/.

8. Kyle Pope, "Meet Your New Public Editors," *Columbia Journalism Review,* 11 June 2019. https://www.cjr.org/public_editor/meet-your-new-public-editors.php

9. At the time of this writing, only the Quebec Press Council, which deals with complaints in the province where French is the predominant language, continues apart from the NNC. The Alberta Press Council closed on December 31, 2018, and the NNC has picked up most of its members, according to NNC Executive Director John Fraser.

10. Kathy English, "New Era for Media Accountability in Canada: Public Editor," *Toronto Star,* 11 September 2015, https://www.thestar.com/opinion/public_editor/2015/09/11/new-era-for-media-accountability-in-canada-public-editor.html.

11. Leveson Inquiry, *Report into the Culture, Practices and Ethics of the Press* (London: Department for Digital, Culture, Media & Sport and Leveson Inquiry, 2012).

12. CRA is an organization of London crime reporters, who frequently interact with the Metropolitan Police. It does not include members from other parts of the United Kingdom. Most British tabloids operate out of London.

13. John Twomey declined to be re-interviewed because he no longer serves as head of the CRA. He recommended the current chair of the organization.

14. College of Policing, "Engagement and Communication," College of Policing, 24 May 2017, https://www.app.college.police.uk/app-content/engagement-and-communication/media-relations/#introduction.

15. College of Policing, "Engagement and Communication."

16. These regulations were an update of both the 2010 Communications Advisory Group's guidance and the College of Policing's 2013 Guidance on Relationships with the Media. College of Policing, "Guidance on the Relationships with Media," College of Policing, 1 May 2013, https://www.npcc.police.uk/documents/reports/2013/201305-cop-media-rels.pdf.

17. College of Policing, "Engagement and Communication."

18. College of Policing, "Engagement and Communication." It makes clear that members of the police force ought not to leak to the press. Instead, the site offers contact information for whistleblowers through the charity Public Concern at Work.

19. Romayne Smith Fullerton and Maggie Jones Patterson, "Comparing Crime Coverage Rituals in Sweden, Holland, England and North America," in *Media and Public Shaming: Drawing the Boundaries of Disclosure*, ed. Julian Petley (London: IB Tauris, 2013), 115–144.

20. Contempt of Court Act 1981 (U.K.), 1981, c. 49.

21. John Woodhouse, "Press Regulation After Leveson," U.K. Parliament, 27 July 2018, https://researchbriefings.parliament.uk/ResearchBriefing/Summary/CBP-7576#fullreport.

22. British broadcasters are regulated by the Office of Communications (OFCOM), a government agency that has wide-ranging powers over television, radio, telecoms and the postal sectors; it sets a steep bar for ethical standards. Public trust in television is higher than in newspapers, and trust in radio is highest among media outlets in the United Kingdom. See: Dominic Ponsford, "Survey Finds That U.K. Written Press (By Some Way) the Least Trusted in Europe," *Press Gazette*, 26 May, 2017, https://www.pressgazette.co.U.K./survey-finds-that-U.K.-written-press-is-by-some-way-the-least-trusted-in-europe/.

23. This applies only to printed material in Britain. Broadcast is regulated separately by OFCOM and is generally well respected and largely without serious criticism.

24. One legislative change in particular was supposed to incentivize publishers to join a recognized regulator: Section 40 of the Crime and Courts Act 2013 would have made it easier for the public to challenge media because if an organization did not belong to an approved regulator, it would have to pay both sides' legal costs, regardless of court outcome. This section was withdrawn in 2018. See: Woodhouse, "Press Regulation After Leveson"; BBC News Staff, "Press Regulation: What You Need to Know," *BBC News*, 13 April 2016, https://www.bbc.com/news/uk-politics-36034956; Jim Waterson, "Why Is UK Press Regulation Back in the Headlines?," *The Guardian*, 8 May 2018, https://www.theguardian.com/media/2018/may/08/why-is-uk-press-regulation-back-in-the-headlines.

25. For example, see: Ben H. Bagdikian, *Double Vision: Reflections on My Heritage, Life and Profession* (Boston, MA: Beacon Press, 1997); Edward Herman and Noam Chomsky, *Manufacturing Consent: The Political Economy of the Mass Media* (New York: Random House, 2010), Edward Herman and Robert McChesney, *The Global Media: The New Missionaries of Corporate Capitalism* (Washington, DC: Cassell, 1997); Robert McChesney, "The Political Economy of the Global Communication Revolution," in *Capitalism and the Information Age: The Political Economy of the Global Communication Revolution*, ed. John Bellamy Foster and Ellen M. Wood (New York: Monthly Review Press, 1998), 1–26.

26. Waterson, "Why Is UK Press Regulation Back in the Headlines?"

27. Jack Katz, "What Makes Crime 'News'?" *Media, Culture & Society* 9, no. 1 (1987): 47–75.

28. Romayne Smith Fullerton and Maggie Jones Patterson, "Crime News: Defining Boundaries" in Clifford G. Christians and Bo Shan, *The Ethics of Intercultural Communication* (New York: Peter Lang, 2015), 183–198.

29. Al Tompkins, "'Cynics Might Call the Perp Walk the Crime Reporter's Red Carpet': How We Justify Images of Accused IMF Chief in Handcuffs," *Poynter*, 17 May 2011, https://www.poynter.org/reporting-editing/2011/is-it-ethical-to-use-perp-walk-images-of-dominique-strauss-kahn-imf-chief-accused-of-attempted-rape/.

30. Angela Diffley, "French Huffington Post Will Run Strauss-Kahn Stories, Says Editor Anne Sinclair," *RFI English*, 19 January 2012, http://en.rfi.fr/americas/20120119-french-huffington-post-will-run-strauss-kahn-stories-says-editor-anne-sinclair.

31. Diffley, "French Huffington Post Will Run Strauss-Kahn Stories."

32. Martin Innes, "'Signal Crimes': Detective Work, Mass Media and Constructing Collective Memory," in *Criminal Visions: Media Representations of Crime and Justice*, ed. Paul Mason (Cullompton, Devon, U.K.: Willan, 2003), 52.

33. The following are the relevant parts of the Press Council of Ireland Code of Practice: "5.1 Privacy is a human right, protected as a personal right in the Irish Constitution and the European Convention on Human Rights, which is incorporated into Irish law. The private and family life, home and correspondence of everyone must be respected. 5.2 Readers are entitled to have news and comment presented with respect for the privacy and sensibilities of individuals. However, the right to privacy should not prevent publication of matters of public record or in the public interest. 5.3 Sympathy and discretion must be shown at all times in seeking information in situations of personal grief or shock. In publishing such information, the feelings of grieving families should be taken into account. This should not be interpreted as restricting the right to report judicial proceedings." See: Press Industry Code Committee, "Code of Practice: For Newspapers and Periodicals," *Irish Times*, 6 December 2006, https://www.irishtimes.com/news/code-of-practice-for-newspapers-and-periodicals-1.1034235.

34. Horgan retired in 2014 and was replaced by Peter Feeney.

35. Reporters Without Borders, "2018 World Press Freedom Index," Reporters Without Borders, n.d., https://rsf.org/en/ranking. The 2018 rankings are as follows: Ireland 16; Canada 18; United Kingdom 40; United States 45.

36. Stephen Dunne, "Policing the Press: The Institutionalisation of Independent Press Regulation in a Liberal/North Atlantic Media System" (Ph.D. diss., Dublin City University, 2017). For specifics about Quebec, Canada, see: Hemmings Pritchard, *Holding the Media Accountable*. For the United States, see: Ugland and Breslin, "Minnesota News Council"; Ugland, "The Legitimacy and Moral Authority of the National News Council." In the United Kingdom, sees: O'Malley and Soley, *Regulating the Press*, as well as in England, see specifically: Frost, *Journalism Ethics and Regulation*; Frost, "The Press Complaints Commission"; and, Frost, "A Crisis of Ethics."

37. The Leveson Inquiry interviewed Ombudsman John Horgan so he could offer his insights into the Irish model, and Leveson suggested their system was a good model for England to emulate.

38. Dunne, "Policing the Press," 264.

39. We interviewed Fraser just after the NNC's "soft" launch in September 2015, when it opened to hear complaints about media behavior; however, at that time, the council was still hiring staff, writing a constitution, and establishing a board, as well as working to increase membership. It launched in January 2016. As of January 2019, Fraser said they had nearly 600 media outlet members, and the website noted its roster "includes most daily and community newspapers, news magazines and online news organizations across Canada, with the exception of Quebec, which is served by a separate provincial press council." See: National NewsMedia Council, "About Us," National NewsMedia Council, n.d., https://mediacouncil.ca/about-us-ethics-journalism/.

40. See: Dunne, "Policing the Press," Chapter 7, for more. Complaints are filed in one of four categories: accuracy or bias; attribution; opinion; sensitive issues. Pat Perkel, executive director of NNC since its inception, noted the number of complaints the council receive is increasing as people become aware the service exists. Also, the type of concerns shift over time: "There was a period where maybe they were influenced by American politics, when they read something they did not like, or didn't believe, they wanted it not to be in the paper," Perkel said, and they'd ask the council to have it removed. "There was a lack of tolerance for difference of opinion, or of contrary opinion. . . . Now, it's too much personal information in stories, and the question of just because the information is accessible, should it all be reprinted, or should it be judged what material you print or don't print?" She noted this in particular reference to court cases where there are documents about parole boards, sentencing hearings, Special Investigations Unit (SIU) reports (in which the civilian agency SIU investigates serious allegations against police), and so on. It is a key question, Perkel says, for journalists: "Do you become a stenographer and reprint all these details, or do you use journalistic discretion and keep in mind the feelings, the sensitivities, of the victims?"

41. For example, the NNC were signatories to the Canadian Journalists for Freedom of Expression's petition, Journalism Is Not a Crime, which urged withdrawal of criminal charges against independent journalist Justin Brake, who followed Indigenous protestors onto a hydroelectric site in Eastern Canada in 2016. See: Canadian Journalists for Free Expression, "Journalism Is Not a Crime," Canadian Journalists for Free Expression, 17 March 2017, https://www.cjfe.org/journalism_not_a_crime.

42. In New Zealand, the death of British backpacker Grace Millane shocked people in both countries. At the request of his lawyer, the accused, a New Zealand man, had a temporary ban placed on his name in order that he might have a fair trial, with a jury of peers chosen who had no or very little knowledge about the case. Some countries, however, defied New Zealand's court ruling, and published his name: in England, see: Jonathan Pearlman, Mark Broatch, and Jack Hardy, "Grace Millane Murder Suspect Revealed: Jesse Kempson, 26, Described Backpacker as 'Radiant' Just Minutes Before She Was Last Seen," *The Telegraph*, 10 December 2018, https://www.telegraph. co.uk/news/2018/12/10/alleged-killer-british-backpacker-grace-millane-pictured-first/. *The Guardian* did not name the accused but published a piece where New Zealand "rebukes Google" for sending out his name in a mass email. See: Kate Lyons,

"Grace Millane Murder: New Zealand Rebukes Google for Emailing Out Suspect's Name," *The Guardian*, 19 December 2018, https://www.theguardian.com/world/2018/dec/19/grace-millane-new-zealand-rebukes-google-for-emailing-out-suspects-name. In December 2018, Australian authorities threatened to lay charges against foreign media that named an Australian priest convicted in the first of two trials for child sexual abuse; his name and the outcome was protected under a publication ban to ensure a fair trial at the second of these court cases. See: Dorothy Cummings McLean, "Australian Prosecutor Threatens US Media for Breaking Publication Ban on Cdl. Pell's Trial," *Life Site*, 13 December 2018, https://www.lifesitenews.com/news/australian-prosecutor-threatens-us-media-for-breaking-publication-ban-on-cd. The first in Canada was the case of Karla Homolka and her then husband, Paul Bernardo. The pair kidnapped, sexually assaulted, and then murdered school girls Leslie Mahaffy and Kristen French in the 1990s. In 1993, Homolka, as part of a plea bargain, pleaded guilty to two counts of manslaughter and agreed to testify against Bernardo. To protect his presumption of innocence, the Canadian court that heard Homolka's plea protected the details of her statements under a publication ban, and most of the information about the teens' abductions, rapes, and deaths did not come into the public realm until Bernardo's trial. However, this was the early days of the Internet, and some American media outlets came to Homolka's trial and disseminated the information, protected in Canada under the gag order, to its American audiences. The same possibility arises in any high-profile case in Canada. The details of Vancouver's Willy Pickton's trial were of similar interest across the border in the United States and were published or broadcast, despite Canadian restrictions.

43. Richard Sambrook, "'Rat-Like Cunning, A Plausible Manner and Little Literary Ability': Time to Prove Nick Tomalin Wrong?," in *After Leveson?—The Future for British Journalism*, ed. John Mair (Suffolk, U.K.: Abramis Academic, 2013), 94.

44. Dewey quoted in Walter R. Fisher, "Narration, Reason, Community," in *Writing the Social Text: Poetics and Politics in Social Science Discourse*, ed. Richard Brown (New York, NY: Routledge, 2017), 308.

45. Fisher, "Narration, Reason, Community," 314.

46. See Sandra Borden, *Journalism as Practice: MacIntyre, Virtue Ethics and the Press*, (Hampshire, U.K., and Burlington, VT: Ashgate Press, 2007).

47. Walter R. Fisher, *Human Communication as Narration: Toward a Philosophy of Reason, Value, and Action* (Columbia: University of South Carolina Press, 1989).

48. Carol Gilligan, *Mapping the Moral Domain: A Contribution of Women's Thinking to Psychological Theory and Education* (Cambridge, MA: Harvard University Press, 1988).

49. The PCC was replaced in 2014 by IPSO, which is similarly contentious. While most of the country's newspapers have joined, *The Guardian* and *The Observer*, as well as their affiliates, are noticeably absent because their editors continue to believe this is a sham group. For more, see: Roy Greenslade, "Why *The Guardian's* Decision Not to Sign Up to IPSO Makes Sense," *The Guardian*, 4 September 2014, https://www.theguardian.com/media/greenslade/2014/sep/04/press-regulation-ipso.

50. Tom Felle, "Ireland Press Regulation: An Irish Solution to a British Problem," in *After Leveson—The Future for British Journalism*, ed. John Mair (Suffolk, U.K.: Abramis Academic, 2013), 165–175.

Chapter 8

1. Andrei Khalip, "Portuguese Ex-PM Arrested in Corruption Probe," *Reuters*, 22 November 2014, https://www.reuters.com/article/portugal-corruption-socrates-idUSL6N0TC04K20141122.

2. One newspaper, *Correio da Manhã*, did gain access to the records for a time through a legal maneuver that is explained later in this chapter.

3. Luís De Sousa, "'I Don't Bribe, I Just Pull Strings': Assessing the Fluidity of Social Representations of Corruption in Portuguese Society," *Perspectives on European Politics and Society* 9, no. 1 (2008): 8.

4. De Sousa, "'I Don't Bribe, I Just Pull Strings,'" 8.

5. De Sousa, "'I Don't Bribe, I Just Pull Strings,'" 9.

6. Prosecutors released a 4,000-page document on 11 October 2017 in what was dubbed "Operation Marqués." Sócrates denied all wrongdoing. Peter Wise, "Former Portuguese PM Jose Sócrates Charged with Corruption," *Financial Times*, 11 October 2017, https://www.ft.com/content/ca71ca96-ae89-11e7-aab9-abaa44b1e130.

7. On 28 January 2020, the Associated Press reported: "A Portuguese magistrate is deciding whether there is enough evidence to put a former prime minister and two dozen other once-powerful figures on trial for corruption, money laundering and other crimes." "Magistrate Considers Major Corruption Trial in Portugal," https://apnews.com/facad73714154dd2bfaa11bc3071aa0a. The case was due to be heard in April 2020. Natasha Donn, "Former PM José Sócrates Sues Portuguese State for €50,00," *Portugal Resident*, 9 January 2020, https://www.portugalresident.com/former-pm-jose-socrates-sues-portuguese-state-for-e50000//.. In a similar example of police leaks, a press scrum was waiting at the apartment of Rodrigo Rato, former president of the International Monetary Fund, when he was taken into custody by Spain's tax authorities in 2015. He began serving a four-year sentence in October 2018 for embezzlement. "Ex-IMF Head Rodrigo Rato's Home and Office Searched in Spain," BBC, 16 April 2015, https://www.bbc.com/news/world-europe-32335842. "Ex-IMF Head Rodrigo Rato Starts Jail Term in 'Black Cards' Case," *Reuters*, 25 October 2018, https://www.reuters.com/article/spain-corruption/ex-imf-head-rodrigo-rato-starts-jail-term-in-black-cards-case-idUSL8N1X569K.

8. See: Carlos Maciá-Barber and María-Ángeles Galván-Arias, "Presumption of Innocence and Journalistic Ethics: The Aitana Case," *Revista Latina de Comunicacion Social* 67 (2012): 356–387. Similar unqualified accusations can be found in Italian newspapers.

9. Daniel C. Hallin and Paolo Mancini, *Comparing Media Systems: Three Models of Media and Politics* (Cambridge, U.K.: Cambridge University Press, 2004).

10. While an in-depth discussion about the differences among the legal systems of the ten countries under consideration lies beyond the capacity of this text, we would note that in Spain, Portugal, and Italy, the justice system employs an inquisitorial rather than an adversarial approach to trials. The latter is embraced by the Watchdog countries of the United States, Canada, England, and Ireland. One of the central differences between these two systems is that the inquisitorial approach puts more emphasis on the discovery of truth in its largest sense. Under adversarial criminal procedure model, there is clear "willingness to recognize other criminal procedure goals beyond the naked pursuit of truth." See: Elisabetta Grande, "Italian Criminal Justice: Borrowing and Resistance," *American Journal of Comparative Law* 48, no. 2 (2000): 249.

11. Paul Manning, *News and News Sources: A Critical Introduction* (Thousand Oaks, CA: Sage, 2001), 17.

12. This is not to suggest that police and journalists in the Protector or Watchdog countries have transparent relationships and there are no blurred lines or information links. Indeed, we explore the current situations and concurrent challenges in both the Watchdog and Protector parts of this book.

13. This legislative act followed the 1983 arrest of well-known TV personality Enzo Tortora, who was widely shown in handcuffs. Tortora was accused of drug trafficking and being associated with the Camorra by two gangsters who were cooperating with the judiciary. Tortora was later exonerated and released in 1987. He returned briefly to his popular television show before dying of cancer in 1988.

14. Elisa Giomi and Fabrizio Tonello, "Moral Panic: The Issue of Women and Crime in Italian Evening News," *Sociologica* 7, no. 3 (2013): 15.

15. Romayne Smith Fullerton and Maggie Jones Patterson, "Murder in Our Midst: Expanding Coverage to Include Care and Responsibility," *Journal of Mass Media Ethics* 21, no. 4 (2006): 304–321.

16. Smith Fullerton and Patterson, "Murder in Our Midst."

17. The account here is taken from two reports that appeared in England's *The Guardian*. The first is Rosie Scammell, "DNA Evidence and Family Secrets Snare Italian Child Murderer," *The Guardian*, 2 July 2016, https://www.theguardian.com/world/2016/jul/02/yara-gamirasio-murder-massimo-bossetti-dna-evidence-italy-guilty-verdict. And the second story is Tobias Jones, "The Murder That Has Obsessed Italy," *The Guardian*, 8 January 2015, https://www.theguardian.com/world/2015/jan/08/-sp-the-murder-that-has-obsessed-italy.

18. In 2015, a scientific adviser to the Italian court suggested there could be an error in matching the DNA, and, at appeal, the lawyers for Bossetti, who has always maintained his innocence, asked for the sample to be retested. The court denied this application and upheld the conviction. For more, see: Bergamo Chronicle Staff, "Yara, parla la Procura: 'Quel Dna è di Bossetti'" [Yara, the public prosecutor speaks: "That DNA is from Bossetti"], *Bergamo Chronicle*, 28 January 2015, https://bergamo.corriere.it/notizie/cronaca/15_gennaio_28/yara-parla-procura-quel-dna-bossetti-503b2b2c-a6e0-11e4-93fc-9b9679dd4aa0.shtml?refresh_ce-cp;   Carmelo Abbate, "Yara, l'avvocato Salvagni: Ecco lo sporco gioco contro Bossetti" [Yara, the lawyer Salvagni: Here is the dirty game against Bossetti], *Panorama*, 2 February 2015, https://www.panorama.it/news/cronaca/yara-bossetti-avvocato/.

19. According to the journalistic ethics manual, "Carta di Roma," Italian journalists should not identify, interview, or show pictures of children without written authorization by parents. But sources reported it was often violated.

20. After the publication of the photo of Alan Kurdi, a three-year-old child found dead on a Turkish beach while his family attempted to reach Greece in 2015, hundreds of articles appeared in the Italian press. Now a private ship named for him patrols the Mediterranean on search-and-rescue missions. Another iconic picture of a Moroccan boy saving his schoolbooks while police officers expelled his family in Rome moved public opinion in 2019: A non-profit NGO, "Famiglie Accoglienti," collected thousands of euros in 24 hours to help him continue his studies.

21. Not all scholars agree that this term is appropriately applied to journalists. The term is used by political scientists to describe access to resources and favors provided to "clients" in exchange for "deference and various kinds of support" to "patrons." Reporters may not need to show to magistrates the "deference and support" expected by patrons.

22. Daniel C. Hallin and Stylianos Papathanassopoulos, "Political Clientelism and the Media: Southern Europe and Latin America in Comparative Perspective," *Media, Culture & Society* 24, no. 2 (2002): 184–185.

23. Hallin and Mancini, *Comparing Media Systems*, 137.

24. See: Maggie Jones Patterson and Romayne Smith Fullerton, "Credibility: The Best Currency in Journalism," in *The Sage Guide to Key Issues in Media Ethics and Law*, ed. William Babcock and William Freivogel (Thousand Oaks, CA: Sage, 2015), 81–92.

25. See: Eurostat Staff, "Intentional Homicide Victims in EU," *Eurostat*, 22 February 2018, https://ec.europa.eu/eurostat/web/products-eurostat-news/-/EDN-20180222-1.

26. Jones, "The Murder That Has Obsessed Italy."

27. Giomi and Tonello, "Moral Panic," 15.

28. Gaye Tuchman, *Making News* (New York: Free Press, 1978).

29. Italy is a civil law state, governed by codified law. The criminal procedure adopted in 1988 is considered somewhere between the inquisitorial and the adversarial court systems. Investigation is a pretrial process, separated from the trial, which is closer to the adversarial system. The inquisitorial system was partly abandoned. In Italy, the suspect arrested must be arraigned within five days. Nicola Canestrini, "Basic Principles of Italian Criminal Law," *Canestrini Lex*, 26 March 2012, https://canestrinilex.com/en/readings/italian-criminal/.

30. Canadian and British reporters, who enjoy greater access to police and court documents, complained much more about unobtainable police and court documents.

31. Hallin and Mancini, *Comparing Media System*.

32. Hallin and Mancini, *Comparing Media Systems*, 135.

33. Hallin and Mancini, *Comparing Media Systems*, 138.

34. Hallin and Mancini, *Comparing Media Systems*, 138.

35. Mario Calabresi, "Millennials Wary of Corrupt Media Reporting," Markkula Center for Applied Ethics at Santa Clara University, n.d., https://www.scu.edu/ethics/focus-areas/journalism-ethics/resources/the-trust-issue-in-italy/.

36. Calabresi, "Millennials Wary of Corrupt Media Reporting."

37. De Sousa, "'I Don't Bribe, I Just Pull Strings.'"

38. Katrin Voltmer, *The Media in Transitional Democracies* (Hoboken, NJ: John Wiley & Sons, 2013), 198–199.

39. Ana Pinto Martinho, Gustavo Cardoso, and Miguel Paisana, "Portugal," in *Digital News Report 2018*, ed. Nic Newman, Richard Fletcher, Antonis Kalogeropoulos, David A. L. Levy, and Rasmus Kleis Nielsen (Oxford: Reuters Institute for the Study of Journalism, 2018), 96–97.

Chapter 9

1. Katrin Voltmer, *The Media in Transitional Democracies* (Hoboken, NJ: John Wiley & Sons, 2013), 198.

2. Voltmer, *The Media in Transitional Democracies*.

3. Anton Rosa, "Benítez: Un símbola contra la especulación en El Raval," *El Nacional*, 8 October 2018, https://www.elnacional.cat/es/sociedad/benitez-un-simbolo-contra-la-especulacion-en-el-raval_312021_102.htm>.

4. Account taken from Michael Ray and from the recollections in interviews of Jorge Tuñón Navarro, and other Spanish journalists. See: Michael Ray, "Madrid Train Bombing of 2004," *Encyclopædia Britannica*, 10 March 2010, https://www.britannica.com/event/Madrid-train-bombings-of-2004.

5. Bill Kovach and Tom Rosenstiel, *The Elements of Journalism: What Newspeople Should Know and the Public Should Expect* (New York: Three Rivers Press, 2014), 95.

6. Kovach and Rosenstiel, *The Elements of Journalism*, 98.

7. Stephen Ward, *Ethical Journalism in a Populist Age: The Democratically Engaged Journalist* (Lanham, MD: Rowman & Littlefield, 2018).

8. Tobias Jones, "The Murder That Has Obsessed Italy," *The Guardian*, 8 January 2015, https://www.theguardian.com/world/2015/jan/08/-sp-the-murder-that-has-obsessed-italy.

9. Elisa Giomi and Fabrizio Tonello, "Moral Panic: The Issue of Women and Crime in Italian Evening News," *Sociologica* 7, no. 3 (2013): 1–30.

10. Giomi and Tonello, "Moral Panic," 7.

11. Giomi and Tonello, "Moral Panic," 3.

12. According to United Nations Office on Drugs and Crime, which ranks national murder rates in six categories. Italy is in the lowest rankings on par with Spain and the Netherlands. Portugal (1.2% murder rate), Canada (1.4%), and England (1%) are all in the second-lowest category, and the United States (3.4%) in the third lowest. See: Enrico Bisogno, Jenna Dawson-Faber, Michael Jandl, Kristiina Kangaspunta, Labib Kazkaz, Lucia Motolinia Carballo, Serena Oliva, and Felix Reiterer, *Global Study on Homicide 2013* (Vienna: United Nations Office on Drugs and Crime, 2013). For European murder rates, see: Eurostat, "Homicides Recorded by the Police, 2002–12," *Eurostat*, 3 June 2014, https://ec.europa.eu/eurostat/statistics-explained/index.php/File:Homicides_recorded_by_the_police,_2002–12_YB14.png.

13. All three Ambivalent countries were perceived by experts and businesspeople as having the highest level of corruption in the public sector among all the other nations in our sample on the "Corruptions Perceptions Index 2017," compiled by Transparency International, a nonprofit research organization headquartered in Brussels. Transparency International, "Corruption Perceptions Index 2017," Transparency International, 21 February 2018, https://www.transparency.org/news/feature/corruption_perceptions_index_2017.

14. In 2007, American Amanda Knox was convicted in Italy of the murder of her British roommate, Meredith Kercher. Knox spent nearly four years in jail before she was acquitted by the Italian Supreme Court of Cessation. The case highlighted for the public, and for legal scholars, the different emphases an inquisitorial versus and adversarial court system puts on a case. For more, see: Julia Grace Mirabella, "Scales of Justice: Assessing Italian Crime Procedure Through the Amanda Knox Trial," *Boston University International Law Journal* 30, no. 1 (2012): 229–260.

15. The 34% figure comes from: European Commission, "Europeans and Their Languages," Special Eurobarometer 386, 2012, https://web.archive.org/web/20190617170303/http://ec.europa.eu/commfrontoffice/publicopinion/archives/ebs/ebs_386_en.pdf

16. The story of the Panama Papers is told in: Frederick Obermaier and Bastian Obermayer, *The Panama Papers: Breaking the Story of How the Rich and Powerful Hide Their Money* (New York: Simon and Schuster, 2017).

17. Investigative Reporting Project Italy, "About Us," Investigative Reporting Project Italy (IRPI), n.d., https://irpi.eu/en/about-us/.

18. Branco noted that many youths in Portugal do not remember how challenging it was to practice the craft of journalism in a dictatorship, and she found it frightening how accepting some young people are about a potential slide away from democracy. This disaffected attitude about the importance of democracy is shared by young people in many countries around the world. Many dismiss its values and virtues, and its underlying democratic cultural norms, like compromise, tolerance, dialogue, and a shared desire for impartial facts. Canadian political scientist Paul Howe, for example, has studied how many Millennials (those born between the early 1980s and late 1990s) are unenthused about, or indifferent to, democracy. International survey data suggest they might be willing to consider other forms of governance. See: Paul Howe, "Eroding Norms and Democratic Deconsolidation," *Journal of Democracy* 28, no. 4 (2017): 15–29. Yascha Mounk, a lecturer on government at Harvard University, has studied what he argues is a shift from a democratic to a more authoritarian style of government. Among Americans born in the 1930s and 1940s, more than two-thirds believe that living in a democracy is central; that figure drops to one-third among Americans born in the 1980s. He is interviewed about some of these ideas on CBC Radio's Ideas program. See: Paul Kennedy, "The People vs Democracy," *CBC Radio*, 13 December 2018, https://www.cbc.ca/radio/ideas/the-people-vs-democracy-1.4944953. He also has a recent book about global trends in support for democracy. See: Yascha Mounk, *The People Vs. Democracy: Why Our Freedom Is in Danger and How to Save It* (Cambridge, MA: Harvard University Press, 2018).

Chapter 10

1. Lawrence Kohlberg, *Essays on Moral Development: The Psychology of Moral Development* (San Francisco: Harper & Row, 1981); William G. Perry, *Forms of Intellectual and Ethical Development During the College Years* (New York: Holt, Rinehart & Winston, 1970) ; Belenky, Mary Field, Blythe McVicker Clinchy, Nancy Rule Goldberger, and Jill Matluck Tarule, *Women's Ways of Knowing: The Development of Self, Voice and Mind* (New York: Basic Books, 1986); Carol Gilligan, *In a Different Voice: Psychological Theory and Women's Development* (Cambridge, MA: Harvard University Press, 1982).

2. Carlos Maciá-Barber and María-Ángeles Galván-Arias, "Presumption of Innocence and Journalistic Ethics: The Aitana Case," *Revista Latina de Comunicacion Social* 67 (2012): 356–387.

3. This account is derived from various Spanish news sources and from Maciá-Barber and Galván-Arias, "Presumption of Innocence and Journalistic Ethics."

4. Jennifer Jiménez, "Condenados 'ABC' y 'La Opinión de Tenerife' por llamar asesino y violador a un hombre inocente," *CanariasAhora*, 2 July 2017, https://www.eldiario.es/canariasahora/tribunales/Condenados-ABC-Opinion-Tenerife-inocente_0_609989559.html.

5. Maciá-Barber and Galván-Arias, "Presumption of Innocence and Journalistic Ethics," 362.

6. Commission of Arbitration, Complaints, and Deontology of Journalism Staff, "Código Deontológico" [Code of Ethics], Commission of Arbitration, Complaints, and Deontology of Journalism, 22 April 2017, http://www.comisiondequejas.com/codigo-deontologico/.

7. Commission of Arbitration, Complaints, and Deontology of Journalism Staff, "Código Deontológico" [Code of Ethics].

8. Maciá-Barber and Galván-Arias, "Presumption of Innocence and Journalistic Ethics," 359–360.

9. Daniel C. Hallin and Paolo Mancini, *Comparing Media Systems: Three Models of Media and Politics* (Cambridge, U.K.: Cambridge University Press, 2004), 90

10. Hallin and Mancini, *Comparing Media Systems*, 298.

11. Hallin and Mancini, *Comparing Media Systems*, 298.

12. Clifford G. Christians, Theodore Glasser, Denis McQuail, Kaarle Nordenstreng, and Robert A. White, *Normative Theories of the Media: Journalism in Democratic Societies* (Urbana and Champaign: University of Illinois Press, 2010).

13. Christians et al., *Normative Theories of the Media*.

14. Christians et al., *Normative Theories of the Media*, 134.

15. Hallin and Mancini, *Comparing Media Systems*, 58.

16. Lee Wilkins and Renita Coleman, *The Moral Media: How Journalists Reason About Ethics* (New York: Routledge, 2005); Kohlberg, *Essays on Moral Development*.

17. See, for example: Maggie Jones Patterson and Megan Williams Hall, "Abortion, Moral Maturity and Civic Journalism," *Critical Studies in Media Communication* 15, no. 2 (1998): 91–115; Wilkins and Coleman, *The Moral Media*.

18. Kohlberg, *Essays on Moral Development*; Belenky et al., *Women's Ways of Knowing*; Gilligan, *In a Different Voice*; William G. Perry, *Forms of Intellectual and Ethical Development During the College Years*.

19. Belenky et al., *Women's Ways of Knowing*; Gilligan, *In a Different Voice*.

20. Wilkins and Coleman, *The Moral Media*.

21. Wilkins and Coleman, *The Moral Media*.

22. Lee Wilkins and Renita Coleman, "Journalists' Moral Development: Thinking Through Both Rights and Care in a Professional Setting" (presentation, Association for Education in Journalism and Mass Communication [AEJMC], Toronto, August 4–7, 2004).

23. Patterson and Hall, "Abortion, Moral Maturity and Civic Journalism."

24. Algarve Daily News Staff, "2017 Will Be a Very Bad Year for Journalism in Portugal," *Algarve Daily News*, 18 January 2017, https://algarvedailynews.com/news/10838-2017-will-be-a-very-bad-year-for-journalism-in-portugal.

25. As we explained in Chapter 8, *Correio da Manhã* published a series of disclosures begrudgingly picked up by various news outlets, which had no other way to get the information. These revelations included accounts about the spending habits of Sócrates' family members. Sócrates accused the newspaper of invading his privacy, and, in October 2015, *Correio da Manhã's* fortunes were reversed when a judge ordered that the entire Cofino media empire cease publication of *any* stories about the Sócrates case.

26. The limitations of our space and focus on ethics prevent us from further detailing possible reforms and setbacks; however, low salaries for entry-level and freelance journalists, which in some places are set by unions, are especially critical. As a result, many young journalism graduates seek new professions or move abroad. Licensing of journalists, especially in Italy, can also erect roadblocks to a new generation who could help erase the institutional memory of a press under political control.

27. Frank La Rue, *Report of the Special Rapporteur on the Promotion And Protection of the Right to Freedom of Opinion and Expression* (New York: United Nations General Assembly, 2011); Algarve Daily News Staff, "2017 Will Be a Very Bad Year for Journalism in Portugal."

28. Freedom House, an independent watchdog agency located in Washington, reported in 2016: "Freedoms of expression and the press are constitutionally guaranteed and generally respected" in Italy. However, "defamation is a criminal offense, punishable by a fine of no less than €516 ($570) or six months to three years in prison." See: Freedom House, "Italy," Freedom House, 2016, https://freedomhouse.org/report/freedom-press/2016/italy. Italy's criminal defamation legislation remained the target of international criticism. The report cited a recent case in *Panorama* magazine that resulted in an €800 fine and €45,000 in damages after the magazine published an article that alleged links between the governor of Sicily and organized crime groups.

29. The Council of Europe (Council of Europe Parliamentary Assembly 199321; Council of Europe and Commissioner for Human Rights 2011) has defined ethical journalism as a public good with a mission to provide information needed for "the formation of citizens' personal attitudes and the development of society and democratic life."

See: Assembly of the Council of Europe on July 1st, 1993, 42nd Sitting. The Council of Europe's 2011 resolution seeks to protect journalism from constraints that restrict the scrutiny of public figures and government, and "to protect the rights of people to be properly informed against the imposition of rules that may be intended to protect communities, but can be used to reinforce secrecy and undermine civil liberties." It also insists that ethical journalism clearly distinguishes between news and opinion. See: Thomas Hammarberg, *Human Rights and a Changing Media Landscape* (Strasbourg, FR: Council of Europe, 2011), 74.

30. La Rue, *Report of the Special Rapporteur.*

31. Il Corriere della Sera Staff, "Defamation in Italy: A Draft Law to Be Changed," Council of Europe, 8 June 2014, https://www.coe.int/en/web/commissioner/-/defamation-in-italy-a-draft-law-to-be-changed.

32. Michele Giacomelli, "Remarks Following Alert No. 48/2020," in a message addressed to Matjaz Gruden, director, Directorate of Democratic Participation, Council or Europe, 26 May 2020. https://rm.coe.int/09000016809e7ac3.

33. As interpreted for us by a lawyer for the Portuguese paper, *Publico*, Francisco Teixeira da Mota.

34. The concept of innocent until proven guilty was not introduced in Spain until the new Constitution took effect in 1978. Italy's dictator Benito Mussolini fell in 1943; Spain's Francisco Franco fell in 1975; and Portugal's dictatorship under António de Oliveira Salazar lasted from 1932 to 1968 and was followed by Marcello Caetano until the Carnation Revolution in 1974.

35. Katrin Voltmer, *The Media in Transitional Democracies* (Hoboken, NJ: John Wiley & Sons, 2013), 198.

36. Gabriela Bravo Sanestanislao, "Presunción de inocencia y cultura democrática," *El País*, 11 December 2009, https://elpais.com/diario/2009/12/11/opinion/1260486011_850215.html.

37. Alberto Jabonero, "Mañana podemos ser nosotros," *El País*, 1 December 2009, https://elpais.com/diario/2009/12/01/sociedad/1259622002_850215.html; Manuel Jiménez-de-Parga, "Los nefastos 'juicios paralelos,'" *ABC*, 4 August 2009, https://www.abc.es/opinion/abci-nefastos-juicios-paralelos-200908040300-923068256978_noticia.html.

38. Jabonero, "Mañana podemos ser nosotros."

39. Stephen Ward, *Ethical Journalism in a Populist Age: The Democratically Engaged Journalist* (Lanham, MD: Rowman & Littlefield, 2018).

40. Christians et al., *Normative Theories of the Media*, 91.

41. Christians et al., *Normative Theories of the Media.*

42. Christians et al., *Normative Theories of the Media*, vi; italics in original.

43. Christians et al., *Normative Theories of the Media*, 123.

44. Voltmer, *The Media in Transitional Democracies*; Hallin and Mancini, *Comparing Media Systems.*

45. Voltmer, *The Media in Transitional Democracies*, 199–200.

46. Hallin and Mancini, *Comparing Media Systems*, 41.

47. Hallin and Mancini, *Comparing Media Systems*, 41.

48. Kovach and Rosenstiel contest the common interpretation of objectivity as "free of bias. . . . The call for journalists to adopt objectivity [circa 1920s] was an appeal for them to develop a consistent method of testing information—a transparent approach to evidence—precisely so that personal and cultural biases would not undermine the accuracy of their work." Bill Kovach and Tom Rosenstiel, *The Elements of Journalism: What Newspeople Should Know and the Public Should Expect* (New York: Three Rivers Press, 2014), 81–82. Objectivity is not a fundamental principle of journalism, they declare. Rather, the familiar neutral voice in newswriting is often a helpful device to convey that the information was obtained by objective means (83). Hellmueller, Vos, and Poepsel also suggest that the online formats may be pushing younger U.S. journalists toward a greater reliance on transparency than objectivity as their measure of credibility. See: Lea Hellmueller, Tim P. Vos, and Mark A. Poepsel, "Shifting Journalistic Capital? Transparency and Objectivity in the Twenty-first Century," *Journalism Studies* 14, no. 3 (2013): 287–304.

49. Carol Gilligan and Jane Attanucci, "Two Moral Orientations: Gender Differences and Similarities," *Merrill-Palmer Quarterly* 34, no. 3 (1988): 232.

50. Gilligan and Attanucci, "Two Moral Orientations," 232–233.

51. Gilligan, *In a Different Voice.*

52. Gilligan and Attanucci, "Two Moral Orientations," 233.

53. Nona Plessner Lyons, "Two Perspectives: On Self, Relationships, and Morality," *Harvard Educational Review* 53, no. 2 (1983): 125–145.

54. Plessner Lyons, "Two Perspectives," 136.

55. Because the masculine, justice perspective is more widely recognized, their American research subjects skewed somewhat toward it in their decision-making. But more women included a care focus than did the male subjects.

56. Perry, *Forms of Intellectual and Ethical Development During the College Years.*

57. Gilligan and Attanucci, "Two Moral Orientations," 236.

Chapter 11

1. Clifford G. Christians, "The Ethics of Being in a Communications Context," in *Communication Ethics and Universal Values,* Clifford G. Christians and Michael Traber, editors, Thousand Oaks, CA: Sage Publications, 13.

2. Daniel C. Hallin and Paolo Mancini, *Comparing Media Systems: Three Models of Media and Politics* (Cambridge, U.K.: Cambridge University Press, 2004), 3.

3. A point we made in Part 3 about the Watchdogs.

4. See, for example: Michael Brüggemann, Sven Engesser, Florin Büchel, Edda Humprecht, and Laia Castro, "Hallin and Mancini Revisited: Four Empirical Types of Western Media Systems," *Journal of Communication* 64, no. 6 (2014): 1037–1065; Daniel C. Hallin and Paolo Mancini, "Comparing Media Systems: A Response to Critics," *Media & Journalism* 17, no. 9 (2010): 52–67; Hallin and Mancini, "Ten Years After Comparing Media Systems: What Have We Learned?," *Political Communication* 34, no. 2, (2017): 155–171; Pippa Norris, "Comparative Political

Communications: Common Frameworks or Babelian Confusion?" *Government and Opposition* 44 no. 3 (2009): 321–340; Jesper Strömbäck and Óscar G. Luengo, "Polarized Pluralist and Democratic Corporatist Models: A Comparison of Election News Coverage in Spain and Sweden," *International Communication Gazette* 70, no. 6 (2008): 547–562.

5. Hallin and Mancini, " 'Comparing Media Systems': A Response to Critics," 55.

6. Hallin and Mancini write that most countries in Western Europe subsidize newspapers although those subsidies have not been sufficient to stem the downward market trends that motivated them. In the Democratic Corporatist countries, they have been used to keep weaker newspapers alive and support pluralism by helping those that represent political parties or minority populations. The debate over subsidy systems always included the issue of whether subsidies would make newspapers subject to pressure from the state and less willing to play a watchdog role. There does not seem to be evidence that this has occurred in the Democratic Corporatist countries. Hallin and Mancini, *Comparing Media Systems,* 162–163.

7. Brüggemann et al. "Hallin and Mancini Revisited," 1043.

8. James Carey, *Communication as Culture: Essays on Media and Society* (London, U.K.: Routledge, 2008), 84.

9. Stephen J. Ward, *Ethical Journalism in a Populist Age: The Democratically Engaged Journalist* (Lanham, MD: Rowman & Littlefield, 2018), 3.

10. Lennart Weibull and Britt Börjesson, *Publicistiska seder: Svensk pressetik i teori och praktik 1900–1994* [Publishing traditions: Swedish press ethics in theory and practice 1900–1994]. Stockholm: Tidens förlag, 2006.

11. Maggie Jones Patterson and Megan Williams Hall, "Abortion, Moral Maturity and Civic Journalism," *Critical Studies in Mass Communication* 15, no. 2 (1998): 91–115, 108.

12. Recent surveys of the public's trust in media show it plummeting in some parts of Europe and North America. But the overall surveys are hard to interpret because they often include social media. However, studies do show that trust is increasing in some parts, and trust in public television remains high in much of Western Europe. See, for example, Julia Stoll, "Trust in Media in Europe—Statistics And Facts," *Statista*, 18 March 2019, https://www.statista.com/topics/3303/trust-in-media-in-europe/, and "Fact Sheets: News Media and Political Attitudes in Western Europe," Pew Research Center, 17 May 2018, https://www.pewresearch.org/global/collection/news-media-and-political-attitudes-in-western-europe/.

13. Re: "legal restrictions": For example, in Canada, journalists saw publication bans, which only temporarily restrict reporting to protect an accused person's presumption of innocence or in trials involving minors or sexual assault victims, as not entirely defensible. Many said they would prefer a more American system with less restriction.

14. Among our sample countries, only the Watchdogs routinely use juries in criminal trials.

15. Re: "blue hats": This term is used in right-wing conspiracy theories to describe U.N. troops allegedly poised to confiscate Americans' guns when a global government is formed.

16. Rich Lord, "How Robert Bowers Went from Conservative to White Nationalist," *Pittsburgh Post-Gazette*, 10 November 2018, https://www.post-gazette.com/news/crime-courts/2018/11/10/Robert-Bowers-extremism-Tree-of-Life-massacre-shooting-pittsburgh-Gab-Warroom/stories/201811080165.

17. Lord, "How Robert Bowers Went from Conservative to White Nationalist."

18. U.S. Supreme Court Justice Oliver Wendell Homes famously wrote in a 1919 opinion: "You can't yell 'fire' in a crowded theater." The sentence has been widely used since then to refer to a legally acceptable limit on free speech. For a discussion, see Ken White, "Fire in a Crowded Theater," Legal Talk Network, 18 June 2018, https://legaltalknetwork.com/podcasts/make-no-law/2018/06/fire-in-a-crowded-theater/.

19. Sissela Bok, "Lies: They Come with Consequences," *Washington Post*, 23 August 1998, C1.

20. Anita L. Allen, *Why Privacy Isn't Everything: Feminist Reflections on Personal Accountability* (Lanham, MD: Rowman & Littlefield, 2003).

21. Patrick L. Plaisance, *Media Ethics: Key Principles for Responsible Practice* (Thousand Oaks, CA: Sage, 2009).

22. For more, see: Gemma Richardson and Romayne Smith Fullerton's "Rob Ford," IN *Scandal in a Digital Age*, ed. Hinda Mandell and Gina Masullo Chen (New York: Palgrave and Macmillan, 2016), 145–158. Also Maggie Jones Patterson and Romayne Smith Fullerton, "'Out' versus 'About': News Media, Politicians' Privacy, and Public Discussion," in *The Sage Guide to Key Issues in Mass Media Ethics and Law*, eds. William A. Babcock and William H. Freivogel (Thousand Oaks, CA: Sage, 2015), 287–301.

23. Peter Edwards, crime reporter, *Toronto Star*.

24. Ward, *Ethical Journalism in a Populist Age*, 23.

25. For more about Merkel's policy, and its effects, see: James McAuley and Rick Noack, "What You Need to Know About Germany's Immigration Crisis," *Washington Post*, 3 July 2018, https://www.washingtonpost.com/news/worldviews/wp/2018/07/03/what-you-need-to-know-about-germanys-immigration-crisis/?utm_term=.09ffd1f25fef.

26. Andray Domise, "The Rise of an Uncaring Canada," *Macleans*, April 2019, https://www.macleans.ca/news/canada/the-rise-of-an-uncaring-canada/.

27. See the Dutch press code here: https://www.rvdj.nl.

28. Marshall McLuhan, *Understanding Media: The Extensions of Man* (Toronto: McGraw-Hill,1964), 7.

29. Harold Innis, cited in James Carey's "Tribute to Harold Innis," in *Communication as Culture: Essays on Media and Society* (London: Routledge, 2008), 160.

30. Yvonne Jewkes and Chris Greer, "Extremes of Otherness: Media Images of Social Exclusion," *Social Justice*, 32, no. 1 (2005): 20–31.

31. Jewkes, and Greer, "Extremes of Otherness," 20

32. George Gerbner, Larry Gross, Michael Morgan, Nancy Signorielli, and James Shanahan, "Growing Up with Television: Cultivation Processes," in *Mediaeffects: Advances in Theory and Research*, ed. J. Bryant and D. Zillmann (Mahwah, NJ: Lawrence Erlbaum Associates, 2002), 43–67.

33. Renita Coleman and Esther Thorson, "The Effects of News Stories That Put Crime and Violence into Context: Testing the Public Health Model of Reporting," *Journal of Health Communication* 7 (2002): 401–425.

34. Elena Holodney, "Traffic Fatalities in US Have Been Mostly Plummeting for Decades," *Business Insider,* 20 April 2016, https://www.businessinsider.com/traffic-fatalities-historical-trend-us-2016-4.

35. Martin Innes, "'Signal Crimes': Detective Work, Mass Media and Constructing Collective Memory," in *Criminal Visions: Media Representations of Crime and Justice,* ed. Paul Mason (Cullompton, U.K.: Willan, 2003), 51–69, 53.

36. Lawrence Lanahan, "What *The Wire* Reveals About Urban Journalism," *Columbia Journalism Review,* January/February 2008, https://archives.cjr.org/cover_story/secrets_of_the_city.php.

37. Jeffrey W. Murray, "The Other Ethics of Emmanuel Levinas: Communication Beyond Relativism," in *Moral Engagement in Public Life,* ed. Sharon Bracci and Clifford Christians (New York: Peter Lang, 2002), 171–195.

38. Wade Davis, quoted in *The Wayfinders: Why Ancient Wisdom Matters in the Modern World,* https://www.azquotes.com/quote/353042

Bibliography

Abadi, David, Leen d'Haenens, Keith Roe, and Joyce Koeman. "Leitkultur and Discourse Hegemonies: German Mainstream Media Coverage on the Integration Debate Between 2009 and 2014." *International Communication Gazette* 78, no. 6 (2016): 557–584.

Abbate, Carmelo. "Yara, l'avvocato Salvagni: Ecco lo sporco gioco contro Bossetti" [Yara, the lawyer Salvagni: Here is the dirty game against Bossetti]. *Panorama*, 2 February 2015. https://www.panorama.it/news/cronaca/yara-bossetti-avvocato/.

Adam, G. Stuart. "Foreword." In *Communication as Culture: Essays on Media and Society*, edited by James W. Carey, ix–xxiv. London: Routledge, 2008.

Ahmed, Akbar. *Journey into Europe: Islam, Immigration, and Identity*. Washington, DC: Brookings Institution Press, 2018.

Akbar, Jay, and Sofia Petkar. "Who Is [Full Name]? Countess of Chester Hospital Nurse Arrested on Suspicion of Murdering Eight Babies." *The Sun*, 8 July 2018. https://www.thesun.co.U.K./news/6688782/lucy-letby-nurse-arrested-murder-eight-babies-hospital/.

Algarve Daily News Staff. "2017 Will Be a Very Bad Year for Journalism in Portugal." *Algarve Daily News*, 18 January 2017. https://algarvedailynews.com/news/10838-2017-will-be-a-very-bad-year-for-journalism-in-portugal.

Allen, Anita L. *Why Privacy Isn't Everything: Feminist Reflections on Personal Accountability*. Lanham, MD: Rowman & Littlefield, 2003.

Altschull, J. Herbert. *Agents of Power: The Role of the News Media in Human Affairs*. Harlow, U.K.: Longman, 1984.

Amsterdam Info Staff. "Amsterdam Newspapers." Amsterdam Info. N.d. https://www.amsterdam.info/newspapers/.

Asylum Information Database. "Overview of the Main Changes Since the Previous Report Update." Asylum Information Database. 1 March 2018. http://www.asylumineurope.org/reports/country/germany/overview-main-changes-previous-report-update.

Bagdikian, Ben H. *Double Vision: Reflections on My Heritage, Life and Profession*. Boston, MA: Beacon Press, 1997.

Baker, Edwin C. *Media Concentration and Democracy: Why Ownership Matters*. Cambridge, U.K.: Cambridge University Press, 2006.

Barthes, Roland. *Mythologies*. Translated by Annette Lavers. New York: Hill and Wang, 1972.

BBC News Staff. "Ex-IMF Head Rodrigo Rato's Home and Office Searched in Spain." BBC News, 16 April 2015. https://www.bbc.com/news/world-europe-32335842.

BBC News Staff. "German Nurse 'Admits Killing 30' with Fatal Overdoses." BBC News, 8 January 2015. https://www.bbc.com/news/world-30732841.

BBC News Staff. "Grace Millane: New Zealand Anger over Google Naming Murder Suspect." BBC News, 13 December 2018. https://www.bbc.com/news/world-asia-46548574.

BBC News Staff. "Mission, Values and Public Purposes." BBC, n.d. https://www.bbc.com/aboutthebbc/governance/mission.

BBC News Staff. "Press Regulation: What You Need to Know." BBC News, 13 April 2016. https://www.bbc.com/news/U.K.-politics-36034956.

Belenky, Mary Field, Blythe McVicker Clinchy, Nancy Rule Goldberger, and Jill Matluck Tarule. *Women's Ways of Knowing: The Development of Self, Voice and Mind.* New York: Basic Books, 1986.

Bell, Emily. "What 2,000 Job Cuts Tell Us: The Free Market Kills Digital Journalism." *The Guardian,* 2 February 2019. https://www.theguardian.com/media/2019/feb/02/what-2000-job-cuts-tell-us-the-free-market-kills-digital-journalism.

Bennhold, Katrin. "Bavaria: Affluent, Picturesque—and Angry." *New York Times,* 30 June 2018. https://www.nytimes.com/2018/06/30/world/europe/bavaria-immigration-afd-munich.html.

Bennhold, Katrin. "Crosses Go Up in Public Offices: It's Culture, Bavaria Says, Not Religion." *New York Times,* 30 May 2018. https://www.nytimes.com/2018/05/30/world/europe/bavaria-germany-crucifix-migrants.html.

Bennhold, Katrin. "German Intelligence Agency Says It Will Track Members of Far-Right Party." *New York Times,* 16 January 2019. https://www.nytimes.com/2019/01/15/world/europe/alternative-for-germany-investigation.html.

Bennhold, Katrin. "Grappling with Death in a Small German Town." *New York Times,* 17 January 2018. https://www.nytimes.com/2018/01/17/insider/kandel-germany-mia-v-murder.html.

Bergamo Chronicle Staff. "Yara, parla la Procura: 'Quel Dna è di Bossetti'" [Yara, the public prosecutor speaks: "That DNA is from Bossetti"]. *Bergamo Chronicle,* 28 January 2015. https://bergamo.corriere.it/notizie/cronaca/15_gennaio_28/yara-parla-procura-quel-dna-bossetti-503b2b2c-a6e0-11e4-93fc-9b9679dd4aa0.shtml.

Bertrand, Claude-Jean. *Media Ethics and Accountability Systems.* London: Transaction, 2000.

Bettelheim, Bruno. *The Uses of Enchantment: The Meaning and Importance of Fairy Tales.* New York: Vintage, 2010.

Beusekamp, Willem. "Suspicious Abduction Melchers Dissatisfied." *de Volkskrant,* 14 August 2006. https://www.volkskrant.nl/nieuws-achtergrond/verdachte-ontvoering-melchers-ontevreden~bedd340e/.

Bisogno, Enrico, Jenna Dawson-Faber, Michael Jandl, Kristiina Kangaspunta, Labib Kazkaz, Lucia Motolinia Carballo, Serena Oliva, and Felix Reiterer. *Global Study on Homicide 2013.* Vienna: United Nations Office on Drugs and Crime, 2013.

Blatchford, Christie. "Christie Blatchford: Why I Can't Completely Share the Outrage over Mcclintic's Healing Lodge Transfer." *National Post,* 1 October 2018. https://nationalpost.com/opinion/christie-blatchford-why-i-cant-completely-share-the-outrage-over-mcclintics-healing-lodge-transfer.

Bok, Sissela. "Lies: They Come with Consequences." *Washington Post,* 23 August 1998, C1.

Bok, Sissela. *Lying: Moral Choice in Public and Private Life.* New York: Vintage, 1999.

Borden, Sandra. *Journalism as Practice: MacIntyre, Virtue Ethics and the Press.* Hampshire, U.K. and Burlington, VT: Ashgate Press, 2007.

Brainard, Curtis. "What Kind of News Do People Really Want?" *Columbia Journalism Review,* 31 August 2007. https://archives.cjr.org/behind_the_news/what_kind_of_news_do_people_re.php.

Brandeis University Staff. "Louis D. Brandeis Legacy Fund for Social Justice." Brandeis University. N.d. https://www.brandeis.edu/legacyfund/bio.html.

Bravo Sanestanislao, Gabriela. "Presunción de inocencia y cultura democrática." *El País*, 11 December 2009. https://elpais.com/diario/2009/12/11/opinion/1260486011_850215.html.

Brown, Lesley. *The New Shorter Oxford English Dictionary on Historical Principles*. Oxford: Oxford University Press, 1993.

Brüggemann, Michael, Sven Engesser, Florin Büchel, Edda Humprecht, and Laia Castro. "Hallin and Mancini Revisited: Four Empirical Types of Western Media Systems." *Journal of Communication* 64, no. 6 (2014): 1037–1065.

Calabresi, Mario. "Millennials Wary of Corrupt Media Reporting." Markkula Center for Applied Ethics at Santa Clara University. 27 August 2015. https://www.scu.edu/ethics/focus-areas/journalism-ethics/resources/the-trust-issue-in-italy/.

Canadian Journalists for Free Expression. "Journalism Is Not a Crime." Canadian Journalists for Free Expression. 17 March 2017. https://www.cjfe.org/journalism_not_a_crime.

Canestrini, Nicola. "Basic Principles of Italian Criminal Law." Canestrini Lex. 26 March 2012. https://canestrinilex.com/en/readings/italian-criminal/.

Carey, James W. *Communication as Culture: Essays on Media and Society*. London: Routledge, 2008.

Carey, James W. "A Cultural Approach to Communication." In his *Communication as Culture: Essays on Media and Society*, 13–36. London: Routledge, 2008

Carlyle, Thomas. *On Heroes, Hero-Worship, and the Heroic in History*. Oakland: University of California Press, 1993.

Carr, Nicholas. *The Shallows: What the Internet Is Doing to Our Brains*. New York: W. W. Norton, 2011.

Carter, Bill. "The F.B.I. Criticizes the News Media After Several Mistaken Reports of an Arrest." *New York Times*, 17 April 2013. https://www.nytimes.com/2013/04/18/business/media/fbi-criticizes-false-reports-of-a-bombing-arrest.html.

Christians, Clifford G. "The Ethics of Being in a Communications Context." In *Communication Ethics and Universal Values*, edited by Clifford G. Christians and Michael Traber, 3–23. Thousand Oaks, CA: Sage, 1997.

Christians, Clifford G., John P. Ferré, and P. Mark Fackler. *Good News: Social Ethics and the Press*. Oxford: Oxford University Press, 1993.

Christians, Clifford G., Theodore Glasser, Denis McQuail, Kaarle Nordenstreng, and Robert A. White. *Normative Theories of the Media: Journalism in Democratic Societies*. Urbana and Champaign: University of Illinois Press, 2010.

Christians, Clifford G., and Bo Shan. *The Ethics of Intercultural Communication*. New York: Peter Lang, 2015.

Citizens Information Staff. "Children and the Criminal Justice System." Citizens Information. 3 May 2017. https://www.citizensinformation.ie/en/justice/children_and_young_offenders/children_and_the_criminal_justice_system_in_ireland.html.

Clifford., Sadie, J. "Expressions of Blame: Narratives of Battered Women Who Kill in the Twentieth Century *Daily Express*." Ph.D. diss. Cardiff University, 2009.

Cohen, Stanley. *Folk Devils and Moral Panics*. London: Psychology Press, 2002 (1972).

Coleman, Renita, and Esther Thorson. "The Effects of News Stories That Put Crime and Violence into Context: Testing the Public Health Model of Reporting." *Journal of Health Communication* 7 (2002): 401–425.

College of Policing. "Engagement and Communication." College of Policing. 24 May 2017. https://www.app.college.police.U.K./app-content/engagement-and-communication/media-relations/#introduction.

College of Policing. "Guidance on the Relationships with Media." College of Policing. 1 May 2013. https://www.npcc.police.U.K./documents/reports/2013/201305-cop-media-rels.pdf.

Commission of Arbitration, Complaints, and Deontology of Journalism Staff. "Código Deontológico" [Code of Ethics]. Commission of Arbitration, Complaints, and Deontology of Journalism. 22 April 2017. http://www.comisiondequejas.com/codigo-deontologico/.

Cook, David. "Monitor Shifts from Print to Web-based Strategy." *Christian Science Monitor*, 29 October 2008. https://www.csmonitor.com/USA/2008/1029/p25s01-usgn.html.

Craig, David A. "Communitarian Journalism(s): Clearing Conceptual Landscapes." *Journal of Mass Media Ethics* 11, no. 2 (1996): 107–118.

Crouch, David. "The New 'People's Home': How Sweden Is Waging War on Inequality." *The Guardian*, 17 July 2017. https://www.theguardian.com/inequality/2017/jul/17/peoples-home-sweden-waged-war-inequality-rich-poor-gothenburg.

Da Fonseca-Wollheim, Corinna. "750,000 Germans Fled East Prussia in 1945. A Novelist Imagines One Family's Exodus." *New York Times*, 25 May 2018. https://www.nytimes.com/2018/05/25/books/review/walter-kempowski-all-for-nothing.html.

Dahl, Robert A. *On Democracy*. New Haven, CT: Yale University Press, 2008.

Davis, Wade. Quoted in *The Wayfinders: Why Ancient Wisdom Matters in the Modern World*. https://www.azquotes.com/quote/353042.

Department of Justice. "Publication Bans." Government of Canada. 5 March 2015. https://www.justice.gc.ca/eng/cj-jp/yj-jj/tools-outils/sheets-feuillets/publi-publi.html.

De Sousa, Luís. "'I Don't Bribe, I Just Pull Strings': Assessing the Fluidity of Social Representations of Corruption in Portuguese Society." *Perspectives on European Politics and Society* 9, no. 1 (2008): 8–23.

Deutscher Presserat. "Section 8: Protection of Personality." In *German Press Code*. Berlin: Deutscher Presserat, 2013.

De Volkskrant Staff. "Hans Melchers Establishes Press Victims Foundation." *de Volkskrant*, 21 October 2006. https://www.volkskrant.nl/nieuws-achtergrond/hans-melchers-richt-stichting-slachtoffers-pers-op~b82912ad/.

Dewey, John. *The Public and Its Problems: An Essay in Political Inquiry*. Edited by Melvin L. Rogers. University Park: Pennsylvania State Press, 2012.

Die Welt News Staff. "Germany's NSU Neo-Nazi Trial Verdict Sparks Protests, Calls for Investigation." *Die Welt*, 11 July 2018. https://p.dw.com/p/31JDB.

Diffley, Angela. "French Huffington Post Will Run Strauss-Kahn Stories, Says Editor Anne Sinclair." *RFI English*, 19 January 2012. http://en.rfi.fr/americas/20120119-french-huffington-post-will-run-strauss-kahn-stories-says-editor-anne-sinclair.

Domise, Andray. "The Rise of an Uncaring Canada." *Macleans*, April 2019. https://www.macleans.ca/news/canada/the-rise-of-an-uncaring-canada/.

Donn, Natasha. "Former PM José Sócrates Sues Portuguese State for €50,00." *Portugal Resident*, 9 January 2020. https://www.portugalresident.com/former-pm-jose-socrates-sues-portuguese-state-for-e50000//.

Dörr, Dieter, and Eve Aernecke. "A Never Ending Story: Caroline v Germany." In *The Right to Privacy in the Light of Media Convergence*, edited by Dieter Dörr and Russell L. Weaver, 114–124. Berlin: De Gruyter, 2012.

Dunne, Stephen. "Policing the Press: The Institutionalisation of Independent Press Regulation in a Liberal/North Atlantic Media System." Ph.D. diss. Dublin City University, 2017.

Elshtain, Jean Bethke. *Public Man, Private Woman: Women in Social and Political Thought.* Princeton, NJ: Princeton University Press, 1993.

English, Kathy. "New Era for Media Accountability in Canada: Public Editor." *Toronto Star*, 11 September 2015. https://www.thestar.com/opinion/public_editor/2015/09/11/new-era-for-media-accountability-in-canada-public-editor.html.

Entman, Robert M. "Framing: Toward Clarification of a Fractured Paradigm." *Journal of Communication* 43, no. 4 (1993): 51–58.

Ericson, Richard V., Patricia M. Baranek, and Janet B. L. Chan. *Representing Order: Crime, Law, and Justice in the News Media.* Milton Keynes, U.K.: Open University Press, 1991.

European Commission. "Europeans and Their Languages." Special Eurobarometer 386. 2012. https://web.archive.org/web/20190617170303/http://ec.europa.eu/commfrontoffice/publicopinion/archives/ebs/ebs_386_en.pdf.

European Federation of Journalists Staff. "Freelance Journalist Facing Alone Lawsuits After Publication of Articles on Italian Businessman." European Federation of Journalists. 21 April 2017. https://europeanjournalists.org/blog/2017/04/21/freelance-journalist-facing-alone-lawsuits-after-publication-of-articles-on-italian-businessman/.

Eurostat Staff. "Homicides Recorded By the Police, 2002–12." Eurostat. 3 June 2014. https://ec.europa.eu/eurostat/statistics-explained/index.php/File:Homicides_recorded_by_the_police,_2002–12_YB14.png.

Eurostat Staff. "Intentional Homicide Victims in EU." Eurostat. 22 February 2018. https://ec.europa.eu/eurostat/web/products-eurostat-news/-/EDN-20180222-1.

Eva Matsa, Katerina. "Across Western Europe Public News Media Are Widely Used and Trusted Sources of News." Pew Research Center. 8 June 2018. https://www.pewresearch.org/fact-tank/2018/06/08/western-europe-public-news-media-widely-used-and-trusted/.

Expatica Staff. "Media in the Netherlands: Expat Guide to The Netherlands." Expatica. 15 November 2018. https://www.expatica.com/nl/living/telecommunications/media-in-the-netherlands-106958/.

Farhi, Paul. "An Australian Court's Gag Order Is No Match for the Internet, as Word Gets Out About Prominent Cardinal's Conviction." *Washington Post*, 13 December 2018. https://www.washingtonpost.com/lifestyle/style/an-australian-courts-gag-order-is-no-match-for-the-internet-as-word-gets-out-about-prominent-cardinals-conviction/2018/12/13/5137005c-fef5-11e8-83c0-b06139e540e5_story.html?utm_term=.a0da49bcf32c.

Felle, Tom. "Ireland Press Regulation: An Irish Solution to a British Problem." In *After Leveson?—The Future for British Journalism*, edited by John Mair, 165–175. Suffolk, U.K.: Abramis Academic, 2013.

Fengler, Susanne, Tobias Eberwein, Gianpietro Mazzoleni, Colin Porlezza, and Stephan Russ Mohl. *Journalists and Media Accountability: An International Study of News People in the Digital Age.* New York: Peter Lang, 2014.

Fielden, Lara. *Regulating the Press: A Comparative Study of International Press Councils.* Oxford: Reuters Institute for the Study of Journalism, 2012.

Fisher, Walter R. *Human Communication as Narration: Toward a Philosophy of Reason, Value, and Action.* Columbia: University of South Carolina Press, 1989.

Fisher, Walter R. "Narration, Reason, Community." In *Writing the Social Text: Poetics and Politics in Social Science Discourse*, edited by Richard Brown, 199–219. New York: Routledge, 2017.

Freedom House. "About Freedom House." Freedom House. N.d., https://freedomhouse.org/about-us.

Friedrichsen, Gisela. "Fast alles, was Hussein K. erzählt hat, war gelogen" [Almost everything that Hussein K. said was a lie]. *Welt*, 3 February 2018. https://www.welt.de/vermischtes/plus174127866/Vergewaltigung-in-Freiburg-Fast-alles-was-Hussein-K-erzaehlt-hat-war-gelogen.html.

Frost, Chris. "A Crisis of Ethics: Breaking the Cycle of Newspaper Irresponsibility." In *The State in Transition: Essays in Honour of John Horgan*, edited by Kevin Rafter and Mark O'Brien, 78–100. Dublin: New Island Press, 2015.

Frost, Chris. *Journalism Ethics and Regulation*. Essex, U.K.: Pearson, 2000.

Frost, Chris. "The Press Complaints Commission: A Study of Ten Years of Adjudications on Press Complaints." *Journalism Studies* 5, no. 1 (2004): 101–114.

Gans, Herbert. *Deciding What's News: A Study of CBS Evening News, NBC Nightly News, Newsweek and Time*. New York: Pantheon, 1979.

Gerbner, George, Larry Gross, Michael Morgan, Nancy Signorielli, and James Shanahan. "Growing up with Television: Cultivation Processes." In *Media Effects: Advances in Theory and Research*, edited by J. Bryant and D. Zillmann, 43–67. Mahwah, NJ: Lawrence Erlbaum Associates, 2002.

German Press Council Guidelines for Journalistic Work. Section 12.1. Accountable Journalism. 2006. https://accountablejournalism.org/ethics-codes/Germany-Press-Council.

German Press Council Guidelines for Journalistic Work. Section 12.1, as of 2017. Presserat (German Press Council), https://www.presserat.de/files/presserat/dokumente/download/Press%20Code.pdf.

Gillespie, Bruce. *News Writing and Reporting: An Introduction to Skills and Theory*. Oxford: Oxford University Press, 2018.

Gilligan, Carol. *In a Different Voice: Psychological Theory and Women's Development*. Cambridge, MA: Harvard University Press, 1982.

Gilligan, Carol. *Mapping the Moral Domain: A Contribution of Women's Thinking to Psychological Theory and Education*. Cambridge, MA: Harvard University Press, 1988.

Gilligan, Carol, and Jane Attanucci. "Two Moral Orientations: Gender Differences and Similarities." *Merrill-Palmer Quarterly* 34, no. 3 (1988): 223–237.

Giomi, Elisa, and Fabrizio Tonello. "Moral Panic: The Issue of Women and Crime in Italian Evening News." *Sociologica* 7, no. 3 (2013): 1–30.

Glaser, Barney G., and Anselm L. Strauss. *The Discovery of Grounded Theory*. Hawthorne, NY: Aldine, 1967.

Glendon, Mary Ann. *Abortion and Divorce in Western Law*. Cambridge, MA: Harvard University Press, 1987.

Globe and Mail Staff. "About Us." *The Globe and Mail*, n.d. https://www.theglobeandmail.com/about/.

Grande, Elisabetta. "Italian Criminal Justice: Borrowing and Resistance." *American Journal of Comparative Law* 48, no. 2 (2000): 227–259.

Greenslade, Roy. "Eight Newspapers Pay Libel Damages to Christopher Jefferies." *The Guardian*, 29 July 2011. https://www.theguardian.com/media/greenslade/2011/jul/29/joanna-yeates-national-newspapers.

Greenslade, Roy. "See You in Court—Dominic Grieve Lays Down Law on Contempt." *Evening Standard*, 30 November 2011. https://www.standard.co.U.K./business/media/see-you-in-court-dominic-grieve-lays-down-law-on-contempt-6373540.html.

Greenslade, Roy. "Why Cliff Richard's Case Against the BBC Should Worry Us All." *The Guardian*, 17 April 2018. https://www.theguardian.com/commentisfree/2018/apr/17/cliff-richard-bbc-court-case-police-press-media.

Greenslade, Roy. "Why *The Guardian's* decision Not to Sign up to IPSO Makes Sense." *The Guardian*, 4 September 2014. https://www.theguardian.com/media/greenslade/2014/sep/04/press-regulation-ipso.

Greer, Chris, and Yvonne Jewkes. "Extremes of Otherness: Media Images of Social Exclusion." *Social Justice* 32, no. 1 (2005): 20–31.

Grieco, Elizabeth. "Newsroom Employment Dropped Nearly a Quarter in Less Than 10 Years, with Greatest Decline at Newspapers." Pew Research Center, 30 July 2018. https://www.pewresearch.org/fact-tank/2018/07/30/newsroom-employment-dropped-nearly-a-quarter-in-less-than-10-years-with-greatest-decline-at-newspapers/.

The Guardian Staff. "The Guardian's Editorial Code." *The Guardian*, 5 August 2015. https://www.theguardian.com/info/2015/aug/05/the-guardians-editorial-code.

Gunter, Joel. "Chris Jefferies Wins 'Substantial' Libel Damages from Newspapers." *Journalism.co.U.K*, 29 July 2011. https://www.journalism.co.U.K./news/chris-jefferies-wins-substantial-libel-damages-from-newspapers/s2/a545392/.

Habermas, Jürgen. *The Structural Transformation of the Public Sphere*. Translated by Thomas Burger and Frederick Lawrence. Cambridge, U.K.: Polity, 1989 (1962).

Hallin, Daniel C., and Paolo Mancini. *Comparing Media Systems: Three Models of Media and Politics*. Cambridge, U.K.: Cambridge University Press, 2004.

Hallin, Daniel C., and Paolo Mancini. "'Comparing Media Systems': A Response to Critics." *Media and Journalism* 17, no. 9 (2012): 53–57.

Hallin Daniel C., and Pablo Mancini. "Ten Years After Comparing Media Systems: What Have We Learned?" *Political Communication* 34, no. 2, (2017): 155–171.

Hallin, Daniel C., and Stylianos Papathanassopoulos. "Political Clientelism and the Media: Southern Europe and Latin America in Comparative Perspective." *Media, Culture & Society* 24, no. 2 (2002): 175–195.

Hammarberg, Thomas. *Human Rights and a Changing Media Landscape*. Strasbourg, FR: Council of Europe, 2011, 74.

Hansen, Felix, and Sebastian Schneider. "Facts & Figures About the NSU Trial—An Overview." NSU Watch. 23 September 2017. https://www.nsu-watch.info/2017/09/facts-figures-about-the-nsu-trial/.

Hellmueller, Lee, Tim P. Vos, and Mark A. Poepsel. "Shifting Journalistic Capital? Transparency and Objectivity in the Twenty-first Century." *Journalism Studies* 14, no. 3 (2013): 287–304.

Herman, Edward, and Noam Chomsky. *Manufacturing Consent: The Political Economy of the Mass Media*. New York: Random House, 2010.

Herman, Edward, and Robert McChesney. *The Global Media: The New Missionaries of Corporate Capitalism*. Washington, DC: Cassell, 1997.

Hobbes, Thomas. *Leviathan*. G. A. J. Rogers and Karl Schuhmann, eds. London: Continuum, 2006.

Hodges, Lou. "Privacy and the Press." In *The Handbook of Mass Media Ethics*, edited by Lee Wilkins and Clifford Christians, 276–287. New York: Routledge, 2009.

Holodney, Elena. "Traffic Fatalities in US Have Been Mostly Plummeting for Decades." *Business Insider*, 20 April 2016. https://www.businessinsider.com/traffic-fatalities-historical-trend-us-2016-4.

Hooper, Anthony, David C. Ormerod, and Duncan Atkinson. "Section F19 Inferences from Silence and the Non-Production of Evidence." In *Blackstone's Criminal Practice*, 2709–2733. Oxford: Oxford University Press, 2012.

Horgan, John. *Irish Media: A Critical History Since 1922*. London: Routledge, 2001.

Howe, Paul. "Eroding Norms and Democratic Deconsolidation." *Journal of Democracy* 28, no. 4 (2017): 15–29.

Il Corriere della Sera Staff. "Defamation in Italy: A Draft Law to Be Changed." Council of Europe. 8 June 2014. https://www.coe.int/en/web/commissioner/-/defamation-in-italy-a-draft-law-to-be-changed.

Innes, Martin. *Investigating Murder: Detective Work and the Police Response to Criminal Homicide*. Oxford: Oxford University Press, 2003.

Innes, Martin. "'Signal Crimes': Detective Work, Mass Media and Constructing Collective Memory." In *Criminal Visions: Media Representations of Crime and Justice*, edited by Paul Mason, 51–69. Cullompton, Devon, U.K.: Willan, 2003.

Innes, Martin, and Nigel Fielding. "From Community to Communicative Policing: 'Signal Crimes' and the Problem of Public Reassurance." *Sociological Research Online* 7, no. 2 (2002): 1–12.

Investigative Reporting Project Italy. "About Us." Investigative Reporting Project Italy (IRPI). N.d. https://irpi.eu/en/about-us/.

Irish Times Staff. "About the Irish Times." *Irish Times*, n.d. https://www.irishtimes.com/about-us/the-irish-times-trust.

Jabonero, Alberto. "Mañana podemos ser nosotros." *El País*, 1 December 2009. https://elpais.com/diario/2009/12/01/sociedad/1259622002_850215.html.

Jerkins, Morgan. "The Genius Behind Nameless Protagonists." *Book Riot*, 14 March 2015. https://bookriot.com/2015/03/14/critical-linking-march-14-2015/.

Jewkes, Yvonne, and Chris Greer. "Extremes of Otherness: Media Images of Social Exclusion." *Social Justice* 32, no. 1 (2005): 20–31.

Jiménez, Jennifer. "Condenados 'ABC' y 'La Opinión de Tenerife' por llamar asesino y violador a un hombre inocente." *CanariasAhora*. 2 July 2017. https://www.eldiario.es/canariasahora/tribunales/Condenados-ABC-Opinion-Tenerife-inocente_0_609989559.html.

Jiménez-de-Parga, Manuel. "Los nefastos 'juicios paralelos.'" *ABC*, 4 August 2009. https://www.abc.es/opinion/abci-nefastos-juicios-paralelos-200908040300-923068256978_noticia.html.

Jones, Tobias. "The Murder That Has Obsessed Italy." *The Guardian*, 8 January 2015. https://www.theguardian.com/world/2015/jan/08/-sp-the-murder-that-has-obsessed-italy.

Katz, Jack. "What Makes Crime 'News'?" *Media, Culture & Society* 9, no. 1 (1987): 47–75.

Kennedy, Paul. "The People vs Democracy." CBC Radio podcast. 13 December 2018. https://www.cbc.ca/radio/ideas/the-people-vs-democracy-1.4944953.

Khalip, Andrei. "Portuguese Ex-PM Arrested in Corruption Probe." Reuters, 22 November 2014. https://www.reuters.com/article/portugal-corruption-socrates-idUSL6N0TC04K20141122.

Knowlton, Steven, and Bill Reader. *Moral Reasoning for Journalists*. Westport, CT: Praeger, 2008.

Koene, Daphne C. *Press Councils in Western Europe*. Diemen, The Netherlands: AMB, 2009.

Kohlberg, Lawrence. *Essays on Moral Development: The Psychology of Moral Development*. San Francisco: Harper & Row, 1981.

Kovach, Bill, and Tom Rosenstiel. *The Elements of Journalism: What News People Should Know and the Public Should Expect*. New York: Three Rivers Press, 2014.

Krotoszynski Jr, Ronald J. *The First Amendment in Cross-Cultural Perspective: A Comparative Legal Analysis of the Freedom of Speech*. New York: New York University Press, 2006.

La Rue, Frank. *Report of the Special Rapporteur on the Promotion and Protection of the Right to Freedom of Opinion and Expression*. New York: United Nations General Assembly, 2011.

Lanahan, Lawrence. "What *The Wire* Reveals About Urban Journalism." *Columbia Journalism Review*, January/February 2008. https://archives.cjr.org/cover_story/secrets_of_the_city.php.

Langer, Lorenz. *Religious Offence and Human Rights: The Implications of Defamation of Religions*. Cambridge, U.K.: Cambridge University Press, 2014.

Laver, Nicola. "Contempt of Court Act 1981." *Inbrief*, n.d. https://www.inbrief.co.U.K./legal-system/contempt-of-court-act/.

Lepore, Jill. "The Rise of the Victims'-Rights Movement." *The New Yorker*, 14 May 2018. https://www.newyorker.com/magazine/2018/05/21/the-rise-of-the-victims-rights-movement.

Leveson Inquiry. *Report into the Culture, Practices and Ethics of the Press*. London: Department for Digital, Culture, Media & Sport and Leveson Inquiry, 2012.

Levinas, Emmanuel. *Ethics and Infinity*. Translated by Richard Cohen. Pittsburgh: Duquesne University Press, 1985.

Lord, Rich. "How Robert Bowers Went from Conservative to White Nationalist." *Pittsburgh Post-Gazette*, 10 November 2018. https://www.post-gazette.com/news/crime-courts/2018/11/10/Robert-Bowers-extremism-Tree-of-Life-massacre-shooting-pittsburgh-Gab-Warroom/stories/201811080165.

Lyons, Kate. "Grace Millane Murder: New Zealand Rebukes Google for Emailing out Suspect's Name." *The Guardian*, 19 December 2018. https://www.theguardian.com/world/2018/dec/19/grace-millane-new-zealand-rebU.K.es-google-for-emailing-out-suspects-name.

Lyons, Nona Plessner. "Two Perspectives: On Self, Relationships, and Morality." *Harvard Educational Review* 53, no. 2 (1983): 125–145.

Lyotard, Jean-Francois. *The Differend: Phrases in Dispute*. Translated by G. Van Den Abbeele. Minneapolis: University of Minnesota Press, 1988.

Maciá-Barber, Carlos, and María-Ángeles Galván-Arias. "Presumption of Innocence and Journalistic Ethics: The Aitana Case." *Revista Latina de Comunicacion Social* 67 (2012): 356–387.

"Magistrate Considers Major Corruption Trial in Portugal." *Associated Press News*, 28 January 2019. https://apnews.com/facad73714154dd2bfaa11bc3071aa0a.

Manning, Paul. *News and News Sources: A Critical Introduction*. Thousand Oaks, CA: Sage, 2001.

Marek, Michael, and Marie Todeskino. "German Hostage Drama: The Day the Press Became the Story." *Deutsche Welle*, 16 August 2018. https://www.dw.com/en/german-hostage-drama-the-day-the-press-became-the-story/a-17025034.

Martinho, Ana Pinto, Gustavo Cardoso, and Miguel Paisana. "Portugal." In *Digital News Report 2018*, edited by Nic Newman, Richard Fletcher, Antonis Kalogeropoulos, David

A. L. Levy, and Rasmus Kleis Nielsen, 96–97. Oxford: Reuters Institute for the Study of Journalism, 2018.

"Master of Media Circus for Madeleine McCann." *The Daily Telegraph*, 24 April 2008. https://www.telegraph.co.U.K./news/1902515/Master-of-media-circus-for-Madeleine-McCann.html.

Matsuda, Mari. "Critical Race Theory and Critical Legal Studies: Contestation and Coalition." In *Critical Race Theory: The Key Writings that Formed the Movement*, edited by Neil Gotanda and Garry Peller, 62–79. New York: New Press, 1995.

Matthews, Sibella, Vincent Schiraldi, and Lael Chester. "Youth Justice in Europe: Experience of Germany, the Netherlands, and Croatia in Providing Developmentally Appropriate Responses to Emerging Adults in the Criminal Justice System." *Justice Evaluation Journal* 1, no. 1 (2018): 59–81.

McAuley, James, and Rick Noack. "What You Need to Know About Germany's Immigration Crisis." *Washington Post*, 3 July 2018. https://www.washingtonpost.com/news/worldviews/wp/2018/07/03/what-you-need-to-know-about-germanys-immigration-crisis/?utm_term=.09ffd1f25fef.

McChesney, Robert. "The Political Economy of the Global Communication Revolution." In *Capitalism and the Information Age: The Political Economy of the Global Communication Revolution*, edited by John Bellamy Foster and Ellen M. Wood, 1–26. New York: Monthly Review Press, 1998.

McCracken, Grant. *The Long Interview*. Newbury, CA: Sage, 1988.

McKercher, Catherine, and Carman Cumming. *The Canadian Reporter: News Writing and Reporting*. Scarborough, ON: Nelson Thompson Learning, 1998.

McLean, Dorothy Cummings. "Australian Prosecutor Threatens US Media for Breaking Publication Ban on Cdl. Pell's Trial." *Life Site*, 13 December 2018. https://www.lifesitenews.com/news/australian-prosecutor-threatens-us-media-for-breaking-publication-ban-on-cd.

McLuhan, Marshall. *Understanding Media: The Extensions of Man*. Toronto: McGraw-Hill, 1964.

McQuail, Dennis. *McQuail's Mass Communication Theory*. Thousand Oakes, CA: Sage, 2010.

Meaney, Thomas, and Saskia Schäfer. "The Neo-Nazi Murder Trial Revealing Germany's Darkest Secrets." *The Guardian*, 15 December 2016. https://www.theguardian.com/world/2016/dec/15/neo-nazi-murders-revealing-germanys-darkest-secrets.

Merrill, John Calhoun. *The Imperative of Freedom: A Philosophy of Journalistic Autonomy*. New York: Hastings House, 1974.

Mill, John Stuart. "Utilitarianism." In *Seven Masterpieces of Philosophy*, edited by Steven M. Cahn, 337–383. New York: Routledge, 2016.

Milton, John. "Areopagitica." In *The Complete Poetry and Essential Prose of John Milton*, edited by William Kerrigan, John Rumrich, and Stephen M. Fallon, 923–966. New York: Modern Library, 2007.

Mirabella, Julia Grace. "Scales of Justice: Assessing Italian Crime Procedure Through the Amanda Knox Trial." *Boston University International Law Journal* 30, no. 1 (2012): 229–260.

Mitchell, Amy, Katie Simmons, Katerina Eva Matsa, and Laura Silver. "Global Publics Want Politically Balanced News, but Do Not Think Their News Media Are Doing Very Well in This Area." Pew Research Center. 11 January 2018. https://www.pewglobal.org/2018/01/11/publics-globally-want-unbiased-news-coverage-but-are-divided-on-whether-their-news-media-deliver/.

Molla, Rani. "The 'Trump Bump' In *The New York Times*' Digital News Subscription Growth Is Over." *Vox*. 9 August 2018. https://www.vox.com/2018/8/9/17671000/new-york-times-trump-subscribers-news-slower-growth.

Morgenstern, Christine. "Judicial Rehabilitation in Germany—The Use of Criminal Records and the Removal of Recorded Convictions." *European Journal of Probation* 3, no. 1 (2011): 20–35.

Morlino, Leonardo. *Changes for Democracy: Actors, Structures, Processes*. Oxford: Oxford University Press, 2012.

Mounk, Yascha. *The People vs. Democracy: Why Our Freedom Is in Danger and How to Save It*. Cambridge, MA: Harvard University Press. 2018.

Murray, Jeffrey W. "The Other Ethics of Emmanuel Levinas: Communication Beyond Relativism." In *Moral Engagement in Public Life*, edited by Sharon Bracci and Clifford Christians, 171–195. New York: Peter Lang, 2002.

National NewsMedia Council. "About Us." National NewsMedia Council. N.d. https://mediacouncil.ca/about-us-ethics-journalism/.

New York Times Staff. "Standards and Ethics." *New York Times*, n.d. https://www.nytco.com/who-we-are/culture/standards-and-ethics/.

Noack, Rick. "Leaked Document Says 2,000 Men Allegedly Assaulted 1,200 German Women on New Year's Eve." *Washington Post*, 11 July 2016. https://www.washingtonpost.com/news/worldviews/wp/2016/07/10/leaked-document-says-2000-men-allegedly-assaulted-1200-german-women-on-new-years-eve/?noredirect=on&utm_term=.6aa3be390ffc.

Noack, Rick. "Sexual Assaults Challenge Germany's Welcoming Attitude Toward Refugees." *Washington Post*, 6 January 2016. https://www.washingtonpost.com/news/worldviews/wp/2016/01/06/sexual-assaults-challenge-germanys-welcoming-attitude-toward-refugees/?utm_term=.4fd111e72dd5.

Norris, Pippa. "Comparative Political Communications: Common Frameworks or Babelian Confusion?" *Government and Opposition* 44 no. 3 (2009): 321–340.

O'Malley, Tom, and Clive Soley. *Regulating the Press*. London: Pluto, 2000.

Osborne, Samuel. "[Full Name]: Police Search Home of Nurse After Arresting Health Care Worker on Suspicion of Murdering Eight Babies." *The Independent*, 4 July 2018. https://www.independent.co.U.K./news/U.K./crime/lucy-letby-baby-murders-countess-cheshire-hospital-neo-natal-unit-arrest-police-a8430196.html.

Parveen, Nazia. "Nurse Arrested over Cheshire Baby Deaths Released on Bail." *The Guardian*, 6 July 2018. https://www.theguardian.com/U.K.-news/2018/jul/06/nurse-arrested-over-cheshire-baby-deaths-released-on-bail-lucy-letby.

Patterson, Maggie Jones, and Romayne Smith Fullerton. "Credibility: The Best Currency in Journalism." In *The Sage Guide to Key Issues in Media Ethics and Law*, edited by William Babcock and William Freivogel, 81–92. Thousand Oaks, CA: Sage, 2015.

Patterson, Maggie Jones, and Romayne Smith Fullerton, "'Out' versus 'About': News Media, Politicians' Privacy, and Public Discussion." In *The Sage Guide to Key Issues in Media Ethics and Law*, edited by William Babcock and William Freivogel, 287–301. Thousand Oaks, CA: Sage, 2015.

Patterson, Maggie Jones, and Megan Williams Hall. "Abortion, Moral Maturity and Civic Journalism." *Critical Studies in Media Communication* 15, no. 2 (1998): 91–115.

Patterson, Maggie Jones, and Steve Urbanski. "What Jayson Blair and Janet Cooke Say About the Press and the Erosion of Public Trust." *Journalism Studies* 7, no. 6 (2006): 828–850.

Pearlman, Jonathan, Mark Broatch, and Jack Hardy. "Grace Millane Murder Suspect Revealed: Jesse Kempson, 26, Described Backpacker as 'Radiant' Just Minutes Before She Was Last Seen." *The Telegraph*, 10 December 2018. https://www.telegraph.co.U.K./news/2018/12/10/alleged-killer-british-backpacker-grace-millane-pictured-first/.

Perry, William G., *Forms of Intellectual and Ethical Development During the College Years*. New York: Holt, Rinehart & Winston, 1970.

Pew Research. "Fact Sheets: News Media and Political Attitudes in Western Europe, 17 May 2018. https://www.pewresearch.org/global/fact-sheet/news-media-and-political-attitudes-in-the-united-kingdom/.

Plaisance, Patrick L., *Media Ethics: Key Principles for Responsible Practice*. Thousand Oaks, CA: Sage, 2009.

Ponsford, Dominic. "Survey Finds That U.K. Written Press (By Some Way) the Least Trusted in Europe." *Press Gazette*, 26 May 2017. https://www.pressgazette.co.U.K./survey-finds-that-U.K.-written-press-is-by-some-way-the-least-trusted-in-europe/.

Pope, Kyle. "Meet Your New Public Editors." *Columbia Journalism Review*, 11 June 2019.

Press Industry Code Committee. "Code of Practice: For Newspapers and Periodicals." *Irish Times*, 6 December 2006. https://www.irishtimes.com/news/code-of-practice-for-newspapers-and-periodicals-1.1034235.

Press Ombudsman of Sweden. "How Self-regulation Works." Allmänhetens Pressombudsman Pressens Opinionsnämnd [The Press Ombudsman and the Press Council]. N.d. https://po.se/about-the-press-ombudsman-and-press-council/how-self-regulation-works/.

Press Reference Staff. "Netherlands Press." *Press Reference*, n.d. http://www.pressreference.com/Ma-No/Netherlands.html#ixzz5dl9feTuj.

"Pretrial Publicity Has Little Effect on the Right to a Fair Trial." Reporters Committee on Freedom of the Press. N.d. https://www.rcfp.org/journals/pretrial-publicitys-limited/.

Pritchard, David Hemmings, ed. *Holding the Media Accountable: Citizens, Ethics, and the Law*. Bloomington: Indiana University Press, 2000.

Public Policy Forum. *The Shattered Mirror: News, Democracy and Trust in the Digital Age*. Ottawa, ON: Public Policy Forum, 2017.

Puxley, Chinta. "A Look at How Canadian Courts Handle Young People Charged with Murder." *The Canadian Press*, 26 January 2016. https://globalnews.ca/news/2476202/a-look-at-how-courts-handle-youth-murder-suspects/.

Raad voor de Journalistiek. "Developments." Raad voor de Journalistiek. N.d. https://www.rvdj.nl/english.

Raad voor de Journalistiek. "Guidelines of the Netherlands Press Council." Raad voor de Journalistiek. 1 June 2018. https://www.rvdj.nl/english/guidelines.

Ramelsberger, Annette. "Eine schrecklich normale Entwicklung" [A terribly normal development]. *Süddeutsche Zeitung*, 6 May 2018. https://www.sueddeutsche.de/politik/nsu-prozess-wo-es-wehtut-1.3966494.

Ray, Michael. "Madrid Train Bombing of 2004." *Encyclopedia Britannica*. 10 March 2010. https://www.britannica.com/event/Madrid-train-bombings-of-2004.

Reiner, Robert. "Crime and Control in Britain." *Sociology* 34, no. 1 (2000): 71–94.

Reiner, Robert. "Media, Crime, Law and Order." In *Policing, Popular Culture and Political Economy: Towards a Social Democratic Criminology*, edited by Robert Reiner, 235–254. New York: Routledge, 2017.

Reiner, Robert. "Media Made Criminality: The Representation of Crime in the Mass Media." In *The Oxford Handbook of Criminology*, edited by Mike Maguire, Rodney Morgan, and Robert Reiner, 376–418. New York: Oxford University Press, 2002.

Reiner, Robert. "What's Left? The Prospects for Social Democratic Criminology." *Crime, Media, Culture* 8, no. 2 (2012): 135–150.

Reiner, Robert, Sonia Livingstone, and Jessica Allen. "From Law and Order to Lynch Mobs: Crime News Since the Second World War." In *Criminal Visions: Media Representations of Crime and Justice*, edited by Paul Mason, 13–32. Cullompton, Devon, U.K.: Willan, 2003.

Rengers, Merijn, and John Schoorl. "'Verbijsterde' Paarlberg on Appeal." *de Volkskrant*. 8 June 2010. https://www.volkskrant.nl/economie/verbijsterde-paarlberg-in-hoger-beroep~b4948088/.

Reporters Without Borders. "2018 World Press Freedom Index." Reporters Without Borders. N.d. https://rsf.org/en/ranking.

Reuters Staff. "Ex-IMF Head Rodrigo Rato Starts Jail Term in 'Black Cards' Case." *Reuters*, 25 October 2018. https://www.reuters.com/article/spain-corruption/ex-imf-head-rodrigo- rato-starts-jail-term-in-black-cards-case-idUSL8N1X569K.

Richardson, Gemma, and Romayne Smith Fullerton. "Rob Ford." In *Scandal in a Digital Age*, edited by Hinda Mandell and Gina Masullo Chen, 145–158. New York: Palgrave and Macmillan, 2016.

Richmond, Randy. "More Than Six Years After Her Child Was Slain, Tara Mcdonald Is Helping Bring New Life to Others." *The London Free Press*, 30 July 2015. https://lfpress.com/2015/07/30/more-than-six-years-after-her-child-was-slain-tara-mcdonald-is-helping-bring-new-life-to-others/wcm/4922a06a-58a4-6d8b-99ed-e57190cc2b0c.

Rosa, Anton. "Benitez: Un simbola contra la especulación en el Raval." *El Nacional*, 8 October 2018. https://www.elnacional.cat/es/sociedad/benitez-un-simbolo-contra-la-especulacion-en-el-raval_312021_102.html.

Rosen, Jay. *What Are Journalists For?* New Haven, CT: Yale University Press, 1999.

Rossmann, Andreas. "Learning from the Mafia Means Learning to Be Silent." European Centre for Press and Media Freedom. 3 May 2017. https://ecpmf.eu/news/ecpmf/learning-from-the-mafia-means-learning-to-be-silent.

Sambrook, Richard. "'Rat-Like Cunning, a Plausible Manner and Little Literary Ability': Time to Prove Nick Tomalin Wrong?" In *After Leveson?—The Future for British Journalism*, edited by John Mair, 88–97. Suffolk, U.K.: Abramis Academic, 2013.

Sandel, Michael J. *What Money Can't Buy: The Moral Limits of Markets*. London: Macmillan, 2012.

Scammell, Rosie. "DNA Evidence and Family Secrets Snare Italian Child Murderer." *The Guardian*, 2 July 2016. https://www.theguardian.com/world/2016/jul/02/yara-gamirasio-murder-massimo-bossetti-dna-evidence-italy-guilty-verdict.

Schudson, Michael. *Why Democracies Need an Unlovable Press*. Cambridge, U.K.: Polity, 2008.

Scialabba, Nicole. "Should Juveniles Be Charged as Adults in the Criminal Justice System?" American Bar Association. 3 October 2016. https://www.americanbar.org/groups/litigation/committees/childrens-rights/articles/2016/should-juveniles-be-charged-as-adults/.

Siebert, Fred S., Theodore Peterson, and Wilbur Schramm. *Four Theories of the Press*. Urbana: University of Illinois Press, 1956.

Shaer, Matt. "A Monster Among the Frum." *New York Magazine*, 2 December 2011. http://nymag.com/news/features/levi-aron-2011-12/.

Silverman, Craig, and Lawrence Alexander. "How Teens in the Balkans Are Duping Trump Supporters with Fake News." *Buzzfeed News*. 3 November 2016. https://www.

buzzfeednews.com/article/craigsilverman/how-macedonia-became-a-global-hub-for-pro-trump-misinfo#.pudrdwbM1.

Silverman, Craig. "Last Press Council in U.S. Will Close Next Month." *Poynter*, 10 April 2014. https://www.poynter.org/reporting-editing/2014/last-press-council-in-u-s-will-close-next-month/.

Sjøvaag, Helle. "The Reciprocity of Journalism's Social Contract: The Political-Philosophical Foundations of Journalistic Ideology." *Journalism Studies* 11, no. 6 (2010): 874–888.

Skelton, Chad. "There Are Fewer Journalists in Canada Than 15 Years Ago—But Not as Few as You Might Think." *J-Source*, 4 May 2018. https://j-source.ca/article/canadian-journalists-statistics/.

Smith, Sydney. "Where Is the Outrage? Dutch Newspaper Interviews 9-year-old Plane Crash Survivor from His Hospital Bed." iMediaEthics. 10 May, 2010, https://www.imediaethics.org/wheres-the-outrage-dutch-newspaper-interviews-9-year-old-plane-crash-survivor-from-his-hospital-bed/.

Smith Fullerton, Romayne, and Maggie Jones Patterson. "Comparing Crime Coverage Rituals in Sweden, Holland, England and North America." In *Media and Public Shaming: Drawing the Boundaries of Disclosure*, edited by Julian Petley, 115–144. London: IB Tauris, 2013.

Smith Fullerton, Romayne, and Maggie Jones Patterson. "Crime News: Defining Boundaries." In *The Ethics of Intercultural Communication*, edited by Clifford G. Christians and Bo Shan, 183–198. New York: Peter Lang, 2015.

Smith Fullerton, Romayne, and Maggie Jones Patterson. "'Killing' the True Story of First Nations: The Ethics of Constructing a Culture Apart." *Journal of Mass Media Ethics* 23, no. 3 (2008): 201–218.

Smith Fullerton, Romayne, and Maggie Jones Patterson. "Murder in Our Midst: Expanding Coverage to Include Care and Responsibility." *Journal of Mass Media Ethics* 21, no. 4 (2006): 304–321.

Spiegel Staff. "Neo-Nazi Evil Has an Ordinary Face." *Spiegel*, 7 May 2013. https://www.spiegel.de/international/germany/german-press-reaction-to-start-of-nsu-neo-nazi-trial-a-898557.html.

Staudenmaier, Rebecca. "NSU Victims' Families Sue Government over Investigation Errors." *Die Welt*, 18 June 2017. https://p.dw.com/p/2etKY.

Stoll, Julia. "Trust in Media in Europe—Statistics and Facts." 18 March 2019. https://www.statista.com/topics/3303/trust-in-media-in-europe/.

Strömbäck, Jesper, and Óscar G. Luengo. "Polarized Pluralist and Democratic Corporatist Models: A Comparison of Election News Coverage in Spain and Sweden." *International Communication Gazette* 70, no. 6 (2008): 547–562.

Swedish Institute. "20 Milestones of Swedish Press Freedom." Swedish Institute. 1 October 2018. https://sweden.se/society/20-milestones-of-swedish-press-freedom/.

Taylor Wessing Staff. "German Personality Rights in 2012." Taylor Wessing LLP. 1 February 2013. https://www.taylorwessing.com/download/article_germanpersonalityrights.html#.XIfWUC0ZPUo.

Tompkins, Al. "Cynics Might Call the Perp Walk the Crime Reporter's Red Carpet: How We Justify Images of Accused IMF Chief in Handcuffs." *Poynter*, 17 May 2011. https://www.poynter.org/reporting-editing/2011/is-it-ethical-to-use-perp-walk-images-of-dominique-strauss-kahn-imf-chief-accused-of-attempted-rape/.

Tonry, Michael. "Preface." In *Crime and Justice in Scandinavia*, edited by Michael Tonry and Tapio Lappi-Seppälä, vi–x. Chicago: University of Chicago Press, 2011.

Tonry, Michael, and Catrien Bijleveld. "Crime, Criminal Justice, and Criminology in the Netherlands." In *Crime and Justice in the Netherlands*, edited by Michael Tonry and Catrien Bijleveld, 1–30. Chicago: University of Chicago Press, 2007.

Tonry, Michael, and Tapio Lappi-Seppälä. "Crime, Criminal Justice, and Criminology in the Nordic Countries." In *Crime and Justice in Scandinavia*, edited by Michael Tonry and Tapio Lappi-Seppälä, 1–32. Chicago: University of Chicago Press, 2011.

Toronto Star. "About the Star." *Toronto Star*, 27 November 2018. https://www.thestar.com/about/aboutus.html#c.

Transparency International. "Corruption Perceptions Index 2017." Transparency International. 21 February 2018. https://www.transparency.org/news/feature/corruption_perceptions_index_2017.

Tuchman, Gaye. *Making News*. New York, NY: Free Press, 1978.

Turner, Nicholas, and Jeremy Travis. "What We Learned from German Prisons." *New York Times*, 6 August 2015. https://www.nytimes.com/2015/08/07/opinion/what-we-learned-from-german-prisons.html.

Ugland, Erik, and Jack Breslin. "Minnesota News Council: Principles, Precedent, and Moral Authority." *Journal of Mass Media Ethics*, 15, no. 4 (2000): 232–247.

Ugland, Erik. "The Legitimacy and Moral Authority of the National News Council." *Journalism* 9, no. 3 (2008): 285–308.

Verhovnik, Melanie. "School Shootings in Media Coverage: Why Media Play an Important Role in the Genesis of School Shootings." *The International Journal of Interdisciplinary Studies in Communication* 10, no. 3 (2015): 31–46.

Voltmer, Katrin. *The Media in Transitional Democracies*. Hoboken, NJ: John Wiley & Sons, 2013.

Von Uexkull, Ole. "Opinion: Proposed Law Change Threatens to Erode Sweden's Press Freedom." *The Local Sweden*, 13 March 2018. https://www.thelocal.se/20180313/opinion-proposed-law-change-threatens-to-erode-swedens-press-freedom.

Wagner, Peter, and Wendy Sawyer. "States of Incarceration: The Global Context 2018." Prison Policy Initiative. 1 June 2018. https://www.prisonpolicy.org/global/2018.html.

Ward, Stephen. *Ethical Journalism in a Populist Age: The Democratically Engaged Journalist*. Lanham, MD: Rowman & Littlefield, 2018.

Ward, Stephen. "Philosophical Foundations for Global Journalism Ethics." *Journal of Mass Media Ethics* 20, no. 1 (2005): 3–21.

Ward, Stephen. *Radical Media Ethics: A Global Approach*. Hoboken, NJ: John Wiley & Sons, 2015.

Washington Post Staff. "Policies and Standards." *Washington Post*, 1 January 2016. https://www.washingtonpost.com/news/ask-the-post/wp/2016/01/01/policies-and-standards/?utm_term=.522f55ae655e.

Waterson, Jim. "Cliff Richard Wins £210,000 over BBC Privacy Case." *The Guardian*, 18 July 2018. https://www.theguardian.com/music/2018/jul/18/cliff-richard-wins-damages-from-bbc-over-police-raid-footage.

Waterson, Jim. "Why Is U.K. Press Regulation Back in the Headlines?" *The Guardian*, 8 May 2018. https://www.theguardian.com/media/2018/may/08/why-is-U.K.-press-regulation-back-in-the-headlines.

Weibull, Lennart, and Britt Börjesson. *Publicistiska seder: Svensk pressetik I teori och praktik 1900–1994* [Publishing traditions: Swedish press ethics in theory and practice 1900–1994]. Stockholm: Tidens förlag, 2006.

Weibull, Lennart. "Press Law of 1766, Sweden." In *Encyclopedia of Political Communication*, edited by Lynda Lee Kaid and Christina Holtz-Bacha, 645–646. Thousand Oaks, CA: Sage, 2007.

Weibull, Lennart, and Britt Börjesson. "The Swedish Media Accountability System: A Research Perspective." *European Journal of Communication* 7, no. 1 (1992): 121–139.

White, Ken. "Fire in a Crowded Theater." Legal Talk Network. 18 June 2018. https://legaltalknetwork.com/podcasts/make-no-law/2018/06/fire-in-a-crowded-theater/.

Wilkins, Lee, and Renita Coleman. "Journalists' Moral Development: Thinking Through Both Rights and Care in a Professional Setting." Paper presented at the Association for Education in Journalism and Mass Communication (AEJMC), Toronto, August 4–7, 2004.

Wilkins, Lee, and Renita Coleman. *The Moral Media: How Journalists Reason About Ethics*. New York: Routledge, 2005.

Wise, Peter. "Former Portuguese PM Jose Sócrates Charged with Corruption." *Financial Times*, 11 October 2017. https://www.ft.com/content/ca71ca96-ae89-11e7-aab9-abaa44b1e130.

Wollacott, Mark. "Differences Between Libertarian & Social Responsibility Models of the Press." *Bizfluent*, 26 September 2017. https://bizfluent.com/info-8109528-differences-social-responsibility-theories-press.html.

Woodhouse, John. "Press Regulation After Leveson." U.K. Parliament. 27 July 2018. https://researchbriefings.parliament.U.K./ResearchBriefing/Summary/CBP-7576#fullreport.

Youth Justice Legal Centre Staff. "Which Court?" Youth Justice Legal Centre. 20 January 2015. https://yjlc.U.K./which-court/.

Index

For the benefit of digital users, indexed terms that span two pages (e.g., 52–53) may, on occasion, appear on only one of those pages.

Note: Tables are indicated by *t* following the page number